Libya and the United States

Libya and the United States

Two Centuries of Strife

Ronald Bruce St John

PENN

University of Pennsylvania Press

Philadelphia

Copyright © 2002 University of Pennsylvania Press
All rights reserved
Printed in the United States of America on acid-free paper

10 9 8 7 6 5 4 3 2 1

Published by
University of Pennsylvania Press
Philadelphia, Pennsylvania 19104-4011

Library of Congress Cataloging-in-Publication Data

St John, Ronald Bruce.
    Libya and the United States : two centuries of strife / Ronald Bruce St John.
        p.   cm.
    Includes bibliographical references (p.) and index.
    ISBN 0-8122-3672-6 (cloth : alk. paper)
        1. United States—Foreign relations—Libya. 2. Libya—Foreign relations—United
States. I. Title
    E183.8.L75S7   2002
    327.730612'09—dc21   2002018049

To Carol

Contents

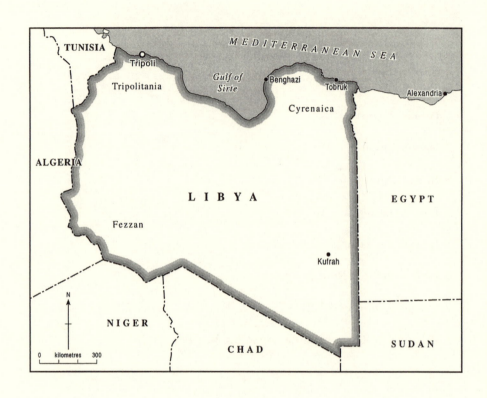

Chapter 1
Dismal Record

Bilateral relations between Libya and the United States have been active, engaged, and positive for no more than twenty out of the last two hundred years, a dismal record with few parallels in the annals of American diplomatic history. Commercial and diplomatic intercourse between the United States and Libya began on a low note after the failure of desultory negotiations in the late eighteenth century led to armed conflict at the beginning of the nineteenth. Following a hiatus of almost a century and a half, diplomatic exchange expanded with expectation and promise, particularly on the Libyan side, in the aftermath of World War II. A little more than two decades later, relations between Libya and the United States entered the Qaddafi era, a period characterized from the outset by political tension and mutual mistrust that later deteriorated into open hostility.

No issue of foreign relations since American independence in 1776 has confounded and frustrated the policy makers of the United States more completely, repeatedly, and over a longer period of time than the problems of the Middle East. Washington has repeatedly tried and failed since 1945 to mediate lasting solutions, prevent recurrent crises, and secure its own national interests in a region that became increasingly important to the United States. The root cause of this failure was the inability of successive presidential administrations from Truman to Bush, often because of domestic political considerations, to harmonize and synthesize America's four major interests in the Middle East—access to oil, the security of Israel, containment of communism and Soviet expansionism, and adherence to the principles of self-determination and the peaceful settlement of disputes. The preservation of the status quo was the real thrust and practical intent of all four of these objectives.

United States foreign policy toward Libya in the immediate postwar period mirrored American policy toward the Middle East and the world as a whole. In support of a Cold War strategy, grounded on a chain of air bases in the eastern Mediterranean and the Middle East, Washington's first priority in Libya was to ensure long-term Western access to existing military facilities, especially Wheelus Field outside Tripoli. In support of this objective, the United States adamantly opposed Soviet attempts to secure similar facilities in Tripolitania. It also rejected a proposed UN trusteeship over Cyrenaica, the Fezzan, and Tripolitania because the administrator of a trust territory, under the UN system, could not establish military bases except in the case of a strategic trusteeship; and the Soviet Union was sure to veto in the Security Council any attempt to create a strategic trusteeship. As its options narrowed, the Truman administration later supported the Bevin-Sforza plan to establish a series of Western trusteeships over Libya. When this approach failed, Washington viewed an independent Libya as the best option available to achieve its strategic objectives in the region. Platitudes voiced at the time by American officials in support of self-determination and self-government were, at best, secondary considerations packaged as window dressing to disguise the real intent of U.S. policy. As the Cold War heated up, the primary interest of the United States was to secure a base agreement in Libya as soon as possible and preferably before independence strengthened the Libyan negotiating position.

With North Africa commanding the southern approaches to Europe and the western approaches to the Middle East, Arab nationalism, especially in the wake of the creation of Israel in 1948, was seen in Washington as a potent force that threatened Western interests in the region. Misreading the intent of Arab nationalists, American policy makers expressed mounting concern with the potential for communist infiltration of the region in conjunction with Arab nationalist activities. As a result, the United States, in a policy doomed from the start, opposed Arab nationalist movements in Libya for the first two decades of Libyan independence on the faulty premise that such movements would necessarily facilitate the spread of communism. In so doing, American officials throughout the 1950s and 1960s continually underestimated or ignored the potential impact of Arab nationalist movements on an isolated Libyan monarchy with transparent ties to the West. Viewing Libya after independence as a strategic asset as opposed to an important but sovereign ally, the U.S. government encouraged the regime of Sayyid Muhammad Idris al-Mahdi al-Sanusi to adopt foreign policy positions that were unpopular in the Arab world and thus contributed to the popular perception of Libya as a Western dependency. The discovery of oil in marketable quantities in the late 1950s offered an opportunity for Washington to reassess its regional policies; nevertheless, American policy toward Libya ended the decade of the 1950s exactly where it had begun.

As a result, the economic, military, and political dependence of Libya on the United States reached a dangerous level in the second decade of Libyan independence. This situation was the product of internal factors, forces, and interests in Libya together with the pursuit by the United States of its own economic, military, and political objectives. It was not the product of a Libyan commitment to Western ideals or traditions; on the contrary, the monarchy sought to minimize the impact of Western social structures and mores on the Libyan people. The Libyan government chose to maintain a close relationship with the United States and its allies because it believed they were in the best position to guarantee Libyan security. The monarchy's position in this regard was later borne out in September 1969, when it asked the British government to intervene and restore it to power, an action the Labour government of Harold Wilson refused to take.

Under the circumstances, the position of the United States in Libya was rendered more and more paradoxical. As American foreign policy heightened the awareness of both governments as to the intricacy of their interests and relations, a growing number of Libyan citizens increasingly distrusted the United States and resented its extensive presence in significant aspects of Libyan internal and external affairs. The conflicting demands of Arab nationalism, and the need for ongoing cooperation with the United States to achieve many of Libya's foreign and domestic goals, contributed to the growing ambiguity that characterized this complex and convoluted relationship.

In turn, policy makers in Washington saw Libya, together with the remainder of North Africa and the Middle East, as falling within a highly sensitive security zone. For this reason, Libyan foreign policy, despite Libya's formal sovereignty, was effectively constrained by the bounds of U.S. tolerance. This left the Idris regime free to follow any policy it desired so long as its actions did not affect the security interests of the United States as defined by Washington. For the first decade of independence, Tripoli successfully accommodated itself to these restrictions; however, in the 1960s, a combination of developments inside and outside Libya posed an entirely new challenge for Washington. Mounting oil revenues reduced the dependency of the Libyan government on military base payments but increased the complexity of its socioeconomic and political problems. As economic conditions improved and social mobility increased, the Libyan people, especially the younger, urban population, yearned for political change coupled to a coherent new ideology. The Idris regime, detached and remote, attempted to respond to these needs but failed to understand them, just as it failed to comprehend and satisfy the demands of Arab nationalists. American officials, committed to the status quo in the region, also failed repeatedly to recognize the pressing need to accommodate Arab nationalist positions. In this sense, the policies of the United States and its Western allies made a major contribution to the political bankruptcy of the Idris regime in 1969.

After the overthrow of the monarchy, Mu'ammar al-Qaddafi articulated an increasingly comprehensive ideology which had strong Libyan antecedents but also enjoyed similarities with the ideologies of other Arab revolutionary movements. He skillfully blended the threads of nationalism, anti-imperialism, and pan-Islamic loyalties, which had emerged in Libya at the beginning of the twentieth century, with contemporary movements for Arab nationalism, Arab socialism, and Arab unity. Qaddafi based his variant of Arab nationalism, the central element of his ideology, on a glorification of Arab history and culture that conceived of the Arabic-speaking world as the Arab nation. Libya became the heart, the vanguard, and the hope of the Arab nation and thus the custodian of Arab nationalism. In the early months of the revolution, Qaddafi focused on highly symbolic acts of national independence, most especially an early termination of the base agreements with the United Kingdom and the United States. Once the bases were emptied, Qaddafi declared March 28, the day the British evacuated the Al-Adem Base, and June 11, the day the Americans evacuated Wheelus Field, official national holidays and commemorated them annually with popular festivities and a strongly nationalistic address.

If Arab nationalism was the core element of Qaddafi's ideology, the concept of *jihad* (holy war) was the action element of that Arab nationalism. Qaddafi saw jihad as a means to achieve social justice inside and outside Libya. His unique approach to the traditional concept of jihad led the Libyan leader to support publicly an extremely wide range of liberation movements from the Irish Republican Army to militant Black groups in the United States to the African National Congress. In most of these cases, Libyan support was neither a question of doctrine nor of national interest; instead, Qaddafi saw such support as a practical means to strike at colonialism and imperialism.

The Libyan concept of jihad found its most pragmatic expression in early support for a variety of Palestinian groups. In Qaddafi's mind, Palestine was an integral part of the Arab nation; and the latter could never be truly free and united until Palestine was completely liberated. The enemy was Zionism, together with the colonialist and imperialist powers, most especially the United States, responsible for visiting this indignity upon the Arab people. Qaddafi's prolonged advocacy of the use of force against Israel later contributed to a bitter feud with Palestine Liberation Organization Chairman Yasser Arafat and also had an adverse impact on the Libyan leader's aspirations to regional and international leadership. His support for liberation movements also brought Qaddafi into prolonged contact with groups and activities that the United States and its Western allies associated with terrorism. Consequently, he spent considerable effort in the 1980s and 1990s trying to differentiate between revolutionary violence, which he continued to support, and terrorism, which he purportedly opposed. American officials generally proved unable, at least officially, to differentiate between the two policies. On the other hand, Qaddafi was feted by fellow African heads of state, during the sanctions era and even more so once the UN sanctions on Libya were suspended, out of respect for a revolutionary leader whose support for liberation movements helped end colonialism on the continent.

The doctrine of positive neutrality was also an integral component of Qaddafi's ideology. Critical of both capitalism and communism, which he described initially as two sides of the same coin, he rejected foreign influence or control in any form. As a result, early Libyan policy toward both the Soviet Union and the United States followed a dichotomous pattern. Highly critical of American foreign policy, the Libyan government maintained close ties with the West, selling oil to its European allies and using the proceeds to import massive amounts of Western technology. At the same time, Qaddafi criticized the Soviet Union, especially its policy of allowing Jews to immigrate to Israel, but purchased Soviet armaments in growing quantities.

At the outset of the One September Revolution, key American policy makers mistakedly believed the revolutionary government could become an ally in support of American policy to keep Soviet influence and communism out of the Middle East. This brief honeymoon period soon ended as Libya's approach to the Arab-Israeli conflict and the Palestinian question quickly soured the prevailing policy mix. Before long, Libyan foreign policy was challenging the status quo in Africa and the Middle East at every opportunity. In so doing, the Qaddafi regime came into direct conflict with the four core interests of American foreign policy in the region. The 1973 October War, which was followed by Libyan nationalization of American oil interests, proved a watershed event in American-Libyan relations, which rapidly deteriorated in the second half of the decade.

Fundamental, long-standing policy differences were at the heart of the mounting impasse, the most significant being the Palestinian issue. The centrality of the Palestinian question to Qaddafi's ideology and his approach to a resolution of the issue, particularly his open support of guerrilla movements, quickly dissipated whatever official or unofficial constituency existed in the United States for improved diplomatic relations. With the trashing of the U.S. embassy in Tripoli at the end of 1979, common ground for discussion disappeared. State-sponsored terrorism, according to the White House, was a weapon of unconventional war against the democracies of the West, a weapon that took advantage of their openness to build political hostility toward them. The subsequent closure of the U.S. embassy in 1980, together with the closure of the Libyan People's Bureau (embassy) in Washington in 1981, proved the catalyst for a sharp deterioration in American-Libyan relations.

Falsely describing Libya as a Soviet puppet, the Reagan administration increased diplomatic, economic, and military pressure on the Qaddafi regime in a very systematic fashion. Eager to reassert American power and influence in the world, particularly in the Middle East, the confrontational policies of the U.S. government eventually led to the American bombing of Benghazi and Tripoli in 1986. A major difference between Reagan's attack on Libya and Thomas Jefferson's attack on Tripoli almost two centuries earlier was that Reagan appeared to target a head of state for destruction. Otherwise, the two actions were similar in that both administrations chose to punish a relatively weak, minor player in the region in support of broader policy objectives. For no apparent reason, Qaddafi hoped the end of the Reagan era would offer a window of opportunity for improved diplomatic relations with the United States. The first Bush administration soon dampened such enthusiasm with its adoption of the Rogue Doctrine.

It is instructive at this point to recall that the overwhelming majority of the European partners of the United States refused to support a confrontational approach to Libya. They had their own interests at stake and were not prepared to sacrifice them for what they saw as an American obsession. While few European governments denied that Qaddafi was often a negative influence, they argued that it was a mistake to isolate him by closing all Western doors to Libya. In their view, the punitive policies employed by Washington often exacted serious costs in human lives and credibility, yet failed to change regime behavior. Meanwhile, European companies, before and after the period of UN sanctions, remained well positioned to enjoy the lucrative contracts that Washington's hardline approach denied their American counterparts. To this degree, the Libyan case clearly highlighted the need for closer consultation with European governments to involve them more directly in key decisions of American foreign policy. Diplomacy involving pressure on foreign governments to make decisions in American interests, but not in the interests of those foreign governments, might enjoy short-term success. Unfortunately, the Libyan example suggested it would often do so at the expense of longer-term relationships.

A difficulty facing most African and Arab societies in the latter half of the twentieth century was the establishment of a meaningful relationship between aspirations and accomplishments. This was especially true of Libya under the Qaddafi regime. An enormous gap existed between the ideas, beliefs, and myths that constituted Qaddafi's ideology and the respective realities they purported to describe or explain. This lacuna was especially wide in the areas of regime policy and performance but existed throughout the entire ideological spectrum. In part for this reason, Qaddafi's ideology was greeted with widespread disbelief and disinterest throughout the Arab and African worlds where its anachronistic character was largely rejected. Qaddafi pursued energetically a stage larger than a nation of only a few million people, but his superficial treatment of worn ideas, in the end, effectively confined him to the Libyan playhouse.

In the post-Cold War period, elements of U.S. foreign policy, much like Qaddafi's policies in the 1970s, became anachronistic. There was no longer a Cold War global system, a Cold War military, or a Cold War public. American foreign policy was more about managing weakness, the weakness of China, Japan, and the Commonwealth of Independent States, as opposed to projecting power and force around the world. All three of these world powers experienced wrenching internal adjustments to globalization that made the potential collapse of the Commonwealth of Independent States, in particular, more threatening to the United States than its former strength. Globalization itself, in terms of the speed, interconnectivity, and economic impact of global markets, was also a new and not clearly understood force. The Internet, in particular, offered the potential to become a powerful enabling device for nongovernmental organizations to influence in the future foreign policy formulation and execution to a far greater extent than in the past.

The United States in the post-Cold War world was not just a superpower but in reality the only superpower. In France, for example, analysts referred to the United States as a "hyperpower" to emphasize its unique position in the world. American military might was unrivaled, and its information technology was the envy of the entire world. At the same time, it was not omnipotent and was not capable of solving all the problems of the world. Attempts to do so were deeply resented by America's allies as well as by its enemies. Other countries increasingly called on Washington for leadership, but at the same time they envied and resented the U.S. more than ever. No one could afford to be America's enemy, but few wanted to be seen as its close friend and ally. As a result, whenever Washington proposed a bold initiative that threatened vested interests abroad, it risked a ferocious backlash from friends and rivals alike. For example, repeated American attempts to label the Qaddafi regime and other governments as "rogue states" and to punish them for alleged transgressions increasingly had the opposite effect. The strong-arm tactics employed by Washington, in the end, contributed to declining international support for multilateral sanctions instead of the American objective, which was to build support for them.

American observers, in this regard, seldom recognized that the policy of confrontation initiated by the United States in the 1980s often did not serve American interests in the Middle East or in Libya. The imposition of the American embargo resulted in the lost sale to European allies and others of an enormous quantity of goods and services, from capital equipment to consumer goods to consulting contracts. Politically, it strained American relations with key partners in Europe, like France, Germany, and Italy, as well as with allies in Africa and the Arab world. Academically, it stifled research by Americans in Libya and choked the flow of Libyan students to the United States. It also had a deleterious impact on the 1990s generation of American students of the Middle East and North Africa. Within Libya, on the other hand, U.S. policy served Qaddafi's interests as it made it easier for him to survive, albeit with some modification in behavior. When American policy makers spoke of "sanctions fatigue" in the late 1990s, they were really acknowledging the bankruptcy of the confrontational policies initiated by President Reagan and later adopted by the Bush and Clinton administrations.

From the outset of the American-Libyan relationship, most Americans viewed Libya from the vantage point of the distant and deep cultural differences characterized as Orientalism by the contemporary Palestinian-American writer Edward W. Said. Together with the remainder of the Western world, Americans regarded Libya, if they were even aware of its existence, as a country shrouded in mystery and cloaked in the exotic, a mirror of their own dreams, desires, and extremes. Orientals in general and Libyans in particular were viewed as irrational, depraved, childlike, or simply different when compared to Westerners, who were rational, virtuous, mature, and normal. The Commission of Investigation dispatched to Libya by the Council of Foreign Ministers in 1948, for example, described the Libyan people as backward, childlike, and immature in their understanding of the responsibilities of independence. Contemporary American observers mirrored these attitudes. Benjamin Rivlin, a Harvard University professor and former employee of the State Department and the United Nations, wrote in the *Middle East Journal* in January 1949 that the Libyan populace was a "predominantly backward and illiterate people" who were "politically unsophisticated, unorganized, and inarticulate."[1] This short-sighted and ultimately arrogant attitude, with its frequent concentration on the exotic elements of Libyan society to the exclusion of anything remotely familiar, amounted to paying lip service to diversity while being concerned with only selected aspects of a foreign culture.

For more recent American observers, businessmen, diplomats, journalists, and travelers, Libya was a place, not to be studied and understood, but to be exploited, first, as a site for air bases, and later, as a source of high quality petroleum. In an article published in the *Middle East Journal* in winter 1958, Louis Dupree, a professor of anthropology at Pennsylvania State University, captured the prevailing American attitude:

Most American servicemen are apathetic to service in Libya and almost never leave the air base. Others, when they do leave, make asses of themselves. Few understand or even attempt to understand the history, culture or problems of the United Kingdom of Libya. The native population is referred to as "Mohab," and rumors are spread that Christians are killed in the Old City of Tripoli. All Libyan customs are interpreted—and compared, always unfavorably—in terms of the air conditioned, skyscrapered culture of the United States.[2]

In short, American policy makers have had limited knowledge of, as well as limited interest in or appreciation of, Libya for most of the two hundred-plus years of their intercourse. The level of interest increased after independence in 1951, and especially after the discovery of commercial petroleum deposits in 1959; however, knowledge and understanding continued at very low levels. As recently as the late 1970s, when the author first visited Libya, English language books in print on Libya could be counted on one hand, and the available information focused on narrow segments of the economy and particular aspects of the society as opposed to broader surveys of the rich culture and history of the country. In this context, the charismatic Qaddafi, more often than not described today in the American press as bizarre, erratic, remote, or quixotic, was only the most recent manifestation of Orientalism, with a long line of Libyan antecedents stretching from Yusuf Karamanli to Sidi Umar al-Mukhtar to Sayyid Muhammad Idris al-Mahdi al-Sanusi. The caricatures found in modern popular culture also continued to be propagated at the box office in movies like *Iron Eagle* (1986) and *The American President* (1995). Viewed in Washington as hostile and unpredictable leaders of marginal states, Orientals like Qaddafi existed to be put back in their box, as Secretary of State George Shultz commented in the aftermath of the 1983 crisis in the Sudan, anytime or anywhere they challenged American policies and interests.[3]

In a very real sense, Libya was a victim of the apathy that had long characterized the American public's approach to many aspects of foreign affairs, especially in the post-Cold War era. Broadly supportive of an internationalist foreign policy, the American public seldom demonstrated notable intensity over individual foreign policy issues. This apathetic internationalism encouraged Washington politicians to neglect foreign policy and to gravitate, instead, toward the domestic issues that appeared to matter most to their constituents. It also empowered the squeaky wheel in that American politicians catered to those groups with narrow but intense interests. To cite a more recent example, after the Department of State dispatched four consular officials to Libya in March 2000 to assess travel safety for Americans, Secretary of State Madeleine Albright indicated that she would be inclined to lift the ban on travel to Libya if the safety assessment team recommended that action. Many months later, in a time in which tens of thousands of Europeans and others had visited Libya, the issue was still pending because representatives of the victims of the Lockerbie disaster, supported by a few members of Congress, had effectively stonewalled what appeared to many to be a relatively simple, clear-cut decision.

The widening conflict between Libya and the United States also drew attention to the asymmetrical nature of their total relationship. Due to its location, size, and power, the United States loomed large on the Libyan horizon. After independence in 1951, diplomatic and commercial relations with the United States were a principal concern of every Libyan government and a matter of interest to informed, articulate Libyan citizens. Commercially and politically, any move in Washington could and often did have an impact on Libya. Viewed from the opposite direction, the case was quite different. The United States in the second half of the twentieth century, especially during the Idris regime, generally viewed Libya as a relatively remote and unimportant country. Relations with Libya seldom had any significant influence on U.S. foreign or domestic policy and seldom gained the attention of the American public. Consequently, what was good for Libya not only was not necessarily good for the United States, but often was of no interest to the United States. The failure of Libyans, most especially Qaddafi, to understand these differing perspectives repeatedly led them to expect too much from U.S. policy.

The factors underlying American-Libyan relations during the Qaddafi era also contributed to their contradictory nature. Bilateral economic ties were shaped in large part by mutual economic interests, but political dialogue was determined by forces external to that relationship. Libya never ranked high on the American political agenda, and Qaddafi was generally viewed as a non-actor. He was ignored whenever possible and made an example when he proved too troublesome. A calculated policy of hostility and stern retribution, when employed, seldom proved effective in redirecting Libyan foreign policy; but it did focus attention on a major irony in the American-Libyan relationship. Experience would suggest that a major world power, by employing military force against a minor power, more often than not projects an image of the bully, as opposed to the policeman or peacemaker, and thus simply adds to the international stature of its opponent. This was clearly true in the Libyan case. Due to his esteem for American power and prestige, Qaddafi often betrayed a need for U.S. recognition of his position and importance. Punitive acts like the 1986 bombing raid alienated most American allies and did little to modify the policy of the Qaddafi regime, but they clearly generated the international attention and recognition craved by Qaddafi. At the same time, a policy of confrontation on the one side begat a policy of confrontation on the other.

The foreign policies of both Libya and the United States were marked by a notable consistency throughout most of the Qaddafi era. In the light of changed circumstance, in and out of Africa and the Middle East, the time appeared ripe, at the outset of the George W. Bush administration, to rethink those policies as part of a broader reevaluation of the U.S. role in the region and the world. Despite the spotlight on Qaddafi for more than three decades, misconceptions about his aims, conduct, and theories were rife. Fundamental errors regarding the history of Libya were repeated ad nauseam, and a confused picture of the historical, economic, and political perspectives dominating Libya were recurrent. On both sides, it appeared time to recognize that the American-Libyan relationship was an important one, commercially, politically, and culturally, certainly far more important than recent U.S. conduct would suggest.

Given the opportunity, there was some indication in the early days of the second Bush administration that American policy toward Libya would be modified if not overhauled. Administration officials and their British counterparts met with Libyan representatives to discuss the actions Libya would have to take to end UN sanctions. At the same time, the White House initiated a review of U.S. sanctions policies. Arguing that sanctions were often ineffective and needlessly harmed American companies, the Bush administration advocated more flexibility than Congress later proved willing to approve. Whereas the White House favored a renewal of the Iran-Libya Sanctions Act for two years only, Congress voted overwhelmingly for a five-year extension, although it did offer a small concession in the form of a review of the act after two years. The 11 September 2001 terrorist attacks on the World Trade Center and the Pentagon, followed by a heightened threat of bioterrorism, later destroyed any immediate opportunity for a more thorough rethinking of Libyan policy. Despite Qaddafi's measured response to the attacks and the bombing of targets in Afghanistan, Libya's close association with terrorism in the 1980s and early 1990s, especially its alleged attempts to develop chemical weapons, made any immediate change in U.S. policy improbable if not impossible.

The American-Libyan relationship over the last half century offered insight into the Arab-Muslim reaction to American policy in the Middle East in general and to the 11 September terrorist attacks in particular. Washington was successful in forming a fragile coalition in support of a military response to terrorism; however, moderate governments across the Arab-Muslim world remained circumspect in voicing public support for American policy, torn between a fear of fundamentalism and a revulsion at civilian casualties. Washington responded, as it had often done in the past, with pressure on friendly governments in the Arab-Muslim world to support foreign policies unpopular in those countries, strengthening the widespread image of many as Western dependencies. Vital U.S. allies like Pakistan and Saudi Arabia faced potential revolutions, not unlike Qaddafi's 1969 overthrow of King Idris, if the bombing in Afghanistan continued too long. The bombing campaign itself, like the 1986 air strikes on Benghazi and Tripoli, increased political support in many areas of the world for the very targets it meant to destroy.

American policy toward Libya over the last half century was in many respects a case study of U.S. policy toward the wider Arab-Muslim world. Afghanistan, the Taliban, and Osama bin Laden, from this perspective, were relegated to a sideshow in the real campaign against global terrorism, an American foreign policy that recognized and promoted legitmate ambitions, diversity, opportunity, and respect in the Arab-Muslim world. Precisely because the moment looked so bleak, it offered a fresh opportunity for a serious reassessment of U.S. foreign policy.

Chapter 2
Desert Kingdom

Libyan foreign policy today is strongly influenced by forces originating in the past. The early history of Libya is one of colonialism and neocolonialism under the Phoenicians, Greeks, Romans, and Turks. Several centuries of Ottoman rule were followed by three decades of Italian occupation and nearly a decade of French and British occupation. The Italian domination of Libya was especially traumatic, as it was marked by two bloody wars followed by a decade of exploitation that only ended with the defeat of Italy in World War II. Italian policy included the seizure of choice lands together with the dislocation of nomads and peasants. Independence finally came in 1951, not because of internal action although there was discontent, but because it suited the strategic purposes of the Western powers. Even then, the boundaries of the new state were defined by the partition lines of the remaining imperialist powers in North Africa, the United Kingdom in Egypt and France in Algeria and Tunisia.

Limits of Political Geography

Located on the north central coast of Africa, modern-day Libya comprises the former provinces of Tripolitania, Cyrenaica, and the Fezzan. It is bordered on the east by Egypt and the Sudan, on the west by Tunisia and Algeria, and on the south by the republics of Niger and Chad.[1] Libya's long frontier with Egypt has been especially influential. In fact, Libya is sometimes described as Egypt without the Nile. Its proximity to one of the Arab world's traditional leaders has increased its visibility on the world stage and given its external relations an importance they would not otherwise have had. The Mediterranean Sea borders Libya on the north, providing it with over 1,100 miles (1,775 kilometers) of shoreline. Its closeness to the oil markets of Europe gives Libya a distinct marketing advantage over other Middle East oil-producing states.[2]

With an area of 680,000 square miles (1,760,000 square kilometers), Libya is both the fourth-largest country in Africa and the fourth-largest in the Arab world. One-quarter the size of continental United States, it is larger than the combined areas of France, Germany, Italy, and Spain. Libya contains three climatological-geographic zones. The Mediterranean littoral is the most heavily populated and the most suitable for agriculture, but it is also the smallest, only 3 percent of the total. Some 6 percent is semidesert chiefly suitable for grazing; the remaining 90 percent is a desert zone containing a few fertile oases. An impression of the arid nature of Libya is conveyed by the fact that no stream in the entire country has a permanent flow. To correct a popular misconception, less than 20 percent of the desert area of Libya is covered by sand dunes. A much greater part is occupied by rocky and gravel plain.[3]

Libya rests on the periphery of three worlds—Arab, African, and Mediterranean. This location has given it some flexibility as to where it will play a role as well as creating uncertainty as to exactly where it belongs. For most of its history, Libya has lacked the human and material resources to impact simultaneously on all three areas. Consequently, the focus of its diplomacy has oscillated from one world to the other depending on where opportunities—or obstacles—were greatest.

Relative to the Arab world, Libya straddles the Maghrib (western Islamic world) and the Mashriq (eastern Islamic world). This political division is reflected in the physical split of the nation's two major provinces by the Gulf of Sirte and the great Sirte Desert. Before independence, Cyrenaica tended to look eastward toward Egypt, while the focus of Tripolitania was westward toward Algeria, Morocco, and Tunisia. Southern Libya extends well into the Sahara and shares selected socioeconomic features with the bordering African countries of the Sahel. To a degree, the Fezzan region of Libya has a natural role in Saharan affairs which accounts in part for Libya's involvement in recent decades in the politics of central and eastern Africa.[4]

Population and Labor

Demography has compounded the limits that geography imposed on the Libyan state. For a large and ambitious country like Libya, a population of approximately five million citizens concentrated in a few detached urban centers was debilitating. Compared to Egypt, for example, Libya has 75 percent more territory but only some 7 percent as many people. Consequently, it has proved difficult for the Libyan government to meet its development targets and build the military force it feels necessary to promote the national interest. The nation's limited demographic resources underlay a number of controversial security policies over the last few decades, including universal conscription and the recruitment of mercenaries into the so-called Islamic Legion.

The Libyan government's dependence on imported labor, especially after the discovery in 1959 of significant deposits of petroleum, reversed regional labor practices long characterized by a substantial emigration of Libyan workers to Egypt and Tunisia. Whereas there were only 17,000 expatriate workers in Libya in 1964, the total had risen to 223,000 in 1975 and 562,000 by 1983, representing approximately half the total work force. And official figures probably underestimated the size of the foreign work force because they did not take into account illegal and undocumented migration. But even though foreigners accounted for around 20 percent of the Libyan population in 1983, it should be noted that the situation in Libya was still very different from that in the Gulf States, where foreigners outnumbered nationals. One of the major international issues related to the expatriate work force has been the problem Libya faced in maintaining politically acceptable host countries. For example, large-scale repatriations of both Tunisian and Egyptian workers occurred in the 1970s as the result of political crises between their governments and Libya. There was also the question of the political vulnerability of the groups who migrated to Libya, since the Libyan government has often tried to organize and indoctrinate its expatriate work force.[5]

On the other hand, the social significance of the presence of such a large alien work force has appeared to be minimal. Expatriate workers have generally adjusted relatively well to the austere living conditions of revolutionary Libya, while the Libyan population has mostly remained detached from these workers. The periodical crises that plagued the Libyan economy over the last two decades have been the cause of occasional adjustments in the size of the foreign work force. The dramatic fall in oil prices after 1981 sharply reduced government revenues, resulting in the expulsion in the summer of 1985 of tens of thousands of expatriate workers, including large numbers of Egyptians and Tunisians. In late 1995, the Libyan government requested permission from the United Nations to use aircraft to repatriate more than a million African workers. The government cited the poor state of the economy in support of its request, but some observers also viewed the policy as a form of protest against the UN sanctions in place at the time.[6]

The problem of underpopulation was aggravated by the generally low educational attainment of the Libyan labor force. Over 90 percent of the population was illiterate in 1952, and the illiteracy rate was still above 60 percent as recently as 1973. Consequently, it should come as no surprise that both the monarchy and the revolutionary government emphasized educational development. Broadening the educational policies of the monarchy, the revolutionary government achieved significant advances in the number of educational facilities and the size of the student body. The impact of the revolution on the quality of education was more difficult to assess. Education in revolutionary Libya was not a goal in itself but a means to create a new kind of citizen. The Libyan government announced a new round of educational reforms in mid-1992, for example, which constituted yet another redefinition of the role education should play in Libya. The new law defined the role of universities to be the development of citizens with specialized scientific training and the ideological convictions necessary to perform their obligations to the Arab nation and the *jamahiriya*. University students were described in the reforms as the vanguard in the awakening of Arab and Islamic civilization.[7]

Libyan Economy

At the outset of the independence era, Libya was judged by the World Bank to be one of the least developed nations in the world. Its capacity to generate foreign exchange earnings was so limited that a significant contribution came from the export of esparto grass, used in the manufacture of cordage, paper, and shoes, as well as the scrap metal collected from disabled World War II armored vehicles. Eighty percent of the population were engaged in agriculture and animal husbandry; however, insufficient rainfall, poor soil, and limited usable groundwater restricted most agriculture to dry farming. Libya was aptly referred to as the desert kingdom.[8]

The discovery of petroleum in commercially viable quantities at the end of the decade modified the Libyan economy quickly and drastically. A number of international oil companies arrived in Libya after 1955 and began investing substantial amounts of capital in oil exploration. In spring 1959, Esso Standard Libya Incorporated, an affiliate of Standard Oil of New Jersey, made the first major oil strike. Oil production at the Zelten oil field increased almost twenty-three-fold in 1961-64, and the production of associated natural gas increased nearly twenty-four-fold. By 1966 Libya was exporting 1.5 million barrels of oil a day. Since the mid-1960s, petroleum sales have accounted for upward of 99 percent of annual export earnings and have never dropped below 90 percent. In this sense, Libya can be considered a distributive state, as opposed to a production state, in that its income is derived from the sale of a commodity as opposed to extracting taxes from the population. At current levels of production, Libya's estimated oil reserves are expected to last well into the twenty-first century.[9]

Exploding oil revenues affected Libya's external relations in a number of significant ways. The new income freed the monarchy from its former dependence on foreign base revenues and thus made possible new policies that were inconceivable less than a decade earlier. Oil revenues also increased Libya's political influence beyond its frontiers by permitting it to dispense aid to less fortunate neighbors and to rebuild and rearm its armed forces. Finally, Libya's new status as an oil-producing state increased and diversified its political relations with other countries and made those relations more important. The early impact of oil on Libya's external intercourse can be easily demonstrated by comparing the number of countries that purchased Libyan crude oil in 1961 (six) to the number in 1971 (twenty-two).[10]

A number of different forces, including the imposition of economic sanctions by the United States and the United Nations, falling demand, OPEC quotas, and aging fields, affected Libyan oil production in the 1990s. Only a few new oilfields were put into production after the mid-1970s, and the Libyan government did not issue detailed field reserve or production figures for them. Despite these difficulties, oil production in 1990 was estimated at 1.372 million barrels a day, the highest output since 1980. Annual production remained between 1.361 million and 1.483 million barrels daily for the remainder of the decade. In fact, the Libyan oil industry became in some ways more robust because of the economic sanctions imposed. The National Oil Company took considerable, and justifiable, pride in being a survivor, in keeping the oilfields abandoned by the Americans in 1986 under production, and in finding secure markets for its exports. The sanctions also helped cement stronger links, both upstream and downstream, with European companies. From this perspective, the ability of the Qaddafi regime to maintain production at a relatively high level throughout the decade represented something of an achievement, albeit one the government chose not to publicize. Instead, it emphasized the damage to the economy done by the sanctions.[11]

Islamic Foundations

Islam penetrated North Africa as a result of the Arab conquest in about A.D. 642-643. Thereafter, the North African shore, especially Libya, assumed a distinct Arab-Islamic character. In the second quarter of the nineteenth century, Muhammad Bin Ali al-Sanusi founded the influential Sanusi order in Cyrenaica. Born in Algeria in 1787, al-Sanusi spent his early life in the Maghrib studying in and around his home town of Mustaghanim. He then moved in 1809 to Fez in Morocco, the intellectual capital of the Maghrib and one of the great centers of learning in the Islamic world. Accounts of his subsequent movements are imprecise; however, he first traveled to the Hijaz after 1815 and later returned for an extended period, following an interlude in Egypt around 1826. Returning to the Maghrib around 1840, al-Sanusi founded his first lodge at al-Bayda in Cyrenaica in 1841.[12]

Al-Sanusi was a Sufi, seeing this as the basis for his religious experience, as well as a prolific and renowned scholar and author of some fifty books, eight of which have survived together with a collection of prayers, a poem, and other fragments. His interests and activities centered on the religious, scholarly world as opposed to the temporal, political realm. He became one of the most influential Islamic leaders of nineteenth-century North Africa. Creating an organization that spread over most of the central Sahara and desert edge, he had a profound and lasting impact on the nomadic society of what is today called Libya.[13]

Centered in Cyrenaica, the Sanusiya became well established in the Fezzan but never achieved the widespread following in Tripolitania that they had in eastern and southern Libya. More a religious than a political movement, the Sanusiya aimed at purifying Islam and educating the Libyan people in Islamic principles. By the late 1920s, there were 146 Sanusi lodges scattered throughout North Africa and the Middle East, with one-third of them located in Cyrenaica. Administered by the Sanusi brothers or *ikhwan*, the Sanusi lodges constituted the socioeconomic and administrative structure of the order and formed the core of a de facto state.[14]

When the Italians invaded Libya in 1911-12, the Libyans considered it an attack against Islam; consequently, it was religious zeal rather than nationalism in the European sense that provided the motivation to resist Italian occupation. Sidi Umar al-Mukhtar, born of the Minifa tribe and educated in Sanusi schools at Janzur and Giarabub, was an active and highly effective guerrilla leader after 1923 and a major hero of the Cyrenaican resistance movement. With his capture and execution in 1931, effective Libyan resistance to Italian colonization ended. In the wake of the Italian occupation of Cyrenaica, the Sanusi order largely ceased to exist as a religious, political, or social organization in the territories occupied by French and Italian colonial forces. Nevertheless, Islam, as epitomized by the Sanusi brotherhood, gave continuity and legitimacy to the hereditary monarchy established in 1951. Muhammad Idris al-Mahdi al-Sanusi, the grandson of Muhammad Bin Ali al-Sanusi, was the first head of state of the independent United Kingdom of Libya, formed under the auspices of the United Nations. The role of religion as a legitimizing force steadily declined in the following two decades for a number of reasons including increased education and urbanization.[15]

The strong role of religion in Libya's traditional Islamic society remains an important influence on government policies. Conservative attitudes dominate, and people's values and behavior are very much a function of their religious background and attachment. The resistance wars were motivated by the demands of the true faith as part of national expression and emancipation, and religion was also central to the Arab League's efforts to motivate the Libyan populace to demand independence from the Commission of Investigation that visited the country in 1948. In short, Islam continues to play a most influential role in determining the direction and content of public policy as well as being a political symbol of great importance in controlling and mobilizing the masses.[16]

Chapter 3
In the Beginning

From the halls of Montezuma to the shores of Tripoli,
We fight our country's battles on the land as on the sea.
— U.S. Marine Corps Hymn

Even though Libya and the United States entered into a formal treaty relationship as early as 1796, diplomatic relations from the outset were characterized by discord, misunderstanding, and confusion.[1] Commercial interests in the newly independent United States of America, eager to expand commerce and trade, were in direct conflict with a government in Tripoli seeking to increase revenues through the traditional practice of privateering in the eastern Mediterranean.[2] Once this issue was resolved, diplomatic and commercial contacts between the two states were minimal for the remainder of the century. At the same time, events in Libya in the late nineteenth and early twentieth centuries set the stage for the nationalist independence movements eventually successful after World War II. In turn, events leading up to independence in 1951 had a strong impact on relations between Libya and the United States in the second half of the twentieth century.

Karamanli Dynasty

Contemporary Libya was Ottoman territory for most of the period from 1551 to 1911. The Ottomans governed Libya through a pasha appointed by the sultan in Istanbul. In turn, the pasha was dependent upon the janissaries, an elite military caste stationed in Libya to support Turkish rule. In matters of taxation and foreign affairs, the sultan allowed the local divan or council considerable autonomy. After 1661, Turkish power declined and the janissaries, together with local pirates, increasingly manipulated the divan. Eventually, the janissaries began designating among their own number a bey (dey) or local chief. Between 1672 and 1711, some twenty-four different beys struggled to control the increasingly chaotic political situation in Libya.[3]

In 1711, Ahmed Karamanli, an officer in the Turkish army, led a popular revolt against the ruling bey; in the process, he founded the Karamanli dynasty, which governed Libya for the next 124 years. After seizing Tripoli, Karamanli purchased his confirmation as pasha-regent from the Sublime Porte, as the Ottoman government was known, with goods stolen from Turkish officials murdered during the coup. Although he continued to recognize nominal Ottoman suzerainty, Karamanli created an independent hereditary monarchy with a government largely Arab in composition. Reigning from 1711 to 1745, he pursued an active foreign policy with the European powers while extending his political authority into Cyrenaica and the Fezzan. The Karamanli regime began a slow decline following the death of Ahmed who was succeeded by his son Muhammad, the pasha until 1754. The reign of Ali I, which stretched from 1754 to 1793, was especially corrupt and inefficient and led to a confused civil war at the end of the century. Finally, Yusuf Karamanli, one of three sons of Ali I, installed himself as pasha in 1795. In a throwback to the reign of Ahmed, Yusuf tamed the tribes of the interior and defied both British and Ottoman naval power, supporting Napoleon Bonaparte in his 1799 Egyptian campaign.[4]

At the outset of the nineteenth century, Libya could best be characterized as a quasi-independent Ottoman province, administered as a dynastic military garrison. Largely dependent on long-distance trade, the revenues from the trans-Saharan caravan trade and control of the sea lanes of the eastern Mediterranean combined to allow rulers to conduct commercial and political relations without heavy reliance on revenues from the countryside. Within a year of gaining political control over Tripoli, Yusuf Karamanli moved to raise Libya to a position of enhanced power on the Mediterranean scene. In pursuit of this objective, he adopted the common North African policy which, since the days of Ottoman imperial expansion, had put a premium on naval strength. The Libyan fleet, which in 1798–1800 had no more than eleven ships, had grown by 1805 to twenty-four armed vessels together with several skiffs.[5]

Increasingly recognized as an important maritime power in the Mediterranean, Karamanli called on various European powers, through their resident consuls, to establish appropriate treaty relationships with Libya by forwarding traditional consular presents. Spain was the first to respond, but was soon followed by others, including France and the Republic of Venice. Some European powers, like Denmark, Holland, and Sweden, which failed to respond on the grounds that the demands were too high, found their Mediterranean shipping set upon by Libyan privateers. As a result, in the decade 1795–1805 the new navy became a highly profitable source of revenue for the Tripoli government. Overall naval expenditures were relatively low, which made it possible for the navy to pay for itself and still yield large surplus revenues for the pasha.[6]

America Interests in the Mediterranean

As long as the American colonies remained a part of the British imperial system, American ships engaged in trade around the Mediterranean enjoyed such immunities from Barbary privateering as the British bought by payments of tribute to the rulers of Algiers, Morocco, Tripoli, and Tunis. Protected thus by the Royal Navy, American trade in the region was considerable, involving hundreds of men and thousands of tons of shipping. When the colonies declared independence, however, British protection was immediately withdrawn, with the privateers now proving useful to Britain in throttling the commerce of the rebellious colonies. After the United States won its independence, it continued to face the uncertainties of Mediterranean privateering, as the great maritime powers of the world, including England, did little to assist the new state. In fact, many in England believed the nascent economy of the United States, at the time a rather loose confederation of states with limited central power, could not survive the threat to commerce posed by the Barbary states.[7]

As early as 1784, privateers detained the American ship *Betsy* off the coast of North Africa. The vessel was soon released by Moroccan authorities, even though there was no treaty in existence at the time between the governments of Morocco and the United States. The following year, two American schooners, the *Maria* and the *Dauphin*, were seized by Algiers, triggering an outpouring of concern and consternation from commercial and mercantilist circles in the United States. In anticipation of such problems, the Continental Congress had earlier sought the alliance and protection of the great maritime powers of Europe. For example, in 1776 the Congress approached France with a proposed treaty, one article of which sought explicit protection from the Barbary states, including Morocco. When the treaty was finally concluded in 1778, France agreed to employ its good offices and interposition in cases of depredation by Barbary privateers. Shortly thereafter, in May 1784, the U.S. Congress resolved to send three ministers plenipotentiary, John Adams, Benjamin Franklin, and Thomas Jefferson, to the region to conclude treaties of amity and commerce with the Barbary states.[8]

Following the seizure of the *Maria* and the *Dauphin*, the U.S. government sought to invoke its treaty with France, but the good offices of the latter failed to materialize. With direct negotiations the next obvious resort, Washington through its three ministers plenipotentiary dispatched emissaries to Morocco and Algiers. The mission to Morocco, the outermost and most amenable of the Barbary states, met with early success, and a treaty of peace and friendship was concluded in May 1786 that included a ship signals agreement and a reduction in duty paid by American ships in Moroccan ports. Encouraged by England, the regency of Algiers, the strongest and most bellicose of these powers, proved much more intransigent, and a state of protracted conflict persisted between the Algiers regime and the U.S. government. In London, John Adams and Thomas Jefferson also conducted desultory negotiations in 1786 with a Tripolitanian envoy that proved equally fruitless. The financial demands of the Tripolitanian emissary were far too great to be met by the limited funds the U.S. Congress had put at the disposal of the ministers plenipotentiary. According to Jefferson biographer Thomas Malone, "the meeting with the Tripolitan minister was even more fruitless. That bearded, pipe-smoking emissary calmly asserted that it was the duty of his countrymen to make war on 'sinners' and asked for much more peace money than they [Adams and Jefferson] could pay".[9]

At this point, negotiations between the United States and the Barbary states lapsed; and by the end of 1793, Algerian privateers had captured eleven more American vessels and incarcerated their crews with those of the *Maria* and the *Dauphin*. The conflict with Algiers eventually led to the establishment of the U.S. Navy when in early 1794 Congress authorized the building of six frigates to be launched against that Barbary state. As the frigates were being built, the U.S. government reopened negotiations with the dey of Algiers, and a treaty of peace and amity was finally concluded in September 1795. Through the terms of the agreement, the United States paid a substantial ransom for the release of the American captives and agreed to deliver annual tribute to the dey of Algiers in the form of naval and military stores. In addition, Washington agreed to give Algiers a thirty-six-gun frigate, appropriately named the *Crescent*, which it delivered in 1798. The treaty with Algiers, ratified by the U.S. Senate in March 1796, led to a similar treaty with the regency of Tunis in 1797.[10]

More regular contact between Libya and the United States began in 1796, at the time the pasha was moving to make Tripoli a major maritime power. Since Washington enjoyed no treaty relationship with Tripoli, American shipping in the Mediterranean enjoyed no protection against privateering attacks. Consequently, Tripolitan privateers captured two American vessels, the *Betsy* and the *Sophia*, in August 1796. The latter was soon released because it carried the treaty money America owed the dey of Algiers, but the *Betsy* was converted into a corsair and its crew enslaved. To obtain the release of the captive crew and to protect its Mediterranean commerce, the U.S. government again moved to establish a treaty relationship with Tripoli.[11]

The bey of Tripoli and Joel Barlow, U.S. agent plenipotentiary, finally concluded a treaty of peace and friendship, guaranteed by the dey of Algiers, on 4 November 1796. It promised protection and free passage for the naval vessels of both states and instituted a system of passports to ensure said protection. Commerce between the United States and Tripoli, the reciprocal right to establish consuls in each country, and the privileges, immunities, and jurisdictions to be enjoyed by such consuls were all granted on a most-favored-nation basis. Finally, the treaty recognized the money and presents paid to the bey of Tripoli by the United States as full and satisfactory compensation, stating that no periodical tributes or further payments would be made by either party. The U.S. Senate ratified the 1796 treaty on 10 June 1797, one month before James Leander Cathcart was appointed U.S. consul to Tripoli.[12]

Unfortunately, the 1796 treaty incorporated a serious misunderstanding between the parties that contributed to armed conflict between them in 1801. In articles 1 and 12 of the treaty, the United States demanded that any disputes arising out of the interpretation of the treaty should be referred to the dey of Algiers, described as a mutual friend of the signatories. To Yusuf Karamanli, eager to assert the political independence of Tripoli from Algiers as well as the Sublime Porte, the terms of articles meant simply the arbitration of a mutual friend. Representatives of the United States, on the other hand, misunderstood the relationship between Tripoli and Algiers, viewing Tripoli as a dependency of Algiers and the guarantee of the dey of Algiers as that of a political overlord. From the conclusion of the treaty in 1796 to the outbreak of war in 1801, the pasha repeatedly emphasized in official communications and contacts the need for the United States to treat Tripoli as a sovereign state, while American officials persisted in their view that Tripoli was in fact a dependency of Algiers. American versions of the origins of the 1801 war later emphasized Libyan privateering, but Libyan versions more often focused on the failure of the United States to assess correctly the Algiers-Tripoli relationship.[13]

The United States after 1796 failed to honor fully its treaty obligations with Tripoli in terms of the payment of cash and presents. Consequently, Yusuf Karamanli refused at first to receive James Leander Cathcart, the newly appointed American consul when he appeared in Tripoli harbor in April 1799. In a difficult position, Cathcart soon negotiated a new settlement in which the U.S. government agreed to pay Tripoli $18,000 annually in return for a promise that Tripoli-based privateers would not molest American shipping. While this agreement was similar to others concluded with the rulers of Algiers, Morocco, and Tunis, it contained an important and significant new condition. A 15 April 1799 letter from the pasha to President John Adams emphasized that the new settlement would continue to be valid only so long as the United States treated Tripoli exactly as it did the other regencies of North Africa. The American failure to observe this condition contributed to the incidents that led Tripoli to declare war against the United States in 1801.[14]

When President Adams failed to respond to Karamanli's April 1799 letter, the pasha asked Consul Cathcart whether the letter had been received. The latter confirmed receipt as well as Adam's willingness to treat Tripoli as the equal of the other Barbary states. Despite this assurance, the pasha again felt compelled to write the American president on 25 May 1800, reiterating his position that the United States must treat the regency of Tripoli on the same grounds as the other Barbary states. Again, the pasha received no official response from the American president; and in October 1800 one of the pasha's naval officers captured an American vessel. While this action was apparently taken to demonstrate the conviction among naval officers that Tripoli was a growing naval power and must be respected as such, Yusuf Karamanli intervened, released the ship and its cargo, and dismissed the naval officer concerned. The pasha also took advantage of the incident to lecture the U.S. consul on the need to respect Tripoli as a maritime power.[15]

War with Tripoli

Yusuf Karamanli later demanded a new agreement, including a $250,000 annual stipend; and when Washington refused, the American consulate in Tripoli was attacked and the consul expelled. On 14 May 1801, the flagstaff in front of the American consulate was cut down by order of the pasha, thereby announcing a breach in diplomatic relations. Rightly interpreting these actions to constitute a declaration of war, the U.S. government, bolstered by a growing sense of American nationalism, responded with a more aggressive approach to the privateering activities of the Barbary states. In an action that marked the beginning of a United States naval presence in the Mediterranean, the Jefferson administration dispatched a naval squadron to the region with orders, in the event Tripoli declared war, to destroy as many enemy ships as possible and to initiate a partial blockade of the Libyan coast.[16]

To this point, U.S. policy toward the privateers had resembled the policies of the European powers in that the United States sought to protect its commerce through payment of tribute. Inaugurated on 4 March 1801, Thomas Jefferson had long opposed this traditional approach, arguing that force was the only effective language to employ with brigands of the sea. He did not believe in buying peace with them and became the first chief executive to use force against them. The American consul in Tunis, William Eaton, shared Jefferson's conviction that the use of force was the most appropriate policy for the Barbary powers and repeatedly urged the Jefferson administration to act. In fact, President Jefferson had ordered the squadron of four vessels to the Mediterranean to protect American commerce even before he learned that the flagstaff in front of the Tripoli consulate had been cut down. As the Tripolitan War dragged on, it later proved ironic that the Jefferson administration was criticized for allegedly pursuing an inconclusive and indecisive policy against the Barbary states.[17]

Although it enjoyed the reputation of being a nest of corsairs, Tripoli was not a major privateering port and had never attracted the level of attention of more important centers like Algiers. Most studies today confine Tripoli to a relatively minor role, and this relative weakness, vis-à-vis other Barbary ports, helped explain why the Jefferson administration chose to make it an example of its new policy toward privateering. That said, the small American fleet in the Mediterranean proved inadequate for sustained offensive action; and the intermittent blockade of Tripoli proved relatively ineffective. Disaster struck on 31 October 1803, when the frigate *Philadelphia* struck a shoal in pursuit of Tripolitan cruisers. The crew of the *Philadelphia* was captured and incarcerated, but American sailors later succeeded in penetrating enemy lines and sinking the stranded frigate. American naval forces then proceeded to bombard Tripoli in August–September 1804.[18]

Even as the United States navy prepared to shell Tripoli, Consul Eaton approached Washington with an elaborate plan, first suggested by Consul Cathcart in July 1801, to overthrow the Tripolitanian government. Eaton proposed to organize a political coup in Tripoli that would overthrow the regime of Yusuf Karamanli and replace it with a more compliant government led by his brother, Ahmed. The Jefferson administration hesitated for many months; but eventually in May 1804, appointed Eaton "Navy Agent for the Several Barbary Regencies." More to the point, it agreed to support with arms and men an overland expedition by Eaton to overthrow the Tripoli regime of Yusuf Karamanli. In the spring of 1805, Eaton left Alexandria, Egypt in command of a small military force, seizing the port of Darnah, several hundred miles east of Tripoli, in late April.[19]

Upon seizing Darnah, the Eaton-led force found itself almost immediately besieged by a strong military contingent from Tripoli. The Americans eventually evacuated Darnah in mid-June following the 3 June 1805 termination of hostilities between Tripoli and the United States. Given the general ineffectiveness of their naval operations, American authorities had for some time been searching for an acceptable peace formula. In turn, the continuing blockade, combined with the American capture of the second city of Tripoli, had made a deep impression on Yusuf Karamanli. Preliminary talks between American representatives in Malta and the bey in Tripoli opened in late 1804 but progress was slow because the Americans found Libyan terms—$200,000 for peace and the ransom of American captives plus the unconditional release of all Libyan prisoners of war—unacceptable.[20]

The settlement eventually agreed to in a June 1805 treaty of peace and amity provided for the release of all prisoners on both sides with the United States agreeing to pay the regency of Tripoli an ex gratia payment of $60,000 for the number of Americans held captive in excess of those Tripolitans in American hands. The U.S. government agreed to the withdrawal of American forces, together with the pretender Ahmed, from Darnah; in turn, the bey of Tripoli agreed to the release of Ahmed's wife and children, held captive in Tripoli. Yusuf Karamanli subsequently took four years to honor this particular clause of the agreement. The bey of Tripoli also granted the United States most-favored-nation privileges and relinquished claims to additional tribute. In the event of future hostilities, Tripoli promised to treat American captives as prisoners of war and not as slaves. Given the terms of the 1796 treaty, it was noteworthy that no attempt was made in the 1805 agreement to have the dey of Algiers guarantee the treaty or act as an arbiter of disputes. Overall, the terms of the treaty were relatively favorable to the United States and certainly the most favorable that any Western nation had secured to that date from the regency of Tripoli, or for that matter from any of the Barbary states. Nevertheless, the terms of the 1805 treaty occasioned a bitter partisan debate in the United States; and it was not until 12 April 1806 that the U.S. Senate ratified the agreement.[21]

The outcome of the 1801–5 conflict between Libya and the United States represented a significant achievement for the Karamanli regime. Military success against the United States enhanced Tripoli's international status as a maritime power on the Barbary coast, a key strategic objective of the Libyan government. In addition, the failure of the abortive American scheme to replace Yusuf Karamanli with his brother ensured the continuity of the former's regime. Not only was a dynastic coup safely avoided, but the political existence of Tripoli as a sovereign power was reaffirmed. If Yusuf had been replaced, both Darnah and Tripoli would have likely fallen under American influence, an event that potentially offered serious diplomatic and political consequences for North Africa in general and Libya in particular. If the United States had risen to a position of regional influence in the early 1800s, for example, it might have preceded France by over two decades as a colonial power in North Africa.[22]

The final years of the Karamanli dynasty were characterized by a severe economic crisis compounded by growing social problems and deepening political malaise. In the aftermath of the Napoleonic Wars, American and European powers combined to end the privateering of the Barbary states. Following the War of 1812, two American squadrons, one commanded by Commodore Stephen Decatur, a hero of the war with Tripoli, returned to the Mediterranean to punish Barbary privateers as well as to negotiate successfully new agreements with Algiers, Tripoli, and Tunis. Although the United States maintained a Mediterranean squadron of five to six ships through the first Jackson administration (1829–33), and reinforced it in 1833 with a ship of the line, the activities of the squadron were largely limited to peaceful cruising. The end of privateering led Yusuf Karamanli to neglect his naval forces; in 1823 Tripoli's naval contribution to the sultan's war against Greece was so small that a special envoy was dispatched from Istanbul to reprimand the pasha. In response, Karamanli over the next five years increased the size of the navy by several vessels, and by 1828 Tripoli had reemerged as a regional maritime power. This achievement was short-lived, however, as Tripoli by 1832 had again plunged into bankruptcy and revolution. When the American consul in Tripoli felt himself aggrieved and struck his flag in 1832, the Tripolitanian chief minister called on an American naval officer to adjudicate the dispute, promising in advance to accept the decision.[23]

Ottoman Revival, 1835–1911

The end of the privateering system dealt a devastating blow to the economy of the Karamanli regime. Deprived of tribute payments, the Tripoli government found itself unable to pay for basic imports or to service its foreign debt. The subsequent increase in customs duties and the imposition of extraordinary taxes on luxury commodities and consumer goods, intended to generate the revenues necessary to run the government, provoked considerable domestic opposition which eventually degenerated into civil war. Having exhausted all other means to generate the necessary revenues, Yusuf Karamanli imposed an emergency tax on the *kulughlis*, an auxiliary force comprised of the sons of Ottoman officers and North African women. Viewing the imposition of taxes as an end to their privileged status, this traditionally tax-exempt military contingent mounted an attack on Tripoli. Recognizing the hopelessness of his position, Yusuf Karamanli abdicated in favor of his son, Ali II, who ruled from 1832 to 1835. At that point, the Ottoman government responded to Ali's own appeals for assistance by sending troops to Libya to put down the rebellion and restore public order. In the process, Ali II was bundled aboard a warship that carried him into exile even as Turkish troops restored Ottoman rule in Tripoli.[24]

Ottoman reoccupation marked a turning point in the history of Libya. The restoration of Ottoman rule signaled the end of the long period of decentralized political rule that had prevailed under the Karamanlis. Under the new regime, Libya became more directly responsible to and hence more closely linked to the Sublime Porte. In support of this new policy of consolidating central power over distant provinces, the Ottoman authorities in Libya were expected to use every resource, be it trade, taxes, or otherwise, in support of centralization.[25]

When the Ottomans reoccupied the former autonomous province of Libya, they found a war-torn country, undermined by years of strife and neglect. It took the new governors almost two decades to reestablish order. But by the mid-1850s, Libya had become fertile ground for the reforms that flowered during the Ottoman reform or *Tanzimat* period. For the next twenty-five years, the Ottomans proceeded with administrative, economic, and educational reforms as agriculture slowly supplanted the dying trans-

Saharan commerce. The caravan trade in the course of the eighteenth century steadily declined because European traders along the west coast of Africa diverted the trade in gold and slaves to Atlantic ports. Over the same period, the Mediterranean trade was increasingly dominated by Europeans. The Sublime Porte responded to these changes by governing Libya as a full-fledged province of the Ottoman empire for the remainder of the nineteenth century.[26]

The consolidation of Ottoman control in urban areas set the stage for subsequent developments elsewhere in Libya. Land reform and agricultural development, by encouraging settlement and loosening kinship ties, undermined the tribal organization of nomadic pastoralism. Ottoman administrators, incorporating local sons into the Ottoman bureaucracy, attacked the entrenched power of Libyan tribes in the belief that the traditional decentralization of the Ottoman empire, largely dependent on local notables for the administration of the provinces, was dangerously outmoded. In its place, the reformers sought to create a more efficient administrative system capable of reviving Ottoman power in the face of European expansion. Occurring throughout Libya, the process was especially complex in Cyrenaica due to the administrative role of the Sanusi brotherhood, an influential religious order, in the eastern portion of the province.[27]

American diplomatic and commercial relations with the Ottoman administrators of Libya were minimal throughout the period of Ottoman revival. One observer termed the consulate at Tripoli "one of the finest sinecures in the gift of the President of the United States." When Michel Vidal arrived as the new U.S. consul in September 1870, he found that the pay was good at $3,000 a year plus $800 for expenses, that there were no Americans in residence, and that no American merchantman had called for a generation. The principal activities of the incumbent were to acknowledge circular instructions from Washington and to raise the American flag twice a year on the Fourth of July and on the anniversary of the Battle of New Orleans. When Consul Vidal solicited reappointment in February 1873, he acknowledged in an official dispatch to the State Department that the post could well have been abolished at any time after the Ottoman reoccupation in 1835.[28]

Granted reappointment, Vidal embarked upon an aggressive, multifaceted initiative that eventually led to his recall three years later. Long a proponent of an American coaling station on the Cyrenaican coast, Vidal pushed his government both to maintain its naval strength and to establish a strategic global network of cables, colonies, and coaling stations similar to that maintained by Great Britain. Vidal then linked the problems of an African naval base to a distaste for the slave trade and an affirmation of the nature of American relations with Tripoli. The latter issue concerned the American contention that the Ottoman reoccupation of Libya had not changed the legal status of Libya or the 1805 treaty. In August 1875, after Vidal became involved in an incident with members of a visiting Ottoman naval squadron, matters came to a head when proceedings were filed against him in a civil court. Vidal cabled the State Department, "My home violated by sailors of Ottoman Squadron [sic]. Am insulted. Am threatened by crowd. Denial of redress. Slave trade cause of hostility. Immediate protection desireable."[29]

The State Department soon had two warships on station in Tripoli harbor in support of the consul, and the pasha eventually visited the U.S. consulate to apologize in person. While the U.S. government backed Vidal in time of need, his victory proved bittersweet as he was soon recalled at the insistence of the Sublime Porte. The new consul arrived in October 1876 with instructions from Secretary of State Hamilton Fish that ruled out both a naval base and the emancipation of slaves. "Unlike some, at least, of the European Governments," wrote Fish, "we have no political objects in the Turkish dominions. . . . We covet no occasions to bluster or domineer there, certainly none such as sentimental patronage of benighted Africans would require of us." Under new management, the U.S. consulate in Tripoli returned to the status quo until 1882, when Congress abolished the posting and ended the period in American-Libyan relations that had begun with negotiations between three U.S. ministers plenipotentiary and a Libyan envoy in 1786.[30]

In the end, some eight decades of Ottoman administration produced a significant social and economic transformation of Libya. The policies of a series of Ottoman governors combined to establish order, reorganize administration, encourage settlement, and increase education. Agriculture and pastoralism, which slowly replaced long-distance trade as primary sources of revenue, moved from subsistence to revenue-generating activities. The political consequences of this economic and social transformation were later manifested in Ottoman policies that successfully mobilized popular feeling in defense of the province against European encroachment.[31]

Italian Colonialism, 1911–42

Italy was one of the last European powers to engage in imperial expansion. The Italian city-states were not unified until the second half of the nineteenth century; consequently, the Italian government was unable to exploit effectively the early colonial opportunities that Africa offered neighboring European states. At the end of the nineteenth century, Libya was one of the last African territories not occupied by Europeans, and its proximity to Italy made it a primary objective of Italian colonial policy. The Italian government saw itself carrying on the traditions of the Roman Empire even though Italian unification had occurred only a few decades earlier and Italy was not a leading power at the time. On the other hand, European contemporaries expressed surprise, given the depressed economic state of southern Italy, Sardinia, and Sicily that Italy could "be so indignant at the neglected state of Tripolitania and Cyrenaica or wish to undertake their development before it has undertaken that of the two great Italian islands which might employ all her surplus population, and the development of which is even a peremptory national necessity."[32]

Visionaries in Rome hoped to return Italy to its former greatness by creating a modern empire. In this regard, many Italians believed it was their historic right and obligation to apply Italian sovereignty to those regions in Africa once ruled by the Roman Empire. Italy began to penetrate Ethiopia in 1879, but its expansion there suffered a severe blow with the defeat of Italian forces at Adowa in 1896, even though Eritrea was retained and a protectorate established over much of Somaliland. In part in search of revenge for its humiliating defeat, Italy next turned its attention to Libya. In December 1902, France and Italy created spheres of interest in North Africa when they concluded a treaty that recognized the "special interests" of France in Morocco and Italy in Libya.[33]

In addition to issues of historical right and national pride, many Italians viewed overseas expansion as the best solution to a number of vexing internal problems. At the dawn of the twentieth century, a newly unified Italy still suffered from mutual suspicion and internal conflict. Italian leaders saw a foreign war as a means to divert attention from internal divisions, to unify the population, and to increase pride in the homeland. Moreover, overseas expansion offered a means to test the skills and weapons of the highly rated Italian armed forces.[34]

Many Italians also believed that the colonization of Libya offered an ideal settlement region for countrymen wishing to emigrate. Italian emigration to the United States exceeded 650,000 people in 1910 while emigration to other areas like Argentina was becoming more difficult because of the distance and expense involved. In contrast, Libya was situated close to Italy, enjoyed a pleasant climate with favorable coastal terrain, and was only sparsely populated. Remote myths regarding the fertility of certain areas of Libya only added to the enchantment of what came to be called the *terra promessa* or promised land for emigrants.[35]

Finally, Italy was in need of cheap raw materials and markets for the development of its own economy. Based on limited information, many Italians believed the colonization of Libya would improve this situation. Little did they know that Libya's agricultural potential was poor, its industry limited, and much of its territory empty. In the words of a contemporary student of modern Italian history, "it was ironic to see railroads being built in Africa when some Italian districts had been awaiting them for fifty years. Trade figures by no means justified these colonies . . . they remained a liability." Ironically, the Ottoman authorities inadvertently contributed to the lack of economic information available and thus encouraged one of the principal arguments for the subsequent Italian invasion. Afraid that foreign explorers and tourists would be a first step toward occupation, Ottoman administrators in Libya actively discouraged Westerners in general and Italians in particular from surveying or otherwise touring the country. In consequence, there was very little reliable, up-to-date information available on Libya, with the notable exception of the report of the Jewish Territorial Organization that toured northern Cyrenaica in 1908 and concluded that the area was unfit for large-scale European settlement. In the prevailing situation, "these bogus arguments went on being used in Italy because economic facts were buried under considerations of emotion and prestige."[36]

The Italian government declared war on the Ottoman Empire on 29 September 1911, only four days after it had officially notified the Sublime Porte, in a 26 September ultimatum, that the Ottoman Empire must agree within twenty-four hours to Italian military occupation of Cyrenaica and Tripolitania because of the state of neglect and disorder in which the Ottoman government had left those regions. The Turks responded to the ultimatum, declaring themselves ready to make concessions and asking what guarantees Italy might require; however, the Italians had no interest in dialogue because any delay might give their allies, Austria and Germany, time to intervene and mediate. Seizing Tripoli in October, Italy announced in November its annexation of both Cyrenaica and Tripolitania, and the struggle for control of Libya was fully joined. Although Italy was a signatory to the Hague Conventions of 1899 and 1907, which contained explicit provisions for good offices and mediation to prevent a recourse to force, there is no evidence that the Italian government pursued—or even desired—a peaceful solution to the dispute. On the contrary, Italy rushed to war with the Ottoman government in a deliberate attempt to present the world with a fait accompli in North Africa. In the process, Italy clearly violated the 1856 Treaty of Paris, which provided, in the case of a dispute between the Sublime Porte and one or more signatories, that the former and each of the powers should place the other signatories in a position to prevent a recourse to force by their mediating influence. "Reasons for going to war with Turkey in 1911 there were really none, but such a consideration must be acknowledged essentially extraneous—certainly at the time—and pretexts could always be found."[37]

Embarrassed with the sorry state of provincial defenses, Ottoman authorities sent military officers to Libya to organize resistance to the Italian invasion. By the end of 1911, an important group of Ottoman officers had arrived from Istanbul. Known as the Special Organization, this group functioned as a pan-Islamic secret intelligence unit. Their primary objective was to meet and defeat what the Ottomans considered to be the principal dangers to the empire—local separatist movements and European occupation. Turkish officers took command of military resistance to the Italians; and in the process, their enthusiasm for the defense of the province bolstered Libyan loyalty to pan-Islamic and Ottomanist ideologies. Consequently, early Turkish resistance received growing Libyan support.[38]

By the middle of 1912, the Ottoman government had weakened in its determination to support resistance in Libya. Concerned with events in the Balkans, the Sublime Porte opened negotiations with Italy; a treaty of peace was concluded shortly after the Balkan war broke out in October 1912. The Ottomans did not cede sovereignty over their North African province; however, the sultan did issue a declaration to his Libyan subjects in which he granted them full and complete autonomy. At the same time, he reserved the right to appoint an agent charged with protecting Ottoman interests in Libya and agreed to withdraw Ottoman officers, troops, and civil officials. The Italians, in turn, reaffirmed their annexation of the province, an act not recognized by international law until after the 1924 Allied peace settlement with Turkey. In practice, neither Libyan autonomy nor Italian sovereignty enjoyed convincing validity; as a result, the country's status remained anomalous after 1912.[39]

René Albrecht-Carrié, a recognized authority on Italian history, summed up the situation:

Libya, as it came to be known, was another desert in the Italian collection, certainly no source of wealth for its new rulers, and the source of sad disappointment to those rash enthusiasts in Italy who had thought of it in terms of setting up there a flourishing establishment whither Italian settlers would flock.[40]

Despite the October 1912 treaty in which the Turks abandoned Libya to Italian administration, Libyan forces continued to oppose Italian rule in a struggle that assumed aspects of a holy war. By early August 1915, the Italians controlled little more than the Libyan coastal cities of Tripoli, Benghazi, Darnah, and Tobruk.[41]

The United States government responded to Italy's declaration of war on the Ottoman government with an immediate declaration of neutrality. In a presidential proclamation dated 24 October 1911, President William Howard Taft declared "strict and impartial neutrality between the aforesaid contending powers" and called on all American citizens "to obey in letter and spirit the laws, rules, and principles governing the conduct of neutrals in time of international conflict." One year later, the Italian chargé d'affaires in Washington informed Secretary of State Philander C. Knox that the state of war between Italy and the Sublime Porte had ended with the conclusion of a peace treaty in Lausanne on 18 October 1912; he asked the United States to recognize the sovereignty of Italy over Tripolitania and Cyrenaica as well as to relinquish extraterritorial rights formerly enjoyed by foreigners in those regions.[42]

Secretary of State Knox responded in the affirmative on 28 February 1913, indicating that from 1 November 1912 the disposition of the general law would apply to foreigners in both Tripolitania and Cyrenaica. He also indicated that the American consulate at Tripoli would henceforth be administered subordinate to the consulate general at Genoa under the supervision of the American embassy in Rome. The American ambassadors in both Istanbul and Rome were informed of the changes on 1 March 1913, as was the American consul general in Genoa later in the month. The note to the latter concluded, "You are directed to conform to the legal situation established in Libya through the cessation of the special regime formerly enjoyed by foreigners by virtue of the Capitulations of the Ottoman Empire."[43]

The outbreak of World War I in August 1914 witnessed the reappearance of Ottoman influence in Libya. Although the Ottoman government had formally withdrawn from the province, authorities in Istanbul continued to encourage local Libyan forces in their resistance to the Italians. When Italy entered the war on the side of the Entente powers, the Sublime Porte and its German allies hoped to use the few remaining troops in Libya to spark a revolt against the British, French, and Italian presence in North Africa. A combined Ottoman-Sanusi force took the British garrison at al-Sallum in November 1915, but by March of the following year the British had regained their position, routing the Sanusi forces. The eventual failure of Ottoman efforts to dislodge the European powers occupying Libya, efforts that revealed the continuing importance of pan-Islamic loyalties in Libya, left the province with leaders more interested in solidifying local authority than in developing wider loyalties. By the end of World War I, these local Libyan leaders had largely given up either hope or desire for reincorporation into a larger Ottoman or Islamic political union.[44]

The Italian position in Libya at the end of World War I was not a brilliant one. "Actually, the possession was Italian in little more than name, for effective control by Italian arms and administration was confined to a narrow strip of the coastal region, and not even the whole stretch of coast." From 1917 to 1923, known as the period of accords, the Italian government negotiated with a variety of Libyan factions in an effort to consolidate peacefully its occupation of the country. In the east, the British government, concerned that further upheaval in Cyrenaica would undermine its position in the Western Desert of Egypt, arranged in April 1917 a modus vivendi in which the Italians recognized the autonomy of the Sanusiya in Cyrenaica. The so-called Akramah agreement was welcomed in Tripolitania where it was seen as a starting point from which to negotiate self-determination. For the same reason, President Woodrow Wilson's January 1918 declaration in favor of self-determination was widely and warmly applauded in Libya as well as elsewhere in the Arab world.[45]

The year 1918 also saw the creation of the Tripoli Republic by a group of regional notables desiring to create a broad-based organization to represent all Tripolitanians. Italian recognition of the Sanusiya enhanced the order's standing in Cyrenaica; however, the Tripoli Republic never won formal recognition from Italy. Negotiations between the Italians and various factions in Cyrenaica and Tripolitania continued into 1922, but they eventually broke down because neither side would abandon its claims to control of Libya. This period proved to be a turning point in contemporary Libyan history with important ramifications for American-Libyan relations in the second half of the twentieth century. From the Young Turk revolution of 1908 to the end of the period of accords in 1922, Libya moved from being a "symbol of the Ottoman and pan-Islamic struggle against European encroachment" to a more particularistic approach to resistance in which "nationalism, anti-imperialism, and pan-Islamic loyalties would be clearly and closely associated in Libya."[46]

Because the United States was not at war with Turkey, it was not a signatory to the Lausanne peace treaty of 24 July 1923. Nevertheless, it was represented at the talks by an observer of ambassadorial rank because the Harding administration recognized that it would be practically impossible for the Allies to conduct negotiations without dealing with matters in which the United States was interested. As Secretary of State Charles Evans Hughes emphasized in a telegram to the U.S. ambassador to France, "To permit the Allies to conclude their negotiations without any attempt to present Department's views or to obtain assurances for protection of American interests would leave this Government with a *fait accompli* so far as the relations between the Allies and the Turks were concerned." Therefore, "American observers will be present during the course of the negotiations, ready at any opportune or critical moment to interpose the necessary word for our protection." He then detailed an extensive list of American interests, from the protection of American educational, philanthropic, and religious institutions to the provision of archeological research which he felt were at risk during the peace talks. The disposition of the former Turkish territories, including Cyrenaica and Tripolitania, was noticeably absent from the long list of American interests enumerated by Hughes.[47]

After the Fascist takeover in October 1922, the Italian government of Benito Mussolini implemented a much more rigid colonial policy. In early 1923, the Italian armed forces embarked on a brutal reconquest of Libya. Enjoying an overwhelming superiority in men and equipment, the Italian army had some 20,000 men in the field by 1926, while Libyan guerrilla forces seldom numbered more than 1,000. Tripolitania and the Fezzan were soon pacified, and the struggle then centered on Cyrenaica, where

Sanusi tribesmen effectively employed guerrilla warfare characterized by raids, ambushes, and sabotage. In an effort to deny resistance fighters access to their people, the Italian authorities in turn increasingly emphasized repression and terrorism in which men, women, and children were detained in concentration camps, wells were blocked, and livestock slaughtered. Active resistance in Cyrenaica finally ended in September 1931, when Sidi Umar al-Mukhtar, the most effective Cyrenaican resistance leader, was captured and hanged. On 24 January 1932 the Italian authorities declared an official end to the war begun in 1911.[48]

After 1934, the Libyan territories, consisting of Tripolitania, Cyrenaica, and a military administration in the Fezzan, referred to as South Tripolitania, were administered by a governor general redesignated in 1937 as the first consul. He was supported by a general consultative council and a council of government made up exclusively of Italians. The Libyan population, by the mid-1930s had been cut in half due to emigration, famine, and war casualties. The loss of much of the educated elite and middle class, in the face of a severe disruption of coastal agriculture and domestic trade, was especially significant. When assessing the full impact of Italian colonial practices, it is telling to note that the Libyan population, approximately one and a half million in 1911, was at the same level in 1950. On 9 January 1939, the colony of Libya was incorporated into metropolitan Italy and thereafter considered an integral part of the Italian state until the North African campaigns of World War II left Libya in British and French hands.[49]

Setting the Stage

American policy toward Libya evolved and matured in the four decades after the American revolution. Emulating initially the European policy of appeasement, American diplomats attempted to negotiate treaties of peace and friendship with the bey of Tripoli, but when those agreements proved unsatisfactory to both parties, the Jefferson administration moved to meet force with force. The 1805 treaty of peace and amity was an honorable and satisfactory agreement that reflected significant compromise on the part of both signatories. One decade later, two American squadrons returned to the Mediterranean to discipline the dey of Algiers and to collect indemnity from the bey of Tripoli and the bey of Tunis for losses sustained when British warships seized prize vessels which Americans had taken into Tripolitanian and Tunisian ports during the War of 1812. Thereafter, the United States never again paid annual tribute to a Barbary state.

The early American experience in Libya proved paradoxical. On the one hand, the conflict with Libya, despite the fact that the opening line of the Marine Corps hymn, which appeared in the mid-nineteenth century, referred metaphorically to the war with Tripoli, soon became something of a "forgotten war" in American history. On the other hand, the Tripolitanian War provided an early source of national identity for a nascent American state. Stimulating interest in the concepts of national unity and national identity, events on the Barbary coast eventually became something of a landmark and symbol in the history of American nationalism. A telling example of the often denigrating form this process took can be found in contemporary editions of *Webster's New Collegiate Dictionary* that define the "Barbary Coast" as "a district or section of a city noted as a center of gambling, prostitution, and riotous nightlife."

United States interest in and interaction with Libya was minimal from the early nineteenth century to World War II; nevertheless, events were taking place in and around Libya that would directly affect American-Libyan relations in the postwar era. Italian colonialism fueled nationalist sentiments, which incorporated anti-imperialism and pan-Islamic loyalties, and a strong movement in favor of independence after World War II. Equally significant, the Italian colonial administration deliberately retarded the development of the economic, political, and human resources of Libya which meant this poor North African state would eventually attain independence at mid-century with no experience in self-government, only a handful of college graduates to lead the country, and almost total dependence on foreign aid.

Elsewhere in the region, the rise of British power in the Middle East began in the nineteenth century, with the British establishing themselves in neighboring Egypt in 1882. The British soon developed a certain rapport with the Sanusiya in Cyrenaica, when they opposed French encroachment against the Sanusi center at Kufrah in the early twentieth century. British influence throughout the Middle East, especially on the Sanusi order in Cyrenaica, would play a major role in American-Libyan relations after 1945. Early French policy in the Middle East in general, and in North Africa in particular, also played a significant role in postwar American-Libyan relations. Frustrated by the British in Egypt, the French had occupied Algeria in 1830, Tunisia in 1881, and Morocco in 1912. Morocco and Tunisia were ruled as protectorates, but Algeria was officially assimilated within the French administrative system. Beginning in World War II, the United States pursued an anticolonial policy in Algeria, Morocco, and Tunisia that ran counter to Anglo-French interests in the region. Welcomed by Libyan nationalists, United States policy also encouraged Arab nationalist sentiments that surfaced in the Mashriq in the mid-nineteenth century and grew in strength and influence throughout the Middle East in the interwar period and after World War II.

Chapter 4
Postwar Gridlock

Also, the relevancy of this area to international peace and security cannot be ignored. Names such as Tobruk and Bengasi have not been forgotten, and Egyptian and other Arab states are states entitled to a solution that does not again place them in jeopardy. The future of Libya, indeed, intimately affects the whole strategic position in the Mediterranean and the Near East.

— UN Ambassador John Foster Dulles, 1949

From the closing days of World War II until the end of 1991, when the Soviet Union finally imploded, the United States pursued a hostile policy toward its wartime ally along with the forces of international communism that Washington believed the Soviets controlled and directed. Soon after its creation in 1947, the National Security Council issued secret policy papers that called on the United States to wage economic, political, and psychological warfare to bring about the collapse of the Soviet Union, the overthrow of the Soviet Communist Party, and the dismantling of the Soviet economic, military, and political order. Libya became a pawn in what came to be known as the Cold War even before World War II ended, and it remained in a highly dependent position for much of the next decade. In fluid circumstances, American policy toward Libya was often timid and uncertain as Washington vacillated between an idealistic policy of self-determination and the realistic need to deny the Soviet Union a toehold in northern Africa.

Resettlement of Refugees, 1943–44

In World War II, the North African campaign, which set the stage for the eventual independence of Libya, consisted of three phases. The first opened in September 1940 when a large Italian army under Marshal Rodolfo Graziani invaded Egypt from Libya. There was little serious fighting until December of that year, when the British Army of the Nile, commanded by General Archibald Wavell, chased the Italians back five hundred miles into Libya. Phase two began in spring 1941, when Hitler dispatched the Afrika Korps, commanded by General Erwin Rommel, to assist his Italian allies. The fighting seesawed back and forth across the Libyan Desert for months until Rommel's forces eventually advanced within seventy miles of Alexandria, Egypt. Phase three began in fall 1942, when American and British forces invaded Algeria and Morocco in the west while the British Eighth Army, commanded by General Bernard Montgomery, struck in the east at El Alamein and sent the Axis armies reeling back on one of the longest retrograde movements in history. At the end of its retreat, some 1,750 miles, a distance equivalent to marching from Moscow to Paris, the German army met the British First Army and American forces in the west. Allied forces under the command of General Dwight D. Eisenhower cornered the Afrika Korps in Tunisia, where the last Axis forces surrendered in May 1943.

Once the Axis armies had been routed, the British assumed responsibility for administering Cyrenaica and Tripolitania, initially as the Administration of Occupied Enemy Territory and later as the Military Administration, governing under the terms of the 1907 Hague Convention on the conduct of war. They would continue in this role until Libya eventually attained independence in 1951. France in turn administered the Fezzan until independence. While the French made half-hearted arguments for absorbing the province into their Algerian territories, they did not develop elaborate historical arguments to justify their position. Since Libya was considered occupied enemy territory, its government under international law was on a care and maintenance basis with the institutions and laws in effect at the time of occupation remaining operative. Early Allied diplomacy concerning Libya centered on Cyrenaica and Tripolitania as possible resettlement sites for European refugees, most of whom were Jewish.

President Franklin D. Roosevelt directed the preparation, in early 1943, of a memorandum on the limits of land settlement in Libya to prepare himself for discussions with Prime Minister Winston Churchill at the Third Washington Conference (12–25 May 1943). In response, the Department of State prepared a long and perceptive report that displayed an admirable understanding of the economy and geography of Libya. In a subsection entitled "Possibilities of Future Land Settlement," the 22 May 1943 memorandum emphasized that the "Limits to future land settlement may be set by the technical aspects—the amounts of arable land available, the supply of water and the degree to which the land is already settled." According to the report, the Italian government had acquired, by dispossessing Arab inhabitants, approximately 875,000 acres of land for settlement by 1938. Because large areas of this terrain consisted of rocky land, sand dunes, ravines, and eroded soil, only 360,000 acres, or less than half, were actually developed. The Italians settled 30,000 Italian agriculturists on this land in the 1922–38 period. From this evidence, the report suggested that the best land in Libya had already been used for settlement. While the memorandum concluded that additional settlement of European refugees in Libya was possible, it emphasized that such an effort would necessitate the displacement of existing Italian settlers, an extensive public works program, and prolonged subsidies until such time as the settlers were self-supporting.[1]

It addition to the physical and economic limits to land settlement, the memorandum to President Roosevelt also stressed the political considerations involved, emphasizing that the settlement in Libya of Jewish refugees would meet hostile opposition from local Arabs.

Should additional land be acquired for agricultural settlements, particularly for settlers to whom the Arabs are hostile, the present competition between pastoral Arabs for grazing land for increasing herds and flocks and agriculturists for cultivable land, is likely to break into open conflict. The basic struggle between the economy of the Arabs and of European Jews now existing in Palestine would thus be carried into Libya.[2]

In short, "Libyan Arabs would reject any settlement which would threaten their grazing land and facilitate the infiltration of European Jews into the cities."[3] The report also suggested that opposition to a resettlement program would not be restricted to Libyan Arabs but would undoubtedly extend to other Arab and Muslim countries.

Part of the Arab hostility to Jewish immigration into Palestine has been occasioned by fear that Jews desired to acquire domination of other Arab countries. The establishment of Jews in Libya with the aid of the United Nations would presumably be regarded by Arabs as an indication that those ambitions had received the support of the responsible United Nations, which already are believed by most Arabs to desire the creation of the feared Jewish State in Palestine.[4]

Earlier in the year, the United States chiefs of staff, under pressure from British authorities to establish a refugee camp in North Africa to which refugees in Spain escaping from France could move, had also recommended against the creation of resettlement camps. Citing a shortage of cargo and personnel shipping, the chiefs of staff stressed the additional burden such camps would place on theater commanders and "the possibility of Arab resentment to the influx of Jews which might cause disorder."[5] Nevertheless, British Foreign Secretary Anthony Eden, dismissing the reasons given by the U.S. chiefs of staff as not very convincing, continued to press Churchill on the issue. As for the possibility that resettlement camps might cause Arab resentment, Eden naively opined that "this could surely be eliminated by putting the camp in a place sufficiently remote from important Arab centres."[6] Eventually, President Roosevelt responded to

British pressure by agreeing to transfer some five to six thousand refugees from Spain to French North Africa, and from there to unidentified places of more permanent settlement for the duration of the war. At the time, Cyrenaica and Tripolitania, in addition to Madagascar, remained under consideration as possible sites for the transfer of these refugees once they reached North Africa.[7]

Disposition of Italian Colonies, 1944–45

The occupation of Cyrenaica and Tripolitania by British forces, together with Foreign Secretary Eden's statement in the House of Commons on 8 January 1942 that the Sanusiya would not again fall under Italian domination, naturally raised the question of the future disposition of the Italian colonies. The Sanusi order, which had long resisted Italian domination, quickly allied itself with the British during World War II, forming the core of a small but symbolically important contingent known as the Libyan Arab Force. Although the ultimate implications of Eden's statement in the House of Commons were not clear, his remarks suggested at the time that there might be separate arrangements in the postwar era for the different Libyan territories.[8]

In Washington, it was the August 1941 declaration by President Roosevelt and Prime Minister Churchill known as the Atlantic Charter that best provided a broad definition of early U.S. policy intent in Libya. The Atlantic Charter pledged respect for the self-determination of peoples and progress toward global economic justice. In the new world order, the major powers would promote freer channels of commerce and fuller access to sources of raw materials but would not seek territorial changes that did not accord with the freely expressed wishes of the peoples concerned. Beginning in 1942, President Roosevelt and other U.S. policy makers routinely referred to the Atlantic Charter as a global commitment. For this reason, even if many Europeans remained pessimistic about the immediate future, colonial subjects saw the moment as a highly propitious time to press for autonomy or even independence.[9] The practical implementation of the ideals contained in the Atlantic Charter later left many of these early enthusiasts very disappointed.

The Division of Political Studies at the Department of State, in a memorandum dated 12 May 1943 prepared for the First Quebec Conference (14–24 August 1943), outlined four alternative approaches to the question of Libya. The first and preferred solution, according to this document, was the creation of an international trusteeship to govern Libya as part of a wider North African region. This proposal, put forward by a special subcommittee as early as 26 September 1942, was modified several times before May 1943. The idea was to place the administration of Libya in the hands of an international trusteeship with a governing council composed of Great Britain, France, and Egypt, with Ethiopia, Greece, and Turkey also considered for membership. According to the Department of State, opinion was against the participation of the United States in a trusteeship in this part of the world, although its memorandum was not clear as to exactly where such opposition was centered. In light of subsequent developments, it should also be noted that the State Department memorandum suggested that "in view of the rapid development of air-power . . . it was not important, from a security standpoint, who controlled Libya."[10] The position of the United States on this policy issue would change dramatically over the next few years.

The second alternative explored in the 12 May 1943 memorandum was to divide Libya, with Cyrenaica going to Egypt and Tripolitania to Tunisia. This proposal was opposed on the grounds that the poor administration of Egypt should not be extended to Cyrenaica while adding the Italians in Tripolitania to those already in Tunisia would further disturb the balance between French and Italians in Tunisia. The third alternative was the return of Libya to Italy. While there was little support for this approach, there was general agreement that whatever course of action was adopted should not preclude Italian migration into Libya or the enjoyment of equal opportunities by Italians in Libya. The final alternative discussed was the establishment of Libya as a refuge for Jews. This solution advocated the creation of a Jewish state in Cyrenaica and the settlement of Jewish refugees in villages and farms vacated by Italians as well as on additional land. As suggested earlier, an obstacle in the way of this approach was that little arable land was available in Libya beyond that already occupied by Italian colonists and indigenous cultivators. More to the point, the Department of State readily recognized that it would be extremely difficult to persuade Libyan Arabs to accept Jewish settlement. "An increase in Arab nationalism in Libya has been reported. An attempt to foster Jewish settlement in Libya might result in extending the area of Arab-Jewish conflict without offering any substantial relief to the Jewish refugee problem."[11]

Less than a year later, in spring 1944, the British chiefs of staff advanced a variation of alternative two, the division of Libya. Cyrenaica would become an autonomous principality under Egyptian suzerainty with adequate safeguards for United Nations military requirements, including air and naval facilities in the Benghazi area. Tripolitania would be restored to Italy subject to a guarantee of demilitarization and British retention of the right to use Castel Benito Airfield as a staging point. In response to this proposal, Secretary of State Cordell Hull sent a memorandum to President Roosevelt, who was attending the Second Quebec Conference, arguing that the preferred disposition of Libya would be an international trusteeship over both Cyrenaica and Tripolitania, to be administered by a commission of experts responsible to the United Nations. This approach, Hull added, would not preclude the establishment of an autonomous Sanusi Amirate. If it proved impossible to obtain British agreement to this solution, he suggested to Roosevelt that a feasible, albeit less desirable arrangement would be to establish Cyrenaica as an autonomous Sanusi Amirate under Egyptian (or possibly British) trusteeship, along the lines of the British proposal. Tripolitania could then be placed under an international trusteeship to be exercised by Italy.[12]

A little over a year later, at the Moscow Conference of Foreign Ministers, the Soviet Union complicated the question of the disposition of Italian colonies by pressing for a Soviet trusteeship over Tripolitania. At the time, the British continued to advocate a British trusteeship over Cyrenaica with Italy assuming responsibility for Tripolitania.[13] In support of the Soviet position, Moscow reportedly argued that Great Britain and the United States had plenty of bases around the world and therefore could take Soviet interests into account. When Stalin later suggested that the British appeared unprepared to trust the Soviets in Tripolitania, British Foreign Secretary Ernest Bevin responded that "there was no question of lack of trust but a desire to avoid competition."[14]

In a top-secret briefing book prepared for the 1945 Potsdam Conference (17 July–2 August), U.S. representatives explored alternatives for the former Italian colonies but failed to propose a program for their disposition. Instead, the Truman administration indicated that it would support any one of three solutions, if proposed by another government, in the following order of preference. First, in a reversal of policy, the United States now expressed a preference for the return of Libya to Italian sovereignty, subject to such measures of demilitarization as were devised for Italy. Second, Washington supported partition of Libya into its historic parts, with Cyrenaica established as an autonomous Sanusi Amirate under British or Egyptian trusteeship and Tripolitania retained under Italian sovereignty. Failing either of these solutions, the United States would support the partition of Libya with Cyrenaica established as an autonomous Sanusi Amirate under Egyptian or British trusteeship and Tripolitania placed under international trusteeship exercised by Italy. The State Department report also evidenced a newfound appreciation of the strategic importance of Libya. "Libya is strategically important for control of the central Mediterranean because of its ports and air fields."[15]

The disposition of the Italian colonies, in particular Cyrenaica and Tripolitania, was discussed at some length at the 1945 Potsdam Conference; however, no decision was reached and further discussion was relegated to the foreign minister level. In the course of this dialogue, President Truman indicated on more than one occasion that the United States had no interest in a trusteeship over Libya. Truman added in a humiliating, albeit characteristic aside, "We have enough poor Italians to feed in the United States."[16] Generalissimo Stalin, on the other hand, repeatedly expressed interest in the North African colonies of Italy to the point that Prime Minister Churchill finally—and firmly—stated that the British government had "not considered the possibility of Russia claiming territory in the Mediterranean." On the issue of Jewish settlement, Churchill suggested that there was little enthusiasm among European Jews for resettlement in Libya.[17]

In the immediate aftermath of Potsdam, the respective positions of the major powers on the disposition of the Italian colonies in Libya were surprisingly close. The British favored sovereignty over the territories placed collectively in four powers; the Soviets favored three powers; and the United States appeared generally willing to follow the British lead. While everyone talked of international trusteeships, the Europeans in reality had old-fashioned big-power mandates in mind. Unfortunately, the Soviets had picked Tripolitania for their postwar experiment in tending a Mediterranean outpost, and this was totally unacceptable both to Britain and to a Eurocentric Department of State already bombarding the new president with dire warnings about the resurgence of communism in Europe. While the State Department did not offer specific trusteeship proposals in the months following the end of the war, the context in which suggestions were offered made international arrangements appear less and less attractive. "This was one of the fundamental results of the beginning of the cold war: the paralysis of the creative side of diplomacy out of fear that the Soviets would use any and all multinational entities to subvert order and reason."[18]

Council of Foreign Ministers, 1945–48

In the immediate aftermath of World War II, the agency for the work of the great powers was the Council of Foreign Ministers. Viewed by Italy and the Axis allies as a "society of victors," the Council was approved at the 1945 Potsdam Conference and met from 1945 to 1948 in a series of long and spirited, albeit largely unproductive, sessions. Coexisting with the new United Nations, a promising new path for international planning, the Council of Foreign Ministers was a throwback to older patterns that increasingly reflected the disarray among the big powers. The Council successfully negotiated peace treaties with Bulgaria, Finland, Hungary, Italy, and Romania, but resolution of the colonial issue repeatedly eluded its grasp. Discussions related to the disposition of the Italian colonies, which occasionally offered tantalizing possibilities for compromise and accord, more regularly mirrored the bipolar character of the new world order which defined the postwar era.[19]

At the time, U.S. policy continued to be torn between divided counsels, as was evident when the Council of Foreign Ministers met in London in September 1945. The issue of Italian colonies was not, and had never been, a vital one for U.S. policy makers except insofar as American security might be involved. Europe was the priority, and Italy was not a priority even in Europe. The Office of European Affairs, concerned about the future role of the Soviet Union in the Mediterranean, recommended that the Italian colonies, including Libya, be returned to Italy in the form of trusteeships. The Office of Near Eastern and African Affairs, on the other hand, was inclined to give free rein to the United Nations organization and to implement the principles of international administration.

In the end, on September 15 Secretary of State James F. Byrnes offered a plan for establishing United Nations trusteeships in all former Italian territories. His proposal included a ten-year administration over a unified Libya, after which time the territory would become independent. Meeting privately with his Soviet counterpart, Byrnes reiterated many of the themes expounded earlier in the Atlantic Charter, arguing that the Arabs expected the Allies to honor wartime statements favoring self-determination. The creation of UN trusteeships would demonstrate to the world that the big powers were not seeking to exploit their victory. British Foreign Secretary Bevin accepted the U.S. proposal, but the Soviets continue to oppose it, pressing their claim to Tripolitania. In consequence, the first session of the Council of Foreign Ministers ended with little hope of rapid progress toward a final resolution of the colonial question.[20]

While the Council of Foreign Ministers deliberated in London, *New York Times* columnist James Reston published an article that accurately outlined the State Department's internal dialogue over the colonial issue. According to Reston, the dispute was "essentially one of the relations among the great powers and how they intend to reorganize Europe." Reston described the wrangling over African colonies as in reality a struggle for the mastery of Europe with fundamental issues over the character of a postwar world at stake. Reston's column proved highly influential as it became a common referent for analysts arguing that the disposition of the Italian colonies was a test case of Allied resolve to confront the new world order, rejecting the flawed diplomacy of the past. The chief roadblock to international trusteeship was not the question of revived Italian rule but instead Western fears of Soviet involvement.[21]

One month after the Council of Foreign Ministers completed their first session in London, prolonged anti-Jewish rioting broke out in Tripoli on 4 November 1945. The period immediately following the end of World War II was characterized by a state of euphoria in Libya in which Jewish-Muslim relations, especially in smaller towns and rural areas, seemed to settle down, as both groups evidenced a sincere desire to work peacefully together. Jews joined the city of Tripoli police force, something that had not occurred under Italian rule, and patrolled together with Muslims. At the same time, the establishment of the British administration increased expectations and support for complete freedom from colonial rule. In a charged and uncertain atmosphere, the anti-Jewish riots that broke out in late 1945 left more than 130 Jews and one Muslim dead in several days of rioting in Tripoli and nearby communities. The definitive history of the 1945 pogrom has yet to be written. Nevertheless, most observers agree that the riots constituted, at least in part, a symbolic statement on the part of the Libyan majority claiming the restoration of the proper order of Muslim sovereignty. American officials saw the riots as a clear indication that events in the Near East could quickly deteriorate in this and other ways if the Big Four failed to reach a satisfactory agreement.[22]

After Secretary Byrnes presented a proposal for UN trusteeship at the London session of the Council of Foreign Ministers, the State Department continued to work on an agreement for the Italian colonies with drafts crossing and recrossing the Atlantic from October 1945 to early 1946. A twenty-page proposal, dated 4 April 1946, called for UN administration of a unified Libya. The Trusteeship Council of the United Nations would appoint a chief administrator, neither an Italian national nor a citizen of one of the four members of the Council of Foreign Ministers, to a term of five years. He would have full authority over the internal and external affairs of Libya and would be assisted by an advisory committee composed in part of one representative each from Britain, France, Italy, the United States, and the Soviet Union. The chief administrator would create an international corps of civil servants, who would declare loyalty to the United Nations, to administer Libya. In addition, he would establish an independent judiciary and a police force to maintain order. The proposal also stipulated that Cyrenaica would become an autonomous Sanusi Amirate headed by Sayyid Idris, who would derive his power from the chief administrator acting as UN high commissioner to the territory.[23]

The American draft was an ambitious undertaking, as it sought to implant political rights that had never existed in Libya while committing a UN corps to train native peoples for self-governance of a unified state. By restricting big-power involvement to an advisory group that had few powers, the proposal offered little opportunity for Soviet interference. Envisioning an experimental regime committed to gradualism and evolutionary change, the American proposal in the end came to nothing. The draft American agreement for UN trusteeship was never again formally considered by the Council of Foreign Ministers.

The Egyptian government from the start took a keen interest in the Italian colonies, in particular Libya and Eritrea, because of their geographic proximity and the historical ties between Egypt and these colonies. As soon as the Council of Ministers opened their discussions in London, Egypt submitted a memorandum, dated 12 September 1945, expressing its interest in Libya and Eritrea and requesting that Cairo be consulted on the final disposition of both colonies. Stating that Egypt and Libya were tied by common bonds, the memorandum suggested that a plebiscite be held in Libya to ascertain whether the population preferred independence or union with Egypt. If the Council of Foreign Ministers decided against a plebiscite but in favor of a trusteeship, the Egyptian note recommended that the trusteeship be entrusted to either Egypt or the Arab League. When no decision on Libya was reached at the initial meetings of the Council of Foreign Ministers, the Egyptian government later asked to be present at the upcoming Italian peace conference. Egypt was not invited to the peace conference as a participant, but it was given assurances that its representative would be allowed to submit Egyptian viewpoints as an interested party. The Egyptian government would continue to play an important, albeit often peripheral role in Libyan affairs for the next twenty-five years.[24]

Together with Egypt, the Arab League, formed by Egypt, Iraq, Lebanon, Saudi Arabia, Syria, Transjordan, and Yemen on 22 March 1945 also expressed great interest in the future disposition of Libya. A self-appointed custodian of Arab interests in general, the Arab League aimed to place Libya, if it was not granted independence, under the sole trusteeship of Egypt or the collective trusteeship of the Arab League itself. As early as September 1945, Secretary General Abdul Rahman Azzam circulated a memorandum to League members expressing views very similar to those expressed by Egypt to the Council of Ministers. The Libyan question first appeared on the agenda of the Council of the Arab League on 4 December 1945, at which time the Council supported either Libyan independence or a trusteeship under Egypt or the Arab League. The Council of the Arab League, in subsequent meetings, continued to express its support for Libya whenever the issue was raised.[25]

In the months before the 1946 Paris Peace Conference, the Italian government persistently but unsuccessfully lobbied for a postwar role in its former African colonies, expressing particular interest in a trusteeship. Despite these efforts, the draft peace treaty with Italy failed to meet Italian expectations, with article 17 calling for Italy to renounce "all right and title to the Italian territorial possessions in Africa, i.e. Libya, Eritrea and Italian Somaliland" with the final disposal of these possessions to be determined jointly by the United States, United Kingdom, Soviet Union, and France within one year of the peace treaty coming into force. Given the contents of this proposed article, the Italian ambassador to the United States asked Secretary of State Byrnes in August 1946 to support omission of the Italian renunciation clause with respect to colonies so that the status quo in North Africa could continue for another year. Secretary of State Byrnes responded positively to the Italian suggestion and later proposed to the Council of Foreign Ministers a one-year delay in the final decision on the Italian territories in Africa.[26]

In the end, the provisions concerning the colonies in the Italian peace treaty, signed on 10 February 1947, did not change from the early summer of 1946. The treaty required Italy to renounce all right and title to its former African possessions of Eritrea, Libya, and Somaliland, leaving the respective British military administrations in power. Annex 11 of the treaty stipulated that future arrangements regarding the former Italian colonies would be determined by the joint decision of the United States, Great Britain, Soviet Union, and France. The latter four powers were obliged to arrive at a settlement within a year of the treaty's coming into force, which occurred with an exchange of ratifications on 15 September 1947. Failing that, the big powers were to submit the question to the UN General Assembly. In the interim, the foreign ministers of the four powers were authorized to continue study of the issue, using such investigative commissions as might be required.[27]

While the Council of Foreign Ministers was not the only battleground of the early Cold War, its first and second sessions produced an ongoing and ever more acrimonious exchange that reflected new alignments in international affairs. In this sense, the work of the Council clearly reflected the concerns and limits of Cold War diplomacy. The second Council session in Paris was followed by the Paris Peace Conference and then by additional meetings in New York in late 1946 before the anticlimactic signing of the peace agreements in February 1947. At this point, discussion of the disposition of the Italian colonies was essentially complete. After Italy renounced all claims to its colonies, the territories continued under British administration pending their final disposition by the Council of Foreign Ministers within one year of the peace treaty going into effect. If the Council failed to reach an agreement within this time, the future status of the colonies would be decided by the United Nations.[28]

Libya at the end of 1946 was divided into three zones: a nascent Sanusi Amirate in Cyrenaica, a volatile mix of ethnic groups side by side with a more urbanized culture in Tripolitania, and the French-controlled oases in the Fezzan. Despite the plethora of proposals made during Council sessions, there was little reason at the time to believe that a unified Libya would emerge in the foreseeable future. Great Britain planned to continue its close ties with Cyrenaica but was not interested in overseeing Tripolitania and could see little chance of dislodging the French from the Fezzan. The United States, with no interest in assuming trusteeship responsibilities in Africa, promoted a collective trusteeship plan that had some ideological appeal but generated little real support even at the State Department. In turn, the French were determined to retain control in the Fezzan and see Italy restored in Tripolitania. The Soviets hoped to use the colonial issue first to improve their bargaining position in Europe and later to increase their appeal to the Italian electorate by sponsoring the restoration of Italian rule in its former colonies.[29]

Each of the four powers expressed a desire to reach a solution to the problem of the Italian colonies that ensured the welfare of native peoples and was in the best interests of the international community. Nonetheless, the fate of Libya and the other colonies would be dictated in the end by the character of the power relationships issuing from the diplomatic duel in progress in the eastern Mediterranean. The requirements of modern air warfare and the political adjustments in progress due to the new power relationships arising from World War II combined to give Libya a level of international importance that was unimaginable only a few years earlier.

The end of the war witnessed "the total eclipse of French influence in the eastern Mediterranean and its weakening elsewhere, together with the rapid subsidence of British power, once paramount in the area." Fresh impetus was thereby "given to Zionism, Pan-Arabism, and local Arab nationalist movements, all of which must be taken into account to a degree not customary in the past. . . . At the same time, the recession of the British and French empires has breathed new life into ancient Russian expansionism, emboldened by recent victories and strengthened by the crusading gospel of the Soviets." Finally, the United States, "formerly given to righteous aloftness from the struggles of empire in the Mediterranean and African theatres," now allied itself with Great Britain against the Soviet Union, "for what are, in reality, the paramount stakes of national security." In a word, the Italian colonies in general and Libya in particular had become vital elements in the Cold War balance of power.[30]

The run-up to the Italian general elections in 1948 had a heavy impact on events in Libya as the United States and its allies worried that appreciable numbers of Italian voters could be swayed by the colonial issue. The Soviets weighed in early, in an effort to influence Italian voters, when they announced in mid-February 1948 that they favored an Italian trusteeship over all former colonies. American and British policy makers took a more cautious approach, favoring the postponement of a decision until after the elections. As it turned out, the Italian elections came and went with the Gasperi-Sforza regime demonstrating that it could withstand a communist challenge when sufficiently bolstered by external aid. In Washington, the lesson learned was that there was no need to accept Italian demands for trusteeships over former colonies.[31]

Although strategic considerations had been paramount in the case of Libya since the end of World War II, it was the European crisis in early 1948 that galvanized Anglo-American defense plans. In the aftermath of the Italian elections, the State Department and the Foreign Office pledged not to make public statements about the colonies without first consulting each other. Later, the State Department instructed the American delegation to coordinate its strategy with both British and French colleagues. To avoid appearing obstructionist, American delegates were directed to accept "reasonable compromises" on procedural issues, but on matters of substance there were to be no more East-West compromises. "Those days were over, obliterated by the drumbeat of incidents, confusion, and cold war mobilization epitomized by crackling tension over Berlin and the fate of Germany." A British aide-mémoire in June 1948 called for a full and frank exchange of views with Washington over the Italian colonies; and the French government was later included in the discussions.[32]

Throughout the period, Libya remained the key to the preservation of Anglo-American strategic interests in the eastern Mediterranean. In January 1948 Sir Orme Sargent, British Permanent Under Secretary, had described Cyrenaica as the best aircraft carrier in Africa albeit one lacking manpower and resources. The American base in Tripolitania at Mallaha, better known as Wheelus Field, also took on new meaning at this point. Largely demobilized in 1947, plans for the revitalization of Wheelus as a major postwar base took place in mid-1948. In short, the United States by early 1948 had committed itself fully to British interests in Cyrenaica, and by the summer of 1948, to the development of a major American base at Mallaha. With the European crisis of 1948 serving as a catalyst for American aims, the strategic interests of the two powers were now interlocked.[33]

In concert with the provisions of the Italian peace treaty, the Council of Foreign Ministers dispatched a Commission of Investigation to Libya in spring 1948 to report on the internal conditions of the territories and to ascertain the wishes of the people. Composed of one representative from each of the Four Powers, the Commission was instructed to gather facts but to refrain from making recommendations on the final disposition of the territories. The Commission arrived in Libya on 6 March and departed on 20 May, spending forty days in Tripolitania, twenty-five in Cyrenaica, and ten in the Fezzan. In Tripolitania, rival political parties united to present a declaration of policy embodying three principal points: complete and immediate independence, the unity of Libya, and membership in the Arab League. While interviews with individuals outside the influence of political parties confirmed an almost unanimous desire for independence, the Commission later reported that Tripolitania was not ready for independence because it was not self-supporting with its future existence and economic development dependent on external assistance.

As for the Fezzan, sparsely populated with meager resources, the Commission quickly concluded that it was doubtful it could ever become an independent entity. In Cyrenaica, the last province to be visited, the Commission found strong support, especially among the tribes, for independence under whatever form of government Amir Idris might approve. At the same time, it was again clear that the province was not self-supporting and that foreign assistance would be required for many years to come. Torn by conflicting interests, the members of the Commission were eventually able to agree only on a few fundamentals. The people of Libya were virtually unanimous in their desire for freedom from foreign rule, although a mature understanding of the responsibilities of independence was clearly lacking. A corollary to the general aspiration for independence was the widespread lack of sentiment for a return to Italian rule. At the same time, due to the low level of economic development, the country was certainly not self-supporting; therefore, the Commission concluded it was not yet ready for independence.[34]

On 23 July 1948 President Truman approved National Security Council recommendation NSC 19/1 as the core policy statement for American negotiators. Abandoning any thought of collective administration of the ex-colonies, the document acquiesced in British interest in a trusteeship over Cyrenaica. British governance over Tripolitania was also preferred, and the French should evacuate the Fezzan, although this question was deemed not important enough to warrant serious discord. NSC 19/1 failed to resolve the fate of Libya and was immediately followed by a new State Department plan to postpone discussion of the issue for a year in the hopes of achieving a favorable decision in the United Nations. The document was noteworthy only because it again demonstrated the full extent to which the fate of Libya had become ensnarled in the Cold War. The U.S. government in NSC 19/1 opposed immediate independence for Libya on the grounds that creation of a weak state would invite infiltration and aggression on the part of the Soviet Union.[35]

At the final session of the Council of Foreign Ministers, which opened in Paris on 13 September 1948, the Soviet delegate, in an astonishing shift of policy position, proposed placing the colonies under a UN trusteeship. The administration of the trusteeship, according to the Soviet plan, would then be responsible to a Trusteeship Council assisted by an advisory board that would include the members of the Council of Foreign Ministers. The Soviet initiative reproduced almost verbatim the 15 September 1945 proposal of Secretary of State Byrnes and thus returned the Council to its starting point. The American, British, and French representatives on the Council quickly rejected the Soviet plan as impractical, transferred responsibility for the Italian colonies to the United Nations, and ceased to function.[36]

United Nations Decides, 1948–51

The movement of the Libyan question from the Council of Foreign Ministers to the General Assembly of the United Nations was of decisive importance to the future of Libya. The General Assembly was a body in which no veto could prevail, as it consisted of fifty-eight members voting on the basis of equality and deciding important issues by a two-thirds majority. Resolution of the issue might not be made easier by the change of milieu, but the question in this forum would be addressed under very different rules. Unanimity was no longer a prerequisite; and all debates, with the exception of those in subcommittee, were in public. The net result was that the transfer of proceedings to the United Nations gave all parties involved a larger and more accessible forum in which to plead their case. At the same time, the diversity that marked the United Nations from the outset was quickly reflected in the plethora of formulas, propositions, and proposals put forth to determine Libya's destiny.

The Libyan question was placed on the agenda of the third session of the UN General Assembly, scheduled to meet in Paris in September 1948; however, due to a crowded agenda and the limited time given delegates to consult their governments, the question was deferred to the second part of the third session, which opened in Lake Success in April 1949. It was placed initially on the agenda of the First Committee (Political and Security); the deliberations of the committee soon revealed that the divergent views that had prevailed in the Council of Foreign Ministers would be carried over in greater measure into the United Nations. The Soviet representative argued that peace and security in the area necessitated the withdrawal of British forces from Libya together with the establishment of a UN trusteeship. In turn, delegates from Great Britain and the United States suggested that regional peace could not be maintained through UN administration and instead necessitated the retention of British bases in Cyrenaica and Tripolitania.

In outlining the U.S. position, the American delegate emphasized that a decision on the future of Libya should consider the interests of the inhabitants as "paramount" but also take into account concerns for international peace and security. "The inhabitants seem well advanced toward self-government and independence, and we believe any Assembly decision should put the primary emphasis on achieving early independence." At the same time, he emphasized that "the relevancy of this area to international peace and security cannot be ignored. . . . The future of Libya, indeed, intimately affects the whole strategic position in the Mediterranean and the Near East." While the Egyptian delegate once again took the view that Libya was ready for immediate independence, other delegates questioned the area's preparedness for such a decisive step. When prolonged discussion in the First Committee identified no common ground for action on the Libya issue, a subcommittee was appointed to study and propose a resolution to the opposing viewpoints.[37]

The U.S. government by 1949 was reluctant to see any form of UN trusteeship in the area because it would threaten Washington's plan to develop Wheelus Field into a strategic air base. Henry Serrano Villard, the first U.S. Minister to Libya, later pointed out that the administrator of a trust territory under the UN trusteeship system could not establish military bases except in the case of a strategic trusteeship such as that enjoyed by the U.S. at the time in the formerly Japanese islands of the Pacific. However, strategic trusteeships were subject to veto in the UN Security Council of which the Soviet Union was a member. If Libya passed under any form of UN trusteeship, it would thus become virtually impossible for it to play a role in the defense arrangements of the free world. As an independent entity, on the other hand, Libya could enter into treaties or other arrangements with the Western powers looking to the defense of North Africa and the Mediterranean.[38]

After the subcommittee had been formed, the British and Italian foreign ministers together suggested a compromise formula, often referred to as the Bevin-Sforza plan, which gave ten-year trusteeships to Britain in Cyrenaica, Italy in Tripolitania, and France in the Fezzan. At the end of this period, Libya would be established as an independent state if the General Assembly decided such a step was appropriate. Acknowledging Libyan aspirations for independence, the proposal also safeguarded, at least temporarily, American and British strategic interests in the region. The Bevin-Sforza plan received the support of France, Great Britain, the United States, and the Latin American states, but was opposed by the Arab, Asian, and Soviet blocs on the grounds it ignored the national aspirations of the Libyan people.

Less than six weeks after declaring the interests of the Libyan people to be paramount, the U.S. delegate justified support for the Bevin-Sforza plan on the grounds the approach offered a path to both independence and unity.

Independence will be attained in 10 years unless there are very strong reasons to the contrary at that time. Unity is arranged for in the recommendation that the powers charged with the administration of the three territories should take adequate measures to promote coordination of their activities in order that nothing should be done to prejudice the attainment of an independent and unified Libyan state . . . the truth is that the formula of the resolution contains ample provision for working out the necessary machinery to achieve a unified state at the time of independence.[39]

In the end, U.S. support for the Bevin-Sforza plan was simply another example of strategic concerns outweighing the articulated and recognized interests of the Libyan people. Eventually accepted by the First Committee, the plan was widely criticized by Third World delegates because it originated outside the United Nations, ignored the interests of the native population, and divided Libya into three entities after the principle of unity had been accepted. The Bevin-Sforza plan generated widespread protests in Tripoli and elsewhere in Libya before it was finally and overwhelmingly defeated by the Arab, Asian, and Soviet blocs in a May 1949 General Assembly vote.[40]

With the rejection of the trusteeship proposal, some agreement on independence for Libya became a foregone conclusion. Both the United

States and Great Britain now declared themselves in favor of independence, despite what they considered to be the backwardness of the country, but argued that a preparatory period of three to five years was necessary to lay the groundwork for self-government. Championing the cause of colonial areas, the Soviet Union called for immediate independence, together with the withdrawal of foreign forces and the liquidation of military bases within three months. The Arab and Asian representatives, together with Italy, also favored immediate independence. In support of this objective, in late 1949 the First Committee adopted a draft resolution that called for Libyan independence no later than 1 January 1952. After considerable debate, the General Assembly approved a resolution on 21 November 1949 calling for Libya, comprised of Cyrenaica, the Fezzan, and Tripolitania, to become an independent and sovereign state no later than 1 January 1952.[41]

On 10 December 1949, the UN General Assembly appointed Assistant Secretary General Adrian Pelt as UN Commissioner for Libya with a charter to assist the inhabitants of Libya to draw up a constitution and to establish an independent state. The General Assembly also provided for a ten-member Advisory Council consisting of representatives of Egypt, France, Italy, Pakistan, the United Kingdom, and the United States, together with four Libyan leaders appointed by Pelt, to assist the Commissioner to accomplish his tasks. The Egyptian and Pakistani members on what came to be called the Council of Ten often expressed dissenting opinions in the coming months on questions related to the role of the administering authorities and the constitutional form of the Libyan state. The Egyptian representative was especially forceful on the question of federalism versus unity as his government strongly preferred a unified form of government for Libya. In turn, the United States argued consistently, and in the end successfully, that federation was the form of unity best suited for Libya.[42]

The Soviet Union, to the surprise of many observers, largely disengaged from the Libyan issue in the years immediately after 1949. Intensely involved in the earlier Council of Foreign Ministers discussions, Soviet interest waned after the question passed to the United Nations and debate moved outside the central concern of Moscow, a military base in North Africa. If Soviet interest and involvement had continued in 1949–51 at the same level as before, the outcome of the UN mission would likely have been very different. Aggressive Soviet support for Arab League and Egyptian demands for a unitary Libyan state dominated by Tripolitania, for example, would have affected political attitudes in Cyrenaica and the Fezzan and possibly blocked the creation of a unified Libya.[43]

The Western governments, on the other hand, continued to view Libya within the context of the Cold War and related global strategies. The British government worked to consolidate diplomatic and political relations in Cyrenaica in order to establish a sound foundation for its military bases there.[44] The French repeatedly expressed concern that independence in Libya would destabilize the region by encouraging similar movements elsewhere in North Africa. For strategic purposes, France hoped to retain and strengthen its position in the Fezzan to slow the westward spread of Arab nationalism. In the words of Minister Villard, "France alone was not eager to see the sudden rise of an independent country next door to the nationalistically inclined Arab peoples of the French North African territories."[45] The United States, while supporting independence for Libya, worked to solidify its strategic position at Wheelus Field near Tripoli before independence took place. At the same time, American diplomats remained concerned about the level of communist activity in Libya, a concern that in retrospect was more a barometer of American xenophobia than a recognition of a realistic threat.[46] Finally, the Italians had reconciled themselves to independence for their former colony and now waited patiently for the opportunity to forge new agreements to protect their economic and financial interests in Tripolitania.

On 2 December 1950 the National Assembly of Libya approved a fundamental law that provided for a constitutional, democratic, and representative form of government based on federal and monarchical systems. The assembly offered the throne to Amir Idris of Cyrenaica on the same day, but the Amir preferred to wait until a constitution was promulgated before accepting the throne. On 7 October 1951 the National Assembly proclaimed the Libyan constitution; independence was declared on 24 December 1951. The Libyan constitution established a hereditary monarchy under Muhammad Idris al-Mahdi al-Sanusi with a federal state divided into the three provinces of Tripolitania, Cyrenaica, and the Fezzan. It also provided for executive, legislative, and judicial branches of government with a parliament consisting of a senate and a house of representatives. Parliamentary elections were held in early 1952, and the first session of the new parliament opened on 25 March 1952.

Conflicting Demands of Dependence and Independence

The negotiations over the disposition of the Italian colonies in general, and Libya in particular, were complex, intense, and prolonged. At stake in the decisions were a myriad of convoluted aims and interests. Military and strategic considerations included American and British plans to maintain Libya as a Western base area as well as to keep it out of Soviet hands. The British also hoped to buttress the sagging bulwarks of their imperial system in Africa and the Middle East. The French rightly worried that any decisions taken on Libya or the other Italian colonies might generate nationalist sentiment and unrest in the neighboring French territories in North Africa. The Soviets hoped to gain access to the Mediterranean shore, and when that proved impossible they moved to deprive the British of their strategic foothold. Other considerations included Italian prestige, the British pledge to the Sanusiya of Cyrenaica that they would not be returned to Italian rule, and Arab interests in the Muslim populations of the region. Of course, there were also the expressed interests of the Libyan people themselves, defended by those members of the United Nations that supported the aspirations of colonial peoples, and exploited by Moscow once it became clear the Soviet Union would not gain a position in Tripolitania. And even this complicated list of interests and objectives by no means exhausts the multitude of cross currents and ramifications involved in reaching a decision on the disposition of Libya.

Given the circumstances, it was not surprising that the United States government shifted policy positions frequently in an effort to find a solution that would, from the viewpoint of policy makers in Washington, both guarantee the security of the region and protect American interests. Primary among those interests was the shorter term, tactical need to utilize Wheelus Field near Tripoli as a link in the supply chain for American occupation troops in Europe together with the longer term, strategic need to maintain a position on the Mediterranean coast as a base for the southern flank in the event of a European war. Wheelus Field was soon seen as the essential western anchor in an arc of strategic bases stretching from Libya to Saudi Arabia. Consistent with these objectives, the fundamental aim of American policy was to broker an agreement in Libya, any agreement, as long as it served and supported core American interests.

In the process, the U.S. government, less than a decade after the issuance of the Atlantic Charter in August 1941, compromised and very nearly abandoned its pledged respect for the self-determination of peoples. This conscious redirection of American policy took place despite a clear understanding in Washington as to the interests and wishes of the Libyan people. The work of the 1948 Commission of Investigation, undoubtedly the most systematic effort of its kind conducted in the first half of the twentieth century, went well beyond anything conceived of by the League of Nations under its mandate system. Consequently, the U.S. government, together with the other members of the Council of Foreign Ministers, had a clear picture of existing economic, social, and political conditions in Libya at the end of the decade. In particular, the Commission confirmed in Libya the widespread existence of an exuberant form of nationalism among disparate and mostly illiterate peoples, together with a general preference for immediate independence. Policy decisions made in Washington in this time frame mark the outset of a long-term underestimation of the strength and importance of national aspirations and nationalism in Libya and elsewhere in the Arab world.

The issue of the Italian colonies was never a vital one for the United States government, but Soviet interest in Tripolitania eventually made the disposition of Libya a key strategic issue. Where State Department memoranda drafted at the beginning of the 1940s could suggest that control of Libya was unimportant from a strategic standpoint, the situation had changed completely less than a decade later. The provinces of Cyrenaica and Tripolitania, peopled with outspoken nationalistic groups, assumed an exaggerated strategic value in the immediate postwar world. The fact that the two provinces were loosely linked historically, despite geographic, demographic, and religious divisions, only made their disposition that much more difficult. Consequently, the conflicting policies of the big powers soon became Libya's strongest ally in achieving unity and independence. There was discord within Libya, but there was even more discord in the world outside.

In the end, Libya started down the road to independence because the foreign powers with the most interest in its future could develop no consensus on what that future should be. In this regard, the decision to turn the issue of Libya over to the United Nations marked the total failure of the Big Four to resolve among themselves the question of the disposition of the Italian colonies. And the celebrated decision of the United Nations to give Libya independence, while it reflected the wishes of the Libyan people as confirmed by the Commission of Investigation in 1948, was in fact a stage-managed compromise on the part of three of the Big Four powers—France, the United Kingdom, and the United States—to achieve a solution they were unable to negotiate with the Soviet Union through the Council of Ministers. Libya had become an arena for the interplay of great power rivalry, a contest that predated the outset of the Cold War and was exacerbated by it. More than Iran or other rimland controversies, Libya was center stage in the East-West conflict in the immediate postwar period, and it would remain so for many years to come.

Chapter 5
Independence at a Price

A major US objective in Libya is to retain use of Wheelus Field after Libya becomes independent.
—Secretary of State Dean Acheson, 1950

We cannot afford to lose Libya.
—Vice President Richard M. Nixon, 1957

Granted independence in December 1951, Libya was the first African state to achieve independence from European rule and the first and only state to be created by the UN General Assembly. A fragile product of bargains and compromises, the United Kingdom of Libya was driven by a complex web of internal and external demands and interests. In the end, it was a genuine surprise to most observers that it lasted almost eighteen years, a period in which it brought a certain precarious stability to the eastern Mediterranean. From 1951 to 1969, eleven prime ministers and more than forty different cabinets demonstrated an unexpected resilience in dealing with a succession of domestic and international crises that increasingly involved Libyan vulnerability to the Arab nationalist currents sweeping the Middle East.

Strategic Interests

After World War II, the United States worked to clarify its strategic position in the eastern Mediterranean and Middle East. Comprising Greece, Turkey, Iran, the Arab states, Israel, and Libya, the security of the eastern Mediterranean and Middle East was considered to be "of critical importance to the security of the United States." Accordingly, it became U.S. policy to support the security of the region, including the political independence and territorial integrity of Greece, Turkey, and Iran. President Harry S Truman articulated the American response to the Soviet threat at a joint session of Congress on 12 March 1947. In what came to be known as the Truman Doctrine, the president requested immediate aid for Greece and Turkey on the grounds that the United States must support free peoples resisting subjugation by armed minorities or outside pressures. In implementing this policy, Washington later declared itself willing "to make full use of its political, economic and, if necessary, military power in such manner as may be found most effective." Political and economic means were to be exhausted first, including resort to the United Nations, before turning to force. "Any resort to force should be in consonance with the Charter of the United Nations and in cooperation with like-minded members of the United Nations *in so far as possible* [author's emphasis]."[1]

Recognizing the pivotal role Arab-Israeli relations would play in the achievement of its regional objectives, the Department of State identified a number of fundamental propositions to guide its policy toward Israel and the Arab states. First, it recognized that the political and economic stability of the eastern Mediterranean and Middle East was crucial to the security of the United States. Therefore, the State Department concluded that it was in the national interest to enjoy the goodwill and respect of all peoples of the region, Arab and Jew alike, and to orient those peoples away from the Soviet Union. Third, the differences between the newly established Israeli state and the neighboring Arab states should be reconciled, at least to the extent that the Arab states and Israel would act in concert to oppose Soviet aggression. The best means to achieve this result, according to the Department of State, was for the United States to assert impartial leadership in the resolution of regional economic, social, and political problems. Finally, the close collaboration between the United States and the United Kingdom in evidence throughout the postwar period should continue wherever possible to achieve these core objectives.[2]

At the Department of State, the above appraisal of U.S. security interests in the eastern Mediterranean and Middle East suggested the following strategic requirements. Washington must first deny any foothold in the region to a hostile power, that is, the Soviet Union. It must also maintain friendly relations with the countries involved, promoting and cultivating such relationships with economic and social assistance, together with military assistance as might be practical, to ensure the collaboration of the indigenous peoples in the common defense of the region. Third, the oil resources of the area must be developed by the United States and other countries with a friendly attitude toward the United States. Finally, the United States must take the steps necessary to ensure the right of American military forces to enter military essential areas upon threat of war.

In accordance with these four strategic requirements, the State Department recommended that the United States secure a series of air base facilities in the eastern Mediterranean and Middle East that would be anchored in the east by the air base at Dhahran in Saudi Arabia and in the west by the facility at Wheelus Field outside Tripoli. Concerning Wheelus Field, the State Department emphasized that it was "highly important that we be able to work out satisfactory arrangements for continuing our rights to use this important airbase when a solution in the UN has been attained as regards disposition of the Italian Colonies." The same memorandum also reiterated the importance of British policy to American strategic interests in the region:

We have already undertaken and should continue to coordinate the handling of our common strategic interests in the area with the British as it would be unrealistic for the United States to undertake to carry out its policies unless the British maintained their strong strategic, political and economic position in the Middle East and Eastern Mediterranean and they and we follow parallel policies in that area.[3]

While the British bases in Cyrenaica were not specifically mentioned in this memorandum, they had been the subject of earlier State Department memos and were clearly considered by Washington to be crucial to its strategic interests in the region. As early as 1947, the State Department had supported "arrangements for the establishment of permanent British bases in Cyrenaica" when the final disposition of that territory was decided.[4]

In the run-up to Libyan independence, the strategic interests of the United States remained largely unchanged. If there was a change, it was a growing recognition that British defense potential might prove inadequate to the needs of a region threatened by an adversary so formidable as the Soviet Union. American policy makers eventually concluded that U.S. actions seemed likely to be decisive in the long run here as well as elsewhere in the world. The United States joined the United Kingdom, France, and Turkey in proposing a Middle East Command whose principal efforts focused on bringing Greece and Turkey into the North Atlantic Treaty Organization (NATO) and developing a chain of strategic air bases under American control. At one point, American policy makers even considered including Libya in NATO on the grounds it might prove easier to address defense requirements through a multilateral arrangement of this kind as opposed to bilateral agreements, but the idea was quickly discarded as impractical.[5]

U.S. Policy Toward Libya

In early May 1950, Secretary of State Dean Acheson, concerned there might be "misunderstanding and misinterpretation" concerning U.S. policy toward Libya, summarized that policy in a telegram to the U.S. consulate in Tripoli. He emphasized that the United States had two main objectives in Libya. First, in conjunction with the British, Washington sought to obtain the right to establish U.S. and UK military facilities in the area. And second, the United States looked forward to establishing an independent and sovereign Libya no later than 1 January 1952. "In achieving these objectives," said Acheson, "US desires [to] have so far as possible friendship, understanding and respect peoples inhabiting Libya, of Arab states interested in Libyan problem, and of other members UN. We do not wish [to] have our true intentions, motivations or policy [the] subject of suspicion."[6]

A number of related considerations, many of which were discussed at a North African Diplomatic and Consular Conference in Tangier on 2–7 October 1950, influenced U.S. policy toward Libya at this juncture. First and foremost were the security aspects of the region. "North Africa, that is, the area north of the Sahara, is of considerable strategic importance since it commands the southern approaches to Europe and the western approaches to the Middle East." Arab nationalism, especially after the creation of Israel in mid-1948, was clearly recognized as a potent force and a future threat to security interests. "The conference concluded that nationalism is an important factor in North Africa but one which has been exploited by the Arab League and by intellectual opportunists. Despite these factors, *it constitutes the real force of the future in this area* [author's emphasis]." "All these nationalist elements are strongly anti-French, and since our policies are frequently similar to those of the French because of our coinciding interests, they frequently oppose our policies as well." The report added that the reservoir of goodwill that the United States enjoyed in Libya and elsewhere in North Africa as a result of World War II was receding because the United States was not assisting the nationalists to achieve their goals.[7]

Misreading the intent of many Arab nationalists, the Tangiers report, together with later U.S. policy statements, expressed concern about the potential for communist infiltration of the region, especially in the wake of Arab nationalist activities:

The strength of communism is negligible. We must have and we do have stability in this area against the possibility of military operations. If the Arab nationalist leaders were to attain power, it would inevitably create a situation of instability in this area which might last for years or decades, since there is little evidence that the nationalist leaders are less selfish than the French. Therefore, we cannot project any great advantage to the people of this area in the event that the Arab nationalists were to obtain power.[8]

George C. McGhee, Assistant Secretary of State for Near Eastern, South Asian, and African Affairs, made the State Department's view of the connection between Arab nationalism and communism explicit in a November 1950 memorandum to Secretary of State Acheson:

There continues to be a reservoir of goodwill and respect toward the United States throughout Northern Africa among all elements of the population. . . . There is impatience among the Arabs with our apparent reluctance to give concrete recognition to Nationalist aspirations, and our apparent willingness to side with France in order to buy temporary security against the Russian menace. Our prestige is probably higher in Libya than in any other part of the area, because of U.S. support of Libyan independence.

There is uniform opposition to Soviet expansionism throughout the area, and an admiration for the vigor with which we have countered this threat in Korea and elsewhere. While the Arab Nationalist leaders have occasionally flirted with the Communists, they have done so not because of admiration for Communist tenets or as a reflection of ultimate solidarity with Communists, but opportunistically to achieve their own aspirations.[9]

The United States continued to take a jaundiced view of nationalist movements in Libya for much of the next two decades out of fear that such movements would encourage and facilitate the spread of communism. With the advantage of hindsight, this policy was doomed to failure from the outset. Opposition to Arab nationalist movements, especially when coupled to support for unpopular French policies in neighboring states, facilitated in the end the spread of the very movements it hoped to contain.

The core objectives outlined by Acheson in May 1950, coupled with the State Department's regional assessment as reviewed above, led the United States to take three important interrelated decisions at the outset of the decade. First, the United States recognized that it must continue to coordinate its policies with the United Kingdom if it was to maximize its strategic position in the region. Second, Libya would clearly require ongoing support from the United States if it was to maintain its independence. The Tangier report put it succinctly, "Libya must be propped up with military and economic support if it is to become a viable state."[10] Finally, American policy makers concluded that it would be wise to negotiate a military base agreement before independence, if possible, because the negotiating position of the Libyan government would strengthen after independence and the opposition would be emboldened.

Economic Aid and Base Rights

After largely demobilizing the air field at Mallaha in 1947, the European crisis in early 1948 caused the United States to reverse course and begin in mid-1948 to develop Wheelus Field into a major postwar base. That said, as late as September 1950 the United States still had no agreed upon policy for the negotiation with Libya of a long-term agreement to retain Wheelus as part of the strategic American base system. American reluctance to negotiate base-rights agreements on a quid pro quo basis in return for economic assistance from the United States was a particularly difficult obstacle. Andrew G. Lynch, the American consul general in Tripoli, proved clairvoyant when he observed in May 1950 that the linkage of base rights to financial aid could "lay us open to perpetual blackmail on [the] part [of] any new states, which may evolve, and introduce [a] source of constant friction, particularly on occasions when circumstances forced fluctuations in our direct financial aid."[11] The Libyans, of course, approached the issue from the reverse perspective. They viewed their geographic location as their most tangible—and most negotiable—asset.

Both the State Department and the Department of Defense agreed that providing financial assistance directly to Libya for the use of Wheelus Field could set a dangerous precedent that might well affect U.S. base rights in other parts of the world. In addition, the United States might want to retain the use of such bases for a longer period of time than it might grant economic assistance to Libya or any other country in which they were located. U.S. bomber bases in England were an example cited at the time in support of this rationale, as the intent was to retain them for the long term while Economic Cooperation Administration (ECA) aid to the United Kingdom was scheduled to cease in 1952. James T. Hill, general counsel to the secretary of the air force, in a recently declassified Top Secret memorandum dated 11 July 1951, summarized U.S. policy at the time.

As you know, it is contemplated that in connection with negotiating United States requirements for bases in Libya, the United States will have to agree to make some contribution to the Libyan economy. Estimates indicate that Libya's annual deficit will be in the nature of twelve million dollars and that *one of their few assets is their strategic location* [author's emphasis]. The State Department estimates that in addition to funds which may be made available under the foreign aid program, the United States will have to pay between three-quarters of a million and one and one-half million dollars annually for base rights.

It has been informally agreed by Defense and State, with the knowledge and approval of Mr. [Robert A.] Lovett [deputy secretary of defense] and Mr. [George C.] McGhee [assistant secretary of state for Near Eastern, South Asian, and African Affairs], that there should be no formal connection between base rights and our financial contribution to the Libyan economy, although this will, of course, be a principal subject of discussion in the base negotiations. It has been further agreed that securing from Congress whatever sum may be necessary is the responsibility of Defense, and that this fund will be turned over to Libya in appropriate form by the

State Department as economic assistance. There will be no attempt to disguise the fact that the United States is giving such assistance.[12]

How best to maintain a distinction between obtaining base rights and providing economic assistance to Libya remained a subject of debate within the U.S. government for months on end. With the Libyans approaching the issue from the opposite end, that their strategic location was their primary asset and one for which the United States should expect to pay, the distinction between base rights and economic assistance would prove impossible to maintain.

The optimum timing of base-rights negotiations complicated American policy. With Libyan independence scheduled for no later than 1 January 1952, there was a growing appreciation in policy-making circles that some form of provisional arrangement should be reached in advance of formal independence. Michael Wright, an assistant secretary of state in the British Foreign Office, noted in a September 1950 memorandum of conversation that it was U.S. policy to maintain strategic facilities in Libya; however, it was not yet clear how the Americans planned to accomplish this objective. George McGhee responded,

we would probably want to reach some agreement with the Provisional Government of Libya for obtaining our base rights at Wheelus Field and subsequently to have this agreement ratified by the Libyan state. The exact form the agreement would take was not yet certain and would depend largely on future constitutional developments in Libya.[13]

In the end, U.S. officials decided to press for an early independence date for Libya, with a provisional base agreement in place prior to independence, in the hope this strategy would minimize discussion and criticism in the United Nations of U.S. policy toward Libya.

The question of a base-rights agreement with Libya was further complicated by Washington's ongoing desire to coordinate its policies with those of the British government. In this regard, it will be remembered that the British remained responsible for the administration of Cyrenaica and Tripolitania after World War II. As a result, the U.S. Air Force had been using Wheelus Field under permission from the British government since the end of the war. Anglo-American consultation and cooperation in the Middle East and North Africa worked well in the immediate postwar years, but American policy makers in the early 1950s began to voice concern about long-term British resources and capabilities in the region. The State Department in December 1950 justified in part a top-secret review of Middle East policy on the following grounds. "The UK, which has primary responsibility for the defense of the area, lacks both manpower and resources successfully to defend the area and has no plans for defense of the Saudi Arabian oil fields and the Dhahran Air Base." The review later stated that any reliance on "the time-honored assumption that the U.S. can rely upon the UK to defend the Middle East is to indulge in wishful thinking: British capabilities are too small to be a sound basis for the defense of the U.S. interests in the area."[14]

UN Commissioner Adrian Pelt submitted a report to the UN General Assembly on 17 November 1950 that called for the creation of a National Assembly in Libya no later than 1 January 1951, with the subsequent establishment of a Provisional Government by 1 April 1951. Interest in the report centered chiefly on the constitutional development plans that he prepared and thus went beyond the scope of this study. On the other hand, the debate stimulated by the report was relevant as the Soviet Union and its allies used the report to criticize the United States, United Kingdom, and France on the grounds they were impeding Libyan unity and independence and using their position in Libya for militaristic and aggressive purposes. In commenting on these charges, U.S. policy makers expressed concern that Pelt's report appeared to set a timetable for independence that might limit freedom to maneuver in the future, and the report also put more emphasis on "unity" than did the original (21 November 1949) UN resolution.[15]

In late spring 1950, the National Security Council tabled a State Department progress report on the "Disposition of the Former Italian Colonies" that added considerable insight into U.S. policy for an independent Libya. The membership of the National Constituent Assembly of Libya, the document pointed out, consisted of twenty members each from Cyrenaica, the Fezzan, and Tripolitania which guaranteed that the Emir Sayyid Idris would "wield a preponderant influence in the formation of the new government." Moreover, the Emir had said he would assume the kingship at the appropriate time, presumably after the establishment of a provisional government. In the interim, the British would continue to administer Cyrenaica and Tripolitania until Libya became independent. The first acts of the National Constituent Assembly were to declare that Libya should have a federal form of government and to invite Emir Idris to become the constitutional king of Libya. "The Emir, and his leading supporters, have indicated that they are ready and willing to reach suitable agreements with the United Kingdom and the United States regarding the continued use of military facilities by our respective armed forces."[16]

Washington first broached the idea of reaching an accord on strategic facilities with King-designate Idris on 29 May 1951. The Emir agreed to open negotiations in July after the end of Ramadan. At the same time, he expressed concern in a telling comment that the U.S. negotiating team be limited to no more than two or three people. According to Consul General Lynch, "King designate and FonMin [foreign minister] emphasized

Libya's lack of experience in matters of this kind and FonMin [foreign minister] suggested that we might give them advance draft and adequate time to study it before opening conversations." "Throughout conversation it was apparent that King designate and FonMin [foreign minister] fully expect receive money payments for strategic facilities." "I suggest time now ripe to abandon make-believe of obtaining facilities in return for anything but annual cash payments."17 In a subsequent meeting, the Emir reiterated to Lynch his apprehension over a "team of experts" arriving from the United States to negotiate, as Libya "had no corresponding experts to meet with such a group and took the line that two or three Americans might sit down with FonMin [Foreign Minister] in a friendly way to work situation out."18

After much delay, Washington finally opened negotiations for a formal base-rights agreement with the Provisional Government of Libya in August 1951. Two months later the State Department prepared a draft treaty that called for an agreement to continue in force for a period of twenty years and thereafter until such time as one of the signatories gave notice of termination. A long, involved document, the proposal was highly favorable to the United States in a number of key provisions; others clearly infringed on Libyan sovereignty. For example, article 7 provided for the Libyan government to "make all acquisition of land and other arrangements required to permit occupation and use of the agreed areas," but the United States was not "obliged to compensate the Government of Libya or any Libyan national or other person for such occupation or use."19 Article 16 permitted the United States to "bring into Libya members of the United States forces in connection with carrying out the purposes of the present Agreement" and Libyan law would "not operate or apply so as to prevent admission or departure into or from Libya of [any] member of the United States forces." Article 19 of the draft agreement empowered the United States to make "engineering and other technical surveys in any part of Libya" without the consent of the Libyans as long as the United States notified the former that such a survey was to be made.

In the section governing the status of U.S. personnel and property, article 20 granted U.S. military personnel and their dependents, as well as other U.S. nationals and their dependents subject to U.S. military law, immunity "from the criminal jurisdiction of Libyan courts and in matters arising from the performance of their official duties from the civil jurisdiction of the courts of Libya." Article 22 of the same section gave U.S. military personnel in Libya blanket permission to "possess and carry arms as required in the performance of official duties." Finally, article 25 exempted a broad range of U.S. goods and materials, including construction material and equipment, together with personal effects, household goods, and private automobiles, from the normal purview of Libyan customs authorities.

In mid-1951, France and the United States reached an agreement through which the United States would operate five air bases in Morocco, bases under construction since late 1950. About the same time, agreements with Saudi Arabia ensured continued use of the Dhahran base for a five-year period, with other bases planned or under construction in Crete, Cyprus, and Rhodes. In December 1951, the United States disclosed that it had secured permission from Libyan authorities to retain Wheelus Field, as well as other facilities throughout the country, in advance of the formal proclamation of Libyan independence. The terms of the agreement included payment by the U.S. to Libya of $1 million annually for twenty years in addition to reimbursing Libya with equitable rents for land use. Earlier in the month, Acting Secretary of Defense William C. Foster had told Secretary of State Acheson that the Department of Defense was "prepared to include in its budget the sum of $1,000,000 on a yearly basis for the twenty-year term of the agreement, in addition to any technical and economic assistance which may be provided by the Department of State under the Mutual Security Act." When the United Kingdom of Libya proclaimed its independence on 24 December 1951, the United States government extended full recognition and elevated the American consulate general to the status of a legation. Henry S. Villard was appointed the first U.S. minister to Libya.[20]

United Kingdom of Libya

An exchange of diplomatic correspondence only weeks before Libya attained its independence provided a vivid snapshot of the political climate prevailing in the country at the time. The U.S. consul general in Tripoli reported to the State Department on 30 October 1951 that he had just learned from the commanding officer of Wheelus Field that some 2,000 U.S. Air Force troops were scheduled to arrive in Tripoli over a one-month period beginning in early December. Since their arrival would coincide almost exactly with the achievement of Libyan independence, the consul general expressed concern that the troop deployment could have serious local political repercussions.

US now undergoing serious propaganda attacks in local anti-govt [government] Arabic press. We are being accused of being new imperialists who plan to take over all of Libya. . . . Opposition to govt [government] is strong and antiforeign line popular one.

The consul general added that a premature troop deployment would "play into [the] hands [of the] Soviet bloc and Arab League and might be "politically disastrous" to American friends in Libya. "It might also adversely affect chances ratification Libyan American defense agreement now under negotiation which will come before Parliament early 1952." Shortly thereafter, the U.S. secretary of defense advised Secretary of State Acheson that the scheduled deployment, in view of the tense political situation in Libya, would be postponed.[21]

Less than a year later, the Central Intelligence Agency authored an assessment of Libya which emphasized that it was extremely poor and devoid of natural resources. "Because of its economic weakness, Libya is almost wholly dependent on foreign aid. Great Britain has been Libya's main support since it occupied the area in World War II." In return for various concessions, Britain was underwriting the major part of Libya's budget deficit, which was currently about $3–5,000,000, as well as its adverse balance of payments. France was doing the same on a much smaller scale for its sphere of influence in the Fezzan. Six months of independence, the report added, had brought "little change in the fundamental disunity of the Libyan kingdom." Tripolitania had accepted the concept of a united kingdom out of fear of renewed domination by Italy. Cyrenaicans remained largely separatist in outlook, fearing domination by the more populous Tripolitania. Time had only widened this breach while King Idris I, a reluctant head of state, constantly reasserted his preference for Cyrenaica.[22]

On the subject of external relations, the September 1952 CIA assessment emphasized the pro-Western orientation of the new Libyan government due to its need for foreign aid and the strong ties developed with Great Britain during the war. Since that time, British influence had been predominant in Libya with the British government providing the bulk of outside economic assistance and British advisers forming the backbone of the administration. At the same time, U.S. influence in Libya appeared to be growing. The assessment also suggested that Libya had "only slight relations, at present primarily cultural in nature, with Egypt and the Arab states. The King and most Cyrenaicans fear the ascendancy of adjacent Egypt and have shown little desire to join the Arab League." The report also suggested that Egypt appeared to have ambitions to dominate the new kingdom although its influence had recently declined. "However, various Tripolitanian urban elements and a few politically conscious Cyrenaicans still regard Egypt as their champion against Sanusi conservatism and Western 'imperialism' and call for closer ties with the Arab world." In two short paragraphs, this CIA assessment captured the essence of the conflict which was to confront and confound Libya for much of the next two decades.[23]

Less than a year later, a draft policy statement prepared for the National Security Council Planning Board articulated a post-independence policy for Libya that mirrored, if not guided, U.S. foreign policy until 1969. Calling on the United States to avoid actions that might weaken the British and

French positions in Libya, the draft statement called on the United States to act in concert with its allies to the greatest extent practical. On the other hand, it called on the United States to be prepared to assume an increased share of responsibility toward Libya if that proved necessary to safeguard American interests. "The United States should be ready to provide promptly appropriate economic, technical and possibly military assistance, if necessary to prevent the development of any political vacuum that might result from failure or inability of the interested Western European powers to assure the Western orientation of Libya." In addition, the NSC staff paper called on the United States to exercise its influence to prevent the weakening or disintegration of the unity of the Libyan state.[24]

The successful pursuit of the policy outlined in the 1953 NSC paper would prove to be a serious challenge for American diplomacy. On the one hand, as pointed out in an August 1954 National Intelligence Estimate, Libya after independence was unable to establish firm foundations for economic or political stability. "The poverty and economic underdevelopment of the country, the unresolved Tripolitanian-Cyrenaican differences, the weakness of the parliament and the bureaucracy, and the limited support for the ruling dynasty, all make for an unstable future." On the other hand, Libya was almost totally dependent on foreign financial and technical assistance to carry out even a minimal development program. "The UK at present provides over ten million dollars annually to Libya, which also receives some technical aid from the UN and the US."[25]

It was already clear in the early 1950s that British influence was in decline, which opened the prospect for a partial vacuum to develop in Western economic and political influence. In part for this reason, according to the August 1954 National Intelligence Estimate, King Idris had begun to express an interest in a closer relationship with the United States, with Washington becoming Libya's chief benefactor and protector.[26] Elsewhere, there was strong Libyan resentment over French influence in the Fezzan, French repression of Moroccan and Tunisian nationalist movements, and French policy in Algeria. Franco-American relations were under stress in part due to long-term differences over French policy in North Africa.[27] The Soviet Union had not yet opened diplomatic relations with Libya; however, the latter had joined the Arab League in early 1953 although its membership had not yet resulted in any fundamental change in its pro-Western orientation. "Libya uniformly endorses the Arab League's pronouncements on Israel and on North African nationalism, but plays only a secondary role in the League and has frequently adopted an independent attitude." "However, growing Libyan political and cultural ties with Egypt constitute an increasing challenge to the Western position. Nevertheless, Libya will remain fearful of Egypt's greater power." The August 1954 National Intelligence Estimate concluded with a simple but powerful thought, one with enormous ramifications for U.S. policy in Libya and the region. "*In the long run, however, Libya is likely to follow the lead of the other Arab states* [author's emphasis]."[28]

Even though King Idris expressed interest in a closer relationship with the United States, this significant shift in Libyan foreign policy did not allay widespread criticism in Libya of the terms of the 1951 base rights agreement. Shortly after independence, the Libyan government began to signal its discontent with the pact hastily negotiated at the end of 1951; and in September 1952, it officially informed the U.S. legation that it wished to renegotiate both the duration of the agreement and the amount of financial compensation provided. Members of the Libyan Parliament, government supporters and opposition alike, charged that the treaty infringed on Libyan sovereignty and in effect constituted an occupation of Libya by the United States. Minister Villard reported in January 1953, for example, that Libyan deputies had recently approached the legation's Arab secretary and "criticized [the] articles giving United States Forces freedom of movement throughout Libya and freedom from jurisdiction [in] Libyan courts."[29]

At one point, Prime Minister Muntasir even charged that he had been pressured into signing the 24 December 1951 agreement, a charge emphatically denied by Andrew Lynch, chargé d'affaires in Tripoli at the time and U.S. signatory to the base agreement. The details of the renegotiation of the original base agreement, which were the focus of Libya-United States diplomatic relations for almost two years, will not be discussed here, as the talks themselves added nothing new to the issues and policies under discussion. Suffice it to say that the negotiations were long, tedious, and frustrating. Minister Villard, the senior U.S. diplomat in Libya throughout this period, later captured the strength of the U.S. commitment to a successful renegotiation of the 1951 agreement. "From our first glimpse of Wheelus to the last, the American stake in this fragment of foreign territory was to be a paramount concern of the Legation and one of the principal subjects of discussion in my daily dealings with the Libyan government."[30] The central question that prolonged the talks, the appropriate compensation to be paid to Libya by the United States, was complicated by other issues like the definition of the appropriate status of Americans residing on the base. On this subject, Minister Villard commented at one point, in an obvious note of exasperation, that the attitude of the Libyan government was "tantamount to blackmail and showing little change from [the] barbary pirate tradition."[31]

A new agreement on base rights and economic assistance was finally reached in Washington on 20 July 1954, more than two and one-half years after Libya attained its independence. The new agreement granted the United States the use of Wheelus Field and other designated facilities in Libya for military purposes until 24 December 1970 or after that date until such time as one of the signatories gave notice of termination. In a quid pro quo for the use of Libyan military facilities, the United States agreed to pay $4 million annually for six years and $1 million annually thereafter to 1970. In addition, Washington offered $7 million in development assistance and 24,000 tons of grain for drought relief. While the State Department described the agreement as "an important contribution to the defense of the free world" and an instrument designed to "strengthen the ties of amity which bind together the people of the two countries," Secretary of State Acheson later complained that there was little or no U.S. press coverage of the event. In the wake of the French defeat at Dien Bien Phu, American interest and concern at the time centered on the peace conference underway in Geneva together with the prospect of armed Chinese intervention in Vietnam. Libya in the summer of 1954 was simply not on the radar screen of most Americans.[32] The formal agreement was signed in Libya on 9 September and entered into force on 30 October 1954. In his memoirs, Minister Villard described the agreement in the following terms. "The United States-Libyan Agreement of 1954, regulating the conditions under which American armed forces are stationed in Libya, is the keystone of the bridge between the two countries and the best example of Libya's orientation toward the West."[33] On 25 September 1954, the United States announced that the legation in Libya had been elevated to the status of an embassy with John L. Tappin appointed the first U.S. Ambassador to Libya.

Arab Nationalism and Communism

Less than four months after he presented his credentials, Ambassador Tappin, authored a glowing report in which he described Libya as "unequalled in the Near East and North Africa for the establishment not only of a secure bastion for defense of the area, but also of a springboard for swift and massive retaliation against any aggressor." Suggesting that the twenty-year base agreement had the full consent of the Libyan people, he stated there was no "ascertainable internal opposition" in Libya that viewed the base agreement as a reason for attacking the ruling elite or for accusing it of supporting imperialism. Emphasizing that there was "no active or sizeable Communist Party in Libya nor is there in fact any Communist influence," Tappin went on to say, "Our hands are, to date, completely clean in Libya." Nowhere in the report did he mention the growing force of Arab nationalism in the Middle East, the developing relationship of the Libyan government with Egypt, or the potential impact Arab nationalist movements might have on an aging monarchy with transparent ties to the West. While the Libyan government, from the outset of independence, was on the defensive vis-à-vis pan-Arabism, the United States saw the real threat in Libya, not as Arab nationalism but as the Soviet Union. Ambassador Tappin's report exemplified and highlighted a policy dichotomy that plagued American-Libyan relations for much of the next fifteen years.[34]

In his memoirs, Prime Minister Ben-Halim described a series of meetings with Egyptian President Nasser that began in June 1954, nine months before Tappin authored his report, in which Egypt and Libya moved to coordinate their respective policies. "From there [Ankara] I went straight to Cairo and had a long and comprehensive discussion with President Nasser in which we laid the foundations of an intimate friendship and honest understanding between us. The result was co-operation between Egypt and Libya which lasted for many years." According to Ben-Halim, President Nasser encouraged him to cultivate diplomatic relations with the United States because it did not have a colonial policy, unlike Great Britain and France, and because it was a wealthy country that could assist Libya. The meetings between Ben-Halim and Nasser reportedly stretched from mid-1954, shortly after Ben-Halim took office, until his departure from office in mid-1957.[35]

When Libya announced on 25 September 1955 that it had established diplomatic relations with the Soviet Union, the U.S. embassy in Tripoli sought to minimize the importance of an event it had worked actively to block since 1951.

The Libyan decision to exchange diplomatic representatives with the USSR was not made because of any feeling of friendship for Communism or support of the Soviets. Rather it was based on (1) a desire to refute charges that Libya is subservient to the West and (2) the belief that Western aid to Libya would be increased if we felt that she might turn to the USSR for aid.[36]

In response to concerns expressed by Ambassador Tappin, Secretary of State Dulles suggested that Soviet policy in Libya was patterned after efforts elsewhere in the world to undermine independent countries. He added that Tappin could expect the Soviets to "arrive in large numbers, propose economic assistance," and raise questions of base rights and related matters. The Secretary of State concluded as follows: "When one remembers that these steps [are] under [the] auspices of [Soviet Foreign Minister Vyacheslav] Molotov, [the] same person who proposed that Libya be assigned as [a] trust territory to [the] Soviet Union, eventual goals of Soviet Union self-evident.[37]

While the goals of the Soviet Union might have appeared self-evident to Secretary of State Dulles, the appropriate response of the U.S. government was less clear. Ambassador Tappin spent the next two years locked in negotiations with Tripoli and Washington over the former's repeated demands for increased economic assistance. Throughout these negotiations, the Libyan government exploited Washington's fear of communism to the fullest extent possible to wring maximum economic concessions from the Eisenhower administration. Rightly or wrongly, Ambassador Tappin responded positively to the Libyan pressure, becoming an increasing vocal advocate for increased aid levels. He wrote Deputy Assistant Secretary of State Palmer on New Year's Day 1957, for example, stressing that "her pressing needs makes [sic] Libya a veritable bargain basement, where extraordinary values can be had at a very low cost."[38] Increasingly frustrated with Washington's failure to agree fully with his policy recommendations, Tappin cabled the Department of State three months later that "Libyans feel they have been good children and cannot understand why Santa Claus came with instruction to leave scooter when they needed and had asked for bicycle."[39]

In February 1955, Turkey and Iraq concluded a mutual cooperation agreement that eventually became the Baghdad Pact after Iran and Pakistan, together with Great Britain, adhered to the treaty. Washington viewed the Baghdad Pact, which highlighted the fundamental continuity in the Middle East policies of the Truman and Eisenhower administrations, as one more step in its policy of surrounding the Soviet Union with Western-controlled alliance systems. Nevertheless, the United States never formally adhered to the Baghdad Pact, largely out of fear of antagonizing revolutionary Arab states, particularly Egypt. Because it provoked a strong negative reaction in Egypt and elsewhere in the Arab world, the pact proved counterproductive, causing a chain reaction that deepened the cleavage between Arab nationalists and the United States. By early 1956, the United States and United Kingdom had tired of Egyptian President Nasser's incessant criticism of the Baghdad Pact as an instrument of Western imperialism and resolved to distance themselves from Cairo. In the wake of an Egyptian decision to purchase Soviet bloc arms from Czechoslovakia, American and British officials agreed to shelve plans to provide aid for the Aswan High Dam. Cancellation of Aswan High Dam aid prompted Nasser to nationalize the Suez Canal Company in late July 1956, an action that provoked the so-called Suez Crisis. In a three-hour harangue in Alexandria on 26 July, the day he proclaimed the nationalization, Nasser denounced imperialism, alliances in general, and the Baghdad Pact in particular; he spoke of Britain as a mere satellite of the United States.[40]

After fighting broke out on 29 October, the United States imposed sanctions on both the United Kingdom and France because President Eisenhower believed the war threatened vital Western interests in the Third World. The crisis inflamed passions throughout the Arab world, liquidating much of the remaining British influence. The British after Suez were never again able to pursue a foreign policy in the Middle East independent of the United States. And in no Arab country were the effects of Suez more severe than in Libya, where a government allied with the British became an immediate target of Arab wrath. In the aftermath of the Suez Crisis, when the British signaled their intent to reduce financial assistance to Libya, the U.S. government finally agreed to assume a heavier financial burden. A May 1957 National Security Council memorandum captured President Eisenhower's thoughts on the issue. "The President commented that in view of its strategic location, its proximity to Egypt, and the evident weakness of its economy, Libya would have to be helped. The United States would be 'in an awful fix' if we ever lost Libya."[41]

With U.S. policy makers focused on the Soviet Union and the global communist threat, there was only occasionally some recognition in Washington of the challenge Arab nationalism posed for the Libyan monarchy and in turn for United States interests in Libya. Under Secretary of State Herbert Hoover, Jr., in a November 1955 letter to the secretary of defense, recognized that "Libya, as an Arab State and neighbor to Egypt, is obviously susceptible to the influence of Egypt and appears to be under strong temptation to adopt Egyptian tactics in the conflict between East and West."[42] In a similar vein, a National Intelligence Estimate, dated 19 June 1956, viewed Libya as "sympathetic with the anticolonial and anti-Western feelings of the Arab world, and subject to extensive Egyptian influence. Libyan leaders fear Egyptian domination and suspect Egyptian intentions, yet they will cooperate with Egypt in various policies, some of which are hostile to Western interests."[43] And in June 1957 a National Security Council statement of U.S. policy on Libya pointed out that Egypt had since 1951 continuously sought to bring Libya into the Egyptian orbit. "The Libyan Government and the King have become fearful of Egyptian motives and have initiated steps to counteract Egyptian influence."[44]

Representatives of the U.S. government were especially concerned with the political influence of the several hundred Egyptian teachers then working in Libyan secondary schools. A related concern centered on the political doctrines and tactics that Libyan students studying in Egyptian universities might bring home upon graduation. The Office of the Director of the International Cooperation Administration summarized the situation in a 30 November 1956 memorandum to the White House.

One of the most effective means of Egyptian penetration in Libya has been through the provision by Egypt of some 700 subsidized Egyptian teachers for Libyan schools. Recent events, culminating in civil disturbances led by Egyptian teachers, have brought home to the Libyan Government the seriousness of this problem, and it has closed the secondary schools of the Province of Tripolitania, requested that we help recruit Arabic-speaking, non-Egyptian teachers to replace the Egyptian teachers and is considering the withdrawal of the approximately 300 Libyans who are studying at the University of Cairo.[45]

In response to the Libyan government's request, the U.S. government queried its diplomatic missions in India, Iraq, Lebanon, Pakistan, Tunisia, and Turkey as to the availability of Arabic-speaking teachers willing to work in Libya. The response was disappointing, and the large number of Egyptian teachers in Libyan schools continued to represent a political challenge to Libya and the United States.

President Eisenhower, concerned with communist penetration of the Arab world in the aftermath of the Suez affair, Western disunity resulting from the Suez debacle, the attendant collapse of British influence in the area, and the resurgence of Arab nationalist hostility toward the West, addressed Congress on 5 January 1957, requesting a three-part grant of authority. In what came to be known as the Eisenhower Doctrine, the president asked for $200 million in economic assistance to preserve the independence of any nation or group of nations in the Middle East, military assistance for the same countries, and permission from Congress to use military force to protect any Middle East state requesting such aid against overt armed aggression from a country controlled by international communism. Aimed principally at the Arab world, the Eisenhower Doctrine complemented the Truman Doctrine enunciated ten years earlier since the latter had focused on the threat to the non-Arab Northern Tier. It differed from the Truman Doctrine in that the Eisenhower Doctrine committed American forces to defend the threatened countries.[46]

While the Eisenhower Doctrine appeared to be a logical corollary to earlier American policies and statements, it proved a poor fit for the political situation existing in the Arab world at the time. Direct Soviet aggression in the Middle East was a most unlikely scenario. Indirect Soviet penetration was most likely in places like Egypt and Syria, the very states most unlikely to request aid from the United States. In pro-Western countries, such as Lebanon, Libya, and Jordan, the main threat to independence came from the rising strength of Arab nationalism, as personified by Nasser, and not from international communism. The Eisenhower Doctrine in practice became simply another instrument of a status quo policy aimed as much at stopping militant pan-Arabism as preventing the Soviet Union and its agents from upsetting friendly and legally established regimes in the Arab world.[47]

Over the next few years, the U.S. government, continuing to view Libya largely in terms of its role as a strategic asset, remained concerned about the potential spread of communism. After Vice President Richard M. Nixon visited Libya in 1957, for example, he reported to President Eisenhower that Libya occupied "a key strategic position with respect to North Africa and the flank of NATO. We cannot afford to lose Libya."[48] Nonetheless, a memorandum of information drafted less than six months later by

Deputy Director of Naval Intelligence Rear Admiral Charles B. Martell spoke of a "gradual deterioration" in U.S.-Libyan relations. The memo blamed the situation on the "weak and ineffectual" government of Prime Minister Abdul Majid Kubaar. While "not decidedly anti-American or anti-West," Kubaar had reportedly adopted a more pro-Egyptian policy than his predecessor, one that encouraged other cabinet members, notably the defense minister, favoring closer ties with Egypt and a greater independence from Western affiliations. Seeing an opportunity, the Soviet Union had reportedly increased its activities in Libya with concerning results for U.S. policy objectives.

The Soviets have stepped up their activity in Libya and have registered definite gains among the populace. An Embassy was established recently in Benghazi. The Soviet Ambassador is the only chief of mission to state his intention of moving to Benghazi when the Federal Government moves there in October. Rumors of Soviet aid offers, including the equipping and training of men for the Libyan Army, are frequently heard, and may even be encouraged by the Libyan Government. The Soviet Union can be expected to encourage Libyan nationalism in an effort to increase the opportunities for Soviet military and economic aid. Such changes would serve the Soviets by compromising the security of the U.S. Sixth Fleet.[49]

Two years later, as the National Security Council discussed the development of the nascent Libyan oil industry, Nixon again emphasized the importance of Libya, alluding to the many political problems faced by the monarchy.[50]

There is ample evidence to suggest that the Eisenhower administration recognized the importance of Libya, albeit more as an air base than as a sovereign state. Therefore, it remains difficult to understand why the United States in this period repeatedly pressured the monarchy to take foreign policy positions that were unpopular in the Arab world and thus contributed to the widespread image of Libya as a Western dependency. In July 1958, for example, President Eisenhower wrote King Idris a personal note asking him to support publicly the U.S. intervention in Lebanon. Washington also pressured Libya on several occasions in this time frame to support U.S. policy in favor of a six-mile territorial sea when Libya, together with the Arab bloc, favored a wider exclusive zone. The Libyan government's position on this issue at the Geneva Conference on the Law of the Sea rested firmly on Libyan domestic law, which made it an especially sensitive domestic political issue. Both issues, in particular the width of the territorial sea, would be resurrected a decade later following the monarchy's overthrow.[51]

Major oil deposits were discovered in Libya in 1959, when American prospectors confirmed their location at Zelten in Cyrenaica. The policy ramifications of this development, once the extent and magnitude of the oil fields became known, were manifold, complex, and long-lasting. The Libyan government sensed the possibility of eliminating foreign aid, and this prospect affected its attitude toward continued American presence at Wheelus Field and other installations in the country. The development of oil production also had widespread domestic political effects, as it placed a premium on economic power and affected central-provincial government relations. In addition, the discovery of oil aggravated socioeconomic problems in Libya and thus contributed to the crisis in the monarchical system. Petroleum development affected international relations as the countries in the region, most especially Egypt, increased their efforts to control the Libyan government. Compounding this problem, the oil companies competed for skilled and trainable labor, which was in short supply in Libya; consequently, large numbers of expatriates, including many Egyptians, were imported to handle technical jobs. All this took place in a country which the State Department continued to view as a "weak reed" politically. In short, the discovery of oil in exportable quantities improved the economic situation in Libya but radically complicated the political situation.[52]

A secret National Security Council report entitled "Implications of Petroleum Developments on U.S. Operations in Libya," dated 23 September 1959, did an excellent job of outlining the internal and external challenges Libya would face as oil revenues increased. Rightly viewing oil production as a major catalyst for change, the report concluded with an unwarranted optimism as to the impact of petroleum developments on U.S.-Libyan relations.

The economic and political ferment discussed above probably will accelerate present Arab nationalist trends in Libya. Coupled with reduced dependence on our assistance, this will tend to make the Libyans more uncooperative regarding those matters which may be at issue between us, such as the use of Wheelus Air Base, particularly if it becomes expedient to use the U.S. as a scapegoat for any Libyan mishandling of oil revenues. At the same time, realization of their dependence on Western petroleum marketing arrangements and anticipated unwillingness to share their wealth with their Arab brethren may help to balance these trends. While the effects of large petroleum assets may be politically and economically unsettling, and create difficult problems for U.S. operations, new opportunities also are being created for the achievement of U.S. objectives and should be capitalized on wherever possible.[53]

Given the swiftly changing milieu, American policy toward Libya at the end of the 1950s appeared due for a major reevaluation; unfortunately, it concluded the decade exactly where it had begun. A National Security

Council Report dated 15 March 1960 described the underlying political situation in Libya as "unstable," with the death of King Idris likely to precipitate a "chaotic free-for-all." While there were no political parties in Libya, "Pan-Arab nationalism has considerable appeal," especially among younger urban elements. The influence of the United Kingdom had declined while that of the United States had increased. Egypt continued to have designs on Libya, "at a minimum for paramount political influence," and had "demonstrated a capacity for fomenting trouble there." Soviet influence, on the other hand, had never been significant, and had declined since the coolness between the United Arab Republic and the Soviet Bloc. In light of the above, according to the NSC report, American policy in Libya had two related objectives: first, continued availability and use of U.S. and allied military facilities in Libya, and second, a stable central government. The latter objective was defined as a central government able and willing to do three things: (1) permit Western access to Libyan oil reserves; (2) minimize communist and other anti-Western influence in Libya; and (3) cooperate generally with the United States and its allies. These policy objectives, with the addition of access to Libyan oil reserves, were identical to those outlined by Secretary of State Acheson in 1950.[54]

President Eisenhower, in his televised farewell address to the nation on 17 January 1961, spoke of war and peace, of police states and of freedom, in a speech whose theme was the Cold War. He told Americans they were locked in a global conflict that "absorbs our very beings" and "promises to be of indefinite duration." Consequently, the U.S. government was "compelled to create a permanent armaments industry of vast proportions" together with large and costly armed forces. Three days later, President John F. Kennedy proclaimed in his Inaugural Address that the torch had "passed to a new generation" that had been "tempered by war" and "disciplined by a hard and bitter peace." Unfortunately, the generational change touted by Kennedy lacked clear definition. Although his youth was striking, Kennedy turned to elders like Dean Acheson and Clark Clifford for counsel and advice. Moreover, the notion of a torch passed in itself presumed continuity.[55]

In the end, the Kennedy and Johnson administrations largely followed the same course as their predecessors in and outside the Arab world. Familiar arguments about the communist menace were recast to fit the conditions of the moment, and the Soviets continued to be portrayed as aggressive and menacing. The Kennedy and Johnson administrations most feared "not communism, which was too fragmented, or the Soviet Union, which was too committed to detente, or even China, which was too impotent, but rather the threat of embarrassment, of humiliation, of appearing to be weak."[56]

Decade of Change

To say that little had changed in U.S. policy is not to say that little had happened in Libya. As Confucius once observed, the only constant is change, and this was never more true than in the United Kingdom of Libya. At the beginning of the 1960s, economic, social, and political conditions in Libya were changing rapidly; and these developments put new pressures on the Libyan government. Oil revenues reached a level that assured future income for the government, while the combination of new long-range aircraft and reduced international tensions meant that Libyan air bases were no longer central to Western defense strategies. A briefing paper prepared for President Kennedy in October 1962 described the primary mission of Wheelus Air Base as being the operation of a weapons training center for forces assigned to the U.S. Air Force command in Europe. "In brief, the Center provides and supervises a program of gunnery, rocketry and training in special and conventional weapons delivery techniques for tactical fighter and fighter-interceptor squadrons." The report continued to describe Wheelus as "the only currently available facility of its type in that part of the world" and suggested that much of its value derived from the year-round good flying weather conditions that prevailed in Libya. Wheelus Air Base, together with associated firing ranges and support facilities, totaled 27,245 acres at the time with a total population of 10,536 military and civilian personnel.[57]

At the same time, growing oil revenues, accompanied by improved economic conditions and greater social mobility, increased demands, especially among younger Libyans, for a coherent and comprehensive ideology that would satisfy new, albeit vaguely understood, political and spiritual yearnings. The United Kingdom of Libya under the conservative traditional monarchy of King Idris I attempted to respond to these needs but failed to understand and accommodate them, just as it failed to satisfy the growing demands of Arab nationalists in and outside Libya. A distinctive feature of the absolutist system in place continued to be its isolation from society at large. Detached and remote, King Idris preferred to remain in Cyrenaica, where he was secluded from the daily pressures of government.[58]

An overview of the policies of the Libyan government in the 1960s highlights the rapidly changing landscape faced by successive administrations. Muhammad Bin Uthman, a self-made man and prominent Fezzan politician, took office in October 1960. Recognizing the need for foreign capital and expertise, he tried to dispel the widespread belief that the foreign oil companies attracted to Libya were only interested in exploiting the resources of the country to their own advantage. Bin Uthman also worked to sustain good relations with the Western powers together with Egypt and the Maghrib states. On the other hand, his administration provided only lukewarm support for a 1961 unity plan with Algeria, Morocco, and Tunisia. During his tenure, King Idris moved his administrative capital to the remote location of al-Bayda, which added to the general confusion and lack of cohesion in the governance of the country. During Ben Uthman's administration, Crown Prince Hasan al-Rida al-Sanusi, a nephew of King Idris, paid an official visit to the United States. A memorandum from Robert W. Komer, a National Security Council staff member, to President Kennedy captured the U.S. strategy at the time.

Crown Prince Hasan of Libya is here as part of our effort to build him up as an effective successor to 72-year-old King Idris. The UAR is very active in Libya; there are also a number of contending domestic factions. We fear that Idris' death may lead either to chaos or a coup endangering our hold on Wheelus Base and our growing oil interests.[59]

Muhiaddin Fekini, successor to Bin Uthman in March 1963, favored reaching an accommodation with both Algeria and the United Arab Republic. He also questioned a 1955 Franco-Libyan Agreement that covered airfields, radio stations, and other military facilities in southwest Libya, on the grounds that the recent independence of Chad and Niger rendered obsolete the need for such facilities. However, he was unable to negotiate a complete French withdrawal as long as British forces remained in the coastal area. Many of Fekini's policies were a source of grave concern for the U.S. Embassy in Tripoli. As the prime minister prepared to visit Washington, U.S. Ambassador Lightner cabled the following observations to the Department of State:

I do not wish to disguise my concern regarding the course that Fikini is following: his undue catering to extremist voices that call for the cancelation of the Wheelus agreement (and the British treaty), his invoking the Addis Ababa disarmament resolution and the alleged pressure from neighboring Arab countries to explain the failure of the GOL [government of Libya] to stand up in public support of its foreign base agreements. He is walking a tight rope to stay in office and needs popular support, since he has no tribal or other partisan backing. Maybe that explains his wishy-washy handling of all matters connected with the U.S. and British military presence in Libya. The result, regardless of cause, is an attitude of uncertainty which articulate opponents have exploited and will continue to exploit. Playing on nationalistic, pan-Arab emotions and the namby-pamby attitude of the Government, these forces may be expected to succeed in drumming up stronger and stronger anti-Wheelus sentiments among the population. . . .
    Bearing in mind that Fikini is vain and ambitious as well as pro-Arab, pro-Egyptian, pro-African, anti-Israel, anti-foreign base, anti-colonial, and a neutralist in the

East-West struggle, the USG [United States government] should make an effort during his forthcoming trip to the United States to influence his thinking and if possible to get from him an expression of his policy toward Wheelus base.[60]

The talking paper circulated to prepare President Kennedy for Fekini's visit differed in tone but not in content from the cable dispatched by Ambassador Lightner: "In foreign policy Fekini has tended toward Arab nationalist positions. For example, he has emphasized the Palestine issue, has been less friendly toward Wheelus Air Base and has concluded Libya's first trade agreement (a small one) with the U.S.S.R."[61]

Prime Minister Fekini met with President Kennedy at the White House on 30 September 1963. Kennedy noted recent press attacks in Libya on Wheelus Field and emphasized to Fekini that the "base was important to [the] stability of [the] area and [a] kind of guarantee of Libya's continued independence and stability." Asking Fekini's support in reducing the press attacks, President Kennedy suggested it was not wise to "make Wheelus [a] great dominant political issue." Less than four months later, demonstrations in support of the Palestinian cause broke out in several Libyan cities, leaving some students injured and eventually leading to Fekini's resignation. The demonstrations in January 1964 were largely a reaction to the decision of King Idris, under strong pressure from the United States and other Western governments, not to attend a summit of Arab heads of state in Cairo. American opposition to his participation in the Arab summit, together with ongoing American pressure to support controversial policies like the Eisenhower Doctrine and diplomatic recognition of Taiwan, only contributed to the growing isolation of the monarchy.[62]

Mahmud al-Muntasir took office in late January 1964, a move the government-controlled media in Egypt interpreted as signifying an intent to perpetuate the Anglo-Libyan treaty due for revision in 1964. In a Unity Day speech in February, Egyptian President Nasser depicted the foreign bases in Libya as a threat to the United Arab Republic and to the Arab cause in general and called for their liquidation. "No country can claim independence unless the military bases on its territories are liquidated. What guarantees are there for us that American and British bases in Libya will not be used against the Arabs in the event of a clash with Israel?" Expanding on this theme, Cairo Radio falsely alleged that the foreign bases in Libya had been used against the Egyptians during the Anglo-French invasion of the Suez Canal in 1956. The Libyan government hurriedly responded to Nasser's request with a statement indicating it had no intention of renewing or extending its military agreements with either the United Kingdom or the United States. Libya was in full agreement with the views expressed by President Nasser, added the statement of the Libyan government, and would never allow its foreign bases to be used as a source of aggression against its Arab brothers. The contradiction between this statement and the terms of Libya's treaties with the United Kingdom and United States was obvious and could not be ignored.[63]

In March 1964, a small group of pro-Nasser deputies in the Libyan parliament introduced a resolution calling for abrogation of the treaties and liquidation of the bases, a move the Muntasir government, accurately reading public opinion, was not strong enough to oppose. Instead, the prime minister issued a statement promising that the government would demand termination of the treaties and set a time for the withdrawal of Anglo-American forces. The timing of the statement, issued so soon after Nasser's speech, was unfortunate, as it gave the impression the Egyptian president was dictating policy in Libya. The parliamentary resolution and the prime minister's statement deeply upset King Idris, who viewed them as an abject surrender to Egyptian intimidation. The King soon submitted a letter of resignation, which was quickly rejected, but he did nothing to repudiate the parliamentary resolution, leaving it for the Muntasir government to negotiate with the United Kingdom and the United States. The British government, welcoming an opportunity to reduce overseas military expenditures, agreed to withdraw from Tripolitania by 31 March 1966 and from Benghazi one year later. The future of the small garrison at Tobruk and the Al-Adem airfield were left for future consideration.[64]

Nasser's Unity Day speech and the response of the Libyan government to it raised serious concerns in Washington. On 8 March 1964, President Lyndon B. Johnson sent a personal message to King Idris in which he expressed concern that recent events appeared to threaten their mutually beneficial cooperation centered on Wheelus Field. A memorandum signed jointly by Special Assistant for National Security Affairs McGeorge Bundy and Robert W. Komer of the National Security Council staff on 17 March 1964 expressed the concerns of the White House in more explicit terms:

There seems little alternative but to agree now to renegotiate our Libyan base agreement, in hopes this will defuse the issue. Our best friends in the Libyan Government (the King and PM) plead that we do so. They've panicked in the face of an outburst of Libyan nationalism, and face an aroused Parliament demanding prompt abrogation of the US/UK treaties. Nasser started off the parade by criticizing the bases, but clearly both his action and Libyan popular hysteria were stimulated by the Arab-Israeli issue.

Our ability to resist is undermined by UK agreement to renegotiate its base rights. . . . We want to save this regime (the best we could have), and also protect our oil investment, now $670 million. So State, our Embassy, and our Libyan friends recommend we be forthcoming now to sidetrack demands for abrogation. We would then hope to spin negotiations, and finally agree to a reduced tenure which will buy us three-five more years.[65]

Under pressure from the Libyan government, Washington at first agreed to accept the principle of withdrawal from Wheelus Field with no dates mentioned. Later the Libyans agreed to allow the Americans to remain until the 1954 base-rights agreement expired in December 1971.[66]

After Muntasir resigned due to ill health, Hussein Maziq took charge of the government in March 1965, completing the base rights negotiations with the United Kingdom and United States initiated by his predecessor. Increasingly fearful of the political threat from Nasser's brand of Arab nationalism, King Idris requested assurances that the United States would help defend Libya in the event of external aggression. Responding to his concerns in a 1 September 1965 letter that National Security Council staff member Komer described as "very carefully drafted," President Johnson assured King Idris "that the United States could not remain indifferent to an unprovoked and aggressive attack on Libya." In such an event, Johnson promised that the U.S. government would consult with the Libyan government "and other interested governments on the necessary and appropriate steps to meet the situation within the framework of the international obligations and constitutional procedures of all concerned."[67]

When the Six-Day War between Egypt and Israel broke out in June 1967, Libya suffered a fate similar to its experience during the 1956 Suez crisis. The swift, overwhelming defeat of Egyptian forces, blamed by Cairo Radio on the United Kingdom and United States, made Libya with the presence of foreign bases an easy target. Huge demonstrations took place in Benghazi and Tripoli, U.S. offices were attacked, and Jewish property was destroyed.[68] With the situation tense for weeks on end, it was readily apparent that pan-Arabism, as preached by Cairo Radio, had undermined much of the political support for the Idris regime. Walter W. Rostow, a senior administration official, captured the seriousness of the situation in a short note to President Johnson:

Herewith a fear that will mount: a Nasser takeover of Libya after U.S.-U.K. bases are withdrawn. The takeover could be either from within or without, probably the former. It would put Nasser on easy street with oil and bring great pressure to bear on Tunisia. But, as the second attached report indicates, we shall try to buy time on the bases. A good deal depends on whether the King can sweat it out.[69]

Following the resignation of Maziq and a short interim administration by Abdel Qadir Badri, the King turned to Abdel Hamid Bakkush to serve as prime minister. A young, energetic reformer, Bakkush assumed a more assertive stance, aligning Libya more closely with Arab nationalist policies. Many observers at the time felt Libya had finally bestirred itself and might now embark on a mainstream course to modernization. Unfortunately, Bakkush's innovative policies were cut short by King Idris upon the recommendation of his conservative advisers, many of whom saw in the prime minister's initiatives a challenge to royal hegemony. Reportedly, the King himself was especially troubled by Bakkush's insistence that he be allowed to select new cabinet ministers more attuned to his policies and goals. The aging monarch simply could not bring himself to delegate authority even for such modest changes to governmental policy and practice.[70]

As a series of governments failed in their attempts to reform and modernize Libya, the Libyan economy took off fueled by the rapid expansion in oil production. Per capita gross national product rose more than twenty-five-fold, from around $40 in the early 1950s to over $1,000 in 1967. In the latter year alone, per capita GNP increased by 42 percent over 1966. Libya eventually became the most dramatic example of economic growth in the decade, and one of the most dramatic examples in the century. Concomitant with unprecedented economic growth came dramatic change in the nation's social fabric. Swept up in the oil boom, farmers sought the fruits of new jobs in the petroleum industry with the result that a country once self-sufficient in food production became a net importer of foodstuffs. Rapid urbanization put revolutionary demands on housing, health services, and educational facilities. The demand for skilled labor far outstripped supply, while a general condition of unemployment and underemployment prevailed in the ranks of unskilled labor. In the process, social discontinuities everywhere served as frequent reminders that social change could be both idiosyncratic and destabilizing. As the decade ended, xenophobia against the West combined with a crisis in values to produce a growing identity crisis in Libya and a resulting *crise de l'ancien régime.*[71]

On 12 June 1969, the aging King Idris left Libya for rest and medical treatment in Greece and Turkey. Capitalizing on his absence, a group of approximately seventy army officers executed a successful coup d'état on 1 September 1969, one year after the resignation of Prime Minister Bakkush. Public response to the overthrow of the monarchy was surprisingly mute. The public at large reacted with a combination of bewilderment and jubilation. The available evidence suggests that the army officers who led the September 1969 coup were only one of several groups at the time plotting the overthrow of the Idris regime.

Three decades later, with the release of official papers first made public on 1 January 2000, it was learned that the British government had rejected an appeal from its old ally, King Idris, to intervene on his behalf in 1969 when Mu'ammar al-Qaddafi led the military revolt against him. According to official documents released by the Public Record Office in London, the king secretly asked then Prime Minister Harold Wilson to help restore him to power, but Britain's Labour government decided to remain neutral. Foreign Secretary Michael Stewart warned it would be "dangerous and wrong" to intervene in the coup d'état. Within days of the overthrow of the monarchy, Stewart reportedly noted that the sooner the United Kingdom got on reasonable terms with the revolutionary government, the greater would be its chances of protecting its essential interests in Libya.[72]

Conclusions

Monarchical Libya, especially in the period before the discovery of oil, was a thoroughly penetrated economic and political system in that external actors, both governmental and nongovernmental, played significant roles in the formation of the monarchy's domestic and foreign policies. Moreover, those policies largely consisted of adjusting to the interests, pressures, and actions of others. Conversely, the monarchy had little or no impact on the policies of other states, although the revenues from oil exports later increased its influence to a very limited degree.

It must also be emphasized that the potential impact of oil revenues on the monarchy's foreign policy was far greater than the actual impact. Although the monarchy indicated in 1964 that it would not extend or renew the base agreements with the United Kingdom and the United States when they expired in the early 1970s, it continued to maintain a close relationship with the Western powers. The approach of the Libyan government was based, not on any widespread commitment to Western ideals and traditions, but on the monarchy's belief that the Western powers remained in the best position to guarantee Libyan security. On the contrary, the monarchy throughout the 1960s sought to minimize the impact of Western social structures and mores on Libyan society. The Libyan government also remained detached from Nasser's radical Arab nationalism, as evidenced by the firm steps it took to quell the serious domestic disturbances precipitated by the 1967 Arab-Israeli war. Even when the monarchy employed its economic largess as a political tool, the strategy it pursued remained a reactive, defensive one that used its growing financial resources to reduce political agitation from surrounding countries.

Although the revenues from petroleum exports had a minimal impact on the monarchy's foreign policy, those same revenues created the domestic preconditions for the September 1969 revolution, a development that is often misunderstood or ignored. By 1969 oil production exceeded three million barrels a day, and per capita income had increased almost six-fold since 1962. The socioeconomic change that accompanied this oil revolution precipitated a demand for political change that the monarchy was unable or unwilling to accommodate. On the contrary, the evidence suggests that by the mid-1960s King Idris was increasingly out of touch with the political demands and realities of Libya and the region. Unfortunately, American diplomats mostly reinforced the viewpoints of the king instead of encouraging him to promote the social, economic, and political changes demanded by his subjects.

Ironically, a primary source of growing Arab nationalism in Libya was the government's policy of supplementing its underdeveloped educational resources with Egyptian teachers and textbooks. Libyan students demonstrated in defiance of the police in 1964, for example, and the first conference of the Libyan Students' Union was held in 1966. At the conference, the students opted for a leftist tendency within the Arab nationalist movement, pledged support for the Vietnam revolution, demanded a more radical approach to the Palestinian problem, criticized the government's oil policy, and demanded liquidation of the foreign military bases. By the end of the decade, increasing numbers of Libyans, especially the younger, more articulate sectors, had concluded the Libyan government was corrupt and parochial and should be replaced.

The end of World War II brought the United States into North Africa and the Middle East to a degree theretofore unknown. Concomitantly, it reshaped U.S. priorities in the region. That said, it is important to realize that the United States had no clear-cut, well-defined policy for the Middle East at the end of the war. Possessed of enormous power, both absolutely and in relative terms, the United States could travel down any one of several roads in the Arab world. With the advent of the Cold War, America's strategic options, in perception if not reality, narrowed sharply. North Africa and the Middle East became a central arena in a zero sum game in which any advance by the Soviet Union was viewed by Washington policy makers as a defeat for U.S. interests.

In this context, the policies of the Western governments, in particular the United States, before and after independence in 1951 contributed mightily to the state of political bankruptcy reached by the monarchy in 1969. In so doing, these governments must bear a major burden of responsibility for the revolutionary government headed by Mu'ammar al-Qaddafi that took power on 1 September 1969. The United States government and its allies pressured the monarchy to accept long-term base agreements that became an increasingly grating symbol of Western imperialism, especially after the discovery of oil propelled Libya virtually overnight from rags to riches. Not content with the occupation of Wheelus Field and other military facilities, American policy makers also pressured Libya repeatedly to support regional and international policies, like the Baghdad Pact, the Eisenhower Doctrine, and the intervention in Beirut, that clearly were not in the best interests of an Arab state. Libyan support for such policies played well in Washington but were deeply resented throughout the Arab world.

Chapter 6
One September Revolution

> Freedom means the social, economic, and political freedom of the citizen. Freedom is not a slogan we call for or raise—it is an activity we must carry out and achieve by carrying it out.
>
> —Mu'ammar al-Qaddafi, 1969

The overthrow of the monarchy on 1 September 1969 was planned and executed by the Libyan Free Unionist Officers' Movement, and its central committee of twelve officers immediately designated themselves the Revolutionary Command Council (RCC). While the composition and leadership of the RCC was at first anonymous, the organization soon issued a terse statement which announced the promotion of Captain Mu'ammar al-Qaddafi to the rank of colonel together with his appointment as commander-in-chief of the Libyan armed forces. Thereafter, the RCC remained a largely closed organization, but it was soon apparent that Qaddafi was its chairman and the de facto head of state.[1]

Background and Goals

Colonel Qaddafi, his colleagues on the RCC, and indeed most members of the Free Unionist Officers' Movement shared similar backgrounds, motivations, and world views. Most came from poorer families and minor tribes, and almost all attended the Libyan military academy at a time when a military career offered less-privileged segments of Libyan society the widest possible opportunities for education and advancement. The product of an oasis environment, Qaddafi emphasized in a poignant short story published some years later the influence his rural background had on his world view and approach to life.

Depart the city and flee to the village, where you will see the moon for the first time in your lives. You will change from being worms and rats, exiled from social companionship and ties, and become true human beings in the village, oasis or countryside. Leave the cemetery neighbourhoods for God's wide and wondrous land.

You will see constellations in the sky that will make you despise the chandeliers made of sand that used to hang above you in the city. . . .

The village is peaceful, clean, and friendly; everyone knows everyone else. People there stick together through thick and through thin. There is no stealing in the village or countryside; everyone knows everyone else. One takes into account the reputation of his family, his tribe, and himself before doing anything that might cause harm. . . . Moreover, social solidarity and networks in the countryside and village take care of the needs of the needy, and prevent them from having to beg or steal. Rural life is simple, humble, and satisfying, far removed from the desires and luxuries of city life. . . . Villagers do not suffer from tension and complexities, or lusting after wealth. Thus, their lives are calm and easy, innocent of any pains of desire.[2]

The language of RCC members was the language of Arab nationalism, guided by the precepts of the Koran and the Islamic Sharia (religious law), and strengthened by the conviction that only the RCC spoke for the Libyan people. The members of the RCC were convinced that they spoke not only for the Libyan people but for those throughout the Arab world and beyond who felt restricted in their exercise of self determination.

The planning and execution of the One September Revolution bore many similarities to Gamal Abdul Nasser's 1952 coup in Egypt. This was not surprising since the latter had served as a model for the former from its earliest stages.[3] Following the overthrow of the Libyan monarchy, the members of the RCC, together with most members of the Free Unionist Officers' Movement, described themselves as students of Nasser or simply Nasserists. The debt owed by the RCC to the Egyptian experience became even more pronounced once the RCC began to issue new foreign policy statements. The Revolutionary Command Council emphasized that the new Libyan republic was an Arab republic that would be neutral in superpower disputes and would act against any form of colonialism or imperialism at home or abroad. In a similar vein, the RCC announced its intention to play a much more aggressive role in espousing Arab nationalism and supporting the Palestinian cause against Israel. "We pledge all our material and moral capabilities to the Palestine cause. Our relations with other states will be on the basis of the position of these states on the Palestine cause."[4]

The Constitutional Proclamation, issued on 11 December 1969, reflected the goals, philosophy, and policies that first motivated the Libyan revolution. Consisting of a preamble and three parts, this short document helped place the core elements of the One September Revolution in perspective. The preamble detailed the causes for the revolution; the legitimation of the regime; the nature of Arab nationalist philosophy; and the ideals of freedom, socialism, and unity. The preamble deserves to be quoted at length as it provides a sense of the ideological background and emotion the RCC brought to the revolution.

The Revolutionary Command Council, in the name of the Arab people of Libya, who vow to recover their liberty . . . who are determined to break all the fetters which restricted their movement and progress, joining the ranks of their Arab brethren throughout the Arab Fatherland in their struggle to liberate every square inch of land desecrated by imperialism and removing the obstacles which impede Arab unity from the Arabian Gulf to the Atlantic Ocean; who believe that peace can be based only upon justice, recognize the significance of the ties binding them with all peoples of the world who struggle against imperialism and realize that the alliance between the reactionary and imperialism is responsible both for the backwardness suffered by them . . . and the corruption prevailing in government bureaucracy . . . recognize their responsibilities for establishing a national, democratic, progressive and unionist government.[5]

Article 1 of the Constitutional Proclamation defined the state, describing Libya as an Arab democratic republic whose people constituted part of the Arab Nation and whose objective was Arab unity. "Libya is a free Arab democratic republic in which sovereignty rests with the people who constitute part of the Arab nation and whose objective is overall Arab unity. Its territory is part of Africa and its name is the Libyan Arab Republic." The proclamation set forth in article 2 and several following articles the concept of a socialist-style planned economy and reaffirmed the establishment of Islam as the state religion. The second part of the proclamation described the system of government, emphasizing in article 18 that all law, except for the Sharia strictures governing inheritances, would be made by the RCC. "The Revolutionary Command Council is the highest authority in the Libyan Arab Republic. It exercises the functions of supreme sovereignty and legislation and draws up the general policy of the state on behalf of the people." The final part consisted of miscellaneous and transitional rules. Most significant here was article 34, in which the RCC assumed the roles of both the monarchy and the parliament."[6]

Ideology and Policy

From the beginning, Arab nationalism was the central element of Qaddafi's ideology and probably his primordial value. Like Egyptian President Nasser, Qaddafi based his variant of Arab nationalism on a glorification of Arab history and culture that viewed the Arabic-speaking world as the Arab nation.[7] Libya was the heart, the vanguard, and the hope of the Arab nation and thus the custodian of Arab nationalism. Acknowl-

edging the "backwardness" of the Arab nation, Qaddafi laid the blame for
the existing situation on four centuries of stagnation under Ottoman rule,
the subjugation and exploitation of first colonialism and then imperialism,
and finally the repression and corruption of reactionary, monarchical rule.
At the very core of his approach to Arab nationalism was the belief that the
Arab people were equal, if not superior, to other peoples of the world and
had the right and duty to manage their own resources and shape their own
destiny.[8] In an interview on United Arab Republic television on 14 October
1969, Qaddafi was asked to explain the origins of the Libyan revolution.

The true causes are not superficial or easy to determine. They are deep-rooted in
history and we must go back several hundreds of years to find them. Libya in particular and the Arab area in general have been subjected to long centuries of injustice, oppression and slavery through foreign occupation, and social backwardness
as a result of reactionary rule and regionalism which has been forcibly imposed on
them. . . . [More] recent causes were the bitter setback to the Arab people of June
1967, the burning of the Aqsa Mosque which violently shook the Arab people . . .
and some internal causes concerning the Libyan armed forces, and the people.
These are all reasons which brought nearer the date of the revolution. The true
causes of the revolution, on the other hand, lay in the backward Arab life which reduced the Arab man to almost complete loss of feeling of affiliation to the twentieth century world.[9]

In building a comprehensive revolutionary ideology, the first stage is
often nationalistic; and this was clearly true in the Libyan case. Qaddafi's
view of freedom incorporated three separate but related concepts: emancipation of the individual from poverty, ignorance, and injustice; liberation of the homeland (Libya) from reactionary, imperialist elements; and
finally, economic, political, and social emancipation of the entire Arab
world. Consistent, closely integrated ideological values governed policies
in all three areas; consequently, developments in all of them tended to be
closely related. As one result, actions or policies that might conventionally
be seen as external or foreign relations frequently were equally pertinent
to domestic internal affairs and vice versa. American observers in the early
years of the revolution frequently misread this close relationship between
domestic and foreign policies.[10]

At the outset of the revolution, Qaddafi focused on highly symbolic,
widely popular acts of national independence that increased the legitimacy of the revolutionary government. For example, on 19 September
1969 the RCC issued an order that all signs, cards, and tickets in Libya
should be printed in Arabic only. Similar restrictions requiring the use of
Arabic had acquired substance under the monarchy, but they were seldom
enforced. As Qaddafi later explained, "it was not a question of changing
street names from foreign languages into Arabic but the essence of the

change is indeed the outward aspect of struggle now existing between Arab culture and Western culture." The RCC later expanded this initiative to include the mandatory translation of foreign passports into Arabic and a campaign for the adoption of Arabic as an international language, recognized officially in the United Nations and other international organizations. At the same time, the RCC banned the consumption of alcohol and any public entertainment that could be construed as "pornographic, obscene, or vulgar." While many of these acts and policies were of little practical value, they had an enormous symbolic impact on Libyans and the Arab world because they epitomized the regime's rejection of nonindigenous values.[11]

Even though the monarchy had announced in February 1964 that Libya would not renew the base agreements with the United Kingdom and United States due to expire in the early 1970s, the base rights question had remained an extremely controversial issue in Libya. Therefore, it came as no surprise when Qaddafi immediately began to pressure both governments for an early termination of the agreements. On 16 October 1969, in an address delivered in Tripoli, Qaddafi made the Revolutionary Command Council's policy toward foreign bases quite clear.

Today's stand towards the Mellaha (American) base which you ask should be eliminated, has become abundantly clear. Our attitude towards this and other bases is no longer equivocal. The Arab people in Libya which rose on September 1 can no longer live with the foreign bases side by side. Nor will the armed forces which rose to express the people's revolution tolerate living in their shacks while the bases of imperialism exist in Libyan territory.

The lifetime of the bases has become limited the same as that of the occupier. The fate of the bases in our land is already doomed for we accept no bases, no foreigner, no imperialist, and no intruders. This is a clear-cut attitude which is understandable to both friend and enemy. We will liberate our land from bases, the imperialist and foreign forces whatever the cost involved.[12]

Despite the fact the United States and United Kingdom put forth several preconditions for diplomatic recognition, including maintenance of the military bases in Libya, the revolutionary government continued to press for immediate withdrawal. Negotiations with the British went smoothly, as they quickly accepted the principle of evacuation, departing from Al-Adem Base at the end of March 1970. Negotiations with the United States concerning Wheelus Field were more prolonged, as Washington at first insisted on fulfilling the terms of the 1954 treaty. Hoping to avoid moving the base to Europe, American negotiators proposed joint use of Wheelus for training exercises; but when Libya rejected this initiative the Americans agreed to evacuate the base within a year. Once American and British forces departed, 28 March, the day the British evacuated Al-Adem Base, and 11 June, the day the Americans evacuated Wheelus Field, became official national holidays in Libya, commemorated annually with popular festivities and usually highlighted by a strong nationalistic address by Qaddafi. In a similar vein, 7 October 1970, the day Italian-owned assets were confiscated and the Italian community expelled from Libya, was also declared a national holiday.[13]

As the United States and United Kingdom discussed with Libya the closure of the military bases, their ally France was negotiating the sale to the revolutionary government of sophisticated new weapons such as the monarchy had not purchased. Within six weeks of the successful coup, the French government offered to sell Libya one hundred Mirage warplanes on three conditions. First, the French insisted the planes not be used against France or any of its friends, which Paris reportedly defined as Chad, Niger, and Tunisia. Second, Libya could not station or transfer the planes or their parts to another state; this point was later clarified to mean permanent transfer as opposed to deployment or temporary stationing. Third, the planes could not be used on orders of another country. With French approval, Libya eventually agreed to purchase 110 instead of the original 100 Mirages over a period of three years at a cost of $300 million. As part of the deal, France also agreed to train pilots and technicians on a rotating basis in France.[14]

Nationalistic moves in the financial sector began within two weeks of the seizure of power, when the RCC issued a resolution requiring foreign banks to form Libyan joint stock companies with a minimum 51 percent of their shares owned by the government. In contrast, the initial approach of the RCC toward the petroleum sector was almost conciliatory. Even as the revolutionary government prepared for dramatic changes in oil policy, it reassured foreign governments and oil producers alike that major changes were not being contemplated. Although the revolutionary government preached conciliation, it was obvious to informed observers that its intent was to increase control of Libya's petroleum sector. A debate was raging at the time throughout the oil-producing world as to whether to seek broader control through a strategy of greater participation with the oil companies or outright nationalization. The RCC opted initially for the first strategy but soon adopted the second approach.[15]

By summer 1970, Abdel-Salam Jalloud, the RCC member who had negotiated the early withdrawal of American and British forces from Libyan base facilities, was increasingly in charge of oil price negotiations. His appointment was a clear indication that the RCC put the highest possible priority on its negotiations with the oil companies. The Libyan government at the time concentrated its pressure on the independent oil producers, most of which were of U.S. parentage, because Libyan supplies constituted all or a large part of their resources of crude oil outside North America. Moreover, their contracts were generally covered by escalation clauses, and thus they had the least to fear from consenting to posted price and tax increases in a rising market with supply restrictions. Occidental was the first independent oil company to agree to a revised settlement, but similar agreements were concluded over the next few weeks with the other oil companies operating in Libya. Termed the One September Agreement to coincide with the first anniversary of the revolution, the agreement with Occidental marked the first significant increase in the posted price of oil since the formation of the Organization of Petroleum Exporting Countries (OPEC) in 1960.[16]

The global impact of the One September Agreement was enormous. While most OPEC states had stood aloof during the negotiations, an OPEC resolution adopted in December 1970 led to the so-called Tehran Agreement in February 1971 between the oil companies and the oil producing states in the Gulf. The Tehran Agreement stemmed directly from the One September Agreement and incorporated many of the gains won in Libya. Nevertheless, it infuriated the Libyan government because the oil producing states in the pact agreed not to ask individually for better terms after Libya had rejected the principle of collective bargaining. With the conclusion of the Tehran agreement, the limited leadership role that Libya enjoyed in OPEC in autumn 1970 faded. Of even greater significance, Qaddafi in the end misread the whole affair. The lesson he drew from the 1970 oil negotiations was that a defiant posture, buttressed by anti-colonialist and anti-imperialist rhetoric, called the bluff of the cartel of oil companies and consumer nations, shaking out significant additional revenues. Later he applied a similar approach to other aspects of domestic and foreign policy, which were simply not susceptible to such aggressive behavior. This was especially true after 1973, when oil revenues, due to increased oil prices, took a dramatic leap. The net result of sharp policy initiatives in this period proved catastrophic for Libya and its neighbors.[17]

The Libyan government opened new negotiations with the oil companies in early 1971; after difficult talks, in which the Libyan side employed tactics of threat and intimidation, revised terms were agreed to in April. In September the RCC withdrew all Libyan reserves from British banks; two months later, they nationalized the assets of the British Petroleum Company. The Arabian Gulf Exploration Company replaced British Petroleum, and the level of oil production of the other companies operating in Libya was frozen to prevent them from supplying British Petroleum. Decisive action on the part of the RCC at this point set the stage for Libya's growing emphasis over the next two years on participation in the petroleum sector. In June 1973, Libya nationalized the American-owned Bunker Hunt Oil Company, an action Qaddafi described as a slap in the face for the United States because of its support for Israel. By 1 September 1973, the fourth anniversary of the revolution, nationalization had become widespread and affected all the oil companies operating in Libya. In the process, Qaddafi indicated the extent to which the government's policy toward nationalization had changed since its conciliatory statements to the United States and others in the early days of September 1969:

The right to nationalize is one of the rights of the government which owns the oil. There is no law in the world which prevents the country that owns the oil from nationalizing oil resources and from handling oil operations or halting the pumping of oil, taking full control of all oil operations. At the same time, any people already moving on the road of the revolution cannot, in any circumstance, halt in the middle of the road.[18]

These policies and actions epitomized, ideologically as well as practically, the determination of the revolutionary government to liberate Libya from imperialist elements.

The October 1973 war solidified the basic changes in the worldwide oil industry that Libya initiated in 1970. In the course of the conflict, the Arab oil-producing countries imposed oil restrictions; and abandoning any pretense of negotiation over prices, they imposed new price levels by unilateral decree. As might be expected, the Libyan government was at the forefront of the new approach. Even though the Arab states later retreated from the oil boycott, the old system of oil concessions was dead, because the oil companies no longer owned, or could act as though they owned, the producing properties in major oil-producing states. They had become mere buyers in a system in which production levels, and to a lesser extent price levels, were now set by the host governments. The Libyan government had spearheaded these changes in the oil industry, and it enjoyed their fruits for the remainder of the decade.[19]

Qaddafi's early emphasis on freedom and independence at home soon took on regional and international dimensions. He sought to diminish the presence of NATO forces in the Mediterranean region by encouraging Malta to cancel the air and naval facilities it had granted to NATO. The Libyan-Maltese relationship flourished until the late 1970s, when diplomatic relations soured due to a festering dispute over offshore oil rights.[20] Early Libyan initiatives in Africa focused on opposition to colonialism and on undermining the substantial Israeli presence. African governments, in return for Libyan diplomatic and economic support, were encouraged to expel Israeli military and technical advisors and break diplomatic relations. At the same time, Libya moved to reduce Western power and influence on the continent by eliminating Western military bases and undermining moderate African governments opposed to Libyan policies. The Libyan government also provided diplomatic and material support to African liberation movements as well as to radical, anti-Western governments.[21]

Third Universal Theory

By late 1972, Mu'ammar al-Qaddafi had begun to give the tenets of his strain of Arab nationalism a theoretical underpinning with the articulation of what came to be known as the Third Universal Theory. The theory was an attempt to develop an alternative to capitalism and communism, both of which Qaddafi found unsuitable for the Libyan environment. It condemned both communism and capitalism as monopolistic, the former as a state monopoly of ownership and the latter as a monopoly of ownership by capitalists and companies. In an essay entitled "Is Communism Truly Dead?" published after the implosion of the Soviet Union, Qaddafi lucidly summarized his opposition to the world order as he saw it.

Revolution took place in Czarist Russia, and was called the Soviet Union. Stalin said that in order to protect the revolution, apparatuses of oppression were necessary; they were called intelligence, external security, national security, secret police, secret service, security of the revolution, revolutionary courts, etc. Exceptional courts, military courts, political prison . . . all of this in terms of the security issue. . . . It became the fashion to have revolutions or coups, even if against socialist regimes. But these actions would be marked by an iron-willed party, secret police, political prisons, exceptional courts, appropriating freedoms, apparatuses of external and internal security, national security . . . patriotism, nationalism, even America was affected by this. Its Central Intelligence Agency was developed, and deployed outside the country's borders. It committed acts more atrocious than those of the Soviet external security committee, which later became the KGB. Competition reached its summit between the CIA and KGB . . . coups, assassinations, counterfeiting money, forging identity documents and passports, buying agents, from the most worthless person to the president of a country. In order to spite Germany, a Jewish state was established in Palestine, despite the dangerous future it held for the Jews themselves, and its effects on world peace.

After the fall of the Kremlin and the end of the cold war, will all of the related effects also collapse . . . ?

There is no doubt that the old world will fall, from America to the Soviet Union. A new order will certainly arise from these new geopolitical interactions, and not by design, political decision, or by threat of force.[22]

In short, the United States and the Soviet Union, in the early days of the revolution, were grouped together as imperialist countries intent on obtaining spheres of influence in the Middle East. In addition, Qaddafi denounced the atheistic nature of the Soviet regime describing communism as "a political and economic concept void of the Word of the Almighty."[23]

Qaddafi based the Third Universal Theory on nationalism and religion, the two forces considered by him to be the paramount drives moving history and humankind. Nationalism was described as the natural result of the world's racial and cultural diversity and thus both a necessary and a productive force. Arab nationalism was considered to have especially deep and glorious roots in the ancient past. Because the Arab nation was the product of an age-old civilization based on the "heavenly and universal" message of Islam, Qaddafi argued it had the right as well as the duty to be the bearer to the world of the Third Universal Theory.[24] In this sense, Qaddafi's characterization of the Arab man resembled to a striking degree Fouad Ajami's description of the "nativist," the man who believes the whole world should be in the Arab world rather than vice versa.[25] Qaddafi had great difficulty from the start accepting the fact that the Arab world in general, and Libya in particular, were nothing more than a small part of the entire world.

While Qaddafi never produced a coherent, comprehensive discussion of religion, his thoughts in various seminars and statements focused on the centrality of Islam to religion and the Koran to Islam. Considering Islam to be God's final utterance to humanity, he argued that there was nothing in life for which the principles were not found in Islam. For Qaddafi, the essence of religion was the unity of God; consequently, he made no distinction between what he called the followers of Muhammad, Jesus, and Moses. Since there was only one religion and that religion was Islam, he considered all monotheists to be Muslims. Qaddafi firmly believed, not only that Islam was not addressed only to the followers of the Prophet Muhammad, but that Islam meant a belief in God as embodied in all religions. He referred to his contention that anyone who believed in God and his apostles was a Muslim as the divine concept of Islam.[26]

Basing his call for Islamic revival on the Koran, Qaddafi argued that Muslims had moved away from God and the Koran and must return. In the process, he attempted to correct contemporary Islamic practices that were, in his mind, contrary to the faith. For example, he rejected formal interpretation of the Koran as blasphemy and sin, contending that the Koran was written in Arabic so that every Arab could read it and apply it without the help of others. Similarly, he criticized the hadith (traditions of the Prophet Muhammad) on the grounds that the Koran was the only real source of God's word. Qaddafi was also highly critical of the various schools of Islamic jurisprudence, such as the Hanafi, Maliki, and Hanbali, on the grounds they were largely the product of a struggle for political power and thus unconnected to either Islam or the Koran.[27]

While the similarities can clearly be overstated, there were some important continuities between the doctrines of the Sanusi order and the fundamentalist elements of Qaddafi's reformist approach to Islam. To promote Islamic unity, the puritanical Sanusi order accepted only the Koran and the Sunna as the basis for Muslim life and downplayed the role of the various schools of Islamic jurisprudence. Qaddafi emphasized these funda-

mentalist elements in the early years of the revolution because of their legitimizing effect. Later, his approach became increasingly reformist if not
secular.[28]

In the process, the Islamic character of Qaddafi's brand of Arab nationalism and the supposed universal elements of the Third Universal Theory
became increasingly paradoxical. In response, Qaddafi continued to emphasize the centrality of Islam to Arab nationalism while deemphasizing Islam's role in the Third Universal Theory. Although his thoughts on this
complex relationship remained unclear, his argument that the Third Universal Theory was the basis for a new universal civilization centered on the
Arab nation did result in Islam continuing to have a central role. Consequently, any deemphasis of Islam appeared to be little more than a short-
term tactic designed to give the Third Universal Theory wider appeal.[29]

Role of Jihad

Muslims view the struggle to spread the triumph of Islam, often interpreted narrowly to mean holy war in accordance with the Sharia against
non-Muslims, as a permanent duty. In the context of Qaddafi's ideology,
jihad was the action element of his variant of Arab nationalism. In the
broadest sense, he saw jihad as a means to achieve greater social justice in
and out of Libya. From this angle, revolutionary ideology in Libya initially
considered communism and imperialism equal threats to Islam. However,
as the 1970s progressed, it was imperialism that was increasingly identified
as the prime target of jihad.[30]

The concept of jihad found its most practical expression in Qaddafi's
fervent support for the Palestinian movement. In the early 1970s Qaddafi
advocated direct military action against Israel, and on 23 July 1972 he
opened the First Nasserite Volunteers Center, a base for equipping and
training guerrillas in the struggle. He continued this policy after the October 1973 war strengthened the Palestine Liberation Organization (PLO),
and the oil weapon proved to be a much more effective instrument in support of Arab goals. Toward the end of the 1970s, when the creation of ad
hoc, surrogate groups made it possible for many leaders of governments or
movements to pursue the armed struggle while disassociating themselves
from such activities, Qaddafi continued his public support. In the end, in
late 1979, his advocacy of the use of force in support of the Palestinian
cause contributed to a public feud with PLO Chairman Yasser Arafat. It
also adversely affected his aspirations to regional and international leadership. Thereafter, Qaddafi devoted considerable time and attention to differentiating between revolutionary violence, which he continued to advocate, and terrorism, which he allegedly opposed.[31]

Qaddafi's approach to jihad led him to support, at one time or another, a diverse collection of "liberation movements," including the Somali National Salvation Front, the Irish Republican Army, Muslim separatist elements in the Philippines, and Black militant groups in the United States. While government spokespersons later played down Libyan support of liberation movements, Tripoli continued its active encouragement, sponsoring and sustaining terrorist movements as well. With the exception of Islamic minority groups, Qaddafi's support for liberation movements was seldom a question of doctrine or vital national interest. On the contrary, support for liberation movements at the outset of the revolution symbolized the passage of the Arab revolution from the defensive to the offensive. In addition, support for selected liberation movements, like Muslim separatist groups in the Philippines, was a concrete expression of Islamic solidarity. Qaddafi also viewed such support as another means to strike at imperialism and, in the process, to enhance his international status as a leader in the Third World struggle against colonialism and neocolonialism. Finally, Qaddafi used these activities to increase his own legitimacy by enhancing his domestic and international reputation.[32]

In January 1970 the Revolutionary Command Council gave practical expression to Qaddafi's emphasis on jihad with the creation of a Jihad Fund. Its objectives included the support of armed struggle for the liberation of usurped Arab territories from Zionist control. Funded initially from public and private contributions, the RCC soon established a jihad tax to increase the financial strength of the fund. The Jihad Fund exemplified Qaddafi's view that the Palestinian issue was the major threat to the integrity of Islam and the Arab world. He saw Palestine as an integral part of the Arab nation and believed the latter could never be truly free and united until the former was completely liberated. The enemy was Zionism (seen as a European political movement, and not the Jewish people as such), together with the imperialist and colonialist powers responsible for imposing this indignity on the Arab nation. In this sense, Qaddafi's hostility toward the state of Israel, expressed in his support for jihad, encompassed the entire ideological system of Arab nationalism.[33]

Arab Unity

The Revolutionary Command Council, like Gamal Abdul Nasser at the outset of the 1952 Egyptian revolution, proclaimed Arab unity as a core regime goal. According to Salah El Saadany, a former Egyptian ambassador to Libya and a member of the first Egyptian delegation to visit Libya after the overthrow of the monarchy, the initial briefing the Egyptians received from members of the RCC emphasized that the main goal of the Libyan revolution was unity with Egypt. "If Nasser was sacrificing some of Egypt's meager resources to assist the struggle of Algeria, Libya and

Yemen, then the Libyan Revolution should reciprocate and seek the immediate unification of the two countries." In a subsequent meeting with Qaddafi, the Egyptian delegation was told that "Arab unity was a pressing demand." While Qaddafi was aware that Nasser was not in favor of immediate unification without careful planning, he stressed that the RCC "insisted on immediate unity with Egypt, regardless of the consequences."[34]

To comprehend the full significance of Qaddafi's emphasis on Arab unity, the movement must first be placed in historical perspective. In the 1940s, the Syrian Baath Party called for comprehensive Arab unity in the form of a single Arab state stretching from the Atlantic Ocean to the Persian Gulf. The exact means for achieving this end and the operative governmental institutions conveniently were left open. The pan-Arab ideal of the Baath Party later became a goal of Nasser and the United Arab Republic. In stark contrast to the United States and its Western allies, which viewed the Middle East as a land mass vulnerable to communism, Nasser argued that the Arab nations enjoyed a unity of language, religion, history, and culture, which they should take advantage of to create their own system of cooperation and defense. Proponents of this so-called Arab system viewed Israel and not the Soviet Union as the major obstacle to peace in the region. After the collapse of the United Arab Republic in 1961, Arab leaders continued to support the goal of Arab unity, but little substantive progress was made. Pessimism deepened in the aftermath of the June 1967 war, later described by Fouad Ajami as the "Waterloo of pan-Arabism."[35]

King Idris I had carefully limited Libyan participation in the pan-Arab movement while accommodating to and cooperating with the NATO allies. The revolutionary government, on the other hand, quickly moved Libya out of the Western system and into a closer association with the Arab system. Qaddafi's interests focused on the Arab world; and like Nasser, he often referred to the Arab nation, not in geographical terms, but as an expression of conviction and guidance:

The enemies of Arab unity, agents of Zionism and imperialism, occupants of thrones and chairs, those motivated by selfish interests, and the enemies of Arabism and Islam, are a stumbling block on the road to Arab unity. But the people, who have surged forward, broken the shackles and trodden on idols, will impose freedom, socialism, and Arab unity by force on the enemies of Arabism and Islam.[36]

The concept of the Arab nation was an ideological bond for Qaddafi that joined a people with a common cultural history and a faith in their destiny as equal to any race on earth.

At the same time, Qaddafi believed that the present weakness of the Arab people was the direct result of their disintegration into tribal states and regions, a process that the colonial powers encouraged in order to better control and dominate the Arab world. In this light, he saw regionalism as both an innovation of colonialism and the principal reason the Western powers were able to conquer the Middle East. Qaddafi emphasized in a September 1969 speech in the Fezzan, "What is to be abhorred is regionalism, the frittering away of the Arab homeland, and the division of the Arab people's ranks. Regionalism is the innovation that came to be imposed by imperialism and maintained by its agents." Consequently, he felt the Arab people must unite into a single Arab state if they were to regain their former glory and reach their full potential. In this context, the Palestinian issue became simply another manifestation of the lack of Arab unity. Arab divisions enabled Israel to triumph over the Arabs, and the Arab people would first have to unite if they hoped to regain Palestine.

We will arrive at Palestine, Brethren, when we have pulled down the walls which impede the fusion of the Arab people in the battle. We will reach the Holy Land when we have removed the borders and the partitions. We will reach the Holy Land with arms and with men, but only when we have the borders. The battle to free Palestine must extend from Syria to North Africa.[37]

Qaddafi produced a formula for a united Arab politics at his first press conference in February 1970; thereafter, he described the unification of Arab governments into a single state as an absolute necessity. More to the point, he persisted in pursuing practical attempts at Arab unity over much of the next two decades even after the idea was widely discredited elsewhere in the Arab world. In this sense, Qaddafi went through a stage in the 1970s and early 1980s similar to what the Baathists and Nasser had experienced in the previous two decades. Therefore, it was hardly surprising that his idol was the fiery, intractable Nasser of the 1950s and early 1960s as opposed to the more moderate, restrained Nasser of the post-1967 period. Between 1969 and 1974, Qaddafi engaged in union discussions with Egypt (twice), Syria, the Sudan, and Tunisia (twice). His practical approach to Arab unity was unique in that Qaddafi combined oil wealth with pan-Arabism, two forces typically at odds in contemporary Arab history.[38]

While Qaddafi continued to discuss Arab unity after 1974, it was more as a long-term goal than as an immediately recognizable objective. The late 1970s were a period in which Qaddafi appeared to recognize more clearly the rivalries and divisions in the path of Arab unity although he still refused to accept them. Consequently, it came as a surprise when in September 1980 Libya and Syria proclaimed a merger and declared their determination to form a unified government. Their subsequent difficulties in turning the proclamation into reality were not so surprising.[39]

In addition to the Arab world, Qaddafi viewed Libya as an integral part of sub-Saharan Africa, and a central component of his African policy was consistent support for African solidarity and unity. Pan-Africanism took a more practical direction in the late 1970s and early 1980s, when Qaddafi sought political support in and outside Africa for union with Chad. The failure to generate support for his plans did not squelch Qaddafi's ambitions in sub-Saharan Africa. In fall 1982, for example, Qaddafi threatened to establish a rival African movement if efforts failed to reconvene a stalled conference of the Organization of African Unity.[40]

Positive Neutrality in Theory and Practice

Leonard Binder rightly emphasized that "the major element in the Arab conception of neutralism is neither peace nor international responsibility, but the primacy of national independence, self-determination, and nonintervention."[41] Acutely aware of the destructiveness that would ensue from thermonuclear war, the Arabs were never concerned primarily with the Cold War or its demise, something few American policy makers understood. On the contrary, positive neutrality generally meant pursuit of an independent policy in accord with Arab national interests, often defined in terms of the revolutionary trinity of freedom, socialism, and unity.

In this sense, positive neutrality was largely an Arab response to the bipolarization of international power. The Arabs rejected both Eastern and Western blocs on the grounds that they followed diverse but equally misguided ideologies. The United States was viewed as the major opponent to Arab nationalist goals, but the Soviet Union's recognition of Arab neutrality was seen by many Arabs as little more than a tactical device. In a 1973 interview with the French newspaper *Le Monde*, for example, Qaddafi said, "the Russians are exploiting us in spreading hatred for the Americans in the Arab World. We are, of course, against the United States when we speak about it as a colonialist power, but we don't want to serve, in such a manner, the Soviet interest in the region." At the same time, the implementation of the Arab conception of neutralism, in and outside Libya, was never balanced evenly between the two power blocs. Since the basic neutralist position was revisionist, it aimed at the status quo as supported by long-standing Western positions and assumptions in the Middle East. In a word, the primary meaning of neutrality was anti-imperialism in the classical sense of the term.[42]

Qaddafi's ideology from the start incorporated the concept of positive neutrality frequently espoused by Arab revolutionary governments. Like his mentor Nasser, Qaddafi professed to believe in the unity of Third World causes and proclaimed a policy of absolute neutrality between East and West. Point four of the five-point declaration issued by the RCC on 1 September 1969 emphasized that the "Revolutionary Command Council believes in the unity of third-world causes and in the consolidation of the efforts of that world to destroy the yoke of social and economic backwardness."[43] In the following months and years, Qaddafi frequently reiterated his support for positive neutrality and Third World causes. In an October 1969 newspaper interview, for example, he stated that "the foreign policy of my country in the revolutionary era is, in brief, positive neutrality, non-alignment, and support for all liberation causes and for freedom in the whole world."[44] He rejected foreign controls of any form and repeatedly promised vigorous ideological and operational hostility to any form of imperialism, anywhere. He also pursued a leadership role in the nonaligned movement, an ambition he was never able to satisfy.[45]

Harshly critical of both capitalism and communism, Qaddafi initially described them as two sides of the same coin. As a result, early Libyan policy toward the United States and the Soviet Union assumed a dichotomous pattern. Stridently critical of American foreign policy, the revolutionary government maintained close commercial ties with the West, selling most of its oil to the European allies of the United States and using the proceeds to import massive amounts of Western technology, goods, and services. At the same time, Qaddafi criticized Soviet policy, especially its policy of allowing Soviet Jews to immigrate to Israel, but also purchased Soviet technology in increasing amounts.[46]

Window of Opportunity

American policies in the Middle East in the 1970s continued to stem principally from the three dominant global concerns of American foreign policy: containment of communism and Soviet and Chinese expansionism; avoidance of direct superpower conflict; and reinforcement of the Atlantic community. Given this global perspective, Washington aimed to stem the spread of communism in the Middle East, discourage any local conflict that might lead to superpower confrontation, and promote security and prosperity in Western Europe by ensuring continued flow of Middle East oil and unhampered transit through the Suez Canal. In addition, a regional objective involved U.S. commitment to the existence of the state of Israel. In support of these broad strategic goals, American decision makers also pursued three tactical objectives: maintenance of the balance of power; nonaggression; and nonopposition to U.S. global policies. The preservation of the status quo in the Middle East was the practical thrust of all three objectives.[47]

The American embassy in Tripoli had been aware for months that all was not well with the monarchy; nevertheless, the 1969 revolution apparently still came as something of a surprise for the Nixon administration. Ambassador Joseph Palmer, in his first dispatch from Tripoli after the takeover, told President Nixon and Secretary of State William Rogers that the members of the Revolutionary Command Council had promised to protect all Western interests and appeared to be establishing a kind of Muslim welfare state that had raised wages and banned alcohol as a step toward implementation of Koranic law. In the eyes of the American ambassador, early RCC statements suggested the new rulers were anticommunist nationalists who considered Nasser their ideal.[48]

Ambassador Palmer, together with Assistant Secretary of State David Newson, a former ambassador to Libya, subsequently played key roles in the U.S. decision to recognize the new regime. The anticommunist stance of the new government, together with its promise to respect Libya's international commitments, influenced their decision. Both Palmer and Newson saw the revolutionary government as an important asset in support of American policy to keep Soviet influence and communism out of the Middle East. In contrast, according to biographer Adriana Bush, "One portent, [Ronald] Reagan repeated widely in 1969, was the Communist takeover of Libya."[49] National Security Advisor Henry Kissinger was also hostile toward the new regime and favored a more aggressive policy:

There were desultory discussions in the Washington Special Actions Group (WSAG) on what attitude to take toward the new Libyan regime. In a meeting of November 24, 1969, I raised the question whether to have the 40 Committee [interagency committee supervising covert intelligence activities] canvass the possibility of covert action. A study was prepared of economic and political pressure points on Libya; but the agencies did not have their heart in it. All options involving action were rejected, causing me to exclaim that I was averse to submitting to the President a proposition that we could do nothing. My reluctance did not change a consensus along precisely those lines.[50]

The antagonistic policy advocated by Kissinger was rejected by the majority of U.S. policy makers, reportedly on the grounds that hostile acts on the part of the United States might endanger the Americans resident in Libya as well as access to Libyan oil. Concern was also expressed that a more aggressive approach might cause other Arab states to respond with hostile acts of their own. The consensus that emerged from the meeting of the Washington Special Actions Group was captured in a summary statement emphasizing that the optimum course of action was to try to get along with the new Libyan government:

Our present strategy is to seek to establish satisfactory relations with the new regime. The return to our balance of payments and the security of U.S. investments in oil are considered our primary interests. We seek to retain our military facilities, but not at the expense of threatening our economic return. We also wish to protect European dependence on Libyan oil. It is literally the only "irreplaceable" oil in the world, from the point of view both of quality and geographic location.[51]

The official statement of diplomatic recognition was worded very carefully:

The U.S. government has noted the statement of the RCC that all nations maintaining diplomatic relations with Libya are considered as recognizing the new Libyan government. The U.S. is maintaining diplomatic relations with the government of Libya and looks forward to a continuation of traditionally close ties between our two countries.[52]

When Qaddafi came to power, one of his first actions was to assure Americans that their oil companies in Libya would not be nationalized. The U.S. government, in turn, accomplished a speedy withdrawal from Wheelus Field in an effort to remove that irritant from American-Libyan relations and to demonstrate Washington's good intentions to establish a satisfactory relationship with the new government. In addition, eight of sixteen C-130 military transport planes purchased by the monarchy were delivered on schedule with the justification that they represented a "commercial deal" between the previous government and the Lockheed Company. Delivery of some F-5 military aircraft, on the other hand, was delayed. The Libyan government responded positively to these gestures with steps of its own, including the appointment in 1971 of a new Libyan ambassador to the United States.

Over the next three years, American policy makers viewed Libyan policies with an element of detached objectivity. The orientation and conduct of the revolutionary regime was portrayed as largely motivated by Qaddafi's nationalistic convictions and revolutionary zeal. While Libyan policies were often radical and extreme, Washington rightly believed they were not influenced by the Soviet Union. The U.S. government continued throughout this period to view Libya as basically anti-Soviet, a viewpoint reinforced by Qaddafi's reaction to a July 1971 communist coup attempt in the Sudan and by Libyan support for Egyptian President Sadat's expulsion of Soviet advisers, and for Pakistan in its war with India. All these policies, despite the economic and technical agreements later concluded by Libya and the Soviet Union, reinforced Washington's view of Libya as being anti-Soviet. If other issues had not complicated the policy mix, in particular the Arab-Israeli conflict and the Palestinian question, the anti-Soviet attitude of the Libyan government might have served as a solid basis for a long-term, workable relationship with the United States. In any case, the evidence suggests that American officials at the time clearly recognized the convoluted dynamics of Libyan foreign policy.[53]

Assistant Secretary Newson articulated the Nixon administration's view on oil policy when he suggested to Congress in July 1970 that Libya's cutback in production and its demands for higher prices were both justifiable. He argued in part that these issues had been raised by the monarchy before Qaddafi's takeover and thus represented a degree of policy continuity. Washington's policy makers obviously expected the revolutionary government to pursue more aggressive oil policies; however, they did not anticipate the subsequent policy of nationalization. When Libya took steps in the direction of nationalization, its use of petroleum as a political weapon against American companies clouded the official U.S. perception of Qaddafi's oil policies. The Nixon administration responded in July 1973 when it described the nationalization of the Bunker Hunt Oil Company as invalid and not entitled to recognition by other states. Washington viewed the nationalization of the remaining American oil companies in Libya through the same lens; however, its reaction was never strong enough to be characterized as hostile or threatening. On the contrary, the core American interest remained a continuation of the supply of Middle Eastern oil to Western Europe and North America, and Libyan oil was still readily available despite changes in pricing and marketing practices.[54]

It should also be noted that Libya's rapidly expanding revolutionary activities in and outside the Middle East after 1969 received little or no official American attention in the early years of the revolution. According to Mahmoud G. ElWarfally, author of a detailed study of imagery and ideology in American-Libyan relations, words like "terrorist," "subversive," and "destabilizing" were not used by the U.S. government to describe Libya's revolutionary activities in this time frame. Instead, official statements regarding such activities were most often worded in neutral terms. For example, Assistant Secretary Newson, in a July 1971 statement to the House Foreign Affairs Committee, described Libya's involvement in sub-Saharan Africa as follows: "Libya has increasingly interested itself in sub-Saharan Africa through expressions in the past of support for Muslim populations in other states and opposition to what it regards as Israeli influence detrimental to the Arab cause in Africa."[55]

Benevolently neutral toward the revolutionary government, the United States reportedly shielded Qaddafi from internal and external threats on multiple occasions in the early years of the regime. Rumors circulated in 1970–72 that the CIA on three separate occasions informed Qaddafi of plots to overthrow the regime. The first incident supposedly discovered by the CIA and reported to Libya involved a 1970 attempt by a close relative of deposed King Idris to smuggle weapons into southern Libya, where they were to be distributed to tribal elements sympathetic to the monarchy. When the CIA learned of the plot, which Israeli intelligence was tracking and may have been supporting, it reportedly expressed its firm disapproval to its Israeli counterparts. In the second incident, which was reported in the Lebanese newspaper *Al-Nahar* on 1 October 1971 and in the *New York Times* on 3 October 1971, Ambassador Palmer allegedly betrayed a group of army officers plotting a coup d'état by feigning sympathy with the plan and later turning their names over to Qaddafi. A third incident in 1971, generally known as the "Hilton assignment," involved European mercenaries hired by Libyan exiles to overthrow the revolutionary government. When the plot was discovered by the CIA and associated European intelligence agencies, they allegedly informed Qaddafi.[56]

In yet another reported incident, the United States in mid-1972 rejected a proposal to furnish clandestine assistance to Chad to counter Libyan support for Chadian dissident groups. And in November 1972 the United States allegedly pressured Israel, angry with Qaddafi over his support for guerrillas in Lebanon as well as his support for survivors of the Black September attack on Israeli athletes at the Munich Olympics, not to make a retaliatory strike on Libya. The rationale behind U.S. policy in each of these cases, together with the details of U.S. involvement, remain unclear and quite likely will never be known in full; however, U.S. involvement in some or all of them would be consistent with American policy toward Libya in 1969–73. It was a time in which key policy makers in Washington felt U.S. interests in Libya, the region, and the world were best served by reaching a rapprochement with the Qaddafi regime.[57]

Later in the decade, evidence surfaced that several former U.S. government employees, notably Edwin P. Wilson, had been providing military expertise and weapons to the Libyan government in the early to mid-1970s. Wilson's activities first drew public attention in 1977, and he was later sentenced to fifty-two years in prison for various crimes. He was charged with and convicted of shipping twenty-two tons of C-4 plastic explosive to Libya in what was at the time the largest illegal arms deal in U.S. history. His defense was that he had been selling arms to Libya as a cover to gather intelligence for the CIA. At a critical point in his trial, prosecutors presented an affidavit signed by Charles A. Briggs, a top CIA official, which denied that Wilson had been asked "to perform or provide any services, directly or indirectly" for the CIA. The affidavit convinced the lone holdout on the jury of Wilson's guilt, and he eventually was sentenced to more than five decades in prison. Almost twenty years later, through the Freedom of Information Act, declassified documents surfaced to indicate the affidavit was not true and that Wilson had been asked to perform services for the CIA although none of them involved selling C-4 explosives. Declassified documents also indicated that senior officials in the CIA and the Justice Department knew at the time the affidavit was not true.[58]

Politics of Reaction

The years 1973–74 marked a watershed in American-Libyan relations. Beginning in mid-1973, the initial American approach to the Qaddafi regime, given the content and direction of Libyan foreign policy, came under growing pressure. Bilateral relations continued to deteriorate as the

decade progressed. Fundamental, long-standing policy differences were at
the heart of the growing impasse, with the Palestinian issue most important. Libya took an increasingly aggressive role in the Arab-Israeli conflict,
as exemplified by its involvement in preparations for the 1973 October war
and its rejection of American-sponsored peace plans that followed the end
of fighting. At the same time, Qaddafi nationalized four American oil companies in 1973–74 and for the first time employed oil as a political weapon.
Finally, there was the growing rapprochement between Libya and the Soviet Union, which began in mid-1974 with the first major Libyan purchase
of Soviet arms.

The centrality of the Palestinian question to Qaddafi's ideology and his
approach to a resolution of that issue, especially his open support of guerrilla movements, steadily dissipated whatever official or unofficial constituency existed in the United States for an improvement in diplomatic relations. Assistant Secretary Newson, in a 19 July 1972 statement before the
House Subcommittees on Africa and the Near East, accurately and con-
cisely summarized the existing situation.

The Libyan revolution of September 1969 changed the character of Libyan-U.S. relations. The new regime, under the leadership of Colonel Mu'ammar al-Qadhaafi
and a group of young military officers, sees its policies in exclusively Arab terms. It
seeks closer cooperation among the Arab states and sees that cooperation focused
primarily on the cause of the Palestinians and the struggle with Israel. Although
strongly anti-Communist, the regime is at the same time cool to the United States
and Britain because of the stand of these governments on Arab issues.

The present Libyan Government has, at the same time, sought greater control,
greater revenue, and greater participation in the production of its basic resource,
petroleum. U.S. companies which produce 90 percent of Libya's petroleum are
under severe pressure as a result.

The Libyan revolution also ended the previous military relationship with the
United States and Britain. We withdrew at the request of the Libyans from Wheelus
Air Base, as the British withdrew from their base at El Adem. In keeping with the
1954 agreement, permanent construction reverted to the Libyan Government.
Movable property was removed except for a small amount which was sold to the
Libyans after screening our worldwide requirements. By a recent exchange of
notes outstanding agreements were ended and conflicting claims canceled. The
Libyans now use the former base as their principal military base in the Tripoli
area.[59]

From the viewpoint of Qaddafi, the touchstone of Soviet foreign policy,
especially after the 1973 October war, was the latter's position on the Palestinian issue. Even when Qaddafi's criticism of Soviet ideology was vocifer-
ous, he still praised the Soviets for their support of the Arabs in the strug-

gle for Palestine. Libya concluded its first major arms deal with the Soviets in 1974, and a high-level Soviet delegation, headed by Prime Minister Aleksei Kosygin, first visited Tripoli in May 1975. American policy makers worried that the budding Soviet-Libyan relationship might invigorate Soviet diplomacy in the Middle East at a time when Soviet influence was on the decline, as witnessed by the Soviet expulsion from Egypt after the 1973 war with a concomitant increase in American influence in Cairo. Henry Kissinger had by this time moved to the Department of State, and his analysis of world affairs only magnified the potential dangers of a Soviet-Libyan rapprochement, especially one involving large amounts of sophisticated Soviet military equipment.[60]

At the same time, it must be emphasized that ideological affinity played no role in the budding Soviet-Libyan relationship, even though Qaddafi's post-1975 statements about the Soviet system were not characterized by their earlier ideological antipathy.[61] On the contrary, the real key to Soviet-Libyan cooperation was that neither side, particularly the Soviets, insisted on ideological compatibility. Apparently Qaddafi decided that Soviet arms sales and limited technical cooperation in the atomic energy field were of sufficient importance to merit the new relationship. In October 1978, for example, Qaddafi first threatened to join the Warsaw Pact; in July 1981 two Soviet frigates visited the naval base at Tripoli; and in September 1981 Qaddafi commented that it was time for Libya to ally with one of the two superpowers.[62] In the early days of the revolution, it would have been unthinkable for him to take any one of these positions.

Washington first signaled its concern with Libyan policies in early 1973, when it failed to appoint a successor to Ambassador Palmer, who had resigned in late 1972. Thereafter, American relations with Libya were conducted at the chargé d'affaires level until William L. Eagleton, Jr., a noted Arabist who later served as ambassador to Syria, eventually closed the embassy in 1980. The United States also blocked delivery in 1973 of the remaining eight C-130 airplanes, despite the fact that Libya had paid for them. And it elected not to sell Libya military weapons and certain other equipment that could add to Libyan military capabilities. In the wake of the Libyan-Soviet rapprochement in 1974, Washington increased its pressure on Tripoli by delaying the purchase of a $200 million air defense system in January 1975 and later refusing entry of Libyan trainees into the United States for aircraft maintenance training.[63]

In May 1975, a few weeks after the fall of Saigon, Khmer Rouge forces from Cambodia seized the U.S. merchant ship *Mayaguez*. Impatient with diplomacy and with consulting Congress as the War Powers Act required, President Gerald Ford dispatched warplanes and marines to the scene in a flawed rescue attempt that cost forty-one American lives. With both President Ford and Secretary of State Kissinger concerned that America looked dangerously weak, the heart of the mission in retrospect appeared to be the rescue of American credibility and pride as opposed to American sailors. As the distinguished American historian, Michael S. Sherry, later observed, the *Mayaguez* incident set the tone for American foreign policy for much of the next fifteen years. No where was this more true than in Libya.

The incident was illustrative of much that followed, though too minor to be determinative of it. It revealed nostalgia for a presumably bygone era of American muscle, reluctance to employ that power in a serious way, and bewilderment about its utility. Over the next fifteen years, Presidents repeatedly put American forces in harm's way—largely or wholly on their own initiative, despite the War Powers Act and Vietnam's presumed lessons about obtaining national consent—but always in arenas on the periphery of great power conflict, where nuclear confrontation or serious conventional combat was unlikely, and where the stakes for the United States were limited, often largely symbolic.[64]

The Ford administration became so disenchanted with the Qaddafi regime that, when solicited by the Egyptian government in 1976, it gave Cairo a commitment to deter Soviet intervention in the event Egypt launched a military attack on Libya. In the wake of the successful Israeli operation in July 1976 to rescue the Entebbe hostages, Qaddafi reportedly responded in anger by allegedly seeking to instigate terrorist attacks at the 1976 Democratic and Republican conventions. The Ford administration by mid-1976 was suggesting publicly that Libya was supporting and financing international terrorism, and a Department of Defense report released in January 1977 contained a reference that suggested Libya was the fourth-leading enemy of the United States. Economic relations, on the other hand, continued to strengthen throughout this period. Libyan exports to the United States increased from $216 million in 1973 to $2,188 million in 1976, while American exports to Libya over the same period rose from $104 million to $277 million. The United States, by 1977, had become the single largest purchaser of Libyan oil, and it enjoyed this position until after 1980.[65]

The Qaddafi regime welcomed the election of Jimmy Carter because Qaddafi saw the new American president as a moral leader who might move American foreign policy, especially its stand on the Palestinian issue, in a new direction more favorable to Arab interests. A change in American attitude on this issue, from the Libyan perspective, would remove the most serious obstacle to improved ties between Tripoli and Washington. On 11 June 1977 Qaddafi urged Carter to improve diplomatic relations by appointing an American ambassador to Tripoli. Qaddafi's hopes were soon dashed: American policy toward the Arab-Israeli dispute did not change, and the new administration in Washington by mid-1977 had become more antagonistic toward Libya. Publicly accusing Libya of terrorism, the Carter administration blocked the sale of Italian transport planes to Libya on the grounds that the engines for the planes were assembled under license from an American company. Washington also sided with Egypt in its skirmish with Libya in July 1977. While it continued to refuse to sell military equipment to Libya, the Carter administration announced the sale of $200 million in military hardware to Egypt immediately after the Libya-Egypt clash.[66]

In late 1977 the Carter administration discovered evidence of a planned Libyan-sponsored assassination attempt against Herman Frederick Eilts, a well-respected diplomat and U.S. ambassador to Egypt in 1974–79, who had worked diligently since his appointment under the Nixon administration to improve Egyptian-American relations. Qaddafi was deeply upset by what he viewed as a betrayal of the Arab cause and was apparently on a course to take revenge on a visible American participant in the policy change. When Washington learned of the plan, President Carter sent Qaddafi a personal note, indicating that he was aware of the plot and offering enough details to substantiate the claim. The Qaddafi regime denied that any such plan existed; nevertheless, operation Eilts never got off the ground. While some analysts, including John Cooley, have suggested the Eilts affair represented a turning point in the U.S. perception of Libya as a terrorist state, it would appear more accurate to say that the abortive assassination attempt simply reinforced perceptions formed earlier in the Carter administration.[67]

In an unsuccessful effort to deny the United States any pretext for using accusations of terrorism to deny future sales of aircraft and equipment, Libya in 1978 signed the three United Nations conventions relating to terrorism. When this action had little or no impact on U.S. policy, Qaddafi initiated in 1978–79 a direct dialogue with the American people, an initiative consistent with his theory of government which called for the people to rule themselves. Although the targets of this campaign included well-known personalities like Muhammad Ali and Senator William Fulbright, the people-to-people approach concentrated on the citizenry of Georgia, President Carter's home state, and Idaho, the home state of Senator Frank Church, chairman of the Senate Foreign Relations Committee and a vocal opponent to the delivery of the C-130s to Libya. Delegations of farmers and businessmen from both states were welcomed in Libya in 1978, and delegations from Libya visited Idaho and Georgia in 1978–79. The people-to-people initiative also included an Arab-American People-to-People Dialogue Conference in Tripoli in October 1978, which the Libyans used to voice their positions on a variety of issues, including terrorism and the Camp David Accords.[68]

Billy Carter, the president's brother, visited Libya as a member of the Georgia delegation in 1978 and returned in 1979 to attend celebrations commemorating the tenth anniversary of the Libyan revolution. These efforts at people-to-people diplomacy generated considered press coverage in the United States, especially reports that Billy Carter had been photographed with Yasser Arafat and other liberation leaders and had promised to assist in the release of the C-130 airplanes to Libya. When asked whether his relationship with Libya might be criticized by American Jews, Billy Carter reportedly answered, "There are a hell of a lot more Arabs than Jews." Billy Carter was back in the news in 1980 when reports surfaced that he had received $220,000 from the Libyan government. Qaddafi described the money as a loan to President Carter's brother related to business transactions conducted during his visits to Libya in 1978 and 1979. Billy Carter considered the money he received part of a $500,000 loan that he expected to repay from fees earned as a broker for Libyan oil. To avoid a federal grand jury investigation, he eventually registered as an official foreign agent of the Libyan government. He commented at the time, "My main crime, I think, is to show friendship to a country that is not normally shown friendship in the United States, and I have not backed down."[69]

Libyan diplomacy on both the official and unofficial levels combined to result in a moderate improvement in American-Libyan relations in 1978–79, but any change remained superficial and did not touch on sensitive issues like the eight C-130 aircraft, which remained in storage in Marietta, Georgia. The State Department approved the sale of two Boeing 727s to Libyan Arab Airlines in November 1978, following a September 1978 directive by President Carter to "take export consequences fully into account when considering the use of export controls for foreign policy purposes." The deal was followed by State Department approval for the sale of four hundred heavy trucks to Libya by the Oshkosh Truck Corporation of Wisconsin. In March 1979 Washington approved the sale of three Boeing 747s to Libya on condition they be used solely for civilian, commercial purposes, a decision it later reversed after Qaddafi used a Boeing 727 to evacuate troops from Uganda.[70]

In each of these instances, Washington hoped the promotion of commercial relations with Libya would encourage a more constructive dialogue on political issues. While the U.S. image of Libya as a supporter of terrorism improved in this period, Qaddadi continued his attacks on American imperialism in the Middle East and what he described as the defeatist policies of Egyptian President Sadat. In an 11 June 1979 address celebrating the anniversary of the American evacuation of Libyan bases, for example, Qaddafi dwelled on the twin themes of American imperialism and Egyptian support for U.S. policies in a speech that included creative references to the war with Tripoli.

Brothers. Today we celebrate the ninth anniversary of the eviction of the American forces from Libyan soil after the revolution. On this occasion, we greet the friends and brothers who have come to join us in celebrating this historic anniversary.

Today we celebrate the triumph of freedom in Libya. But we feel that Arab freedom will still be incomplete as long as some Arab territories still suffer from the yoke of imperialism. . . . we still feel that freedom is incomplete, since Arab freedom is still incomplete and Arab territory is still not completely purged.

As you are aware, on 11 June 1805, the American forces evacuated Darna [Darnah]. On 11 June 1970, there was an evacuation from this base and other bases which supported this big base.

Thus today we are celebrating a double victory over the invading American forces. . . .

Brothers, history repeats itself. Once more, after over 170 years, the United States fills the Mediterranean with its fleets and practices international terrorism against the peoples. All the people want is to live freely and happily.

Once more, the agents in Egypt strike an alliance with the United States. But the fate of this filthy alliance, this unholy alliance, will be like that of the 1805 alliance between the Egyptian agents and the force of American terrorism in the Mediterranean.[71]

The policy of the Carter administration toward Libya stiffened in the spring of 1979 as a result of Libya's interventionist policy in Uganda. American-Libyan relations reached a new low in December 1979, when large numbers of Libyan demonstrators, in support of Iranian militants holding U.S. hostages in Teheran, sacked and burned the U.S. embassy in Tripoli.[72]

Relations Deteriorate

Following the attack on the U.S. embassy, President Carter summoned Libyan Chargé Ali El-Houdari to the Oval Office and asked him to deliver the following message to Qaddafi:

Please relay the following message to Colonel Qadhafi: 1) I very much appreciate your assistance regarding the hostages [American hostages in Iran]; 2) I am personally very disturbed by the attack on our Embassy. I feel your Government could have prevented it, had it moved with dispatch. The Libyan Government did not treat our Embassy with proper concern and protection. My expectation is that your leaders will give us an apology and repair the damage; 3) I would like to go on with an even closer relationship with Libya in the future, provided that [the] issue can be put behind us. The American people and I feel deeply concerned over what happened, but want you to know that we would like to have a better relationship. That is clearly in our mutual interest.[73]

Chargé Houdari reportedly answered that it was the media that contributed to the poor relationship between Libya and the United States. He asked President Carter to remember that Libya was a developing country that appreciated Carter's decency and religious character. Carter responded:

> I have noticed that Col. Qadhafi has not attacked me personally. I hope that you will tell Col. Qadhafi that I trust he will give this issue his personal attention so that our relationship can be repaired. We will then seek better communication, either through State or directly with Dr. [Zbigniew] Brzezinski.

As Dr. Brzezinski escorted Chargé Houdari from the Oval Office, he told him that an event such as the embassy burning could be a catalyst for either a much better or a worse diplomatic relationship between Libya and the United States. In this case, the trashing of the U.S. embassy proved to be the catalyst for a severe deterioration in American-Libyan relations.[74]

Almost a year later, President Carter, in written testimony before a U.S. Senate subcommittee, characterized American-Libyan relations in the latter half of his administration as follows:

> There are few governments in the world with which we have more sharp and frequent policy differences than Libya. Libya has steadfastly opposed our efforts to reach and carry out the Camp David Accords [between Israel, Egypt, and the United States, signed in 1978 and 1979]. We have strongly differing attitudes toward the PLO and the support of terrorism.[75]

An insightful article written around the tenth anniversary celebrations for the September 1969 revolution and published in the *New York Times* captured the ambivalence which characterized American-Libyan relations throughout much of the Carter administration, especially its later years.

> The display of military might, celebrating the 10th anniversary in power of Col. Muammar el-Qaddafi, seemed to confirm that Libya had become one of the Soviet Union's staunchest Arab clients.
>
> But despite its huge Soviet-supplied arsenal and an ideology vaguely evocative of Marxism, the country still leans economically toward the West, selling oil to the United States and its European allies and purchasing their technology. Libyan students go to universities in the United States, not the Soviet Union.
>
> Relations between Tripoli and Washington remain frosty. Libyan officials and some Western sources contend that the Carter Administration is more responsible for this than Colonel Qaddafi. Libyan attempts over the last two years to improve ties with the West as a counterbalance to links with Moscow have been mostly rebuffed by Washington.[76]

At the time, the State Department estimated some 3,000 Libyan students were enrolled in colleges and universities in the United States. Conversely, fewer than 2,000 Americans were resident in Libya, and the number was declining due to harassment by Libyan authorities.[77]

Diplomatic relations with the United States and its Western allies reached a new low in the wake of a guerrilla attack in early 1980 on the Tunisian town of Gafsa. Following persistent reports of Tunisians receiving guerrilla training in Libya, one such group crossed the border on 27 January 1980 and attacked the Tunisian mining town of Gafsa. Once it had crushed the attacking force, the Tunisian government, convinced the rebel attack had been organized and supported by Libya, withdrew its ambassador from Tripoli and closed both the Tunisian cultural center in Tripoli and the Libyan cultural center in Tunis. Libyan motives for supporting the filibuster remained unclear, but likely included disagreements over a 1974 merger plan and the manner in which it was rejected by the Habib Bourguiba government. Libya and Tunisia were also pressing conflicting claims to oil deposits in the Gulf of Gabès. Finally, Qaddafi hoped to see socioeconomic reforms enacted in Tunisia similar to those he promoted in Libya, and Gafsa appeared a fertile starting point. Situated a long distance from Tunis, Gafsa was economically depressed and widely recognized as a traditional area of political dissent.[78]

Western reaction to the surprise attack was immediate and decisive. France sent two military transport planes and several helicopters to Tunisia and stationed three warships in the Gulf of Gabès as a warning to the Libyans. Washington accelerated its military assistance program to Tunisia by air freighting armored personnel carriers and military helicopters to assist the Tunisian army to patrol a long and largely unprotected border. In response, on 4 February 1980 Libya allowed irate mobs of citizens to ransack and burn both the French embassy in Tripoli and the French consulate in Benghazi. Decrying the passivity of Libyan authorities during these attacks, France withdrew its ambassador and principal aides and asked the Libyan mission in Paris to do the same. Since the U.S. embassy in Tripoli had been sacked earlier, the State Department effectively closed the embassy on 7 February 1980, on the grounds it could no longer accept guarantees from the Libyan government regarding the future safety and security of U.S. diplomats.[79]

In addition, the U.S. government in May 1980 expelled members of the Libyan People's Bureau in Washington under suspicion of harassing anti-Qaddafi Libyan students in the United States. Federal agents said the Libyans had been under surveillance for several months because they were suspected of being members of a terrorist squad charged with killing Libyan students who refused to return to Libya. At the time of their expulsion, President Carter referred to the Libyan diplomats as "would-be assassins." U.S. officials linked the expelled Libyans to a campaign of terror that resulted in the death of several Libyan dissidents in Athens, London, Milan, Rome, and Valletta, Malta in the summer of 1980.[80]

By summer 1980, Libyan fighters were intercepting American planes over the Mediterranean Sea, in some cases "locking on" radar firing controls while in others flying within two hundred yards of U.S. warplanes. American-Libyan relations had reached a level of tension not seen since the American bombardment of Tripoli in 1804. Qaddafi captured the mood in an open letter to President Carter and Ronald Reagan that appeared as a paid advertisement in the *Washington Post* on 22 October 1980. Qaddafi warned the United States "to keep its naval and air forces away from the Libyan Arab borders in the Mediterranean." "Otherwise," he added, "confrontation and the outbreak of an armed war, in the legal term, would regretfully be a possibility within view at any moment. . . . Should a war break out—a possibility which cannot be ruled out—it will be a war forced upon us by America," Qaddafi concluded. Washington spokespersons responded that the air reconnaissance flights off the Libyan coast, which had been conducted since 1972 when Libya began receiving military equipment from the Soviets, would not be affected by Colonel Qaddafi's letter.[81]

New Directions

The geography, history, and social patterns of Libya strongly influenced the domestic and foreign policies of the revolutionary government that seized power from the monarchy in 1969. As the Gulf of Sirte divided the nation geographically, so did Libyan foreign policy oscillate between its search for a wider role in the Mashriq and its more natural affinity to the Maghrib. Historically, the dominant influence on external policy remained the long, difficult experience with colonialism, neocolonialism, and imperialism, an experience the revolutionary government argued ended only with the September 1969 coup d'état. Culturally, a wide variety of factors conditioned the policies of Qaddafi and his fellow members on the RCC with the orthodox religious faith of the people being the most obvious and probably the most important. To comprehend the foreign policy of the revolutionary government in general and its approach to the United States in particular, that policy must be appreciated and investigated as a product of this unique milieu.

Despite the rhetoric, it must also be emphasized that Qaddafi and the RCC continued or expanded many of the policies of the monarchy, something most observers either failed to recognize or ignored. Evidence of considerable support for the Palestinian people was evident in Libya as early as 1947; and over the next two decades, the monarchy supported and encouraged the Palestinian movement to a modest extent. Soon after taking office, King Idris banned all political parties, a ban that continued in effect for the remainder of the monarchy's existence and was then extended by the revolutionary government. In terms of oil policy, the monarchy pressed for government participation in the posted price of oil after 1967 and well before the revolutionary government later reduced production and increased prices. Following the discovery of oil, the monarchy moved to reduce Western presence and influence in the kingdom, in particular the burdensome air bases, and to bring some substance to the image of neutrality. To balance and check the regular army, the King recruited militias drawn largely from tribal forces much like Qaddafi later created a people's army. Finally, both King Idris and Qaddafi carefully circumscribed the power of the *ulama* or religious scholars. The impact of the revolutionary government on the monarchy's policies should not be underestimated; however, it is equally incorrect to assume there was no policy continuity between the two regimes.

At the same time, the RCC distinguished itself through a determined effort to legitimize its three core objectives—freedom, socialism, and unity—placing them within the context of the Libyan heritage and appealing to traditional values, most especially Islam. The rationale employed in pursuit of legitimacy was not dissimilar to that of the monarchy, but both essence and emphasis differed considerably. Stressing brotherhood, the RCC shifted the emphasis from narrow tribal structures, a core constituency of the monarchy, to the larger Arab community. Recalling the heroic struggle against Italian colonialism, the revolutionary government added condemnation of the more recent corruption of the palace together with its collaboration with neocolonialism and imperialism. While the power and sanctity of Islam was invoked repeatedly by the RCC, it was promoted within the context of the orthodox doctrine of right rule and justice as opposed to the parochial lodges and brotherhoods of the Sanusi order. Depicting himself as a devout and austere Muslim, Qaddafi repeatedly expressed a desire to increase the role of Islam as a cultural and religious factor in national life.

Elsewhere, RCC policies proved to be radical departures from those of the monarchy. Abruptly terminating the loose association the monarchy had enjoyed with a Middle East system dominated by the United States, Qaddafi initiated a close, albeit often estranged, association with the Arab system. At the same time, the revolutionary government actively sought opportunities to demonstrate its political independence from the Western governments while retaining the very close economic relationship developed under the monarchy. Qaddafi actively promoted the concept of Arab unity, with the ideal being an eventual union of all Arab governments into a single Arab state. The revolutionary government also pursued a new and much broader audience for its policies. Where the monarchy's foreign policy was largely regional in interest and impact, Qaddafi addressed the wider Arab world as well as sympathetic audiences around the globe. Growing oil revenues enabled the revolutionary government to address this wider audience; however, to its astonishment and dismay, it found its radical message had little appeal outside Libya. In this sense, Libya's relatively small population and limited geopolitical and military strength proved grossly disproportionate to the ambition of Qaddafi and his fellow RCC members. As a result, the revolutionary government repeatedly set domestic and international objectives that its national resources would not allow it to achieve.

While Qaddafi and his fellow RCC members were self-proclaimed Nasserists, the Libyan revolution was not a mirror image of the Egyptian experience. First of all, the Libyan government incorporated Islamic doctrine into its approach to Arab unity to a far greater extent than the Egyptians. The union of pan-Arabism with orthodox Islam into a single strategy of legitimacy was very different from the policy followed by Nasser and most other Arab governments, which typically employed either pan-Arabism or orthodox Islam but not both. Second, Libya's appreciable oil wealth by the late 1960s made it the first, and only, wealthy Arab state to promote Arab unity. Qaddafi's advocacy of a union of the rich with the poor marked a total reversal of a long-standing pattern in the Arab world. Similarly, the oil wealth of Libya meant that Qaddafi did not need a wealthy patron, as Nasser had first needed the West and later the Soviet Union. At the same time, it must be remembered that Libya did use the West as a market for its high grade crude and the Soviets as a source for arms supplies. In fact, Qaddafi's continuing reliance on East and West in this manner led cynical Libyans to suggest that Libya still remained only a pawn between the superpowers. Finally, the congress-committee system of government implanted in Libya by Qaddafi was a totally new form of government that had no precursors in Egypt or elsewhere in the Arab world.

The contradictory nature of many of the policies of the revolutionary government must also be emphasized. The Qaddafi regime preached Arab unity, on the one hand, while severely restricting Arab immigration and harassing Arab expatriates from those Arab states with which it was at odds. It cried for freedom from colonialism, neocolonialism, and imperialism, but implemented one of the most totalitarian systems of government in the second half of the twentieth century. It preached self-determination but actively worked to subvert the governments of neighboring states whenever they disagreed with Libya's sociopolitical and economic theories. Harshly critical of the Western world, Libya was an active participant in the international capitalist system, marketing crude oil in exchange for primary materials, manufactured goods, and foodstuffs. Much of the profit derived from that trade was then invested in the Western economies. Finally, Qaddafi called for a return to orthodox Islam, but took actions that many Muslims, both inside and outside Libya, considered heretical. In so doing, the revolutionary government failed to understand why its pan-Islamic crusade caused such deep divisions and separatist tendencies in countries with large non-Muslim populations.

The remarkable stability and consistency that marked Libyan foreign policy into the second decade of the revolution should also be noted. Early policy statements emphasized the concepts of freedom, socialism, and unity; while subsequent discourse refined and expanded on these ideals, the philosophy and central policies of the Qaddafi regime remained intact well into the 1980s. Unfortunately, the pronounced stability and consistency of Libyan policy proved more of a problem than a solution. Initial foreign policy statements, many of them patterned after the fiery Nasser of the 1950s, were often clearly anachronistic in 1969, and they became only more so in later years. As the policies of other Arab governments evolved in response to changing regional and global conditions, the Libyan government adamantly refused to adapt its central objectives to the changing realities of the Middle East. In consequence, the tenets and objectives of Qaddafi's foreign policy were increasingly removed from the governments and peoples he hoped to lead.

On the other hand, the intellectual shortcomings of Qaddafi's ideology, which were soon obvious to more sophisticated observers, should not mask its political effectiveness in Libya. His success at building legitimacy was all the more impressive given the low level of national identity and the lack of a congruous relationship between ruler and ruled that he inherited from the monarchy. A variety of factors, including a high level of consonance between the new ideology and fundamental values of Libyan political culture, contributed to his success. In addition, Qaddafi articulated an ideology largely composed of absolutes. The regime depicted itself as more Arab, more Islamic, and more socialist than any alternative, and in this world of absolutes there was no room for dissent. Qaddafi also effectively buttressed his ideological appeal with charismatic leadership and a system of political mobilization and participation that added a high level of structural legitimacy as well as central control. Finally, the nation's oil revenues provided the fiscal means to pursue an extravagant, frequently misguided ideology far beyond the point at which more realistic economic circumstances and a more mature body politic would have demanded its abandonment.

American-Libyan relations enjoyed a roller coaster ride throughout the decade of the 1970s. Early American attempts to seek a rapprochement with the Qaddafi regime, in retrospect, were clearly the product of wishful thinking. Certainly, any window of opportunity to retain the level of cooperation that characterized American-Libyan relations during the reign of King Idris I was soon slammed shut by the revolutionary government's pursuit of a foreign policy that challenged the status quo in Africa and the Middle East at every opportunity. Libya's budding relationship with the Soviet Union, including the purchase of massive amounts of Soviet arms, openly challenged the containment policies of the United States and clearly threatened the balance of power in the region. Support of liberation cum terrorist movements around the world, later followed by open intervention in neighboring states from Chad to Tunisia to Uganda, made a mockery of Washington's policy of nonaggression. In sum, Libyan initiatives from the Mediterranean to the Caribbean opposed U.S. global policies on virtually every front.

American policies in themselves contributed to the wild swings in American-Libyan relations after 1969. Preoccupied with the containment of Soviet influence in the Middle East, the Nixon and Ford administrations appeared willing to minimize, if not overlook, Qaddafi's support for what he termed liberation movements in return for an anti-communist regime in Libya. The Carter administration, in contrast, was less concerned with the Soviet threat and more interested in the promotion of human rights together with combating terrorism. Viewed from Tripoli, this shift in policy emphasis appeared to offer a second window of opportunity for improved American-Libyan relations; however, Qaddafi again soon closed the window on himself. Opposition to a negotiated peace to the Arab-Israeli conflict, coupled with links to subversion, destabilization, and terrorism before 1977 and after 1979, left little room for a sustained improvement in American-Libyan relations.

Chapter 7
Reagan Agonistes

Qadhafi deserves to be treated as a pariah in the world community.
—Ronald Reagan, 1986

Reagan has to read history. He reads cheap hollywood scenarios and that is the problem of the world today—namely, a second rate actor becomes the president of the biggest power.
—Qaddafi, 1986

Diplomatic relations between the United States and Libya were not good at any time after 1969, and they became especially strained after 1979, when the Libyan government did little to protect the United States Embassy in Tripoli when it was stormed by Libyan students in the early days of the Iranian hostage crisis. The two governments tried to coexist with a mutually unsatisfactory diplomatic relationship which neither seemed willing either to improve or to terminate. The state of affairs took a turn for the worse with the election of Ronald Reagan. Once in office, Reagan systematically increased diplomatic, military, and economic pressure on Libya. Colonel Qaddafi, unfairly and inaccurately characterized as a Soviet puppet, was labeled an international pariah to be restrained if not replaced. Within a year, the Reagan administration had fundamentally altered U.S. policy toward Libya in both the diplomatic and commercial arenas. In the process, Washington came to recognize Qaddafi not as an inconvenience but as an enemy.

Politics of Confrontation and Repression

At the outset of the Reagan administration, three features characterized U.S. policy in the Middle East. The dominant concern was the threat of Soviet invasion or some form of international aggression in support of Soviet objectives by the Soviet-backed radical states in the region. Given the overriding importance of the Soviet threat, the second characteristic of U.S. foreign policy was the tendency to neglect other problems until they forced themselves to center stage as full-blown international crises. Finally, a lack of clarity and predictability in U.S. policy, especially toward local issues, undermined the American position in the Middle East more than did any question of power or will. This last feature characterized U.S. foreign policy even after September 1982, when the Reagan administration altered course and made progress toward an Arab-Israeli settlement a main priority in the region.[1]

Within the general context of its overall Middle East policy, the Reagan administration pursued a number of interrelated objectives in its increasingly confrontational policy towards Libya. First, it aimed to reassert American power and influence in the world and especially in the Middle East. It hoped a swift and effective response to acts of international terrorism would demonstrate American competence to deal with any challenge of extremism anywhere. Second, Washington aimed to foster credibility with moderate Arab states by restoring international respect for the United States as a reliable friend and ally. At the same time, the Reagan administration intended to send a message to the Soviet Union to the effect that the new administration would not tolerate lawless activity on the part of Moscow or its surrogates. Viewing Qaddafi as little more that a Soviet agent, the Reagan administration believed his elimination would reduce the influence of the Soviet Union in Africa and the Middle East. Finally, the U.S. government aimed to squeeze Qaddafi militarily to deter Libya from the pursuit of what Washington saw as subversive and destabilizing activities.[2]

In contrast to the policies of the Reagan administration, Libyan foreign policy in the early 1980s evidenced no major change in content or direction.[3] The Arab-Israeli conflict in general and the Palestinian issue in particular remained Qaddafi's central concern and the most visible and influential aspect of Libyan foreign policy. No compromise was seen possible with the so-called Zionist enemy; only military force could solve the problem. Arab unity remained the ideal path to Arab victory. The radical oil policies of the 1970s, on the other hand, proved more difficult to pursue in the ensuing decade. A global recession, combined with conservation efforts by the leading industrial states, resulted in a sharp decline in oil prices in 1981. Libyan oil revenues plummeted from $24 billion in 1980 to less than $14 billion in 1981. Lower oil revenues continued after 1982 as world recession and an embargo on Libyan oil by the United States combined with a world oil glut to restrain Libyan oil exports.[4]

Nevertheless, the Qaddafi regime continued with obvious enthusiasm its revolutionary activities abroad. In addition to the Palestinian movement and a wide range of African states, Tripoli provided economic and political support to several Central American states, including El Salvador and Nicaragua, in the early 1980s.[5] Libyan involvement in Chad, which began in the early 1970s, culminated in a full-scale military intervention in late

1980. A Libyan announcement in January 1981 that Chad and Libya were set to merge, an act many governments viewed as annexation not merger, provoked considerable criticism in and outside Africa. It was only in late 1981 that Libyan military forces were forced to withdraw from Chad. When asked whether Libya was acting as a Soviet surrogate in Chad, Chester Crocker, then Assistant Secretary of State Designate for African Affairs, bundled the actions of Libya and the Soviet Union in a manner that became characteristic of the Reagan administration:

It would seem to me that there is some—how should we put it—"overlap" in the interests and motivations of the Soviets and the Libyans. I do not believe the Soviets would claim to have control over Colonel Qaddhafi, and I am certain the Libyans would not accept that formulation. But their purposes may well be compatible in a number of situations, and they wind up achieving results which are not helpful to our interests or to those of many African countries.[6]

Finally, in the wake of alleged Libyan assassination threats on the U.S. ambassadors to France, Italy, and the Sudan, an official U.S. claim surfaced in 1981 that the Qaddafi regime had dispatched an assassination team to Washington to kill President Reagan and top administration officials.[7] Even though this claim was dismissed out of hand by the Libyan government and no evidence to substantiate it was ever produced, Qaddafi was talking publicly as early as 1981 about the right of the Libyan people to assassinate Libyan dissidents living abroad.[8] In testimony before a subcommittee of the Senate Foreign Relations Committee, Assistant Secretary Crocker addressed this issue as he sketched a picture of Qaddafi as an enemy of the United States:

Under Colonel Qadhafi, Libya has adopted a diplomacy of subversion in Africa and in the Arab world. It is a diplomacy of unprecedented obstruction to our own interests and objectives. Qadhafi has tried in every way he could think of to obstruct our efforts to achieve peace in the Middle East. He has sponsored subversion from Africa to the Philippines. He actively has supported international terrorism using assassinations abroad as an instrument of his policy.

Perhaps the most bizarre and pernicious Libyan policy under Gadhafi has been the claim to a right to murder Libyan dissidents on foreign soil anywhere, a claim repeated by Qadhafi again this spring and one which seems to have led to the assassination of Libyan nationals in several countries.[9]

The Soviet-Libyan relationship expanded in these tumultuous times, despite policy differences from Afghanistan to Chad, which in turn increased the apprehension of the Reagan administration. Following an announcement in 1975 that the Soviet Union would provide Libya with its first nuclear reactor, Moscow agreed in 1978 to construct a nuclear power plant and research center with a capacity of 300 megawatts. By 1981 the two governments were discussing a further expansion of their nuclear cooperation efforts to include a power station with two 400-megawatt units. During a 1981 visit to Moscow Qaddafi also concluded additional technical and economic cooperation agreements covering a variety of areas, including oil and gas, nonferrous metals, and irrigation. While Qaddafi never pursued the preposterous 1978 threat to join the Warsaw Pact, there were repeated rumors that Moscow and Tripoli might conclude a twenty-year treaty of friendship and cooperation similar to Soviet accords with Iraq, South Yemen, and Syria. Moreover, Libya continued to buy sophisticated Soviet arms, and in July 1981 two Soviet frigates visited the naval base at Tripoli, the first reported visit by Soviet naval forces to a Libyan base. Speaking at the twelfth anniversary celebration of the One September Revolution, less than two weeks after the United States downed two Libyan jets in the Gulf of Sirte, Qaddafi threatened to attack U.S. nuclear depots around the Mediterranean Sea and stated that Libya might be forced to ally itself with one of the superpower camps:

There is no such thing as neutrality during a time of war or in a widescale confrontation such as the one now between Libya and the United States. If a world war breaks out, there will be nothing called neutrality, because if you are neutral than you would raise a white flag and capitulate.

In the end, our existence is more important than neutrality. The defeat of our enemy is the goal and is more important than neutrality. By God, if we were faced by a small state we would not have any need for alignment or to enter into alliance with others.

But to be attacked by the United States and with the 6th Fleet, by aircraft carriers and nuclear missiles. . . . Therefore, we are forced to reconsider our life. . . . There is no neutrality. In case war breaks out we must join one of the camps and fight our enemy. We must join the enemy of our enemy because he is our friend.

At the forthcoming session of the popular committees, I shall personally present to them the question of discussing Libya's foreign policy and the question of neutrality and our position in the world.[10]

From Words to Action

In its first concrete public step against Libya, the Reagan administration in May 1981 closed the Libyan People's Bureau in Washington. The closure order cited a wide range of Libyan provocations and misconduct including alleged support for international terrorism. In a series of related steps, all Libyan visa applications were subjected to a mandatory security advisory opinion and U.S. oil companies operating in Libya were advised to begin an orderly reduction in the number of American citizens working there.

Other elements of the widening campaign against Libya included enhanced coordination of U.S. policy with its European allies and a calculated threat of military intervention. The NATO allies were requested to reject state visits by Qaddafi and to continue or expand existing embargos on arms deliveries and oil exploration.[11]

Military force was first employed in August 1981, when the U.S. Navy, in the process of challenging Libyan maritime claims to the Gulf of Sirte, shot down two Libyan aircraft. The first of many American-Libyan confrontations in this area of the Mediterranean Sea had occurred as early as March 1973, when Libyan Mirage fighters attacked but did not damage a U.S. Air Force RC-130 reconnaissance plane operating off the Libyan coast. In October 1973 the Libyan government declared that portion of the Mediterranean south of 32 degrees, 30 minutes north latitude, in effect the entire Gulf of Sirte, to be an integral part of the Libyan Arab Republic and under its complete sovereignty and jurisdiction. Libya identified the Gulf of Sirte as a bay, despite the fact its 250-mile wide opening was far in excess of the 24-mile maximum width allowed for a bay in the 1958 Geneva Convention on the Territorial Sea and Contiguous Zone, and argued that it had exercised effective sovereignty throughout history and without dispute. The U.S. government immediately characterized the Libyan assertion of sovereignty over the Gulf of Sirte as a violation of both recognized international law and the long established principle of freedom of the seas. Thereafter, the U.S. Sixth Fleet challenged Libyan claims to sovereignty in the area by conducting periodic air and naval exercises in the Gulf of Sirte. It was during one of these exercises, which had been publicly announced well in advance, that two F-14 Tomcats from the Sixth Fleet downed two Soviet-built Su-22 Fitter ground attack planes in mid-August 1981.[12]

About the same time, reliable reports began to circulate of wider clandestine activity by the United States, including disinformation, propaganda dissemination, sabotage, and support for dissident groups. Claudia Wright, for example, reported in 1981 that officials from Saudi Arabia and Tunisia had confirmed privately that they had been told by Reagan administration officials that Qaddafi would be eliminated before the end of the year.[13] A variety of other news sources also suggested that large-scale operations were under way to overthrow the Qaddafi regime. In addition, a regular stream of disinformation on Libyan terrorism was leaked to the Western press by a variety of sources. The disinformation campaign concentrated on a few selected themes, such as Qaddafi the lunatic, Libya the Soviet proxy, Qaddafi the major source of international terrorism, and repressive Libya, all of which were also reflected increasingly in official statements from the U.S. government. A final element in the covert campaign was the aggressive recruitment and mobilization of Libyan dissidents.[14]

To further isolate Libya, Washington increased its economic and political support for African states, including Egypt, Morocco, Tunisia, and Sudan, resisting Libyan interventionism. The United States also allocated $12 million to support the Organization of African Unity (OAU) peace-keeping force, which arrived in Chad following the withdrawal of Libyan troops, conducted joint military exercises with Egyptian and Sudanese forces, and bolstered the Liberian military regime with an extensive economic and military aid program. The much-publicized adventurism of the Qaddafi regime had clearly provoked an American response; nevertheless, some observers questioned whether Qaddafi's actions warranted such wide-ranging measures and whether the Reagan response was really in the national interest. Critics pointed out that U.S. policies threatened to foster the Soviet-Libyan relationship by increasing Qaddafi's sense of isolation and thus pushing him toward closer ties to Moscow. The actions of the Reagan administration also revitalized a flagging Libyan patriotism at a time when radical socioeconomic and political changes, combined with widespread repression at home and abroad, had increased opposition to Qaddafi and his revolutionary government.[15]

The viewpoint in most Western European capitals differed from that in Washington in at least two significant areas. While acknowledging Qaddafi's anti-Western behavior, many European analysts argued that he was not as dangerous as the Reagan administration maintained. In support of this position, they cited his foreign policy failures in Chad and Uganda together with his alienation of African and Middle Eastern leaders. Second, many West Europeans felt it was a mistake to isolate Qaddafi, setting him up as the prime example of the kind of international behavior that President Reagan refused to accept. Instead, they argued in support of maintaining dialogue with the Libyan government as a means to protect Western economic interests and to keep Libya from developing even closer ties with the Soviet Union.[16]

Over the next several months, the Reagan administration continued to pressure the Qaddafi regime, with much of the emphasis now on bilateral economic relations. In March 1982 the U.S. government, charging that Libya was actively supporting terrorist and subversive activities, announced an embargo on Libyan oil and imposed an export-license requirement for all American goods destined for Libya with the exception of food, medicine, and medical supplies. While the imposition of the oil embargo sparked little informed comment at the time, it marked the end of a policy and a policy process, the separation of American commercial and political policies toward Libya, pursued by successive Republican and Democratic administrations since 1969. Washington also urged its allies in Western Europe to support the imposition of economic sanctions, but for various reasons they all politely declined.[17]

Qaddafi was on a state visit to Austria, his first official visit to a European state, when the American sanctions were announced. In early 1983, the U.S. government dispatched AWACS aircraft to Egypt in response to an alleged Libyan threat to the Sudanese government. Once the aircraft had returned to the United States, Secretary of State George Shultz, when asked what threat Libya now posed for the Sudan, responded that "at least for the moment, Khadaffi is back in his box where he belongs." Although the crisis quickly subsided, the aggressive American response embarrassed the Egyptian government and thus underlined once again the difficulty of sanctioning Libyan policies without incurring the wrath of other Arab and African states. Later in the year, President Reagan again publicly urged Western European governments to curb exports to Libya.[18]

Libyan Vulnerability

The increased pressure of the Reagan administration came at a time when the external policies of the Qaddafi regime were under siege in Africa and the Middle East. After intervening in Chad in the winter of 1980–81, Libyan forces were forced to withdraw some ten months later in the face of heavy Western and African pressure. Moreover, the debacle in Chad was only the first in a series of foreign policy disasters endured by the Libyan government over the next eighteen months. The downing of two Libyan aircraft in autumn 1981 and the March 1982 embargo on Libyan oil exports have already been mentioned. In fall 1982, attempts to convene an OAU summit with Qaddafi as chairman broke down completely, in large part due to widespread opposition to Libyan policies in sub-Saharan Africa. In the course of the negotiations, American diplomats lobbied actively in support of shifting both the venue of the OAU summit and its presidency from Libya. Vice President George Bush later downplayed the role played by the United States in this regard, but he was clearly satisfied with the result:

Well, let me be very clear on Qaddafi. We don't like what Qaddafi stands for, and I'll be very honest in saying that we don't like his support of international terrorism. We are opposed to his destabilization of neighboring countries. Having said that, I will repeat, the deliberations of the Organization of African Unity are for the Organization of African Unity to determine. And we have our differences with Qaddafi, and I'm very happy to go into them for you but since we do not see him as a stabilizing influence anywhere in this continent or any place else, and anyone who avows the international use of terror for political change will have our opposition. . . . Having said that, the deliberations in the past at OAU and who heads it up and all of that, that is a matter for the Organization of African Unity. And that is our position.[19]

Qaddafi contributed to his growing isolation by refusing to attend an Arab summit meeting in Fez, Morocco, and later attacking as treasonable the peace proposals adopted there. When the OAU summit finally opened in Addis Ababa in June 1983, it was chaired by the Ethiopian head of state. Following a cameo appearance, Qaddafi hastily departed the meeting, having suffered the double indignity of being denied the chairmanship and seeing his protégé, the Polisario Front, effectively barred from the conference.[20]

Libyan vulnerability at the time to economic sanctions was less understood but equally important. By 1980, the spontaneous takeover of most economic sectors by militants of the Qaddafi regime, even though the banking and oil sectors were still exempt, was having a chilling effect on relations between the Libyan government and U.S. oil companies. The growing animosity with Libya prompted several American oil companies to reconsider their investments in Libya, although a threshold had not yet been reached that prompted actual disinvestment. The exposed position of the Libyan government at the outset of the decade was not immediately recognizable for two related reasons. Uncertainly in the oil market after the Iranian revolution more than doubled the price of Libyan crude, and a lucrative spot market existed in Amsterdam where excess oil could be dumped at high prices. Nevertheless, Libya appeared vulnerable if the U.S. government initiated a boycott of Libyan oil exports. With its dependence on a few European countries and the United States, fully one-third of national income would be abruptly lost with no readily available alternative markets for Libyan crude oil.[21]

Libya's economic fortunes declined sharply after 1981, which further complicated its diplomatic problems. The Qaddafi regime, faced with a worldwide recession, a world oil glut, and a U.S. embargo on Libyan crude oil, continued to pursue a maximalist pricing policy, with the predictable result that oil production dropped precipitously. From the fourth quarter of 1981 to the first quarter of 1982, oil production dropped some 70 percent while oil revenues from mid-1981 to mid-1982 were less than half those of the previous twelve-month period. The ongoing purchase of sophisticated, expensive military equipment, together with the unscheduled costs of the war in Chad, aggravated Libya's constrained economic circumstances.[22]

Even though military spending was not seriously curtailed after 1981, Libya's economic straits did have a negative impact on several aspects of its external policy. As revenues fell, the Libyan government attempted to settle an estimated $4 billion in debt to foreign contractors by imposing unfavorable barter deals or countertrade oil sales. The ensuing talks, generally conducted on a government-to-government level, were acrimonious and prolonged. At the same time, an element of blackmail often crept into the negotiations, with Libya agreeing to pay the money owed for completed projects but only if the other party agreed to buy more Libyan crude oil.[23]

In February 1983 the General People's Congress registered its intent to reduce the foreign work force, but nothing more was said or done until Libya suddenly initiated massive deportations in August 1984. With alarm mounting over the regime's financial health, some 45,000 workers, mostly Egyptians and Tunisians, were suddenly expelled for the purpose of reducing the level of worker remittances. Although the Libyan government maintained that all foreign workers, with the sole exception of Palestinians, would be affected, in practice almost all deportees were citizens of countries with which Libya had poor diplomatic relations. The deportations underscored the polarization that occurred in the Maghrib following the conclusion of the Algeria-Tunisia Accord in 1983 and the Libya-Morocco Treaty of Oujda in 1984.[24]

Financial constraints also reduced Libya's influence in many countries, especially in Africa, where economic and military aid were more important than the ideology outlined in Qaddafi's *Green Book*. In addition, a number of smaller states south of the Sahara were embittered by the sudden expulsion of workers due to the economic importance of their remittances to local and national economies. Inside Libya, the imposition of austerity measures, coupled with other unpopular domestic policies like liberalized divorce laws, universal conscription, and reduced educational facilities, combined to increase markedly domestic opposition to the Qaddafi government.[25]

Nevertheless, Qaddafi pressed forward with the showpiece Great Manmade River project, an ambitious scheme to transport water from desert aquifers to the coast. In November 1983 the Libyan government awarded the contract for Phase I to the Dong Ah Consortium of South Korea. The project was originally conceived of as a five-year, $25-billion effort in five phases; later estimates pushed the completion date to 2020. Brown and Root (UK), the British subsidiary of an American company experienced in civil engineering work, was the management services and engineering contractor for the project. The nature of the Brown and Root connection later proved controversial because the embargo imposed by the Reagan administration allowed subsidiaries of U.S. companies to earn money in Libya and send the profits home as long as the American parent company had no role in managing the operations and no Americans were involved. As a result, Brown and Root (UK) continued to do business in Libya throughout the embargo years.[26]

Growing internal dissent heightened the vulnerability of the Libyan government in the early 1980s. Informed observers estimated that there were as many coup attempts in 1980–83 as there had been in the previous ten years, and there was no letup in subsequent years. The level of discontent was high and encompassed a diverse cross section of society. Not surprisingly, the elite of the old regime were among the first to separate from the revolutionary government. The next group to become disenchanted were the conservative nationalists, who generally supported Qaddafi's early adherence to Arab nationalist causes and the removal of symbols of Libyan dependence on the West but were anything but social revolutionaries. Disenchantment among the religious establishment grew as Qaddafi implemented the dictates contained in the *Green Book*. His attack on private property, for example, included the religious endowments that provided the financial support of the ulama or religious elite. Concern also grew within the ranks of the military as Qaddafi moved to create a new society without police or traditional armed forces.[27]

Despite the apparent vulnerability of the Qaddafi regime, the economic embargo imposed by the United States in 1982 did not in itself change Libyan behavior. American companies with economic ties to Libya, on the other hand, were among the losers. When the Reagan administration blocked delivery of a large order of Boeing airliners, for example, Libya switched to Europe's Airbus Industrie. In a December 1981 op-ed piece in the *New York Times*, Lisa Anderson, a highly respected academic and observer of the Libyan scene, encouraged the Reagan administration to ignore Qaddafi: "American harassment of Colonel Qaddafi and condemnation of his policies only lend credence to his repeated complaints about interference by the United States in the internal affairs of other countries, a resonant theme in the third world." The Western European allies of the United States largely agreed with her position, and by refusing to participate in the U.S. campaign of economic pressure on Libya they reaped substantial commercial benefit from their policy of inclusion.[28]

The policy of the Reagan administration toward Libya at this time was driven by an inaccurate perception that regional difficulties in Africa and elsewhere were the product of a global strategy planned and organized by the Soviet Union. In contrast to the Carter administration, which tended to emphasize regional sources for regional problems, the Reagan administration viewed Libyan pressure against the Sudan or Tunisia, for example, as simply part and parcel of a broader external challenge orchestrated from Moscow. This globalist approach, with a principal concern for East-West competition, often caused the United States to be insensitive to regional goals and priorities, if not to misread them:

A globalist orientation, which includes an inclination to punish enemies, leads the Reagan administration to an exaggerated sense of threat from the Soviet Union and its perceived military allies, such as Libya. Such a perspective results in irrational, self-defeating policies (the embargo on Libyan oil, for example), which are not the most effective means of containing Soviet influences. When it is remembered that Libya was one of only two Arab states that did not take part in the 1973 oil embargo against the United States, then an oil cutoff that pushes Qaddafi closer to one's superpower rival, and risks future access to petroleum reserves in times of need, seems imprudent.[29]

Although the Reagan administration later approved a large-scale sale of American grain to Libya for the first time since 1982, its policy here proved an aberration on the road to tougher sanctions. Washington in 1984 restricted the movement of Libyan diplomats accredited to the United Nations under the toughest regulations applied to any government delegation. Secretary of State Shultz, when asked to comment on yet another dispatch of AWACS planes to the region, summarized the policy of the Reagan administration:

We see a pattern of behavior on the part of Libya that is outside the pale of internationally acceptable behavior. We have sent our AWACS to the region at request, and they are there in a supportive role, and we have wanted the Libyans and others to know that fact and to know what their role is.[30]

Qaddafi later canceled plans to visit the United Nations in October 1985 to participate in fortieth anniversary celebrations, on the grounds that UN headquarters were located in a country that was an enemy of humanity and a leader in international terrorism.[31] In November 1985 the Reagan administration, under pressure from congressional representatives from the oil-producing regions of the United States, banned the import of all Libyan petroleum products. A series of press reports throughout November indicated that President Reagan had also authorized a CIA covert operation designed to undermine the Qaddafi regime.[32] Robert Gates, acting CIA director at the time, later went on record in a classified document, eventually declassified in 1991, stating that the CIA had not authorized an invasion of Libya in mid-1985. "At no time has Acting Director Gates recommended an invasion of Libya. Moreover, any insinuation that Mr. Gates in July 1985 encouraged such action is unfounded." A handwritten note on the document indicated the statement was "not used—on record—only if asked."[33]

Reagan Response to Terrorism

A series of terrorist attacks on U.S. facilities and citizens in 1985 were behind the escalating pressure of the Reagan administration. In July terrorists with alleged ties to Libya bombed the Copenhagen offices of Northwest Orient Airlines. Two months later an extreme Palestinian group, headed by Abu Nidal and with strong connections to Libya, purportedly bombed a cafe next to the U.S. embassy in Rome. In October terrorists

seized the *Achille Lauro*, an Italian cruise ship, in Egyptian waters and bru-
tally murdered Leon Klinghoffer, an elderly American confined to a
wheelchair. The seizure of the vessel was ordered by Mohammed Abu
Abbas, who later received a hero's welcome in Libya after his release by
Italian authorities. In November Abu Nidal commandos, believed to have
been trained in Libya, seized an EgyptAir jet, with fifty-nine people eventually being killed. Later in the same month a U.S. military post exchange
was firebombed in Frankfurt, Germany. Abu Nidal struck again in late December with coordinated attacks on the Rome and Vienna airports that
killed twenty-five people, including five Americans. The Reagan administration charged Libyan complicity, if not actual involvement, in all these attacks, although concrete evidence was never produced.[34]

In the aftermath of the December 1985 terrorist attacks on the Rome
and Vienna airports, Washington again increased the pressure on Libya by
terminating all direct economic activities, freezing Libyan assets in the
United States, and calling on the 1,000 to 1,500 Americans working in
Libya to return home. At the same time, the Reagan administration urged
the governments of Western Europe to join in imposing economic and political sanctions on Libya and again received a half-hearted response. The
equivocal response of European Community (EC) governments was based
on a variety of interrelated arguments. The thrust of these arguments
could be grouped under a few general headings, but subtle and significant
differences in emphasis and approach often differentiated the policies of
individual governments. In addition, many European states voiced a bifurcated response depending on their interpretation of the impact of specific
American or Libyan policies. To take the French government as an example, Paris refused to allow American aircraft to pass through French airspace on their way to bomb Libyan targets exactly two months after the
French had bombed Libyan-backed opposition forces in Chad. Arguing
first that violence was not an effective approach to oppose terrorism, the
French later opposed the 15 April raid on the grounds that they had favored stronger action.[35]

Commercial relations with Libya obviously affected European policy,
but it was never the dominant factor some Reagan administration officials
and other commentators suggested. Italy and West Germany enjoyed especially strong trading links with Libya, and most of the other states in western Europe depended to some degree on steady supplies of Libyan oil.
Great Britain was the only real exception because, once North Sea oilfields
began producing crude of a similar high quality, it no longer needed
Libyan exports. On the other hand, it was interesting to note that British
exports to Libya showed remarkably little disruption in the wake of the
break in diplomatic relations following the April 1984 Libyan embassy
siege in London and the death of an English policewoman. The question
of trade was then complicated by the relatively large number of European

expatriates residing in Libya whose personal safety was a constant concern. The Foreign Office described the situation succinctly in April 1986, when it warned Britons resident in Libya that there was a distinct limitation to the consular protection that could be provided.[36]

In the aftermath of the collapse in oil prices and the resultant reduction in Libyan development projects, the importance of commercial considerations diminished. While statistics were not always precise, the available information suggested that overall Libyan imports in 1985 dropped around 20 percent over 1984, with those originating in Italy and West Germany falling 23 percent and 36 percent respectively. Moreover, the availability of oil at reduced prices elsewhere, coupled with Libya's poor payment record, reduced the attractiveness of the few development projects still active. At the same time, European creditors like Italy, which in 1986 was owed some $800 million by Libya, remained concerned that EC policies not provoke the Qaddafi regime into ending attempts to settle arrears.[37]

More than one European government also argued that Washington was not really serious in its application of economic sanctions and that such sanctions in any case were not really effective. The governments of France and Italy in particular were reluctant to support the policies of the Reagan administration because they did not believe Washington was serious in its progressive application of economic sanctions. They asked publicly why they should put their relatively greater commercial relations as risk for what they viewed as little more than a symbolic demonstration of disapproval of Libyan policy. The strength of this argument, of course, was later diluted by the Reagan administration's termination on 1 February 1986 of virtually all commercial intercourse between Libya and the United States. More to the point, several European governments, in particular Great Britain, argued forcibly that history had shown a policy of economic sanctions to be seldom effective.[38]

Many EC governments also felt that the overall American approach to terrorism in general and Libya in particular was in error; they believed it addressed only the symptoms of the disease and not the cause, which they saw as the Palestinian question. The governments of France, Greece, and Italy in particular supported the Palestinian cause to a greater degree than did the United States, emphasizing the issue was largely a political one to be resolved through negotiation. In this milieu, the use of force or even the threat to use force by the United States produced widespread dismay across the European political spectrum where it was generally felt that force would not address the issue in a positive way and could result in an increase in the level of terrorism. Finally, a belief that the antiterrorist policies of the Reagan administration were fatally flawed only reinforced the long-standing determination of many European governments to pursue a foreign policy autonomous from the United States.[39]

Selected European governments also pointed to the absence of explicit proof of Libyan complicity in terrorist acts, a connection admittedly often difficult to make with state-sponsored terrorism. Over time, the governments of Austria, Greece, and Italy, in particular, addressed considerable significance to this question. The Italian government in early 1986, for example, took the position that it would maintain its privileged position with Libya until such time as firm proof emerged that the Qaddafi regime was supporting terrorist groups. In a similar vein, the Papandreou government in Athens first agreed to EC measures to reduce diplomatic relations with Libya, but later distanced itself from the accord pending explicit proof of Libyan involvement in state-sponsored terrorism.[40]

In early January 1986, President Reagan stepped up the rhetoric when he termed Qaddafi a pariah who must be isolated from the world community.

On December 27th, terrorists, as we know, attacked the Rome and Vienna international airports. It was the latest in a series of atrocities which have shocked the conscience of the world.

It's clear that the responsibility for these latest attacks lies squarely with the terrorist known as Abu Nidal and his organization. . . .

But these murderers could not carry out their crimes without the sanctuary and support provided by regimes such as Colonel Qadhafi's in Libya. Qadhafi's longstanding involvement in terrorism is well documented, and there's irrefutable evidence of his role in these attacks. The Rome and Vienna murders are only the latest in a series of brutal terrorist acts committed with Qadhafi's backing.

Qadhafi and other Libyan officials have publicly admitted that the Libyan Government has abetted and supported the notorious Abu Nidal terrorist group, which was directly responsible for the Rome and Vienna attacks. Qadhafi called them heroic actions, and I call them criminal outrages by an outlaw regime.

Qadhafi deserves to be treated as a pariah in the world community.[41]

Three weeks later, Assistant Secretary of State for Near Eastern and South Asian Affairs Richard Murphy reiterated U.S. policy toward Libya, adding a stern warning to Qaddafi:

There are three underlying messages of our policy toward Libya. First, the United States made the unambiguous statement that we will not continue to do business with a person who has placed himself far outside the boundaries of civilized conduct. Secondly, the measures announced by President Reagan make the point that Qadhafi's continued support for terrorism carries a cost for Libya. . . .

Thirdly, the steps we have taken to date are not the most severe actions that could be levied against Qadhafi. In light of the heinous nature of terrorist acts, these are modest measures. If Libyan aid to terrorists continues, however, the U.S. has the option of imposing a range of more severe actions.[42]

At this point, President Reagan, for the third time since taking office, examined the option of a military strike against Libya but once more chose to limit his reaction to diplomatic and economic measures in part because the administration was split over the question of appropriate response. Secretary of State Shultz and Secretary of Defense Weinberger strongly disagreed over the advisability of military action. Weinberger disputed Shultz's position that military force should be employed even in the absence of explicit proof of Libyan complicity in a specific terrorist act. Secretary Weinberger argued it would be a mistake to seek instant gratification from a bombing act without worrying about the details. He also raised the basic question of whether the use of force would serve to discourage and diminish terrorism in the future. Other considerations in the president's decision not to employ military force at this time were said to be his concern for the safety of American citizens still living in Libya, the possibility of an anti-American reaction elsewhere in the region, and the loss of American aircraft and lives. On the other hand, covert action against Libya aimed at undermining the Qaddafi regime reportedly increased.[43]

The Reagan administration by early 1986 had clearly singled out Libya as an example of American resolve to combat terrorism with the toughest possible response. Although many observers had concluded that states like Iran and Syria were more important sponsors of terrorism, the Reagan administration focused on Libya because it was considered the softest target:

The despicable Qadhafi was a perfect target, a cartoon character Americans loved to hate. Qadhafi had praised the Christmas 1985 machine gun massacres at the Rome and Vienna airports as "honorable." He had decidedly odd personal habits: he reportedly liked to use makeup, wear women's clothing, and travel with a teddy bear. . . . But for an administration looking for a simple victory in its confused war against terrorism, there was no easier mark. Libya was neither strategically nor militarily formidable. Taking Qadhafi on was the counterterrorism equivalent of invading Grenada—popular, relatively safe, and theatrically satisfying. As the spring unfolded, the White House campaign against him quickened.[44]

United States Attacks Libya

Events in the Mediterranean in spring 1986 moved inexorably toward armed conflict. The casus belli proved to be American determination to contest Libya's claim to sovereignty over the Gulf of Sirte. The U.S. government, as suggested earlier, based its legal position in the dispute on a 1958 convention on the territorial sea and contiguous zone, to which Libya was not a party, that permitted nations to claim coastal embayments only up to twenty-four miles in width. In the face of renewed freedom of navigation maneuvers in the disputed waters, Libya reacted predictably in mid-March 1986 with an attack on the U.S. flotilla that failed to inflict damage. U.S. forces responded in turn with a coordinated attack that sank several Libyan craft and damaged Libyan missile sites. Qaddafi's public response to the worsening crisis was all threat and bombast. Pledging to defend what he termed the "line of death" across the mouth of the Gulf of Sirte, Qaddafi threatened to broaden the struggle against the United States and boasted of plans to confront it militarily. Privately, he took a totally different tack. Using various Arab and European governments, including Saudi Arabia, as intermediaries, Qaddafi attempted to open a dialogue with the Reagan administration. Washington responded that it had no interest in opening any dialogue, either direct or indirect, with the Qaddafi regime.[45]

At this point, a report surfaced in the Western press that U.S. Ambassador to the Vatican William A. Wilson had earlier engaged in freelance diplomacy, making an unauthorized visit to Libya in late 1985. Qaddafi had revealed in a media interview in January 1986 that he had recently met with an official of the American government, but it was not until March that Wilson's visit to Libya became public knowledge. The Department of State, apparently unaware of the Wilson initiative, denied that the ambassador was authorized to speak on behalf of the Reagan administration. Ambassador Wilson, a close personal friend of President Reagan, was otherwise not reprimanded, despite Secretary of State Shultz's insistence that he be recalled. Wilson remained at his post until May 1986.[46]

Following renewed air and naval confrontations in the Gulf of Sirte and the bombing of the La Belle discotheque in West Berlin, on 14 April 1986 U.S. aircraft attacked what the Reagan administration termed centers of Libyan terrorist activity and training in Benghazi and Tripoli. Administration spokespersons claimed they had irrefutable evidence of Libyan involvement in the La Belle attack. Secretary of State Shultz solemnly described the information as the "smoking gun" the administration had been looking for. Eventually, the source of American intelligence, radio intercepts of Libyan communications, was made public, a revelation that undoubtedly weakened future intelligence collection efforts against Libya. The radio intercepts mollified critics at the time, but questions were later raised as to the governments actually responsible for the bombing.[47] President Reagan justified the attacks as appropriate retaliation for the Berlin bombing as well as for dozens of other terrorist acts linked to Libya:

My fellow Americans: At 7 o'clock this evening eastern time air and naval forces of the United States launched a series of strikes against the headquarters, terrorist facilities, and military assets that support Mu'ammar Qadhafi's subversive activities. The attacks were concentrated and carefully targeted to minimize casualties among the Libyan people with whom we have no quarrel.

Our evidence is direct; it is precise; it is irrefutable. We have solid evidence about other attacks Qadhafi has planned against the United States installations and diplomats and even American tourists.

We believe that this preemptive action against his terrorist installations will not only diminish Colonel Qadhafi's capacity to export terror, it will provide him with incentives and reasons to alter his criminal behavior. . . .

We Americans are slow to anger. We always seek peaceful avenues before resorting to the use of force—and we did. We tried quiet diplomacy, public condemnation, economic sanctions, and demonstrations of military force. None succeeded. Despite our repeated warnings, Qadhafi continued his reckless policy of intimidation, his relentless pursuit of terror. He counted on America to be passive. He counted wrong.

I warned that there should be no place on Earth where terrorists can rest and train and practice their deadly skills. I meant it. I said that we would act with others, if possible, and alone if necessary to ensure that terrorists have no sanctuary anywhere. Tonight, we have.[48]

The global response to the April 1986 bombing raid was mixed. The American news media broadly supported the attack, the consensus being that it played well in Peoria. Conducted on a Monday evening during national news, the Reagan attack was the first prime-time bombing in the nation's history. In the course of the raid, U.S. Air Force bombers attacked three targets near Tripoli: the airport, a port facility near Sidi Bilal, and the military barracks at Bab al-Aziziyyah, where Qaddafi was known to reside. Naval aircraft operating from aircraft carriers in the Mediterranean simultaneously attacked military facilities near Benghazi. While American military spokesmen spoke of pinpoint bombing, collateral damage included the French embassy, a chicken farm on the outskirts of Tripoli, and several other civilian areas. Estimates of casualties varied, but as many as one hundred Libyan civilians initially were thought to have been killed or wounded in the raid. Qaddafi escaped the raid largely unhurt but was badly shaken by the attack on his living quarters. His two-year-old adopted daughter was killed and two sons were reported injured by American bombs.[49]

Outside the United States, especially in the Arab, African, and Islamic worlds, the response was generally hostile. The Non-Aligned Movement (NAM) denounced the raid as a blatant, unprovoked act of aggression, and to demonstrate support for the Libyan government, dispatched a delegation to Tripoli less than a week after the attack. OPEC member states condemned the raid but quickly rejected a Libyan demand for an immediate oil embargo against the United States. The more moderate Arab states like Egypt and Jordan found themselves trapped between traditional ties of Arab solidarity and considerable uneasiness over the policies of the Reagan administration.[50]

Many Arab leaders had apparently concluded that Washington must either take decisive action against Libya or leave Qaddafi alone. At the same time, they recognized that no Arab leader could endorse an attack on a fellow Arab state, especially an attack by a superpower, without undermining his own domestic political standing. For this reason, most Arab and Islamic states extended Libya varying degrees of rhetorical support but generally refused to take more practical measures in support of the Qaddafi regime. The United Arab Emirates, for example, canceled the scheduled visit of a trade delegation to Britain to protest British involvement in the raid, and an Afghan resistance leader canceled a visit to the United States to highlight his opposition to an armed attack on a fellow Islamic state. The governments of Saudi Arabia and the Gulf states, in a highly exposed political position because of their close association with the United States, roundly condemned the raid, although they also failed to take more stringent action. The general condemnation of the raid, inside and outside the Middle East, was hardly an endorsement of Libyan foreign policy. On the other hand, it did suggest that the Reagan administration had seriously underestimated the negative political fallout the raid would generate.[51]

Impact on Qaddafi

The Reagan administration also misread the impact of the April raids on the Qaddafi regime. Eager to proclaim victory, Secretary of State Shultz suggested that the bombing raid caused Qaddafi to reorient Libyan foreign policy:

The public response in the United States and Europe supported the president's actions. His standing in public opinion polls soared. That made an impact on congressional critics. More important, Qaddafi, after twitching feverishly with a flurry of vengeful responses, quieted down and retreated into the desert. The Europeans, more alert now to the dangers posed to them by Libya, alarmed at the use of force by the United States and anxious to show cooperation with a popular U.S. action, took action of their own. We had finally gotten their attention. They forced drastic personnel reductions in the Libyan people's bureaus, and the activities of those remaining were restricted and watched. This action alone significantly curbed Qaddafi's terrorist capacities.[52]

While there were significant shifts in the foreign and domestic policies of the Libyan government in the coming twelve months, and some of those changes were precipitated or accelerated by the April 1986 bombing raid, few of them supported the objectives articulated by the Reagan administration when it launched the attack. After a period of seclusion, Colonel Qaddafi returned to the world stage with the major tenets of his policies intact. His support for state-sponsored terrorism might now be more circumspect, but he remained adamantly opposed to the international status quo and determined to employ all of Libya's resources to overthrow it.[53]

Qaddafi made his first major public appearance after the raid in Tripoli on the seventeenth anniversary of the September One Revolution. In his speech, which was said to be much more forceful than the previous year, he displayed a new militancy. Denouncing the United States and defaming Reagan, Qaddafi launched a purge of "American agents" and other opponents of the regime, challenging directly those elements in the Libyan military and elsewhere that the United States had intended to strengthen with the April 1986 raid.

Brothers, in 1969 the revolutionaries moved forward. They challenged in those hours five U.S. bases on Libyan territory and a British military base. They challenged the firmly established royal system which the United States was protecting with its five bases. We who are saying today to hell with America said the same thing at the same time 17 years ago, in 1969, while we were confronting five U.S. bases with the revolutionary will. . . . Today we say, o brother, to hell with America, to hell with colonialism, to hell with imperialism, to hell with Zionism, to hell with agents of colonialism, the agents of imperialism, the agents of Zionism. . . .

Reagan has to read history. He reads cheap hollywood scenarios and that is the problem of the world today—namely, a second rate actor becomes the president of the biggest power. . . .

He [Reagan] does not read history. He reads the scripts of trivial plays which all deal with the smuggling of a handful of dollars outside America. This is his education. But he will pay the price of this education. If America continues to obey Reagan the American people will pay the price of such stupidity and ignorance and of this disregard of convincing facts.

I want to say to him [Reagan] that if you continue your tyranny, insolence, madness, and foolishness against the international community and world peace, then I Mu'ammar al-Qadhdhafi, want to state that I can form an international army consisting of fighters against imperialism and against the United States of America personally—please stop chanting and let me finish what I want to say—I can form an army outside Libya and I can take with me thousands of fighters from among the Libyans. This army will spread out to all corners of the globe and destroy the American presence everywhere.[54]

Domestically, the raid rallied revolutionary elements behind Qaddafi and his regime. Seizing the opportunity, he strengthened the power and authority of the revolutionary committees, watchdog organizations first established in 1976–77 and composed of his most fervent supporters. Members of the revolutionary committees became much more active and outspoken in their efforts to silence voices of internal dissent. Qaddafi's efforts in this regard were so successful that by 1987–88 he was describing the revolutionary committees as overzealous and power-hungry. Even though he later moved to reduce their power and authority, they still remained strongly committed to the existence and operation of the revolution.[55]

On the other hand, the relative impunity with which the raids were executed thoroughly demoralized and discredited the Libyan armed forces, the institution the Reagan administration had counted on to force change in Libya. This encouraged Qaddafi to proceed with plans to abolish the formal military hierarchy and to replace it with a vaguely-defined "people's army." Several senior army officers later "volunteered" to take rank reductions as a step toward the planned elimination of the conventional armed forces. The Libyan government also moved forward with plans to relocate army headquarters from Tripoli to a remote desert region, a decision largely designed to reduce coup attempts. This series of moves added to the growing power of the revolutionary committees and thus was understandably unpopular with the armed forces. In March 1987, several members of the Libyan armed forces commandeered a military aircraft in Chad and flew to Egypt where they requested political asylum.[56]

As some observers had predicted before the April 1986 bombing raid, the American crusade embarrassed exiled Libyan opposition groups, undermining their popularity and weakening their already limited capabilities. There were a number of such groups, none of which provided a real threat to the regime; however, they did provide concrete evidence of widespread dissatisfaction with Qaddafi's revolution. Many of these small organizations, most of which were torn by internal rivalry and dissent, became increasingly concerned that they would be dismissed as nothing more than pawns of U.S. foreign policy. After the raid, one opposition group declared that non-Libyans were free to employ sanctions and boycotts to oppose Qaddafi, but the military option was for Libyans and Libyans alone.[57]

In the aftermath of the raid, Qaddafi also accelerated many of the more radical aspects of his domestic agenda. To accommodate lower oil revenues, salaries, research allowances, and welfare benefits were frozen or reduced. In addition, the regime pressured older white-collar employees without university degrees into blue-collar jobs to offset the expatriate workers sent home. An August 1986 government decree banned the hiring of university engineering graduates on the grounds that no more were needed, suggesting that they join the Libyan armed forces. The government also curtailed the teaching of foreign languages, especially English, and reportedly considered a reduction in the provision of elementary education in favor of home schooling. Finally, the regime abolished money as a form of legal tender, a concept first raised almost a decade earlier. The renewed prospect of a barter economy added to the general confusion and consternation prevailing in Libya.[58]

Finally, the American attack strained Soviet-Libyan relations that could already be described as testy. Due to policy differences and the mercurial nature of the Qaddafi regime, the Soviets had remained hesitant, even as relations with Tripoli expanded in the early 1980s, to move too close to Libya. As the American raid developed, Washington kept Moscow informed of its maneuvers, but the Soviets apparently made no effort to intervene on behalf of Libya. In the aftermath of the attack, Qaddafi again repeated his threat to join the Warsaw Pact, a proposal which had received no serious support from the Soviet Union from the time it was first voiced in October 1978. Moscow condemned the raid, canceling a scheduled meeting between Secretary of State Shultz and Soviet Foreign Minister Shevardnadze, but it limited its practical response to a promise to help rebuild Libya's defensive capability. When Qaddafi's deputy, Abdel Salam Jalloud, visited the Soviet capital in May 1986, the Soviets proved reluctant to extend additional arms credits or to conclude a mutual defense treaty. Instead, they reportedly emphasized the ongoing confusion that existed in differentiating between Libyan support for revolution and terrorism. In short, the Soviet Union remained an aloof and reluctant ally.[59]

The United States Unchanged

The Reagan administration, in turn, heightened its program of diplomatic, economic, and military pressure on the Libyan government. In early June 1986, Washington implemented a previously announced decision, ordering U.S. oil and oil-service companies to stop operations in Libya by the end of the month. These companies had been given a special exemption when President Reagan imposed the trade embargo on Libya in December 1985, following the attacks on the Rome and Vienna airports. The directive required the oil companies to terminate all royalty and tax payments to Libya, barred them from receiving payments from European customers buying Libyan oil, and called on them to cease participation in the management and operation of their Libyan oil concessions. At the time, an administration official was quoted as saying that "we recognize that crude oil flow is really Qadhafi's jugular." The new directive, on the other hand, did not require the companies to renounce their ownership of assets in Libya. Afraid a quick pullout would bestow a financial windfall on the Qaddafi regime, Washington gave the oil companies additional time to negotiate their withdrawal from Libya. The five American companies involved—Amerada Hess, Conoco, Marathon, Occidental, and W. R. Grace—estimated their assets in Libya to approximate as much as $2 billion, but hastened to add that it was impossible to estimate precisely the net book asset value or fair-market value. The decision to order U.S. companies to end operations in Libya was expected in Washington, erroneously as it turned out, to make it easier for the United States to seek European sanctions on Libya.[60]

The withdrawal of the American oil companies from Libya had serious implications for the future of the Libyan oil industry. In the short term, it probably affected exploration more than production, as numerous Libyans had gained some production experience working with the departed U.S. companies. Moreover, the Qaddafi regime recognized that U.S. companies retained claim to their concessions, a claim they might be able to exercise at a later date. Since the oil companies had a vested interest in the well-being of their concessions, they were willing to offer advice on production issues when requested. Initially, the Libyan government gave the oil companies suspended rights to their concessions for three years, and representatives of the oil companies and the Libyan government later held sporadic meetings in an attempt to resolve the complicated legal issues involved.[61]

At the same time, the Reagan administration continued to articulate a globalist viewpoint that saw the Soviet Union and its East European allies orchestrating state-sponsored terrorism around the world through surrogates like Libya. Secretary of Defense Caspar Weinberger developed this theme in a January 1987 address to a conference on terrorism:

We see in state-sponsored terrorism significantly different levels of involvement, support, and accountability. These levels might be called, first, the *policy* level: second, the *logistical* level; and finally the *operational* level.

The Soviet Union supports terrorism at the *policy* level by actively encouraging and helping client states. The Soviets do not engage in terrorism directly. Rather, they provide political and military support from a distance. Thus, Moscow can rely on surrogates and clients to provide the operational arm of terrorism. . . .

At the second level of involvement in terrorism, the *logistical* level, we find Soviet allies, clients, and surrogates like Bulgaria, East Germany, and Cuba providing weapons, training, and material support to terrorism.

Finally, at the third level of involvement, the *operational* level, we find three states directly engaged in terrorism, in pursuit of their own national goals—Syria, Libya, and Iran.

Libya's Muammar Qadhafi remains the most notorious proponent of terrorism. Our actions last spring [14 April 1986 U.S. bombing raid on Libya] had a clear effect on his terrorist activities. Indeed, throughout Europe there was a sharp drop in terrorist activity in the months following the strike. Qadhafi now understands that those who use terrorism must pay a heavy cost. . . .

Our policy was also reinforced by the leaders of the seven industrial nations attending the Tokyo summit. There, with the eyes of the world on them, they denounced Libya as a practitioner of terrorism and, in the strongest language, condemned the use of terrorism as an instrument of state policy.[62]

American policy toward Libya in the aftermath of the April 1986 bombing raid accentuated the very real differences separating the Reagan administration and its NATO allies on the subject of how best to deal with terrorism in general and Libya in particular. Great Britain was the only European country to support the raids, and the Thatcher government seemed most unlikely to support a repeat use of force. The remaining governments of Western Europe were generally critical of the use of force with most suggesting the bombing raid was illegal under international law and more likely to provoke terrorism than to prevent it.[63]

According to a little-known U.S. Department of Defense report only made public in February 2000, the Qaddafi regime responded almost immediately to the April 1986 raid, and its campaign of retaliation continued for up to four years. Reprisals included the execution of two kidnapped Britons and one American in Beirut, an attack on a U.S. embassy employee in the Sudan, and a Libyan missile attack in the direction of a U.S. installation on the Italian island of Lampedusa. These actions, and possibly others, contradicted the popular myth propagated by the Reagan administration that the raid suppressed the Qaddafi regime.[64]

Sensing the mood of its allies, Washington delayed efforts to gain European support to tighten sanctions on Libya. It was only in September 1986 that the American envoy, Vernon Walters, visited a number of European capitals where he reiterated the concern of the Reagan administration for Libyan terrorism and pressed for a comprehensive program of diplomatic and economic sanctions. His message was greeted with widespread skepticism and failed to produce the coordinated sanctions package the United States advocated.[65]

Throughout Europe there was a widespread feeling that the Reagan administration, in its closing years, continued to overestimate the Libyan threat and then overreact to it. In support of this assessment, Europeans continued to feel that U.S. policy was addressing the symptoms of the disease of terrorism as opposed to the cause, which they believed to be the Palestinian issue. European governments also expressed concern that American policy could increase the Soviet threat to NATO by leading to a Soviet naval base at Tobruk or elsewhere on the Libyan coast. At the same time, the Soviet Union's growing influence among members of the Gulf Cooperation Council strengthened related concerns over a possible increase in Soviet influence throughout the region. Finally, commercial considerations weighed heavily on many European governments with up to 10,000 Europeans living and working in Libya at the time, and billions of dollars in Libyan arrears still owed European companies.[66]

From this perspective, the foreign policy setbacks suffered by the Reagan administration in the remaining months of his second term simply confirmed in many European capitals the wisdom of remaining one step removed from Washington. An ill-conceived disinformation campaign against Libya in the fall of 1986 diverted attention from Libya's own actions and exposed a split in administration policy toward Libya. The disinformation campaign, outlined in a secret White House memo dated 14 August, was intended to make Qaddafi think that opposition to him was increasing and that the United States was again about to use military force against him. Calling for a series of coordinated events involving covert, diplomatic, and military actions, the scheme was initially successful as the news media in and out of the United States reported as fact much of the false information generated by the plan. A series of articles appeared around the world alleging renewed Libyan backing for terrorism, Qaddafi's imminent downfall, and a looming, new U.S.-Libya confrontation.[67] When this strategy of deceit was eventually discovered, it prompted a storm of protest from American journalists. President Reagan refused to characterize the plan as a disinformation campaign but admitted that he had approved in August a program designed to make Qaddafi "go to bed every night wondering what we might do" to deter terrorism. The fallout from the disinformation campaign led to the resignation of Bernard Kalb, the State Department spokesperson and a highly respected journalist in his own right, and greatly undermined the credibility of administration pronouncements on Libya.[68]

The Iran-Contra fiasco was even more damaging, as it left the anti-terrorist policy of the Reagan administration in total disarray. The sale of arms to the Khomeini government in Iran, one of the three states (Libya and Syria being the other two) that Washington had most frequently associated with terrorism, contradicted its official policy toward the Iran-Iraq war. Reagan biographer Lou Cannon best captured the bifurcated character of American foreign policy at the time: "Throughout the secret dealings with Iran and the flow of U.S. missiles and military spare parts to the Iranian revolutionary government, Ronald Reagan masqueraded as a resolute foe of terrorism."[69] To many observers, the Reagan administration, to the degree it arranged bilateral deals with radical regimes, appeared to be guilty of that ambiguity toward state-sponsored terrorism of which it had so often criticized its European allies. When the Italian government pressed the issue at the end of 1986, it suggested that the United States earlier had also appeared to be pursuing a dual policy of secret contacts with Libya, citing the Wilson visit to Tripoli, while at the same time advocating isolation of the Qaddafi regime.[70]

The April 1986 bombing raid, designed by the United States to promote the overthrow of the Qaddafi regime, had the opposite effect as it actually strengthened his hold on power. While the attack did little to rally the masses around Qaddafi, it invigorated a radical minority, and at the same time, discredited and demoralized regime opponents in and outside Libya. Qaddafi seized the moment to consolidate his domestic position even as he continued to oppose the international status quo. When King Hassan of Morocco on 29 August repudiated the two-year union, Qaddafi refused to accept the decision, arguing the treaty was still in force because it had been ratified by both peoples. He then traveled to Zimbabwe in September for the Non-Aligned Movement conference where he called for retaliatory measures against the United States. When the conference refused to adopt substantive measures, he accused some of its 101 members of being "spies, puppets, and traitors" linked to the United States and Israel, termed it a "funny movement," and threatened to quit the organization. While Qaddafi did not resign from the NAM, his showmanship did underscore his increasing marginality in much of the world.[71]

Largely unsuccessful in redirecting Libyan foreign policy, the policy of the Reagan administration focused attention on a major irony in the total American-Libyan relationship. In part because of his esteem for American power and prestige, Qaddafi often betrayed a need for U.S. recognition of his importance. In this sense, the policies of the Reagan administration probably encouraged as much as discouraged the Libyan policies it meant to check, because the foreign policy of the former helped generate the international attention so desperately craved by the Libyan leader.[72] John Orman, author of a penetrating analysis of what he termed the "macho" presidential style of Ronald Reagan, had this to say about Reagan's impact on Qaddafi:

Since 1981 Reagan had elevated an obscure Arab leader to celebrity status in the world of superterrorists. Our national media provided Qaddafi with a forum and with the recognition he so desired. Reagan's rhetoric matched Qaddafi's word for word, slur for slur. Suddenly the Arab leader gained Hitlerian status in the United States as the "maddest" of the "mad men." Qaddafi called Reagan's hand with the Gulf of Sidra "Line of Death" challenge and Reagan responded with an easy military "victory." Qaddafi called for a new campaign against Americans and Reagan responded with retaliation for the Berlin disco killing of an American soldier. His response was a bombing raid on Libya. All of this was intended to be a victory for the macho style of the presidency. However, innocent citizens from both sides have died while Reagan and Qaddafi play out their games.[73]

At the beginning of 1988, the final year of the Reagan presidency, the administration announced its intent to maintain economic sanctions against Libya. In so doing, Reagan stated that Libya continued "to pose an unusual and extraordinary threat to the national security and foreign policy of the United States."[74] Two months later the State Department issued a statement in which it argued that the U.S. bombing of Libya, coupled with defeats in Chad and domestic problems, had combined to weaken Qaddafi, but he had "not abandoned his radical and aggressive policies or his support of terrorism and aggression." After citing evidence of recent Libyan support for terrorism, the State Department report continued:

The United States believes the appropriate response to Qadhafi's policies remains one of isolating Libya and minimizing Libya's presence abroad to demonstrate to

Qadhafi the cost of his objectionable policies and to limit his capacity to take harmful actions. The administration recently renewed its wide-ranging economic sanctions against Libya.

Improved relations between the United States and Libya will not be possible as long as Qadahafi continues to support terrorism. What we seek is concrete evidence of a durable change in Libyan policies, not mere words.[75]

Plus ça change, plus c'est la même chose

In a front-page article in the 24 December 1987 edition of the *New York Times*, the Reagan administration charged publicly that Libya was building a factory near Rabta, approximately forty miles southwest of Tripoli, which U.S. officials suspected would be used to produce chemical weapons. In the three years preceding the newspaper article, little attention was paid to chemical weapons; however, the Rabta facility was identified by U.S. intelligence sources as early as 1985 and was subject to considerable scrutiny after that time. The author of the newspaper article, Michael R. Gordon, appeared to have had access to senior administration officials, as he discussed Libyan activities with considerable accuracy and detail. Gordon mentioned reports that Libya had used poison gas in its war with Chad and that the Qaddafi regime enjoyed a trade relationship in chemical arms with Iran. Such developments, if true, pointed to a fresh case of chemical weapons proliferation, a development the Reagan administration strongly opposed. In addition, the construction of a factory capable of producing chemical weapons threatened to destabilize the region.[76]

Qaddafi responded promptly to the charge, denying that the plant under construction at Rabta was intended for the purpose of manufacturing chemical weapons. At the same time, the Jamahiriya News Agency of Libya (JANA), the government news agency, condemned the U.S. embargo, especially what it described as the ban on the sale of medical supplies and medicines to Libya. This charge by Libyan authorities constituted a deliberate distortion of U.S. policy as medical supplies and medicine were clearly included in one exclusion in the administration's embargo. The false charge of the Qaddafi regime established a rationale for the construction of the Rabta facility in which Tripoli argued that the U.S. embargo left it with no choice but to build a factory to produce medicines and pharmaceuticals.[77]

The Reagan administration expanded its charges in September 1988 when it announced that Libya appeared to be nearing full-scale production of chemical weapons. CIA director William H. Webster claimed the following month that the facility being constructed in Libya was the largest chemical weapons plant the CIA was aware of anywhere in the world. By the end of the year, U.S. officials had reportedly ascertained that Libya was planning to construct a large complex at Rabta to manufacture chemical weapons and associated products. Public speculation then emerged that Libya had received support for the Rabta project from up to a dozen European firms together with some Japanese companies. At this point, President Reagan increased the pressure on the Libyan government when he stated in a television interview that his administration was considering some form of military attack on the alleged chemical weapons complex. Given the April 1986 attacks on Benghazi and Tripoli, a threat by the American president to attack Rabta appeared highly credible and was reportedly taken very seriously by Qaddafi. President-elect George Bush immediately supported the administration's position on a possible military attack.[78]

The Qaddafi regime reacted vigorously to the growing U.S. pressure in a variety of domestic and international venues, including bilateral diplomatic contacts, international forums, and a steady stream of press releases. Throughout the period, the Libyan government consistently maintained that the technical complex under construction at Rabta was nothing more than a pharmaceutical factory designed to manufacture medicine. Arguing that their interest in chemical industries was legitimate, the Libyans accused Washington of making false charges and challenged the United States to destroy its own stockpile of weapons of mass destruction. Qaddafi later responded through Italian Foreign Minister Giulio Andreotti to President Reagan's threat of a possible military response with an offer to allow a one-time international inspection of the Rabta plant. The Reagan administration immediately rejected this offer on the grounds that a one-time inspection could not be conclusive because a chemical warfare plant could be easily and quickly modified to appear as a legitimate industrial chemical plant. A subsequent visit to the site in early January 1989 by three busloads of journalists proved inconclusive. Libyan authorities allowed the journalists to view the facility only from a distance of approximately two thousand feet in gathering darkness.[79]

As the United States intensified its public accusations that Tripoli was constructing a chemical weapons factory, it quietly exerted diplomatic pressure on the governments of the companies thought to be involved in the construction of the Rabta complex. Possible links to German firms, in particular, surfaced over a prolonged period; nevertheless, until early 1989 the German government steadfastly maintained that it had no knowledge of any prosecutable offenses. It then issued a report that acknowledged the involvement of several German companies, especially Imhausen-Chemie, in the Rabta project. Washington welcomed the subsequent decision of the German government to tighten export regulations and to increase penalties for violations.[80]

As Libya faced off with the United States over the Rabta issue, Qaddafi continued his pursuit of radical internal and external policies. In September 1987, Chad and Libya, responding to an OAU appeal, agreed to a cease-fire. Qaddafi then declared an end to the war with Chad after claiming military victories at Matan al-Sarra and in the Aouzou strip. Chad and Libya submitted their dispute to OAU mediation later in the month, and one year later, announced plans to restore diplomatic ties.[81] On more than one occasion in 1987, Qaddafi also expressed interest in an Arab atomic bomb. He argued that possession of a nuclear bomb would be a legitimate act of self-defense since Israel had reportedly developed its own nuclear capability.[82] Qaddafi denounced the Muslim Brotherhood in January 1988, describing it as the worst of God's enemies and accusing it of destroying the Arab nation. In August 1988 Libya announced plans to abolish both the regular army and the police and to replace them with an armed people whose service would be voluntary. Two months later, Qaddafi outlined plans to restructure the armed forces into three separate branches, the "Jamahiriya Guards" consisting of regular army units, conscript troops with a compulsory service of two years, and part-time recruits. Continuing attempts at devolution, Qaddafi later called for the dissolution of the Jamahiriya News Agency, the security service, the national sports organization, and several other state bodies.[83]

There was a sudden resurgence of terrorist activity against Americans and other Western targets beginning in mid-1988. Separate attacks in April involved four U.S. Information Agency buildings in three Latin American countries plus a bomb attack on a USO club in Italy in which an American woman and four others were killed. Terrorists struck again in May when a bomb exploded at the Citibank office in New Delhi. While the Japanese Red Army appeared involved in several of these incidents, the Reagan administration suggested Libyan involvement operating behind a cover of Japanese and Palestinian groups. In July the USS *Vincennes* shot down an Iranian Airbus, killing 290 passengers; and in October German authorities arrested sixteen Palestinians after finding a bomb similar to those used in airplane attacks. On 21 December Pan American Airways Flight 103, on a flight from London to New York, exploded over the village of Lockerbie in Scotland, killing all 259 passengers as well as 11 persons on the ground.[84]

The Reagan administration ended its second term with its Libya policy intact. On 4 January 1989, less than three weeks before the inauguration of George Bush, U.S. fighter jets downed two more Libyan aircraft over the Mediterranean Sea. The circumstances surrounding the action were not dissimilar to the downing of two Libyan jets in 1981. Secretary of Defense Frank Carlucci described the event in the following terms:

This morning at about 5 a.m. Eastern Standard Time or 12 a.m. local time in the Mediterranean, two Libyan MiG-23 aircraft were shot down in self-defense by American F-14s with air-to-air missiles. . . .

At the time of the incident, both the ship and its aircraft were conducting training operations in international waters. The two F-14s were providing combat air patrol approximately 50 miles south of the [aircraft carrier U.S.S. *John F.*] *Kennedy,* which is some 70 miles north of the northeast Libyan coast. . . . The MiG aircraft were detected shortly after they left al-Bumbah. . . . The F-14 pilots maneuvered to avoid the closing aircraft. . . . The Libyan aircraft continued to close in a hostile manner. . . . At about 14 miles, the U.S. section leader decided his aircraft were in jeopardy, and they could wait no longer. . . .

The 6th Fleet ship and aircraft were operating in international waters and international airspace at the time of the incident and posed no threat to Libya. These routine operations are of the same type that have been conducted in the same area many times in the past. The 6th Fleet operations have no connection whatsoever with Libya's newly constructed chemical facility. These operations, which were conducted over 600 miles northeast of the plant, had nothing to do whatsoever with that plant. We now consider this matter closed.[85]

Whereas the Reagan administration considered the matter closed, the Libyan government branded the U.S. action a "premeditated act" and an example of "American terrorism." Qaddafi was quoted as saying, "We, as well as the fish, are awaiting them." Libya claimed the two MiGs were unarmed and pressed the UN Security Council to condemn the American attack. In response, a Pentagon spokesperson, after brandishing photos showing the Libyan fighters were armed, labeled the Libyan ambassador to the United Nations a "liar." As the war of words escalated, the Libyan workers at the Rabta facility were reported by the Libyan government to be ready to die in an anticipated American military strike. The UN Security Council, in the end, did not condemn the attack, and the United States did not attack the chemical factory at Rabta. America's allies in Western Europe reportedly agreed with U.S. charges that Libya was building a chemical weapons facility but continued to display uneasiness with the policies of the Reagan administration. About this time, the West German government acknowledged for the first time that investigations had uncovered "indications" that West German companies had made unauthorized exports to Libya. As attention focused on West German involvement in the construction of the Rabta complex, the U.S. downing of the two Libyan MiGs was forgotten.[86]

One of the last official acts of the Reagan administration, concluded the day before the inauguration of George Bush, was to modify the U.S. sanctions against Libya in an effort to eliminate the financial windfall the Libyan government had been receiving under the 1986 standstill agreements:

The President has authorized the Department of the Treasury to modify the special licenses of American oil companies operating in Libya.

In 1986 when the United States imposed broad trade sanctions against Libya, the Department of the Treasury authorized American oil companies operating in Libya to negotiate standstill agreements with the Libyan Government. Those agreements provided for a suspension of company operations in Libya to protect the companies from contractual obligations to work their concessions in Libya. The 1986 standstill agreements expire June 30, 1989.

The President's decision has been taken to protect U.S. interests. It will eliminate the significant financial windfall which Libya has been receiving under the 1986 standstill agreements by marketing the U.S. oil companies' equity shares of oil liftings. . . . The effect of the decision will be to permit the U.S. oil companies, subject to the restrictions on trade and travel which remain in effect, to resume their operations in Libya, transfer operations to foreign subsidiaries, or sell their assets.

The United States trade embargo against Libya and the freeze on Libyan assets in the United States, which were renewed January 7, 1989, for 1 year, remain in effect, as do the bans on travel-related transactions and the use of U.S. passports for travel to Libya.

This decision does not represent a change in the attitude of the U.S. Government toward Libya. We remain deeply concerned about Qadhafi's continued support for terrorism and subversion as well as Libyan efforts to develop a chemical weapons capability.[87]

Conclusions

The confrontation between Libya and the United States, given the globalist viewpoint of the Reagan administration, came as no surprise. As long as Qaddafi confined his radical theories and policies to Libya, he remained relatively safe, isolated from outside interference. Once he projected himself into the international arena with policies that threatened the status quo, the rules of the game changed quickly and dramatically. In short order, the Libyan government found itself in direct conflict with a superpower unwilling to allow a minor actor to challenge the global power system.

The Reagan administration confronted Libya around the world from Central America to sub-Saharan Africa and from Northern Ireland to the Philippines. In so doing, the objective was not necessarily the removal of Qaddafi, although evidence suggests he was targeted in the April 1986 raid. Rather, Washington sought to isolate his regime, benchmarking it as an example of the kind of international behavior the United States found unacceptable. For example, Washington generally opposed the policy of a two-hundred-mile territorial sea that was being articulated by a number of countries around the world, but it was in Libya where it chose to challenge the policy directly and aggressively with a response that included military force. Evidence of Libyan involvement in terrorist incidents was often circumstantial, at best, but unable to find the real culprits, the United States chose to punish the Qaddafi regime. With patriotism in full flower in the White House, Qaddafi became a symbolic surrogate for more dangerous radicals inside and outside the Middle East who were beyond the reach of U.S. power. Like the *Mayaguez* a decade earlier and Tripoli during the Jefferson administration, Libya proved an enticing target, soft and relatively safe, on which to demonstrate American resolve.

The bombing raid on Benghazi and Tripoli, a massive operation in which two American pilots and scores of Libyan civilians died, clearly represented a major change in U.S. policy. The political message encompassed in the raid was clear, and the attack surely got Qaddafi's attention. It also put others in the Third World on notice that it was not wise to target the United States regardless of their antipathy toward the West. The actual military damage, on the other hand, was marginal, consisting largely of a few parked Libyan aircraft. Despite the talk of pinpoint bombing, the April 1986 attack proved again how the best laid plans and the most sophisticated technology can go awry in combat.

At the same time, the aggressive policies of the Reagan administration threatened severe consequences for American policy toward Europe, the Third World, and the Soviet Union. European governments were uncomfortable with the use of force on the grounds that it was unproductive and unwarranted. They also expressed concern that further use of force might strengthen the Soviet-Libyan partnership or force Moscow into a similar strong reaction to maintain its own credibility in the Arab world. While many Arab and Third World governments had little sympathy for Qaddafi, they found it impossible to support a superpower bullying one of their own.

The policy of the Reagan administration toward the Qaddafi regime in the end produced, at best, mixed results. It succeeded in making Libya a symbol of unacceptable international behavior, but it failed to change the direction or emphasis of Libyan foreign policy. The central components of Libyan foreign policy after 1988 were not radically different from those before 1981 although the embargo championed by Washington did impose real limits on Tripoli's freedom action on the world stage. Bringing the full impact of American power and influence on Libya also did not stop terrorism which threw into question the actual role of the Qaddafi regime in many terrorist acts. Finally, where the Reagan administration aimed to foster credibility with moderate Arab states and restore respect for America as a reliable friend and ally, it found it extremely difficult to attack Qaddafi in a way that played as well in Amman, Cairo, or Riyadh as it played in Peoria.

Chapter 8
U.S.-Libyan Relations in the Post-Cold War Era

The United States is an important state in this world, and we can only seek to establish the best of relations with it in the framework of respect and mutual interests.
—UN Ambassador Ibrahim al-Bishari, 1993

We have called them the "rogue states" at certain stages, but basically what they are are states that feel that they not only have no stake in the system but, on the contrary, that their very being revolves around the fact that they want to undo the system, literally throw hand grenades into it to destroy it.
—Secretary of State Madeleine K. Albright, 1998

The 1980s closed with the victory of capitalist democracy over Soviet communism and the end of the Cold War. In the words of the historian Michael S. Sherry, "Those victories proved short-lived, unsatisfying, or contested, however—sufficient to shake the old order but not to define a new one." Abroad, Americans still faced an "untidy world which provided only flickering points of reference." At home, "they saw war's passions surging . . . but there too the reference points were unstable."[1] President George Bush had spent a lifetime preparing to be America's commander in chief in the Cold War, but he lacked the temperament and training to redefine his role and the conduct of the nation under changed circumstances. The desire and capacity of the Clinton administration to develop fresh doctrines and to move American foreign policy into unchartered waters was equally uncertain from the outset. The George W. Bush administration, on the other hand, offered some promise in its early days for improvement in American-Libyan relations. Qaddafi had greeted the advent of the first Bush presidency with cautious optimism in the erroneous belief that a new administration offered an opportunity for better relations between Libya and the United States. In a press conference in Tripoli in early January 1989, Qaddafi invited the incoming Bush administration to conduct talks aimed at resolving the issues that had dogged American-Libyan relations for many years. In his statement, the Libyan leader said he was willing to engage in disarmament negotiations and favored the inspection of weapons factories as long as all countries, including Israel and the United States, accepted the same conditions:

America must start by closing down the factories for atomic bombs, chemical bombs and napalm bombs which it has and end the Star Wars program.

Everyone must agree to abolish weapons and that peace should reign between people. Otherwise it's just confrontation.

Everyone in the world has come to hate America, especially in the last eight years and American policy has suffered.

America must reform its policy and clean up its ruined image as much as possible in the era of the new Bush administration.[2]

In a conciliatory gesture, the Libyan government on 13 January 1989 returned to representatives of the Vatican the body of a U.S. airman shot down during the American raid in April 1986. Later in the month, Qaddafi indicated in a press interview that he was willing to discuss American-Libyan relations in official talks with the Bush administration and to work toward the release of American hostages held in Lebanon. Finally, Libyan Foreign Minister Jadallah Azzuz al-Talhi stated in October 1989 that Libya desired normal relations with the United States as long as they were based on mutual respect and without conditions on the American side.[3]

Even as Qaddafi talked of dialogue and reconciliation, the new administration in Washington moved to expand the policy of diplomatic and economic isolation put in place by its predecessor. Convinced that Libya remained a principal supporter of global terrorism, the Bush administration pressured Tripoli on the issue of chemical weapons development even as it maintained and expanded the U.S. sanctions regime already in place. Later, it orchestrated a UN Security Council resolution imposing an embargo on Libya. President Bush also supported a covert policy to provide military aid and training to several hundred former Libyan soldiers. Set in motion during the final months of the Reagan administration, this covert operation hoped to use Libyan volunteers captured during the 1988 border fighting between Libya and Chad to destabilize the Qaddafi government.[4]

At the same time, the Bush administration perpetuated the bifurcated policy of the Reagan government in which U.S. oil companies honored the sanctions regime yet continued their contacts with the National Oil Company of Libya. Both presidents justified the policy on the grounds that forcing U.S. companies to abandon their operations in Libya completely would result in substantial windfall profits for the Qaddafi regime. Outside observers in Europe and elsewhere took a less charitable view. They noted that U.S. policy toward Libya, despite the bombast and rhetoric, seemed inconsistent and perhaps more reflective of powerful lobbyists and American national interests than of a determined effort to punish Libya for its alleged support of terrorism.[5]

Rise of the Rogue Doctrine

Prior to the decade of the 1980s, concepts and terms related to rogue or pariah states, backlash or maverick regimes, or nuclear outlaws were not in common use in academic or policy making circles. To the extent that such terms were applied, it was generally in the context of a few states, like Pol Pot's Cambodia and Idi Amin's Uganda, whose conduct was widely considered to be totally outside the pale of acceptable behavior. The immediate origins of what later became known as the Rogue Doctrine can be traced to the inauguration by the Department of State of its annual list of countries supporting terrorism, a listing mandated by the Export Administration Act of 1979. Regular issuance of this report during the Reagan administration focused increasing attention on the question of state-sponsored terrorism. In 1985, for example, President Reagan referred to Cuba, Iran, Libya, Nicaragua, and North Korea as outlaw governments that sponsored international terrorism against the United States. Secretary of State Shultz throughout the Reagan era made the issue of state-sponsored terrorism a recurrent theme in his public diplomacy.[6]

By the end of the decade, U.S. policy makers were linking the issues of state-sponsored terrorism and weapons of mass destruction to selected Third World states. The Center for Strategic and International Studies, a conservative Washington-based think tank, issued a report in 1988 entitled *Meeting the Mavericks: Regional Challenges for the Next President,* which warned that a new class of Third World states, armed with modern weapons and hegemonic tendencies, could be expected to create new dilemmas for U.S. foreign policy. A few months later, in early 1989, Secretary of State-designate James Baker told the Senate Foreign Relations Committee that chemical weapons and ballistic missiles were already in the hands of governments with a proven record of aggression and terrorism.[7]

With the Soviet Union in irreversible decline and no equivalent adversary in sight, the Joint Chiefs of Staff were faced in 1989 with the difficult task of defining a new security policy that would maintain U.S. defense spending at near-Cold War levels until a credible threat appeared on the horizon. At the time, many congressional leaders were talking about the "peace dividend," generally defined as a significant reduction in military strength and expenditure, sure to follow the collapse of the Berlin Wall.

Responding to the challenge, General Colin Powell, then chairman of the Joint Chiefs of Staff, initiated a search in late 1989 for a post-Cold War military doctrine that would justify the maintenance of superpower military capabilities in a world in which the United States was the only superpower.[8]

On 15 November 1989, General Powell presented his initial thoughts to President Bush. Given the diminished threat from the Soviet Union, Powell argued that the focus of American strategy should shift from a global war with the Soviets to regional responses to non-Soviet threats. Advancing a "base force" concept consisting of 1.6 million active-duty personnel, sixteen active Air Force tactical fighter wings, and 450 warships, he contended that the United States should retain sufficient military strength simultaneously to fight and win two regional conflicts. While Powell did not advance the rogue state concept or any comparable expression in this outline presentation, the central elements of an anti-rogue posture were present in the November briefing. In the next several months, Pentagon officials talked increasingly of the threat posed by aggressive, well-armed Third World states. Eight months later, General Powell and his staff presented a fully developed base force concept to President Bush and Secretary of Defense Richard Cheney. The President formally approved the plan and instructed aides to prepare a speech outlining its essential parameters.[9]

Bush took advantage of a scheduled appearance at the Aspen Institute on 2 August 1990 to deliver an address introducing the new strategic doctrine. Reiterating the arguments developed by Powell and his associates, the president argued that the future size of American forces, in a world less driven by an immediate threat to Europe or a global conflict, would be shaped increasingly by the threat of regional conflict. Given this new challenge, the United States had to maintain the forces necessary to respond to such threats wherever they might appear around the world:

The changes that I'm talking about have transformed our security environment. We're entering a new era: the defense strategy and military structure needed to ensure peace can and must be different. The threat of a Soviet invasion of Western Europe launched with little or no warning is today more remote than at any other point in the postwar period. And with the emergence of democracy in Eastern Europe, the Warsaw Pact has lost its military meaning. And after more than four decades of dominance, Soviet troops are withdrawing from Central and Eastern Europe.

Our task today is to shape our defense capabilities to these changing strategic circumstances. In a world less driven by an immediate threat to Europe and the danger of global war, in a world where the size of our forces will increasingly be shaped by the needs of regional contingencies and peacetime presence, we know that our forces can be smaller. . . .

What matters now, then, is how we reshape the forces that remain.[10]

President Bush's remarks in Aspen drew far more attention than otherwise might have been the case because they were delivered a few hours after Iraqi forces began pouring into Kuwait:

Outside of Europe, America must possess forces able to respond to threats in whatever corner of the globe they may occur. Even in a world where democracy and freedom have made great gains, threats remain. Terrorism, hostagetaking, renegade regimes and unpredictable rulers, new sources of instability—all require a strong and an engaged America.

The brutal aggression launched last night against Kuwait illustrates my central thesis: Notwithstanding the alteration in the Soviet threat, the world remains a dangerous place with serious threats to important U.S. interests wholly unrelated to the earlier patterns of the U.S.-Soviet relationship. These threats, as we have seen just in the last 24 hours, can arise suddenly, unpredictably, and from unexpected quarters.

In spite of our best efforts to control the spread of chemical and nuclear weapons and ballistic missile technologies, more nations—more, not less—are acquiring weapons of mass destruction and the means to deliver them. Right now, twenty countries have the capacity to produce chemical weapons. And by the year 2000, as many as fifteen developing nations could have their own ballistic missiles. In the future, even conflicts we once thought of as limited or local may carry far-reaching consequences.[11]

Because he referred to the Kuwait situation in his Colorado address, many commentators viewed the speech as a spontaneous response to the Iraqi invasion. On the contrary, the regional strategy incorporated in what became known as the Rogue Doctrine was a response to the fall of the Berlin Wall in November 1989, and not to the more recent Iraqi aggression of August 1990. Following the Iraqi invasion of Kuwait, most members of Congress soon discontinued discussion of a "peace dividend" and abandoned any serious plan for a significant reduction in military expenditure. The sustained effort of the Bush administration after 1989 to reorient American defense policy from global containment to regionalism eventually culminated in the publication of Secretary of Defense Cheney's Regional Defense Strategy in January 1993.[12]

Conceived initially as an interim measure, a means to justify defense spending at near-Cold War levels pending the appearance of a more credible threat, the Rogue Doctrine became the defining paradigm for American security policy for the remainder of the decade. As Army Chief of Staff General Carl E. Vuono later put it, "the second of August 1990 will be remembered for generations to come as a turning point for the United States in its conduct of foreign affairs—the day America announced the end of containment and embarked upon the strategy of power projection."[13] As such, the Rogue Doctrine had a significant influence on American foreign policy toward those governments defined by Washington as rogue states, most especially Iran, Iraq, Libya, and North Korea. Michael T. Klare in a succinct and perceptive analysis later explained why the doctrine eventually became, and continues to be, popular in Washington.

The Rogue Doctrine remains popular in Washington because it points to a clearly identifiable set of enemies—no easy feat in this time of ambiguous threats and shifting loyalties—and because it can be used to justify the preservation of the existing military establishment, which no one in authority would like to alter. In addition, special interests, including the military think tanks and organizations, the manufacturers of high-tech weaponry, and so on, share a common interest in maintaining the status quo. So entrenched has this strategy become that none of its proponents feel the need to subject it to any sort of systematic reassessment based on a considered analysis of the existing world security environment; instead, the Doctrine is treated as unshakable wisdom, sufficient onto itself.[14]

Despite the durability of the Rogue Doctrine and the prominence of rogue rhetoric in the American political system, little real consensus developed as to the essential characteristics of a rogue state. Secretary of State Madeleine Albright, in an address at Howard University in April 1998, described rogue states as a major policy challenge because their sole purpose was to destroy the system. More to the point, she argued that rogue states constituted one of four distinct categories of post-Cold War countries, the other three being advanced industrial states, societies in transition, and "basket cases" or failed states. Other Clinton administration officials promoted related efforts at classification, but they were unable to develop consensus inside or outside the U.S. government as to required policy objectives, appropriate strategies, or acceptable policy instruments in regard to the so-called rogue states. On the contrary, as Robert S. Litwak rightly concluded, "the rogue state designation—that is demonizing a disparate group of states" distorted policy-making and perpetuated "the false dichotomy" that established "containment and engagement as mutually exclusive strategies."[15]

This failure to build consensus on the concept of rogue states as a distinct class of nations in the post-Cold War international system was not surprising. The designation from the beginning remained useful primarily as a tool to win domestic political support for punitive action, as opposed to being a rational path for sound policy development. In effect, Washington took a disparate group of states and demonized them for purposes of political mobilization. An official of the Clinton administration, according to Litwak, "conceded that unless the United States appears 'completely maniacal' about Iran and the other rogue states in multilateral forums, such as the G-8, the Europeans and Japanese will take no meaningful actions to address behavior of concern." As a result, where the Clinton administration talked of a differentiated policy toward rogue states, in practice the political dynamic "pushed it toward a one-size-fits-all strategy of containment and isolation."[16] The governments of Iran, Iraq, Libya, and North Korea were most commonly associated with the term "rogue state," but occasionally Cuba was added to the list. Washington typically accused the rogue states of four wrongdoings: development of weapons of mass destruction, support for international terrorism, domestic human rights violations, and overt animosity toward the United States. This package of real or alleged transgressions proved a near perfect fit for Libyan foreign policy throughout most of the decade.[17]

Chemical Weapons Development

On the issue of chemical weapons production, the Libyan government responded to pressure from the Reagan administration with an aggressive diplomatic initiative in 1988–89 that linked the question of chemical weapons development in the Third World to known stockpiles of similar weapons by several major powers. Although it refused to acknowledge the development of such weapons and continued to refer to the facility at Rabta as a pharmaceutical plant, the Qaddafi regime pointed out that there were no international instruments in existence that prohibited their development and that Libya deserved to be treated like any other member of the international system. As long as other nations possessed chemical weapons, together with the more dangerous nuclear weapons, Libyan spokesmen argued, Libya should have the right to consider such weapons as part of its military arsenal. Finally, Libya linked its anti-Israel policy to the issue of chemical and nuclear weapons in a position credible within the context of contemporary Arab politics. A representative example of the Libyan argument was found in a January 1989 statement by Foreign Minister Jadallah Azzuz al-Talhi:

The United States knows very well where the chemical and nuclear weapons are in the Middle East. The United States knows that the Zionist state is an arsenal of chemical and nuclear weapons, yet has not raised a single question about it. Furthermore, is it not Washington which gives Israel the aid and the capabilities needed for producing such weapons and is it not the Zionist state which, with U.S. backing and knowledge, refuses to abide by the international laws and treaties concluded in connection with these types of weapons?

The whole world knows that Washington is the party which aids and supports Israel so that it can produce and develop nuclear, chemical, and bacteriological weapons and that there is a U.S.-Israeli military treaty under which the enemy state's capabilities in this connection are developed. We therefore urge the world public to ask the United States the meaning of its artificial uproar against us.[18]

The U.S. government in fall 1988 called for an international conference to address questions related to the development and use of chemical weapons especially in the Middle East. While a variety of states including France and the Soviet Union supported the initiative, most Middle Eastern governments were not enthusiastic, arguing that the issue was global in scope and not limited to a single region. French President Mitterrand agreed to host the meeting, and the Paris Chemical Weapons Conference opened in early January 1989. Representatives of 149 nations, including Libya, attended the week-long conference, which unanimously approved an innocuous document as a final declaration. Most observers agreed with Thomas C. Wiegele, an American expert on the development of chemical weapons in Libya, that the results of the meeting were underwhelming:

If the United States conceived of the conference as a mechanism to alert the world to general problems of chemical weaponry, the conference was probably a success. If, however, the aim of the conference was to put pressure on Libya to halt its activities at Rabta, the conference must be considered something short of successful.[19]

At the same time, the Paris gathering reportedly crystallized Arab reluctance to forgo chemical arsenals as a counterbalance to the nuclear weapons believed to be stockpiled by Israel. The Arab position, toned down in the interests of a unanimous communiqué, emerged as a real concern for Washington policy makers, given the combination of ballistic missiles and chemical weapons potentially available to a growing number of Arab states.[20]

American concern with the weapons delivery systems available to Qaddafi heightened in the immediate aftermath of the Paris conference, when reports of a pending sale of Soviet long-range bombers to Libya first surfaced. The Soviet deal, which reportedly involved the delivery of as many as fifteen Sukhoi-24D fighter-bombers, together with refueling capability, would greatly increase Libyan capacity to attack the state of Israel. Around the same time, Libya reportedly concluded a $250 million arms deal with Sudan that involved aircraft, tanks, artillery, and trucks. Collectively, these initiatives reinforced the Bush administration's determination to thwart what it viewed as the terrorist policies of the Libyan government. Consequently, the subsequent efforts of the Qaddafi regime in summer 1989 to woo the Bush administration fell on deaf ears.[21]

In the wake of the German government's admission in 1989 that several German companies had been involved in the Rabta project, the issue of chemical weapons development in Libya lay dormant for almost a year until reports surfaced in early 1990 of new activities at Rabta. Once more employing the *New York Times* as a medium of communication, the U.S. government released information from a Defense Intelligence Agency (DIA) report suggesting that Libya had begun production of limited quantities of mustard gas and aimed to reach full-scale production as soon as possible. The same report suggested that small quantities of the highly toxic nerve agent Sarin were also being manufactured at Rabta. The DIA study estimated that thirty tons of mustard gas had been produced in 1989, and that an expansion to the Rabta facility had been completed which would enable the mustard gas to be loaded into plastic containers. Consistent with the policy of the Reagan administration, President Bush called on the world community to support vigorous efforts to stop the manufacturing operations at Rabta. The White House also highlighted the secondary danger that the chemical weapons produced at Rabta might find their way into terrorist hands, and, like Reagan, Bush refused to rule out the possibility of a military attack if the operations in Libya did not cease.[22]

The U.S. government in mid-March 1990 revealed that the Rabta complex appeared to have been damaged by a massive fire, an announcement that pleased many in Washington as well as in the international community. When the Libyan press agency, JANA, later confirmed this report, it blamed Israel, the United States, and West Germany for the incendiary act. Other sources attributed the fire to a variety of terrorist organizations with at least one Libyan dissident group claiming responsibility for the incident. With independent verification impossible, early assessments of the damage at Rabta varied from minor to very extensive. Officials in the Bush administration initially suggested that the fire had rendered the plant inoperable but soon revised their estimates to suggest the plant was not seriously damaged and that the entire incident might have been a hoax. President Bush, on 19 March 1990, told an audience on National Public Radio, "I am absolutely convinced that the plant was manufacturing bad chemicals, chemicals that would be used for killing people, chemicals that would be used for chemical warfare. And therefore I don't lament what happened, but I can't tell you I know the cause of it".[23] In response to the fire, the Libyan government detained several people, indicating it planned to execute those responsible on the spot where the fire occurred. In addition to denouncing the United States for what it termed "an aggressive campaign of American imperialism," Tripoli also suspended currency transfers to West Germany on the grounds that West German agents might be responsible for the sabotage. The French government, on the other hand, chose this moment to supply three Mirage fighter planes to Libya, an action long opposed by the United States because of Libya's alleged support for terrorism and its armed intervention in Chad.[24]

U.S. intelligence sources later confirmed that the reported fire at the Rabta complex was a hoax, the precise objective of which was never clear. Spy satellite photographs ordered by the Pentagon showed burn marks had been painted on the buildings in an elaborate deception. The available evidence suggested that the Libyans had started a controlled fire, exaggerated its consequences, and later painted portions of the facility to simulate fire damage. After the deception fire, activity at Rabta slowed, possibly in an effort to add credibility to Tripoli's claim that a massive fire had rendered the plant inoperable. Qaddafi did not announce the reopening of the Rabta plant until shortly after Operation Desert Storm. Observers speculated at the time that Qaddafi appeared to think the distraction offered by the withdrawal of coalition forces from Iraq offered him an opportunity to engage in more controversial policies.[25]

Even though the reported fire did little or no damage, the exact nature and scope of chemical weapons activities at Rabta remained unclear. In any case, the lack of concrete evidence that Libya was actually producing mustard and nerve gas at Rabta did not prevent the Bush administration from charging in mid-1990 that China might be selling Libya the chemicals needed to make chemical weapons. Beijing emphatically denied it was helping Libya or any other state to develop chemical weapons and reiterated its policy in favor of a comprehensive prohibition and complete destruction of chemical weapons. Washington later reported that it had received assurances from China that it would not sell chemicals for weapons to Libya. A West German businessman and former executive at Imhausen-Chemie pleaded guilty in mid-June 1990 to a charge of secretly assisting Libya to construct the chemical factory at Rabta and confirmed that the plant was build to manufacture poison gas. The Bush administration, one week later, suggested that Libya might be building a second chemical weapons factory at a remote underground location several hundred miles south of Tripoli in an effort to disperse its overall production capability.[26]

The alleged fire at the Rabta complex defused temporarily the chemical weapons issue; however, the Bush administration by 1991 was again charging that Libya was producing poison gas at Rabta. Washington also suggested that the Qaddafi regime was widening its chemical weapons program and increasing its capacity to manufacture such weapons. The Bush administration in January 1992 cited new evidence that Libya was expanding its chemical weapons program and dispersing chemical stockpiles to avoid detection. American officials suggested the stockpiles were being dispersed out of fear of possible U.S. airstrikes and in preparation for a much-touted international inspection of the Rabta facility. Libya in early 1993 denied subsequent American charges that it was constructing a chemical weapons plant outside Tripoli and invited a neutral international group to inspect the construction site in question. Later in the year, the United States warned its Asian ally Thailand that Thai contractors appeared to be the major companies involved in the construction of chemical weapons plants in Libya. When Bangkok moved to investigate U.S. charges of Thai involvement, the Libyan government, in retaliation, ordered the expulsion of several thousand Thai workers. Libya later pledged, during a visit of the Thai deputy foreign minister to Tripoli, to stop discriminating against Thai workers.[27]

U.S. Intransigence

With the Rabta controversy at its height in the spring of 1990, reports surfaced in the world press indicating that the former communist government of Czechoslovakia had shipped 1,000 tons of Semtex explosive to Libya in the 1980s where it was later distributed to terrorist organizations. The substance, manufactured in Czechoslovakia, was described as a pliable, odorless, and high-yield explosive; and some experts suggested, without providing substantive detail, that 1,000 tons would supply the world's terrorists for 150 years. The former communist government had said earlier that it stopped exporting Semtex in 1982, but news reports suggested it had continued to make deliveries to East Germany and Hungary until 1989. Semtex showed up in Northern Ireland in 1985 as part of a Libyan consignment of weapons to the Irish Republican Army. Reports of Semtex shipments to Libya made headlines in 1990 because the explosive was thought to have been used in the terrorist attacks on Pan Am Flight 103 in 1988 and UTA Flight 772 in 1989.[28]

At the same time, Michael Gordon reported in the *New York Times* that Libya had successfully tested a system to refuel fighter-bombers in flight, an achievement that reportedly represented a major advance in extending the range of the aircraft as well as increasing their ability to carry heavier loads. When combined with allegations that the Rabta facility was a chemical weapons plant, these new revelations conveniently reinforced the anti-terrorism component of the Bush administration's Libya policy. The ousture of President Hissène Habré of Chad at the end of the year by Libyan-supported rebels led by Idriss Deby only reinforced Washington's determination to challenge Libyan foreign policy at every turn.[29]

On a more positive note, Libya joined the Arab Maghrib Union in February 1989, concluded integration pacts with the Sudan in March 1990, and forged a regional grouping intended to promote stability and economic development in the Mediterranean region with five Western European and four North African countries in October 1990. Qaddafi also initiated a policy of reconciliation with Egyptian President Hosni Mubarak, visiting Egypt in October 1989 for the first time in sixteen years; and by the end of 1990, bilateral relations between Egypt and Libya were flourishing. The resumption of relations with Egypt was an especially significant foreign policy decision as it signaled the return of Libya to the Arab fold and the pursuit of a more moderate course vis-à-vis the Arab world. Qaddafi also announced at the end of the decade a new round of political reforms, but the net result here appeared to be more continuity than change. Collectively, this disparate grouping of external and internal initiatives served to enhance Qaddafi's domestic position and greatly reduce his isolation abroad both in the Arab world and in Africa.[30]

The Libyan government also emphasized the economic programs initiated in the late 1980s, focusing on the Great Manmade River (GMR) project. The initial phase of this mammoth $25-billion scheme was finally inaugurated in August 1991. The first part of the second phase of the GMR project was celebrated five years later with the introduction of the first desert water supplies into Tripoli. American participation in the construction of the Great Manmade River, through the British subsidiary of Brown and Root, continued throughout this period. Secretary of Defense Richard Cheney, following the electoral defeat of George Bush in 1992 and a stint at the American Enterprise Institute, became in 1995 the Chief Executive Officer of the Halliburton Company, an energy technology and construction giant that had merged with Brown and Root in 1962. Ironically, the author of the Regional Defense Strategy and one of the earliest proponents of the Rogue Doctrine was thus by the middle of the decade indirectly engaged in commercial relations with Libya, as well as with Iran and Iraq to a lesser degree.[31]

The Bush administration relaxed its ban on travel to Libya in spring 1990 to allow American experts to participate in a campaign to eradicate the screw-worm fly, a deadly pest threatening African livestock and wildlife. However, this positive initiative proved the exception to an American policy of intransigence toward Libya. A State Department spokesman, in responding to a question about Libyan support for Iraq, captured the essence of U.S. policy toward Libya as 1990 closed:

Libya's support for terrorism is nothing new. Libya has been on the U.S. Government's list of state-sponsors of terrorism since 1979. Libya continues to offer extensive support to notorious international terrorist groups such as the Abu Nidal organization.

Further, last May a Libyan-sponsored terrorist group, the Palestine Liberation Front, attempted a terrorist attack on public beaches at Tel Aviv. And as you know from the information we've provided, the attack was launched from Libya and received extensive support from the Qaddafi regime.

The head of the Palestine Liberation Front, Abu Abbas, has publicly threatened to engage in terrorism in support of Iraq in the event of hostilities.

Just to reiterate our policy, we continue to hold terrorists and their state sponsors responsible for acts of terrorism.[32]

In early 1991, officials of the Bush administration acknowledged the failure of a two-year-old covert policy to destabilize the Qaddafi regime with U.S.-trained Libyan commandos. Set in motion during the final months of the Reagan administration, the secret paramilitary program had provided military aid and training to some six hundred Libyan soldiers at a base outside Ndjamena, the capital of Chad. The Libyans were captured during the border fighting between Chad and Libya in 1988 and volunteered for the covert force in exchange for freedom from prisoner of war camps. The operation disintegrated in December 1990, when Libyan-backed guerrillas orchestrated a successful coup in Chad and the commando group was forced into a floating exile. The United States first transferred the Libyans to Zaire; when their welcome there wore thin, most were shifted to Kenya. The State Department originally linked the release in February 1991 of $5 million in military aid to Kenya to an improvement in its human rights record, but it later admitted that the money was granted as an expression of gratitude for providing the Libyans temporary refuge. According to the Bush administration, the force never launched a serious military operation, and in fact, may not have seen any combat at all. In a rare show of candor, American officials quietly admitted that the flawed commando policy had handed Qaddafi a propaganda victory. While some of the Libyan soldiers elected to return to Libya, the majority feared persecution, qualified for the U.S. refugee program, and were eventually resettled in the United States.[33]

The Bush administration continued into 1992 its policy of isolating and pressuring the Qaddafi regime in an effort to diminish Libya's alleged support for international terrorism. In response, a growing number of analysts and observers expressed concern that additional pressure on Libya, especially economic pressure in the form of an oil embargo, would be counterproductive. Many feared the ultimate aim of the American and British governments was the overthrow of Qaddafi, an event that could lead to increased instability in North Africa and the Middle East. One diplomat was quoted anonymously as saying, "If you destabilize Libya, you destabilize North Africa." Qaddafi's well-known aversion to Islamic fundamentalists, whom he had suppressed in Libya, thus forming a barrier to the spread of militant Islam, was at the center of much of the concern. With no clear successor, observers feared the overthrow of Qaddafi could lead to chaos in Libya, where tribal loyalties remained strong and the body politic weak. Other commentators worried that the Bush policy toward Libya was targeted more at domestic U.S. consumption during a presidential election year than at containing terrorism. Analysts pointed out that the evidence available suggested that Libya had reduced or halted its support for many terrorist organizations. Some bases of the Palestinian terrorist Abu Nidal, for example, were said to have been shut down. American officials bristled at this last suggestion, maintaining that Abu Nidal was still in Libya, where Qaddafi continued to operate at least five terrorist training camps and appeared to be making only cosmetic concessions to Western demands that he cease support for international terrorism.[34]

Imposition of Sanctions

The Libyan government was linked publicly to the December 1988 bombing of Pan Am Flight 103 over Lockerbie, Scotland, as early as January 1989, when London newspapers reported the alleged existence of a letter from a former Libyan diplomat to Qaddafi praising the latter for taking revenge against American and British imperialists. Subsequent reports, attributed to U.S. intelligence services, suggested that the bombing was conceived during a meeting of Qaddafi, a radical Palestinian group, and Revolutionary Guards from Iran. Nonetheless, for almost two years after the incident, inquiries into the bombing, focused on evidence that Iran hired a Syrian-sponsored terrorist group, the Popular Front for the Liberation of Palestine—General Command. In October 1990, newly discovered evidence, in the form of a computer chip found in the wreckage, indicated for the first time that Libyan intelligence agents might have assembled and planted the bomb that destroyed the plane. The computer chip, lodged in the bomb's detonator, matched a bomb part carried by a Libyan agent arrested in Senegal in February 1988, ten months before the Pan Am bombing.[35]

In November 1991 the United States and United Kingdom charged two Libyan agents with the 1988 Pan Am bombing and sought their extradition. At the same time, the two governments called on the Qaddafi regime to accept responsibility for the actions of the two agents, make public all it knew about the bombing, and pay compensation to the relatives of the victims. Shortly before, in October 1991, a French magistrate had issued international arrest warrants for four Libyan officials for their alleged involvement in the 1989 UTA bombing. The American, British, and French governments also demanded that Libya cease all terrorist actions. The two sets of indictments formed the basis for American, British, and French demands that the named Libyans be remanded for trial in the United States, United Kingdom, and France according to the indictments.[36]

Qaddafi at first ridiculed the charges in the Lockerbie indictments, describing them as "laughable." He refused to surrender the two Libyan suspects on the grounds there were no operative extradition treaties between Libya, the United Kingdom, and the United States, which was true; however, he did promise to bring them to trial in Libya. In an interview on Italian television, Qaddafi later argued that meteorological conditions, not an explosion, had caused Pan Am Flight 103 to crash. Qaddafi enjoyed public support from the Arab League, which backed Libya in the dispute and warned against economic sanctions or military action. The Group of 77, on the other hand, in a November 1991 meeting refused to adopt a resolution supporting the Libyan position. A few weeks later, the Organization of the Islamic Conference issued a statement affirming full solidarity with Libya and opposing any economic or military action.[37]

Following the indictment of two Libyan citizens as the perpetrators of the attack that brought down the plane, Washington and London aggressively pushed for UN Security Council Resolution 731, eventually passed in January 1992, which called for Libyan cooperation in the investigations in progress over the destruction of both Pan Am Flight 103 and UTA Flight 772. Condemning the destruction of flights 103 and 772, Resolution 731 deplored the fact that Libya had not responded to requests to cooperate in the investigation and urged it "to provide a full and effective response to those requests so as to contribute to the elimination of international terrorism." Finally, the resolution requested the UN Secretary General "to seek the cooperation of the Libyan government" and urged "all states individually and collectively to encourage the Libyan Government to respond."[38]

When Libya failed to meet all the conditions in Resolution 731, the UN Security Council on 31 March 1992 adopted Resolution 748, which imposed limited sanctions against Libya, including an embargo on aircraft and arms sales and air travel as well as a reduction in the staff of Libyan diplomatic missions abroad. Resolution 748 was adopted under chapter 7 of the UN Charter, which provided for action with respect to threats to the peace, breaches of the peace, and acts of aggression, together with article 25 of the Charter, which made it mandatory for UN members to accept and carry out decisions of the Security Council. This was only the second time (the first followed the Iraqi invasion of Kuwait) that the Security Council had imposed sanctions on a state for flouting Security Council demands. Earlier, the Bush administration had announced that it was freezing the U.S. assets of forty-six business that it said were ultimately controlled by Libya. None of these commercial concerns, which included multinationals involved in banking, industry, investment, and petroleum, were headquartered in the United States, but several were based in countries that were close allies, including Britain and the France, cosponsors of Resolution 748. In November 1993 the Security Council passed Resolution 883, which toughened the sanctions in place by freezing Libya's overseas assets, with the exception of petroleum-related assets, banning some sales of oil-related equipment, and tightening the earlier decision to end commercial air links. As it supported the UN sanctions, the U.S. government continued to maintain and extend its own ban on direct economic activities with Libya, which had been in place since December 1986.[39]

Responding to the adoption of Resolution 748, the Libyan foreign minister denounced the UN sanctions and accused Britain, France, and the United States of "leading a crusade against Arabs and Muslims." The Arab League also issued a statement that expressed regret over the Security Council's decision, but at the same time it denounced "international terrorism in all its forms" and signaled its readiness "to cooperate in ending it." The Arab League's half-hearted attempts to settle the dispute, coupled with the tepid support of individual Arab states, added to the growing disillusionment of Qaddafi and the Libyan people with the ideal of Arab unity. Qaddafi later called for compromise, but his government adamantly refused to remand the two suspects in the context of a trial in Britain or the United States. Following several futile Libyan attempts to prevent the imposition of sanctions, the United Nations on 15 April 1992 applied the sanctions provided for in Resolution 748, expelled Libyan diplomats, and turned back Libyan airliners seeking to defy the flight ban. In a generally moderate statement issued in May 1992, the foreign ministers of the Non-Aligned Movement welcomed Libyan acceptance of the UN resolution, calling on Tripoli to cut all links with terrorist movements and urging all parties to settle the dispute peacefully. At the end of the year, the Arab Maghrib Union appealed to the Security Council to revise its resolutions and lift the embargo. Given the limited and selective support Libya received from African and other Third World states, it was hardly surprising that the year 1992 marked the beginning of seven long years of international isolation for the Qaddafi regime.[40]

Shuttered Windows

Qaddafi projected an air of detachment during the 1992 American presidential campaign. In response to a question as to which U.S. presidential candidate he supported, he responded that he supported the will of the American people.[41] However, once the returns were in and Bill Clinton was declared the winner, Qaddafi could hardly restrain his glee. After eight years of Reagan and four years of Bush, he obviously believed that a Democratic administration offered an exciting new window of opportunity to improve American-Libyan relations. In a long address to political science students at al-Fatih University in Tripoli, delivered on 31 December 1992, he roundly condemned the Republican Party and the Reagan and Bush administrations and lauded the Democratic Party and the incoming Clinton administration, which he hoped and expected would take American policy in a new direction. In so doing, Qaddafi displayed a disturbing lack of understanding of the American political system and the platforms of the two major parties. Consequently, it was not surprising that he completely misread the future direction of American foreign policy:

Actually, the results of the American elections showed the emergence of a new page and a new state in the world. We toiled and persevered, we mustered our courage, and we stood our ground until the Republican era, the era of the American Republican Party, had ended. It used to antagonize us. It took part in the aggression against us in 1986. We persevered with patience and courage for four more years after the Republican Party had been in power. . . . We were expecting Bush and not Clinton to win, with the Republicans thus continuing in power for four more years. We said: Well, we will have to endure another four years until this American nightmare is over.

But thanks be to God, what happened during one year of patience, courage, resistance, flexibility, and wisdom? The results of the American elections were announced. They spelled the end of the Republican administration with the Democrats scoring a victory. We and the world which is on our side believe that the American Democratic Party will lead America, America's foreign policy, in the opposite direction to that of the Republican leadership.

In the Reagan era, America began to lose its direction. It made historic mistakes, gripped by recklessness and a lack of foresight. . . . This policy spells danger, and the American nation and the American people, because of this imperialist foreign policy, are being driven to disaster.

When Clinton emerged along with the Democratic Party, he started to say that America must be saved, that one had to look inward, that the American wealth must not be wasted on imperialist policies, that half the American forces in Europe should be brought home, that the military bases should be wound up, and that Reagan's Star Wars program must be abolished.. . . . He raised slogans like these and said that a political revolution should take place in America to make America look inward and that the American people should be saved.

. . . Clinton won and the Democratic administration succeeded. The whole world believes that America will change during the era of the Democratic administration.

The Democrats originally consisted of minorities, the oppressed. We have been defending these people during the Reagan era. Because of this, Reagan's vengeance against us increased, because we used to back the blacks, the Red Indians, the minorities, the workers, and the oppressed, who actually were the foundations of the Democratic Party.

In actual fact, the force that formed the Democratic Party to which Clinton belongs, this force actually is our ally. When it was in opposition, we used to back it.

We thank God for this result and give a deep sigh and the whole world feels really satisfied.[42]

Qaddafi's hopes were soon dashed, as the Clinton administration from the beginning articulated a policy toward Libya that was difficult to distinguish in tone and content from its predecessor. In the course of the campaign, Clinton had promised to adopt radically new foreign and military policies in the wake of the Cold War. In an effort to make good on this promise, Secretary of Defense Les Aspin ordered a bottom-up review of U.S. defense policy. While Aspin suggested that the review would produce a major change in U.S. strategy, the end product bore a striking resemblance to the base force concept developed by General Powell in 1989. The revised doctrine called for sufficient American military force to fight and win two major regional conflicts. The only significant difference between the Aspin and Powell plans was that Aspin called for a capability to fight two major regional conflicts nearly simultaneously where Powell had called for them to be fought at the same time.[43]

The bottom-up review completed by the Clinton administration resulted in the articulation of the Rogue Doctrine in its mature form. Secretary Aspin declared that the new strategy was a product of the need to contain rogue leaders set on regional domination through military means, rogue leaders who were also pursuing biological, chemical, and nuclear weapons capabilities. To meet these threats, the Pentagon intended to project American power into regions important to the United States and to defeat potentially hostile regional powers like Libya. Thereafter, opposition to the policies of rogue states became a defining theme in the foreign policy of the Clinton administration.[44]

Substituting the term "backlash" for "rogue" states, Assistant to the President for National Security Affairs Anthony Lake captured the essence of the Clinton administration's policy toward the rogue states in an article published in *Foreign Affairs* in 1994:

our policy must face the reality of recalcitrant and outlaw states that not only choose to remain outside the family but also assault its basic values. There are few "backlash" states: Cuba, North Korea, Iran, Iraq, and Libya. For now they lack the resources of a superpower, which would enable them to seriously threaten the democratic order being created around them. Nevertheless, their behavior is often aggressive and defiant. . . .

These backlash states have some common characteristics. Ruled by cliques that control power through coercion, they suppress basic human rights and promote radical ideologies. While their political systems vary, their leaders share a common antipathy toward popular participation that might undermine the existing regimes. These nations exhibit a chronic inability to engage constructively with the outside world, and they do not function effectively in alliances—even with those like-minded. They are often on the defensive, increasingly criticized and targeted with sanctions in international forums.

Finally, they share a siege mentality. Accordingly, they are embarked on ambitious and costly military programs—especially in weapons of mass destruction (WMD) and missile delivery systems—in a misguided quest for a great equalizer to protect their regimes or advance their purposes abroad.[45]

Emphasizing that the U.S. government had a unique responsibility to oppose such regimes, Lake then stated that this opposition would be communicated by the Clinton administration in a multitude of overt and covert ways:

As the sole superpower, the United States has a special responsibility for developing a strategy to neutralize, contain and, through selective pressure, perhaps eventually transform these backlash states into constructive members of the international community. . . . In each case, we maintain alliances and deploy military capabilities sufficient to deter or respond to any aggressive act. We seek to contain the influence of these states, sometimes by isolation, sometimes through pressure, sometimes by diplomatic and economic measures. We encourage the rest of the international community to join us in a concerted effort. In the cases of Iraq and Libya, for example, we have already achieved a strong international consensus backed by U.N. resolutions.

The United States is also actively engaged in unilateral and multilateral efforts to restrict their military and technological capabilities. Intelligence, counterterrorism and multilateral export control policies, especially on weapons of mass destruction and their delivery systems, are all being employed.[46]

In the *Foreign Affairs* article and other public statements, Lake and his colleagues in the Clinton administration linked domestic structure and foreign policy and suggested that nondemocratic regimes appeared most likely to violate international norms of behavior. A key element of their analysis was that external behavior, as opposed to internal policy, was the key component for inclusion in the category of rogue states. In the Libyan case, for example, it was Qaddafi's alleged support for international terrorism and his pursuit of weapons of mass destruction, not the oppressive political climate in Libya or Qaddafi's questionable record on human rights, that guaranteed Libya membership in the elite circle of rogue states.[47]

Clinton Application of Rogue Doctrine

U.S. intelligence agencies reported in mid-February 1993 that Libya was building a subterranean chemical weapons plant near Tarhuna capable of producing and storing poison gas. Clinton administration officials described the new project as a source of significant concern, especially since the Libyan government had failed to sign a UN convention banning chemical weapons. The Libyan foreign minister had attended the January 1993 Paris conference convened to sign the accord, but at the last minute refused to add his name to the convention. One month later, Secretary of State Warren Christopher threatened Libya with a global oil embargo because of its refusal to hand over for trial the two Libyans accused of the 1988 Pan Am bombing. With Libya totally dependent on crude oil exports, an oil embargo would have dealt a severe blow to the Libyan economy. It would also have negatively affected several European countries, notably France, Germany, Italy, and Spain, that imported significant quantities of Libyan oil. The UN Security Council renewed the air and arms embargo against Libya in April 1993 but rebuffed U.S. efforts to tighten the sanctions. Qaddafi's public reaction to the renewal of sanctions was predictable as he ordered the masses into the streets to protest. In private, he was reportedly relieved that Europe had resisted U.S. pressure to extend the measures to include an embargo on oil or related technology.[48]

Thereafter, the Clinton administration continued to exert pressure on the Qaddafi regime whenever and wherever possible. In June 1993 Washington moved to block the shipment of rocket fuel ingredients from Russia to Libya, the latest in a series of Russian exports to worry the administration. Two months later, Britain, France, and the United States collectively issued a new warning to Libya to turn over the two suspects in the Pan Am 103 bombing or face new and tougher sanctions. In an unexpected move that highlighted the international complexities of the case, Russia later threatened to veto new Security Council sanctions against Libya unless Britain, France, and the United States agreed to give Russia an interest-free loan to cover a $4 billion debt that Tripoli owed Moscow. In November the Clinton administration again pressed for a global oil boycott if Libya failed to hand over the suspected terrorists. But the new sanctions passed by the Security Council, while they froze assets and banned imports of some forms of oil equipment, again stopped short of a total ban on Libyan oil exports. Under the new sanctions, Belgian, French, Italian, and other foreign oil companies were also free to maintain lucrative gas and oil drilling and exploration contracts in Libya.[49]

Despite mounting evidence to the contrary, the actions of the Libyan government throughout most of 1993 suggested that it continued to believe it could work with the Clinton administration. The Libyan news agency announced on 14 May that Libya was prepared to take three steps to comply with UN Resolution 748: (1) cut all ties with organizations involved in international terrorism; (2) deny the use of its territory for terrorist acts and punish severely anyone involved in such acts; and (3) invite UN representatives to see that there were no training camps in Libya. Two months later, Ibrahim al-Bishari, Libyan representative to the Arab League, reiterated many of the arguments developed by Qaddafi in his 1992 address at al-Fatih University:

The United States is an important state in this world, and we can only seek to establish the best of relations with it in the framework of respect and mutual interests. . . . The two Republican administrations of (Ronald) Reagan and (George) Bush were characterized by using the logic of force in resolving international disputes. Fortunately, President Clinton has arrived amid different conditions. The Cold War ended with the collapse of the Soviet Union. Furthermore, the U.S. President is from a generation which has not participated in any wars, whether World War II or the Vietnam War, in which he refused to participate because of his belief that war achieves no solution. He is an intellectual young man whose vision differs from that of the Republican administration. He belongs to the Democratic Party, which includes minorities, including the blacks, Hispanics, Arabs, and Jews, and sympathizes with the cause of small peoples. We saw in the days of President Jimmy Carter how there were no bloody conflicts between the United States and other states.[50]

Qaddafi in December 1993 termed Libya the "mecca of freedom fighters and their natural ally." The Clinton administration in the same week asked Egyptian President Mubarak for assistance in finding Mansour Kikhia, the former Libyan diplomat and prominent dissident, who had mysteriously disappeared in Cairo a week earlier. His disappearance coincided with a call by basic popular committees in Tripoli to crush traitors and spies and followed a November speech by Qaddafi in which he said that opponents of the regime who had escaped to America were worthy of slaughter. Kikhia lived in Columbia, Missouri, where he operated a real estate agency. His wife and four children were American citizens, and he was scheduled to be granted citizenship in April 1994. His disappearance focused renewed international attention on the alleged terrorism and human rights violations of the Qaddafi regime and also damaged its relations with neighboring Egypt. While Kikhia was never found, the available evidence led many observers to conclude that he had been abducted in Cairo by Libyan intelligence agents and removed to Tripoli. Six months later, his wife reported that a Libyan official had recently offered her money to modulate her campaign of criticism of the Qaddafi government. When taken together, events in late 1993 and early 1994 left no hope for improved American-Libyan relations in the foreseeable future.[51]

The U.S. government after 1993 called repeatedly for a global embargo on Libyan oil sales; however, it was unable to win the support of key European states, especially Germany and Italy, which were heavily dependent on Libyan oil supplies. The Italian government, for example, argued that its refineries could not easily be converted to handle types of crude oil different from that supplied by Libya. Even such a close ally and interested party as the United Kingdom appeared to adopt a more liberal interpretation of the sanctions in place. The Bank of England, after initially refusing to allow British oil companies to send cash to Libyan subsidiaries, began in 1995 to allow them on a case-by-case basis for exploration operations. Equally significant, after Qaddafi threatened to deny the flight ban and quit the United Nations, the United Nations agreed in April 1995 to relax the ban to allow Libyan pilgrims to join the Muslim pilgrimage to Saudi Arabia.[52]

Faced with growing opposition at home, especially from Muslim fundamentalists, Qaddafi later moved to deport thousands of Arab and African workers. His expulsion of Palestinians stemmed officially from his unhappiness with the Palestine Liberation Organization for holding peace talks with Israel, but informed observers suggested the expulsions were also linked to reports of domestic unrest. In addition, the expulsion campaign appeared designed to pressure the United Nations for relief from the sanctions regime, now in place for three years. In a speech that reflected his growing isolation in the Arab world as well as in the West, Qaddafi in November 1995 castigated Arab leaders from Morocco to Saudi Arabia, indicating that he could no longer trust any of them. At the end of the year, Britain expelled the head of the Libyan interest section at the Saudi Arabian embassy in London for having engaged in activities incompatible with his diplomatic status. Foreign Office officials denied that the expulsion was tied to the murder in London the previous month of a prominent Libyan opposition leader; however, Libyan experts pointed out that the expelled diplomat was in charge of monitoring the acts of Libyan dissidents.[53]

In February 1996 the Clinton administration again accused Libya of constructing a chemical weapons plant at Tarhuna, some forty miles southeast of Tripoli. The Libyan government continued its refusal to sign the 1993 convention banning the use, development, and storage of chemical weapons; according to the CIA director, it was one of eighteen nations, including most of the countries in the Middle East, working on chemical weapons programs. U.S. Secretary of Defense William Perry later warned that Washington would not rule out military action to prevent the plant from becoming operational. In April, in a move that mirrored American requests to remand the two Libyans indicted in the Pan Am bombing, Qaddafi demanded that the United States surrender the pilots and planners involved in the 1986 air raids on Benghazi and Tripoli, insisting the United Nations take up the case. Coincidentally, the relatives of the victims of Pan Am Flight 103 filed a $10 billion lawsuit against Libya the same month.[54]

The U.S. House of Representatives in June 1996 passed controversial legislation intended to discourage new foreign investment in the Libyan and Iranian petroleum industries. Although Libya was not the main target of the U.S. move, industry executives and analysts said that the U.S. action would likely deter a number of international oil companies from making new investments in Libya. The legislation angered some of Washington's key European allies, who complained about the extraterritorial reach of the sanctions, maintaining the United States was imposing its foreign policy goals on them. When President Clinton signed the controversial bill into law in early August, the European Union rejected the legislation and vowed to fight it. The legislation required the U.S. president to impose sanctions on foreign companies that invested $40 million or more within a year in the energy sectors of Libya or Iran. Specifically, President Clinton was required by law to impose at least two sanctions from a list of six that included import-export bans, lending embargos from U.S. banks, denial of U.S. export financing, and a ban on U.S. procurement of goods and services from sanctioned companies. Members of the European Union, especially France, condemned the legislation on the grounds it established the unwelcome principle that one country could dictate the foreign policies of another.[55]

As the Clinton administration increased pressure on the Qaddafi regime, evidence accumulated that the negative impact of the sanctions was fanning discontent within Libya. Islamist militants clashed with regime forces on several occasions in 1995–96. A football riot in mid-July 1996 in which crowds shouted anti-Qaddafi slogans left up to fifty persons dead. One month later, Libyan opposition groups, not always a reliable source, reported the ambush of a military convoy in which more than two dozen people were killed. Qaddafi responded with renewed emphasis on revolutionary activity at home together with a crackdown on private business, in an apparent attempt to maintain what one observer termed a perpetual state of organized confusion. Even though Qaddafi later expanded efforts to contain internal dissent, reports of alleged assassination attempts surfaced regularly over the next few years.[56]

Qaddafi Resurgent

By 1997 the UN sanctions, were beginning to crack, with African leaders taking the lead in opposing them. In February the secretary general of the Organization of African Unity called for an end to the sanctions, on the grounds that African states felt Libya had taken several positive steps toward a resolution of the Lockerbie issue. In March the Vatican established full diplomatic relations with Libya in part to recognize what it termed recent "positive results" in Libya in the area of religious freedom. Later in the month, a Libyan Arab Airlines plane carrying Muslims on the annual pilgrimage landed in Saudi Arabia in defiance of UN sanctions. Meeting in Cairo in late September, the Arab League adopted a resolution that invited Arab countries to take measures to alleviate the sanctions on Libya until a just and peaceful solution to the issue could be found. In an explicit rejection of the sanctions, the resolution also called on Arab countries to authorize flights to Libya for humanitarian as well as religious reasons and invited them to lift the freeze on Libyan accounts in Arab banks with the exception of oil funds. South African President Nelson Mandela, an old friend of Qaddafi and the initial recipient in 1989 of the Qaddafi International Prize for Human Rights, visited Libya in October to thank Qaddafi for his support during the years of South African struggle against white minority rule. Although Mandela completed the last leg of his journey by car to avoid violating the UN sanctions, he called during his visit for a lifting of the sanctions and said that the Lockerbie case should be handled by an international tribunal, a view shared by the OAU and the Arab League. The presidents of Gambia, Liberia, Tanzania, and Uganda, among others, also visited Tripoli in this time frame.[57]

The International Court of Justice ruled in February 1998 that it would grant Libya a full hearing into its complaint that the United Kingdom and the United States were forcing Tripoli to surrender two suspects for trial in Scotland for the downing of Pan Am Flight 103. The Libyan government termed the ruling of the court, which rejected arguments by Britain and the United States that it did not have jurisdiction in the case, a clear victory for the Libyan people and for justice. In March a Libyan plane carrying 105 Libyan Muslims arrived in Saudi Arabia, again in clear violation of the UN ban on flights from Libya, and the Libyan news agency reported in April that two Italian planes had landed in Tripoli. In May the Clinton administration 1998 reached a deal with European leaders to ease U.S. restrictions on multinational companies doing business with Cuba, Iran, and Libya. And in July the UN sanctions committee temporarily lifted the air embargo to allow Egyptian President Mubarak to fly to Tripoli to inquire into the health of Qaddafi, who had reportedly been injured in an assassination attempt in June. Finally, in mid-July, the Department of State announced that Britain and the United States would consider the creation of a special court in the Netherlands to try the two Libyan suspects for the 1988 Pan Am bombing. This joint initiative represented a major compromise on the part of the Clinton administration since Qaddafi had been willing to accept its core component, trial in a third country, for several years.[58]

In August 1998 the Libyan government accepted the joint British-U.S. proposal to try the two Libyan suspects in the Lockerbie bombing case at The Hague under Scottish law. Two months later, the UN General Assembly adopted a Libyan-sponsored resolution, aimed at the United States, that called for the immediate repeal of laws that unilaterally imposed sanctions on companies and nationals of other countries. The vote was 80 in favor and only 2 (Israel and the United States) against, with 67 delegations abstaining, an unusually large number in a vote of this kind. In the interim, African delegations, including officials from Chad, Gambia, Nigeria, and the Sudan, visited Tripoli in violation of the UN ban. In the wake of intense diplomacy by representatives of Egypt, Saudi Arabia, and South Africa, together with UN Secretary General Kofi Annan, the Libyan government eventually handed over the two Lockerbie suspects on 5 April 1999. Once Libya had remanded the two suspects, the United Nations suspended its sanctions against Libya, allowing air travel and the sale of industrial equipment to resume.[59]

The complex rationale behind Qaddafi's decision to remand the Lockerbie suspects after resisting that action for seven years was not immediately clear, but it probably included the following considerations. As Mary-Jane Deeb has emphasized, by 1998 Qaddafi seemed to have the domestic political situation under control in Libya and was faced with a stagnant or deteriorating economic situation. Consequently, he no longer feared the domestic political repercussions of remanding the two suspects, on the one hand, and needed to open and invigorate the economy, on the other. A less tangible motive could well have been Qaddafi's love of the international limelight and his weariness with a prolonged period of political isolation. This logic helped explain the mid-1999 diplomatic offensive he unleashed in Africa. Strategically, as Ray Takeyh suggested, Qaddafi may also have been motivated by a desire to rebuild alliances in Africa and elsewhere to prevent Libya from being isolated in any potential future conflict with the United States. Finally, the opportunity to renew and enhance ideological and strategic ties with key African states clearly positioned Libya to pursue longer term objectives in the region.[60]

That said, an objective evaluation of the effectiveness of the UN sanctions on Libya suggests that the results were at best mixed. Even though Qaddafi eventually agreed to the extradition of the two Libyans accused of the Lockerbie bombing, the framework for the trial proposed by the United States and the United Kingdom was very similar to a proposal advocated by Libya as early as 1992. The Western powers also sought an end to Libyan support for international terrorism; however, the evidence suggests that Tripoli had largely, if not totally, ended such support at the end of the previous decade. As for broader issues related to the promotion of the conditions and values required for a more stable international environment, there is no evidence the UN sanctions had any impact on Libyan policy or behavior. The Qaddafi regime ended the decade in power with no noticeable improvement in its respect for human and democratic rights. Quite the contrary, central controls in Libya appeared to tighten at a time when deteriorating socioeconomic conditions increased the dependence of most Libyans on the state.[61]

Once the United Nations suspended its sanctions on Libya, Qaddafi moved quickly to end Libya's diplomatic and economic isolation. As a procession of African heads of state traveled to Libya to pay their respects, he unveiled a series of diplomatic initiatives designed to resolve disputes in the Congo, Horn of Africa, Sierra Leone, and the Sudan. Qaddafi brokered a cease-fire agreement between the presidents of the Congo and Uganda in April 1999 and later hosted a five-nation summit on the Congo. In the interim, he dispatched a controversial peacekeeping force to Uganda. In South Africa, he was welcomed in June 1999 as the last official guest of the Mandela administration and saluted by the South African president as "one of the revolutionary icons of our times." In the Horn of Africa, Eritrea and Ethiopia reportedly accepted a Libyan peace plan to end their border conflict; however, a final solution to the dispute here proved as elusive as in the Congo. Qaddafi also dispatched an envoy to the Sierra Leone peace talks in Togo and met with government and opposition leaders in Sudan in an effort to end the civil war there. Although there was little sign that any of these diplomatic initiatives would yield practical results, Qaddafi clearly sought to take advantage of the sympathetic response he received from African governments when the UN sanctions were in place to play a wider role in regional issues.[62]

The new initiatives in Africa were part of a major shift in Libyan foreign policy from the Arab world to Africa, a shift rooted in part, according to Libyan diplomats, in the reluctance of Arab leaders to support Libya in its conflict with the United States and the United Kingdom over the Lockerbie issue. In what became a motif of the new diplomacy, Qaddafi repeatedly proclaimed that the future was for big spaces, and that Libya was part of the African space. Qaddafi attended the OAU summit in Algeria in July 1999, where he was feted as a long-lost brother by fellow African heads of state. Reviving his vision of African unity, he called at the meeting for creation of a Pan African Congress to boost unity and an Integration Bank to push forward the process for implementation of a treaty for the Economic Community of Africa. He also invited African leaders to attend an extraordinary OAU summit in Tripoli, timed to coincide with the thirtieth anniversary of the September 1969 revolution, to discuss ways to restructure the OAU charter to strengthen relations among member states. In turn, the summit in Algiers called for the complete and immediate lifting of all sanctions against Libya.[63]

Before the September meeting in Libya, most African diplomats voiced caution and emphasized that their leaders had agreed to attend out of respect for a veteran revolutionary whose steadfast support of liberation movements had helped end colonialism on the continent. Few expected concrete actions to emerge from the meeting. In advance of the extraordinary summit, Qaddafi called for creation of a United States of Africa, and he pressed the issue in his address to the conference of foreign ministers that met in advance of the summit. African leaders later fell well short of endorsing his call for a United States of Africa, but they did agree to create a Pan-African Parliament in 2000 and an African Union as early as 2001. The Union was to be based on the OAU charter and the 1991 Abuja Treaty, which had called for creation of an African Economic Community together with related financial institutions by 2025. Qaddafi later reiterated his call for African unity at the EU-Africa summit in Cairo in April 2000.[64]

Clinton Administration Holds Firm

Representatives of the United Kingdom and United States met with the Libyan ambassador to the United Nations in June 1999, the first official meeting of American and Libyan diplomats in eighteen years. When the Libyan diplomat pressed for a permanent lifting of the UN Security Council sanctions as opposed to a temporary suspension, the U.S. representative opposed the move on the grounds that the Lockerbie trial had not yet begun. In the meeting, the U.S. diplomat reportedly outlined tough conditions for American support for a permanent lifting of the Security Council sanctions. The conditions included an end to Libyan support for terrorism, payment of appropriate compensation to the families of Pan Am

Flight 103 victims, acknowledgment of Libyan responsibility for the actions of its officials, and cooperation with the investigation and trial. A few days later, the U.S. Supreme Court, without comment or dissent, rejected an appeal by Libya which argued that the relatives of the victims of the Pam Am 103 bombing could not sue Libya in federal court because U.S. courts lacked jurisdiction in the case. The Clinton administration later announced it would not follow Britain's example, when the latter announced resumption of full diplomatic relations with Libya, and threatened to veto any attempt to lift permanently the UN sanctions against Libya.[65]

Deputy Assistant Secretary of State for Near East and South Asian Affairs Ronald E. Neumann detailed the administration's position in testimony to the House subcommittee on Africa on 22 July 1999. After describing Libya as an area of the world where "patience and our diplomatic initiatives have brought a significant success," he recognized that "sanctions fatigue" had set in and was making it increasingly difficult for the United States to maintain, let alone expand, the existing sanctions regime. Neumann then detailed the difficult negotiations that led Libya to remand the two suspects and the United Nations to suspend its sanctions. In so doing, he emphasized that UN Secretary General Annan was called upon to report to the Security Council members, within ninety days of the suspension, on Libyan compliance with the remaining Security Council requirements as outlined in three separate resolutions. These now familiar requirements called on Libya to renounce and end all support for terrorist activities, acknowledge responsibility for the actions of its officials, cooperate with the trial, and pay appropriate compensation. As a practical matter, Neumann pointed out that no one could be sure that Libya was cooperating fully with the trial until such time as the proceedings were substantially underway. When the secretary general made his report to the Security Council on 30 June 1999, the Council responded with a statement that welcomed the positive signs from Libya, but confirmed the Libyan government had not complied fully with all the necessary requirements and that the sanctions would not be lifted permanently until it had done so. Neumann concluded his statement to the House subcommittee on Africa with a challenge to the Qaddafi regime:

We acknowledge Libya's recent declarations of its intention to turn over a new page, but, given its history, such statements are not enough. Positive actions are essential if Libya is to be re-integrated into the international community, beginning with full cooperation in the Pan Am 103 trial, and full compliance with the remaining UNSC [United Nations Security Council] requirements. We recognize that Libya has publicly declared its intention to play an active, constructive role in regional conflicts. It will be important to test that this rhetoric is supported by constructive and consistent actions. . . .

We expect Libya to fulfill all of the UNSC requirements. . . . Only when Libya has complied fully will we be able to consider lifting U.S. sanctions against Libya. Right now, such steps would be premature. At the same time it is important to make clear that we have no hidden agenda. We have given Libya clear, specific benchmarks that it must meet if it is to become a responsible and constructive member of the international community. We have set goals Libya can meet if it has the will to do so.[66]

U.S. policy toward Libya for the remainder of the year was an intricate mixture of carrot and stick. In mid-July the Clinton administration, under heavy pressure from the U.S. agriculture industry to boost exports to offset a depressed domestic market, modified its sanctions regime against Libya, as well as Iran and the Sudan, to allow the sale of food, medicine, and medical equipment to the three states. Responding positively to the U.S. initiative, the Libyan government four months later made its first purchase of U.S. wheat in more than fifteen years. The Clinton administration in late July approved a request from Occidental Petroleum to visit Libya to inspect assets the company had earlier been forced to abandon and subsequently entertained similar requests from the Marathon Group, Conoco Inc., and Amerada Hess Corp. Conoco completed its inspection of oilfields and production facilities in December 1999. On the other hand, Washington renewed a ban on the use of U.S. passports for travel to Libya and forcibly reiterated its intent not to follow the British lead in reestablishing diplomatic relations with Libya. The Clinton administration also intervened to block the sale of twenty-four airplanes to Libya by the European consortium Airbus on the grounds some of the engine parts and electronic equipment were U.S.-supplied and their sale would violate the provisions of the 1996 Iran-Libya Sanctions Act.[67]

At the same time, the Qaddafi regime continued to expand its commercial and diplomatic ties inside and outside the region. The European Union announced in mid-September 1999 that it was lifting its sanctions against Libya to reward signs that the latter had renounced terrorism, although, much to Libya's dismay, leaving in force an arms embargo. A large UK trade mission visited Libya in early October; and in mid-December Britain's first ambassador to Libya in fifteen years arrived in Tripoli. In early December Italian Prime Minister Massimo D'Alema 1999 became the first Western head of state to visit Libya in eight years. The Italian government in recent times had increasingly assumed the role of European interlocutor with isolated or rogue states, and its foreign minister had visited Tripoli the day after the United Nations suspended sanctions in April. At the time, Qaddafi was quoted as saying that "Libya will become Italy's bridge to Africa and Italy will be for Libya its door into Europe."[68]

D'Alema and Qaddafi, in the course of the Italian prime minister's visit to Libya, issued a joint statement that strongly denounced terrorism but said that the United States should take the next step in improving ties.

When the Department of State responded to the joint statement with an indication that it would continue to monitor the Libyan government's policy toward terrorism, the Qaddafi regime rejected any monitoring of its behavior by the United States or any other government. Boosting Italy's trade relationship with Libya, the Italian prime minister reportedly argued that it was important for Italy to have a dialogue with a country like Libya that was on the way to returning fully to the international community. At the same time, D'Alema ruled out a visit by Qaddafi to Rome in the near future, an event that many observers expected would follow his visit to Tripoli, on the grounds that a Qaddafi visit to Rome would have to wait until the Lockerbie trial had ended and the UN sanctions were permanently lifted. Even as the Qaddafi regime emerged from an extended period of international isolation, a variety of human rights groups continued to condemn the oppressive political climate in Libya, detailing reports of torture and summary executions and calling for the release of prisoners of conscience as well as political prisoners.[69]

The Clinton administration announced toward the end of 1999 that it was continuing the sanctions in place, on the grounds that the crisis with Libya had not yet been fully resolved. The logic behind the U.S. decision was contained in an address by Deputy Assistant Secretary Neumann to the Middle East Institute on 30 November 1999:

In consulting with other nations, we have acknowledged the positive steps that Libya has taken and some of the changes in Libya's public posture. But the picture of Libya's current actions is only slowly coming into focus, and our understanding of Libyan intentions or how the Libyan government sees itself in the world remains quite unclear. [70]

Neumann did acknowledge that Libyan support for terrorism had declined. In support of this observation, he cited the expulsion of the Abu Nidal organization from Libya together with associated steps taken by the Libyan government, including new visa restrictions, to prevent terrorists from entering Libya or using Libyan territories as a safe haven. He also welcomed the transfer of Libyan support from the Palestinian rejectionists to the Palestinian Authority and Chairman Arafat, viewing it as a strong signal of Libyan support for the peace process. On the other hand, Neumann expressed concern that the inflammatory rhetoric from the Libyan leadership remained unchanged which raised questions as to their real intentions. Drawing what he termed a "mixed picture," Neumann concluded as follows:

The chief, current goal of the U.S. government with respect to Libya is full compliance with the remaining U.N. Security Council requirements. These requirements are payment of appropriate compensation, cooperation with the Pan Am 103 investigation and trial, acceptance of responsibility for the actions of its officials, and a renunciation and end to support of terrorism and terrorist groups.

If Libya complies fully with all these requirements, it will have met the demands of the Security Council. We have said consistently that Libya can and should comply with these requirements. . . . Any consideration of lifting U.S. sanctions before Libya has complied fully with international demands would be premature.

While U.S. sanctions were imposed because of concerns about Libyan support for terrorism, there have been other sources of contention in U.S.-Libya relations over the past three decades, including Libyan efforts to obtain missiles and weapons of mass destruction (WMD). . . . We continue to want Libya to find a way to address these concerns. . . .

That said, Libya is not Iraq. We do not seek to maintain sanctions until there is a change of regime in Tripoli. We have seen definite changes in Libya's behavior, specifically declining support for terrorism and increasing support for peace processes in the Middle East and Africa. We hope such changes signal Libya's willingness to behave as a responsible member of the international community.

The new millennium opened with fresh allegations that the Libyan government was continuing efforts to develop ballistic missile capability to deliver biological or chemical weapons outside North Africa. The evidence concerned thirty-two cases of parts for SCUD missiles, a weapon capable of hitting targets in Europe from Libya. The SCUD components, discovered on a British Airways flight at Gatwick airport in transit to Tripoli via Malta in the course of a joint search by customs and intelligence officers, were allegedly sent to Britain from Taiwan in the name of a knitwear company. Paperwork with the parts suggested that earlier shipments from Taiwan had traveled through Britain undetected and arrived safely in Libya. Widely viewed as an embarrassment to both countries, any attempted export of missile technology to Libya was clearly illegal as it breached the European Union arms embargo and violated an international treaty preventing the proliferation of ballistic missiles. The British government protested as "unacceptable" the use of a London airport as a staging post to smuggle missile parts to Libya in defiance of the EU arms embargo. In response, the Qaddafi regime denied it was trying to import banned long-range missile components. The Spanish newspaper *El Pais* later reported that Libya was also attempting to purchase ballistic missiles from North Korea.[71]

American-Libyan Relations Slowly Improve

After the Libyan government agreed to remand the two suspects in the Pan Am 103 bombing, reports persisted throughout much of 1999 that UN officials, as part of the deal, had promised Qaddafi that senior officials in the Libyan government would be immune from prosecution in the Lockerbie bombing case. In late December the chairman of the House International Relations Committee, for the third time, sought assurances from Secretary of State Albright that UN Secretary General Annan had not given Qaddafi assurances that Lockerbie prosecutors would not attempt to undermine the Libyan government. The issue concerned a letter and annex that Annan had sent to Qaddafi in February 1999, the contents of which were not immediately made public, that led Libya eventually to turn over the suspects in April. Secretary Albright responded in mid-February 2000, with a statement denying that the letter contained "any external or negotiated limits to the authority" of Scottish prosecutors; however, she refused to release the letter on the grounds it was private UN correspondence that had subsequently been classified by the Clinton administration. Under mounting pressure, Secretary General Annan eventually released copies of the letter and the annex in late August 2000. In the correspondence, Annan assured Qaddafi that the trial would not be used to undermine the regime, but he also made it clear that normal prosecutorial procedures would be followed.[72]

Throughout spring 2000, the U.S. government emitted a number of policy signals that collectively suggested that it was no longer actively opposing Qaddafi's reentry into the international community and might even be willing to work more closely with Libya in the future. Deputy Assistant Secretary Neumann was quoted in late January as saying that change in regard to U.S. policy toward Libya could now be imagined. One month later, Washington elected not to block Libyan participation in a UN mission to the Democratic Republic of the Congo, the first time in a decade that Libya had joined in an international peacekeeping effort. In March the Department of State dispatched four consular officials to Libya on a lightning tour to assess travel safety for Americans. This decision was announced only three weeks after Department of State press spokesperson James Rubin had emphasized that the passport restriction extended at the end of 1999 was not intended to be a sanction but rather was based on a judgment about security. Assessment of travel safety to Libya for Americans thus appeared to be a necessary first step in the potential lifting of the travel ban. Following the return of U.S. officials, a mission that marked the first announced official U.S. visit to Libya since diplomatic relations were broken in the early 1980s, Secretary Albright said she would be inclined to lift the travel ban on Libya if the safety assessment team recommended the action. The decision to investigate travel safety in Libya generated considerable criticism in Congress and elsewhere; therefore it came as no surprise that months passed with no decision announced.[73]

Even as relations between Libya and the United States seemed to improve, Qaddafi took a number of actions that raised questions as to the direction and intent of Libyan domestic and foreign policy. In early March

2000 the General People's Congress announced yet another major reorganization of the Libyan government that abolished people's committees and transferred their functions to provincial organizations. The energy ministry was one of twelve ministries to be scrapped; and in a surprise move that followed more than two decades of devolution, Qaddafi declared that Libya must have a head of state. Billed as a new step in the popular revolution, most observers agreed that the reorganizations were intended to tighten Qaddafi's grip on power. The Libyan leader then jolted a summit of African and European leaders in Cairo in early April with an anti-Western tirade that embarrassed European Commission President Romano Prodi, who had just praised Qaddafi's newfound moderation. A London-based Islamist group charged in the same week that the Qaddafi regime had recently executed three Islamic militants extradited from Jordan. Later in April, Swiss authorities arrested a man in Zurich airport carrying SCUD missile parts from Taiwan to Libya. The director of the U.S. National Security Agency disclosed at about the same time that the People's Republic of China was also transferring long-range missile technology to Libya. Taken together, this collection of erratic events left many observers in and outside the Clinton administration wondering, as one reporter put it, whether Qaddafi was ready to act civilized. Reflecting such thinking, the Senate on 28 April 2000 passed a nonbinding resolution asking the Clinton administration not to lift the ban on travel to Libya until the end of the Lockerbie trial at the earliest.[74]

Lockerbie Trial

The Lockerbie trial finally opened at Camp Zeist, a former U.S. air base in the Netherlands, on 3 May 2000, almost twelve years after a bomb downed Pan Am Flight 103 and killed 270 people. Scottish prosecutors charged the two Libyans on trial, Abdel Basset Ali al-Megrahi and Al-Amin Khalifa Fhimah, with the murder of 270 people in an alleged conspiracy traced back to 1985. The accused faced three alternative charges—conspiracy to murder, murder, and contravention of the 1982 Aviation Security Act. A common feature of the three charges was that the accused were charged with acting in concert together and with unnamed others. If it was shown in the proceedings that more than one person acted in concert, it then became unnecessary to identify which individual carried out the specific unlawful act or omission, provided it was shown they were acting in concert and that the unlawful act or omission was carried out by one of the group.[75]

Under the conspiracy to murder charge, the accused were alleged to have conspired with others to destroy a civil passenger aircraft and to murder its occupants to further the purposes of the Libyan intelligence services by criminal means, namely the use of explosive devices in the commission of acts of terrorism. In addition to the 259 people on the aircraft, the charge included the eleven Lockerbie residents killed when the jumbo jet crashed on the town. In contrast, the murder charge referred to the completed crime, not merely involvement in a conspiracy to commit murder, and required a higher degree of evidence for conviction. Possible reasons for including both the charge of conspiracy and the completed crime were to allow the evidence of conspiracy to be brought forward and to provide a safeguard in the event that the completed crime could not be proven beyond reasonable doubt. To prove murder, prosecutors were required to demonstrate a physical link between the accused and the explosion and to prove that the accused actually caused the death of the 270 victims. The third alternative, contravention of the 1982 Aviation Security Act, Section 2 (1) and (5), involved the intentional destruction of an aircraft in service, damaging the aircraft so badly that it could not fly or was no longer safe, or committing an act of violence on board an aircraft likely to endanger its safety. The accused could be convicted of only one of the three alternative charges; while punishment for conspiracy to murder was discretionary, the other two charges carried mandatory life sentences.[76]

The accused, who pleaded "not guilty" before the trial began, were alleged by the prosecution to have been members of the Libyan intelligence services who used false identities and fake passports to establish a fake tour business as a cover for obtaining some twenty electronic bomb timers in Switzerland in 1985. One-time employees of Libyan Arab Airlines, the accused allegedly later placed a Semtex bomb, built into a Toshiba RT SF 16 "Bombeat" radio-cassette recorder and activated by one of the electronic timers, in a suitcase stuffed with clothes purchased at a Maltese shop called Mary's House. Programmed to detonate aboard Pan Am Flight 103, the suitcase with the bomb was purportedly placed on an Air Malta flight to Frankfurt, where it was transferred to the Pan Am flight destined for New York with an intervening stop at Heathrow Airport in London. The indictment detailed trips, addresses, hotels, and events in Czechoslovakia, Germany, Libya, Malta, Senegal, and Switzerland. It alleged that the bomb timers had been supplied by a Swiss firm, Mebo Telecommunications, and tested at a special forces training camp at Sabha in the Libyan desert. Beyond suggesting the bombing was intended to further the purposes of the Libyan intelligence services, the indictment made no reference as to a precise motive for the attack on Pan Am Flight 103.[77]

A total of three verdicts were competent in the Lockerbie case under Scottish criminal procedure. In addition to a decision of "guilty" or "not guilty," judges could return a verdict of "not proven" if they believed that the accused were guilty but the evidence was insufficient to convict. An oddity of Scottish law, a verdict of "not proven" was the equivalent of an acquittal and required the accused to be set free. It thus proved ironic that the governments of the United States and the United Kingdom, by insisting on a trial under U.S. or Scottish law, eventually placed themselves in a system of justice that demanded a higher burden of proof than if the trial had been held at the International Court of Justice at the Hague as the Qaddafi regime had proposed. Decisions in criminal cases in Scotland are decided by a majority, and the rules governing the Lockerbie case specifically stated that all decisions, including the verdict, were to be taken by at least two of the three judges.[78]

As the Lockerbie trial opened, Qaddafi launched a well-coordinated campaign to distance himself from the proceedings. In an interview with Sky Television just hours before the start of the trial, Qaddafi dismissed as "absurd" any suggestion that the two Libyans on trial were acting under his direct orders. Emphasizing that he had held no administrative or political responsibility in Libya since 1977 when he handed over all authority to the Libyan people, he said that the court in the Netherlands would try only the two Libyan defendants and that the accused would bear individual responsibility for the bombing if found guilty. Describing the issue as a legal as opposed to a political one, he stressed that he would not accept further investigations into the bombing in Libya even if the suspects were found guilty.[79]

Qaddafi repeatedly argued over the next few weeks that Libya had modified its policies in the post-Cold War world; and he encouraged the Clinton administration to follow suit. In the colorful language so often characteristic of the Libyan leader, he encouraged the U.S. government, in an interview published in *USA Today*, to stop "chewing its cud and thinking about the past." Although he occasionally lapsed into old complaints about "Zionism" and "American imperialism," Qaddafi's remarks were generally upbeat and optimistic during the interview, as he emphasized the challenges and opportunities of globalization and the younger generation taking charge around the world. The previous week, U.S. sanctions had prevented American oil companies from participating in a meeting of some forty international oil companies, hosted by the Libyan National Oil Corporation to discuss new oil exploration and production sharing agreements in Libya. In drawing attention to the importance of the Libyan market in the post-sanctions era, the Qaddafi regime appeared to be attempting to marginalize the Lockerbie trial through the lure of new oil blocks and first gas exports. In a subsequent interview at the end of May, Qaddafi accused the United States of cruise missile diplomacy and dismissed the Pan Am Flight 103 bombing as something of the past.[80]

After a twelve-year investigation and eighty-four days of trial, the three Scottish judges sitting in the special court at Camp Zeist found only one of the two Libyan defendants guilty of murder in the bombing of Pan Am Flight 103. Abdel Basset Ali al-Megrahi, a Libyan intelligence agent, was found guilty, but Al-Amin Khalifa Fhimah, a former airline manager, was freed. In an eighty-two-page written decision, the three judges admitted that the case of the prosecution contained "uncertainties and qualifications," but concluded unanimously that there was "nothing in the evidence that left" them "with any reasonable doubt as to the guilt" of al-Megrahi. The American and British governments welcomed the verdict but said that sanctions against Libya would only be lifted when Tripoli abided by outstanding UN resolutions. The Libyan government, which quickly expressed its dismay with the verdict, tried to walk a fine line between saying it respected the court deliberations and distancing itself from a twelve-year issue it hoped the case would close. The Libyan ambassador to the United Nations, for example, commented that his government respected the verdict but denied any involvement in the bombing.[81]

From Rogue State to State of Concern

As President Clinton neared the end of his second term, the policy of his administration toward Libya appeared poised for major change, yet the future direction of that policy remained unclear. In the 1999 annual "Patterns of Global Terrorism" report, issued on 1 May 2000, the Qaddafi regime received a decidedly mixed assessment:

In April 1999, Libya took an important step by surrendering for trial the two Libyans accused of bombing Pan Am flight 103 over Lockerbie, Scotland in 1988. . . . At yearend, however, Libya still had not complied with the remaining UN Security Council requirements. . . . Libyan leader Qadhafi repeatedly stated publicly during the year that his government had adopted an antiterrorism stance, but it remained unclear whether his claims of distancing Libya from its terrorist past signified a true change in policy.

Libya also remained the primary suspect in several other past terrorist operations, including the La Belle discotheque bombing in Berlin in 1986 that killed two US servicemen and one Turkish civilian and wounded more than 200 persons. The trial in Germany of five suspects in the bombing, which began in November 1997, continued in 1999.

In 1999, Libya expelled the Abu Nidal organization and distanced itself from the Palestinian rejectionists, announcing that the Palestinian Authority was the only legitimate address for Palestinian concerns. Libya still may have retained ties to some Palestinian groups that use violence to oppose the Middle East peace process, however, including the PIJ [Palestinian Islamic Jihad] and the PFLP-GC [Popular Front for the Liberation of Palestine-General Command].[82]

In responding to questions about the report, Ambassador Mike Sheehan, the Department of State counterterrorism coordinator, discussed what the Libyan government needed to do to improve its record:

The key issue for Libya is the trial of Pan Am 103, which the Secretary [Madeleine K. Albright] said starts this week. There were UN resolutions put on Libya in 1992 regarding the bombing of Pan Am 103, and Libya, in fact, is not in compliance with two of those aspects of that resolution: first, to cooperate throughout the extent of the trial—and since it hasn't started it would be impossible to gauge their full cooperation in that trial, a trial that should have started a long, long time ago for an event that happened December 21st of 1988; and, secondly, for full compensation of the families. So Libya will remain on the list. Libya must comply with the UN Security Council resolutions. If and when they do, we'll then look at that issue and then we'll look at other issues in the future.

But clearly—let me just say this about Libya. I believe that the political pressure and the sanctions that were associated with the UN resolution since '92 have helped drive Libya out of the counter-terrorism business. Although, if you read the report, they do not get a clear—there are some issues remaining—their links to terrorism have dramatically declined since the 1980s.[83]

Observers noted that Ambassador Sheehan was careful not to suggest that Libyan compliance with the UN Security Council resolutions in itself would necessarily be sufficient to remove them from the State Department's list of state sponsors of terrorism. In answering a question later in the press conference, he expanded and clarified the administration's position on this point: "For Libya right now, the road map that I will get into at this point is complying with the UN Security Council resolutions. Beyond that, we will think about road maps after that. But for right now on Libya, we are focusing on those Security Council resolutions."[84]

Shortly thereafter, Deputy Assistant Secretary Neumann outlined the core elements of U.S. policy toward Libya in a detailed statement on 4 May 2000 to the Senate Foreign Relations Subcommittee for Near Eastern and South Asian Affairs. Describing U.S. policy toward Libya as a continuing story whose ending was not yet clear, Neumann began by emphasizing that U.S. policy goals vis-à-vis Libya had remained consistent throughout the last three presidential administrations. Those goals consisted of ending Libyan support for terrorism, together with preventing Tripoli's ability to obtain weapons of mass destruction; containing Qaddafi's regional ambitions; and ending Libyan opposition to the Middle East peace process. In the wake of the bombing of Pan Am Flight 103, a fourth policy goal was added: to bring to justice those persons responsible for the Lockerbie disaster. Acknowledging that Libya had reduced its support for terrorism and sought to distance itself from terrorist groups, Neumann added that more needed to be done:

On our key concerns—terrorism, opposition to Middle East peace, and regional intervention—Libya no longer poses the threat it once did. On WMD [weapons of mass   destruction] and missiles, our efforts to impede Libya's programs have had substantial success. That said, we must continue to watch Libya closely and will maintain pressure until all of these concerns are fully addressed. Our goal continues to be to deter Libyan policies of concern. An improved bilateral relationship is not, in itself, an end. We will oppose lifting UN sanctions against Libya until we are satisfied that Libya has met all the relevant UN Security Council requirements. The provisions of the Iran and Libya Sanctions Act regarding investment in Libya's petroleum sector will continue to be considered until, as the statute prescribes, the President has determined and certified to Congress that the UNSCR requirements have been met. Also until that time, we expect to maintain core unilateral economic sanctions prohibiting U.S.-Libyan business.[85]

Although Neumann's statement contained nothing new in terms of American policy toward Libya, it was increasingly clear by mid-2000 that the Rogue Doctrine was no longer in vogue in the Clinton administration. After years of directing suspicion and sanctions at so-called rogue states, Secretary of State Albright declared on 19 June 2000 that in effect such states no longer existed. The entities once know as rogue nations had now become "states of concern." The shift in official nomenclature, according to Secretary Albright, signaled an important change in the administration's approach to the unofficial gallery of nations that included Libya. In depicting an evolution in the behavior of states formerly designated as rogue, the Clinton administration adopted the concept of states of concern in the belief that internal reforms might be advanced through the application of a more nuanced vocabulary. The Libyan decision to turn over to the United Nations the two suspects in the Pan Am bombing case was cited by American officials as one example of the new willingness of states formerly designated as rogue to address issues of primary concern to the U.S. government. The Qaddafi regime welcomed the decision in Washington to cease classifying Libya as a rogue state, describing the move as a rational one which symbolized the return of the United States to more just criteria.[86]

In actuality, a number of factors contributed to the decline in popularity of the Rogue Doctrine. First of all, the nations loosely grouped as rogue states for more than a decade had little in common in terms of geographic area, ideology, military capability, or population. While many of them possessed weapons of mass destruction or appeared to be developing them, the available evidence seemed stretched in some cases, including that of Libya. Application of the doctrine relied largely on policies of isolation and punishment of the offending rogue states, policies that proved difficult both to enact and to maintain effectively. The use of unilateral sanctions by the U.S. government to obtain its objectives was checkered at best over the past decade. And multilateral sanctions depended on the ability of Washington to persuade its allies around the world to take diplomatic and economic actions that were often unpopular with their own domestic and international constituencies.[87]

Sanctions and Terrorism

One of the last official acts of the Clinton administration was to notify Congress that it was continuing the state of emergency with Libya declared in January 1986. Citing ongoing concern for Libyan support for terrorism and its noncompliance with UN Security Council Resolutions 731, 748, and 883, President Clinton declared it "necessary to maintain in force the actions taken and currently in effect to apply economic pressure" on the Libyan government. In turn, the George W. Bush administration, after less than two weeks in office, indicated that it intended to move cautiously toward any relaxation of economic sanctions. Under pressure from the relatives of the Lockerbie victims, the new administration stated that Libya must accept responsibility for the bombing of Pan Am Flight 103 and also indicated that the United States would not halt efforts to convict any others who played a part in the operation. In a ceremony welcoming home Al-Amin Khalifa Fhimah, the released defendant in the Lockerbie case, Qaddafi later rejected calls for compensation and railed against the U.S. government and its policies in the Middle East.[88]

In late February 2001, the White House issued a joint statement in which President Bush and British Prime Minister Tony Blair called on Libya to comply with all relevant UN Security Council resolutions. Representatives of both governments later held talks with the Libyan envoy at the United Nations aimed at spelling out what steps Libya should take to end UN sanctions. In exploratory discussions, London and Washington boiled down a series of Security Council resolutions into two core demands—acceptance by Libya of responsibility for the Lockerbie bombing and payment of appropriate compensation to the victims of the families—that had to be satisfied before sanctions would be lifted. Pan Am Flight 103-related discussions between American, British, and Libyan representatives continued throughout the year. When the Canadian government announced its intent to reestablish diplomatic relations with Libya, the White House in July stated that it saw nothing negative in the decision and welcomed having an ally like Canada represented in Libya.[89]

Even though President Bush had emphasized that he had no intention of easing sanctions on Libya, a White House energy policy plan unveiled in May 2001 recommended a review of current unilateral sanctions and their impact on energy policy. A major issue in this regard was the 1996 Iran-Libya Sanctions Act (ILSA), which was up for renewal in August 2001. The White House favored a renewal of ILSA for two years only, on the grounds it would give the administration more flexibility in dealing with Iran and Libya, but Congress voted overwhelmingly for a five-year extension, arguing the shorter extension would send the wrong message. Lawmakers contended that any move to limit the sanctions would signal a lack of resolve by the United States to combat terrorism and the states suspected of supporting it. The House version of the act, which passed by a 409–6 vote, offered a small concession to the administration in that it provided for a review of the law after two years. Both the House and Senate bills imposed tougher sanctions on Libya. Where the existing law was directed at companies that invested more than $40 million annually in Libyan energy production, the new bills reduced the limit to $20 million, the same limit in place for Iran.[90]

ILSA had long been opposed by America's allies in Europe as well as by American oil companies. Extension of the sanctions, on the other hand, was strongly supported by the American Israel Public Affairs Committee and many relatives of victims of the Pan Am Flight 103 bombing, who accused the Bush administration of hypocrisy. Many observers saw the decision to extend sanctions on Libya and Iran as a setback for the Bush administration, which had launched a review of U.S. sanctions policies as one of its first initiatives after taking office. Administration officials argued that sanctions were too often ineffective and needlessly hurt U.S. companies. A Libyan spokesperson termed the ILSA renewal a "cause for dismay and condemnation" and attributed it to "illusions created by Zionist propaganda."[91]

Qaddafi swiftly condemned the 11 September terrorist attacks on the World Trade Center and the Pentagon, expressing sympathy with the many innocent victims. "Despite political differences and conflicts with America, this should not become a psychological barrier against offering assistance and humanitarian aid to U.S. citizens and all people in America, who suffered most from these horrific attacks." In a televised address later in the month, the Libyan leader stated publicly that the United States had a right to take revenge for the terrorist attacks on New York and Washington. Qaddafi also condemned the use of anthrax in the United States, terming it "the worst form of terrorism" and calling for international action to tackle a "very dangerous situation."[92]

Conclusions

Soon after its inauguration on 20 January 1989, the George Bush administration initiated work on an interim security policy intended to continue U.S. defense spending at approximately Cold War levels until such time as a more credible threat surfaced. The product of this initiative, the so-called Rogue Doctrine, argued that regional conflict would shape the new world order in the foreseeable future. To respond to this threat, the doctrine called for the maintenance by the United States of a military force capable of reacting simultaneously to regional contingencies in two different parts of the world. The Iraqi invasion of Kuwait occurred, by coincidence, at precisely the moment the Bush administration was beginning to sell the wisdom and viability of the new doctrine to the American people. The brutality of Saddam Hussein's violation of Kuwait was a great help in marketing the Rogue Doctrine, which was soon widely accepted in the United States with little dialogue or dissent.

At the same time, the Iraqi invasion of Kuwait served to stifle discussion of a possible peace dividend in the form of reduced military spending arising from the fall of the Berlin Wall and the implosion of the Soviet Union. The prevailing circumstances also worked to restrain serious dialogue and analysis of the Rogue Doctrine as a meaningful policy statement. Consequently, little consensus developed as to what constituted a rogue state or what actions were necessarily appropriate and effective when one was encountered. The governments of Iran, Iraq, Libya, and North Korea were most commonly associated with the doctrine; however, they shared very little in the way of background, goals, or ideology. This was clearly demonstrated in their inability to work together or for most of them to work in concert with any other state for any appreciable period of time.

Conceived as an interim measure, the Rogue Doctrine defined American security policy as well as American policy toward the rogue states, especially Libya, for the remainder of the decade. After a cursory review of U.S. defense policy, the Clinton administration wholeheartedly embraced the core elements of the Rogue Doctrine to the extent that the transition of American policy toward Libya from Bush to Clinton was virtually seamless. In regard to Libya, the central concerns of policy makers in Washington for most of the decade were terrorism, opposition to Middle East peace, and regional intervention. These were the same issues that had troubled the Reagan administration as well as earlier American governments. American concern with the potential Libyan development of biological and chemical weapons, together with the ballistic missile systems required to deliver them, was a manifestation of these broader policy issues. The Lockerbie disaster later added a fourth issue to the bag of concerns that determined U.S. policy toward Libya after the mid-1970s. While often treated as a separate question, the Lockerbie issue did not exist as an isolated event but rather was a manifestation of the three central concerns of American policy.

Beginning with the Reagan administration, unilateral sanctions were a key element in the American response to Libyan foreign policy. The first Bush administration pushed for multilateral sanctions after unilateral sanctions proved ineffective, and the Clinton administration later continued the policy of multilateral sanctions as a tactical weapon to substantiate and enforce the Rogue Doctrine. While the Clinton administration hyped multilateral sanctions as an effective means to change the behavior of the Qaddafi regime, declining support for them after 1997–98, coupled with the considerations detailed earlier that compelled the Libyan leader to remand the Lockerbie suspects, suggested that multilateral sanctions were no more effective than their unilateral counterparts. On the contrary, one of the lessons to be learned from the application of UN sanctions against Libya was the difficulty in sustaining Third World support for such actions against a Third World country for any appreciable period of time. The second Bush administration displayed more flexibility on the sanctions issue, but Congress thwarted any substantial change in U.S. policy.

The Qaddafi regime, on the other hand, was guilty of totally misreading the American political scene after 1988. The Libyan leader saw windows of opportunity for improved relations with the United States where none existed. And he believed there was a constituency in America interested in improved relations with Libya where none existed in either the Democratic or Republican parties. On the contrary, the utility of the Rogue Doctrine as a means to justify military spending at something close to Cold War levels was contingent upon maintaining the viability of Libya and other rogue states as credible threats to American and global security. Any form of American rapprochement with Libya thus threatened to undermine the new, post-Cold War security doctrine embraced in the 1990s by the Bush and Clinton administrations. In this milieu, the erratic, often irrational, character of many of Qaddafi's domestic and foreign policies only played into the hands of those American policy makers reluctant to chart a new course toward Libya.

Notes

Chapter 1. Dismal Record

1. Benjamin Rivlin, "Unity and Nationalism in Libya," *Middle East Journal* 3, 1 (January 1949): 31–44, quote 37.

2. Louis Dupree, "The Non-Arab Ethnic Groups of Libya," *Middle East Journal* 12, 1 (Winter 1958): 33–44, quote 44.

3. George P. Schultz, *Turmoil and Triumph: My Years as Secretary of State* (New York: Scribner's, 1993), 677.

Chapter 2. Desert Kingdom

1. Ronald Bruce St John, "The Determinants of Libyan Foreign Policy, 1969–1983," *Maghreb Review* 8, 3–4 (May-August 1983): 96–103; Nathan Alexander [Ronald Bruce St John], "The Foreign Policy of Libya: Inflexibility amid Change," *Orbis* 24, 4 (Winter 1981): 819–46.

2. Ali Muhammad Shembesh, "The Analysis of Libya's Foreign Policy, 1962–1973: A Study of the Impact of Environmental and Leadership Factors," Ph.D. dissertation, Emory University, 1975, 56–60.

3. Gus H. Goudarzi, *Geology and Mineral Resources of Libya—A Reconnaissance*, Geological Survey Professional Paper 660 (Washington, D.C.: U.S. Government Printing Office, 1970), 2–18.

4. Majid Khadduri, *Modern Libya: A Study in Political Development* (Baltimore: Johns Hopkins University Press, 1963), 111–40; John Wright, *Libya, Chad and the Central Sahara* (London: Hurst, 1989); Ronald Bruce St John, "The Libyan Debacle in Sub-Saharan Africa, 1969–1987," in *The Green and the Black: Qadhafi's Policies in Africa*, ed. René Lemarchand (Bloomington: Indiana University Press, 1988), 125–38.

5. R. I. Lawless, "Population Geography and Settlement Studies," *Libyan Studies* 20 (1989): 251–52; J. S. Birks and C. A. Sinclair, "The Libyan Arab Jamahiriya: Labour Migration Sustains Dualistic Development," *Maghreb Review* 4, 3 (June–July 1979): 95–102.

6. Ronald Bruce St John, *Historical Dictionary of Libya*, 3rd ed. (Lanham, Md.: Scarecrow Press, 1998), 86–87.

7. Taoufik Monastiri, "Teaching the Revolution: Libyan Education Since 1969," in *Qadhafi's Libya, 1969–1994*, ed. Dirk Vandewalle (New York: St. Martin's Press, 1995), 67–88; Marius K. Deeb and Mary Jane Deeb, *Libya Since the Revolution* (New

York: Praeger, 1982), 18–51. *Jamahiriya* is an Arabic word coined by Qaddafi, which has no official translation but unofficially is understood to mean "state of the masses," "people's authority," or "people's power." The revolutionary government employs the word to convey a concept of self-rule without interference from state administration. St John, *Historical Dictionary of Libya*, 144.

8. Benjamin Higgins, *Economic Development: Problems, Principles and Policies*, revised edition (New York: W.W. Norton, 1968), 26.

9. Frank C. Waddams, *The Libyan Oil Industry* (London: Croom Helm, 1980), 57–226; Rawle Farley, *Planning for Development in Libya: The Exceptional Economy in the Developing World* (New York: Praeger, 1971), 117–26; P. Barker and K. S. McLachlan, "Development of the Libyan Oil Industry," in *Libya Since Independence: Economic and Political Development*, ed. J. A. Allan (London: Croom Helm, 1982), 37–54.

10. J. A. Allan, *Libya: The Experience of Oil* (London: Croom Helm, 1981), 58–95; Mustafa Sedd El-Ghariani, "Libya's Foreign Policy: The Role of the Country's Environmental and Leadership Factors, 1960–1973," M.A. thesis, Western Michigan University, 1979, 54.

11. Judith Gurney, *Libya: The Political Economy of Oil* (Oxford: Oxford University Press, 1996), 218–25.

12. Knut S. Vikor, *Sufi and Scholar on the Desert Edge: Muhammad b. Ali al-Sanusi and his Brotherhood* (Evanston, Ill.: Northwestern University Press, 1995), 22–180.

13. Nicola A. Ziadeh, *Sanusiyah: A Study of a Revivalist Movement in Islam* (Leiden: E.J. Brill, 1983), 73–98; Vikor, *Sufi and Scholar*, 218–40; Emrys L. Peters, *The Bedouin of Cyrenaica: Studies in Personal and Corporate Power* (Cambridge: Cambridge University Press, 1990), 10–28.

14. E. E. Evans-Pritchard, *The Sanusi of Cyrenaica* (Oxford: Oxford University Press, 1949), 1–28. For context see Lisa Anderson, "Legitimacy, Identity, and the Writing of History in Libya," in *Statecraft in the Middle East: Oil, Historical Memory, and Popular Culture*, ed. Eric Davis and Nicolas Gavrielides (Miami: Florida International University Press, 1991), 75–80.

15. Lisa Anderson, "The Development of Nationalist Sentiment in Libya, 1908–1922," in *The Origins of Arab Nationalism*, ed. Rashid Khalidi, Lisa Anderson, Muhammad Muslih, and Reeva S. Simon (New York: Columbia University Press, 1991), 225–42.

16. George Joffé, "Qadhafi's Islam in Local Historical Perspective," in *Qadhafi's Libya, 1969–1994*, ed. Dirk Vandewalle (New York: St. Martin's Press, 1995), 139–54; Mahmoud Mustafa Ayoub, *Islam and the Third Universal Theory: The Religious Thought of Mu'ammar al-Qadhadhafi* (London: KPI, 1987), Deeb and Deeb, *Libya*, 93–108.

Chapter 3. In the Beginning

1. Although the name Libya is employed as a matter of convenience throughout this narrative, the reader should be reminded that most of the geographical area today recognized as Libya, until its occupation by Europeans, was generally known as Tripoli, the name of its capital city. It was only in 1929, when the separately administered provinces of Tripolitania in the west and Cyrenaica in the east were

united under a single Italian governor, that Libya was adopted as the name of Italy's North African colony.

2. To understand fully the early interaction of the United States and Libya, it is important to distinguish at the outset between piracy and privateering (also known as corsairing), as the concepts differ in theory, legal definition, and practice. Piracy is the practice of attacking ships indiscriminately to loot property or to capture prisoners for ransom, sale, or use. Piracy becomes privateering when governments sanction, license, and authorize the practice. Beginning in the sixteenth century, piratical operations in the Mediterranean were gradually converted over time into privateering. John F. Jameson, *Privateering and Piracy in the Colonial Period* (New York: Macmillan, 1923), ix.

3. Kola Folayan, *Tripoli During the Reign of Yusuf Pasha Qaramanli* (Ile-Ife: University of Ife Press, 1979), 1.

4. Seton Dearden, *A Nest of Corsairs: The Fighting Karamanlis of Tripoli* (London: John Murray, 1976), 25–138; Folayan, *Tripoli*, 1–6.

5. Lisa Anderson, *The State and Social Transformation in Tunisia and Libya, 1830–1980* (Princeton, N.J.: Princeton University Press, 1986), 4, 39–40; Folayan, *Tripoli*, 25–29. On Libya and the African slave trade see Wright, *Libya, Chad and the Central Sahara* (London: C. Hurst, 1989), 55–80.

6. Folayan, *Tripoli*, 29–31.

7. James A. Field, *America and the Mediterranean World, 1776–1882* (Princeton, N.J.: Princeton University Press, 1969), 27–32; Lotfi Ben Rejeb, "To the Shores of Tripoli: The Impact of Barbary on Early American Nationalism," Ph.D. dissertation, Indiana University, 1982, 59–60.

8. Ray W. Irwin, *The Diplomatic Relations of the United States with the Barbary Powers, 1776–1816* (Chapel Hill: University of North Carolina Press, 1931), 20–28; *Naval Documents Related to the United States Wars with the Barbary Powers*, vol. 1 (Washington, D.C.: U.S. Government Printing Office, 1939–45), 22; Field, *America*, 32–33.

9. Dumas Malone, *Jefferson and His Time*, vol. 2, *Jefferson and the Rights of Man* (Boston: Little, Brown, 1970), 27–32, 51–52, quote 51–52. For a copy of the 1786 Treaty of Peace and Friendship Between the United States and the Emperor of Morocco, see Hunter Miller, ed., *Treaties and Other International Acts of the United States of America*, vol. 2, *Documents 1–40: 1776–1818* (Washington, D.C.: U. S. Government Printing Office, 1931), 185–227; Field, *America*, 33–37; Irwin, *Diplomatic Relations*, 37–68; Rejeb, "To the Shores of Tripoli," 64–69.

10. For a copy of the 1795 Treaty of Peace and Amity Between the United States and the Dey of Algiers, see Miller, *Treaties*, 2: 275–317; *Naval Documents*, 1: 107, 221, 239–40; Irwin, *Diplomatic Relations*, 69–81.

11. Folayan, *Tripoli*, 31; Field, *America*, 37–38.

12. For a copy of the 1796 Treaty of Peace and Friendship Between the United States and the Bey and Subjects of Tripoli of Barbary, see Miller, *Treaties*, 2: 349–385. The original treaty was concluded in Arabic and then translated into English by Joel Barlow.

13. Folayan, *Tripoli*, 31–33.

14. Louis B. Wright and Julia H. Macleod, *The First Americans in North Africa: William Eaton's Struggle for a Vigorous Policy Against the Barbary Pirates, 1799–1805* (Princeton, N.J.: Princeton University Press, 1945), 32, 40; Folayan, *Tripoli*, 34.

15. Folayan, *Tripoli*, 34–35.

16. Rejeb, "To the Shores of Tripoli," 73–74; Field, *America*, 48–51; Kola Folayan, "Tripoli and the War with the U.S.A., 1801–5," *Journal of African History* 13, 2 (1972): 261; Irwin, *Diplomatic Relations*, 92–105.

17. Dumas Malone, *Jefferson and His Time*, vol. 4, *Jefferson the President: First Term, 1801–1805* (Boston: Little, Brown, 1970), 97–99, 262–63; Wright and Macleod, *First Americans*, 37, 46–47, 86.

18. *Naval Documents*, 4: 293–307; Stanley Lane-Poole, *The Barbary Corsairs* (London: T. Unwin, 1890), 276–91; Folayan, "Tripoli and the War with the U.S.A.," 262.

19. Field, *America*, 52–54; Irwin, *Diplomatic Relations*, 106–48; Dearden, *Nest of Corsairs*, 173–206; Folayan, *Tripoli*, 37–39.

20. For context see Dumas Malone, *Jefferson and His Time*, vol. 5, *Jefferson the President: Second Term, 1805–1809* (Boston: Little, Brown, 1974), 35–39. The seizure of Darnah obviously affected the bey of Tripoli's decision to sign a peace agreement; however, American scholars have often overemphasized the heroics of Eaton. For example, Wright and Macleod suggest that Yusuf Karamanli was "so frightened" after the occupation of Darnah "that he hastily negotiated a treaty very favorable to the United States before Eaton could carry out his original plan." Wright and Macleod, *First Americans*, v. In a like mode, Robert Rinehart concluded that "Eaton's action compelled Yusuf to conclude peace with the United States and to release the American prisoners." Robert Rinehart, "Historical Setting," in *Libya: A Country Study*, ed. Harold D. Nelson (Washington, D.C.: U.S. Government Printing Office, 1979), 22.

21. For a copy of the 1805 Treaty of Peace and Amity Between the United States of America and the Bashaw, Bey and Subjects of Tripoli in Barbary, see Miller, *Treaties*, 2: 529–56. The original text of the treaty appeared in both Arabic and English. The terms of the 1805 treaty remain a subject of debate, with some scholars arguing that, given the growing strength of the American position, the payment of ransom could probably have been wholly avoided. For example see Irwin, *Diplomatic Relations*, chap. 10. While such revisionist arguments can be attractive, it should be recognized that concern for the fate of American captives, coupled with the demands of a four-year-old war, made the Jefferson administration and the American people eager for any reasonable settlement.

22. Folayan, "Tripoli and the War with the U.S.A.," 270.

23. Field, *America*, 57–58, 207; Folayan, *Tripoli*, 107–8.

24. L. J. Hume, "Preparations for Civil War in Tripoli in the 1820s: Ali Karamanli, Hassuna D'Ghies and Jeremy Bentham," *Journal of History* 21, 3 (1980): 311–22; Folayan, *Tripoli*, 78–168.

25. Anthony J. Cachia, *Libya Under the Second Ottoman Occupation (1835–1911)* (Tripoli: Government Press, 1945), 29–32.

26. Anderson, *State and Social Transformation*, 59–60; Cachia, *Libya*, 74–98. For context see Lord Kinross, *The Ottoman Centuries: The Rise and Fall of the Turkish Empire* (New York: Morrow Quill Paperbacks, 1977), 417–530.

27. Michel Le Gall, "The Ottoman Government and the Sanusiyya: A Reappraisal," *International Journal of Middle East Studies* 21, 1 (February 1989): 91–106; Anderson, *State and Social Transformation*, 87–92. Named after its founder, Muhammad Bin Ali al-Sanusi, the Sanusi order was a late arrival among the Sufi mystical religious brotherhoods active in northern Africa.

28. James A. Field, "A Scheme in Regard to Cyrenaica," *Mississippi Valley Historical Review* 44, 3 (December 1957): 448.

29. Vidal quoted in Field, "Scheme in Regard to Cyrenaica," 445.

30. Field, "Scheme in Regard to Cyrenaica," 445–68, Fish quoted on 467.

31. An anti-Western element of Libyan nationalism surfaced as early as 1881, when the French declaration of a protectorate over Tunisia provoked widespread demonstrations throughout Libya against European colonialism, including the tribes that had previously been most restive under Turkish domination. Cachia, *Libya*, 45.

32. Thomas Barclay, *The Turco-Italian War and Its Problems* (London: Constable, 1912), 12–14, 52–58, quote 12–13.

33. Denis Mack Smith, *Modern Italy: A Political History* (Ann Arbor: University of Michigan Press, 1997), 241–42; Cachia, *Libya*, 54–55.

34. Timothy W. Childs, *Italo-Turkish Diplomacy and the War over Libya, 1911–1912* (Leiden: E.J. Brill, 1990), 29–43; Rachel Simon, *Libya Between Ottomanism and Nationalism: The Ottoman Involvement in Libya During the War with Italy (1911–1919)* (Berlin: Klaus Schwarz Verlag, 1987), 48.

35. Claudio G. Segrè, *Fourth Shore: The Italian Colonization of Libya* (Chicago: University of Chicago Press, 1974), 3–19.

36. Smith, *Modern Italy*, 242–43, quotes 242; *Report on the Work of the Commission Sent Out by the Jewish Territorial Organization under the Auspices of the Governor-General of Tripoli, to Examine the Territory Proposed for the Purpose of a Jewish Settlement in Cyrenaica* (London: n.p., 1909); Simon, *Libya*, 49.

37. René Albrecht-Carrié, *Italy from Napoleon to Mussolini* (New York: Columbia University Press, 1950), 223–25, quote 225; Childs, *Italo-Turkish Diplomacy*, 49–70; Barclay, *Turco-Italian War*, 19–47; Smith, *Modern Italy*, 246.

38. Anderson, "Development of Nationalist Sentiment in Libya," 229; Duncan Cumming, "Libya in the First World War," in *Libya in History*, ed. Fawzi F. Gadallah (Benghazi: University of Libya, 1968), 384.

39. Ahmed M. Ashiurakis, *A Concise History of the Libyan Struggle for Freedom* (Tripoli: General Publishing, Distributing & Advertising Co., 1976), 48–52; Childs, *Italo-Turkish Diplomacy*, 174–230.

40. Albrecht-Carrié, *Italy*, 225–26, quote 225; Denis Mack Smith, *Mussolini's Roman Empire* (London: Longman, 1976), 36–37.

41. Smith, *Mussolini's Roman Empire*, 36–37.

42. The Acting Secretary of State to the American Chargé d'Affaires at Rome, 27 October 1911, File No. 765.67/131a, *Papers Relating to the Foreign Relations of the United States* (hereafter *FR*), 1911 (Washington, D.C.: U.S. Government Printing Office, 1918), 308–9; The Italian Chargé d'Affaires to the Secretary of State, 18 October 1912, File No. 765.67/409, No. 1635, *FR*, 1912, 632; The Italian Chargé d'Affaires to the Secretary of State, 30 October 1912, File No. 765.003, No. 1704, *FR*, 1912, 608.

43. The Secretary of State to the Italian Chargé d'Affaires, 28 February 1913, File No. 765.003, No. 380, *FR*, 1913, 609; The Secretary of State to the American Ambassador, 1 March 1913, File No. 765.003, No. 130, *FR*, 1913, 610; The Secretary of State to the American Consul General at Genoa, 10 March 1913, File No. 765.003, No. 152, *FR*, 1913, 611.

44. Anderson, "Development of Nationalist Sentiment in Libya," 233–34; Cumming, "Libya in the First World War," 385–89; Simon, *Libya*, 155–80.

45. Albrecht-Carré, *Italy*, 237–38, quote 237; Simon, *Libya*, 294–98.

46. Anderson, "Development of Nationalist Sentiment in Libya," 236–41, quote 240–41; Lisa Anderson, "The Tripoli Republic, 1918–1922," in *Social and Economic Development of Libya*, ed. E. G. H. Joffé and K. S. McLachlan (London: Menas Press, 1982), 43–65.

47. The Secretary of State to the Ambassador in France (Herrick), 27 October1922, File No. 767.68119/51a, No. 345, *FR*, 1923, 2: 886–88.

48. Romain Rainero, "The Capture, Trial, and Death of Omar al-Mukhtar in the Context of the Fascist Policy for the Reconquest of Libya," in *Omar al-Mukhtar: The Italian Reconquest of Libya*, ed. Enzo Santarelli, Giorgio Rochat, Romain Rainero, and Luigi Goglia (London: Darf, 1986), 173–87; Ashiurakis, *Concise History*, 67–71.

49. Lisa Anderson, "Legitimacy, Identity, and the Writing of History in Libya, 1908–1922," in *The Origins of Arab Nationalism*, ed. Rashid Khalidi, Lisa Anderson, Muhammad Muslih, and Reeva S. Simon (New York: Columbia University Press, 1991), 76; E. E. Evans-Pritchard, *The Sanusi of Cyrenaica* (Oxford: Oxford University Press, 1949). Anderson calls Evans-Pritchard's study an "illuminating example of scholarship in the service of imperialism" (81), and notes that the book remains one of the best-known studies of Libyan resistance to Italian rule, and it is also a classic in the field of anthropology as well as in Libyan studies and modern Arab and Islamic history. Concerned with those aspirants to nationalist leadership in Libya most amenable to British support, the book exaggerates the vitality of the Sanusiya, neglects the role of Ottoman and later British support, and distorts the struggles of Libyan nationalists who opposed both Italian rule and British influence.

Chapter 4. Postwar Gridlock

1. Memorandum Prepared by the Subcommittee on Territorial Problems of the Advisory Committee on Post-War Foreign Policy, 22 May 1943, Limits of Land Settlement in Libya, Lot 60 D 224, *FR*, The Conferences at Washington and Quebec 1943, 339–41, quote 339; John Wright, "British and Italians in Libya in 1943," *Maghreb Review* 15, 1–2 (January–April 1990): 32.

2. *FR*, The Conferences at Washington and Quebec 1943, 340.

3. Ibid., 341.

4. Ibid., 341–42.

5. Prime Minister Churchill's Chief of Staff (Ismay) to Prime Minister Churchill, 21 May, 1943, Attachment 1: Camp in North Africa for Refugees from Spain, Hopkins Papers, *FR*, The Conferences at Washington and Quebec 1943, 343.

6. The British Foreign Secretary (Eden) to Prime Minister Churchill, 19 May 1943, *FR*, The Conferences at Washington and Quebec 1943, 345.

7. Memorandum by the Assistant Secretary of State (Long) to President Roosevelt, 5 July 1943, File No. 840.48 Refugees/40362/6, *FR*, The Conferences at Washington and Quebec 1943, 322–23.

8. Scott L. Bills, *The Libyan Arena: The United States, Britain, and the Council of Foreign Ministers, 1945–1948* (Kent, Ohio: Kent State University Press, 1995), 15,

20–21. The special relationship between the Sanusiya and the British government dated back to the beginning of the twentieth century when the British intervened to stop the French from occupying the Sanusi center at Kufrah. Eric Armar Vully de Candole, *The Life and Times of King Idris of Libya* (published privately by Mohamed Ben Ghaldon, 1990), 16–17. De Candole was the British representative in Cyrenaica in 1949–52. On early French scholarship on the Sanusiya, much of which inaccurately depicted the order as warlike and anti-French see Vikor, *Sufi and Scholar*, 6–12.

9. Richard W. Leopold, *The Growth of American Foreign Policy: A History* (New York: Knopf, 1962), 576–77; Bills, *Libyan Arena*, 7–8.

10. Memorandum by Mr. Philip W. Ireland, of the Division of Political Studies, 12 May 1943, *FR*, The Conferences at Washington and Quebec 1943, 796–97, quote 797. In contrast, the British recognized at an early date the strategic importance of Cyrenaica, although they felt they had no strategic interests in Tripolitania beyond denying it to a hostile power. Bills, *Libyan Arena*, 22–23.

11. Memorandum by Ireland, *FR*, The Conferences at Washington and Quebec 1943, 798.

12. The Secretary of State to the President, 11 September 1944, Memorandum for the President, Roosevelt Papers, *FR*, The Conference at Quebec 1944, 408–11.

13. Record of Conversation, Prepared by the United Kingdom Delegation at the Moscow Conference of Foreign Ministers, 17 December 1945, File No. 740.00119 Council/12-1745, *FR*, Diplomatic Papers 1945, vol. 2, General: Political and Economic Matters, 629–32.

14. United Kingdom Delegation Record of a Conversation at the Kremlin, 24 December 1945, Moscow Embassy Files: 500 Conference of Foreign Ministers, *FR*, Diplomatic Papers 1945, 2: 774–76, quote 776.

15. Possible Trusteeship for Italian Colonial Territories and Korea, No. 246, 30 June 1945, Briefing Book Paper, File No. 740.00119 (Potsdam)/5-2446, *FR*, The Conference of Berlin (The Potsdam Conference) 1945, vol. 1, 305–6, quote 306. Drawing a parallel with the French position in Algeria, the Italian government lobbied the Truman administration to recognize Libya as an essential part of Italian national territory. The Italian Ambassador (Tarchiani) to President Truman, 6 July 1945, Memorandum for Mr. Truman, President of the U.S.A. on the Position, Wishes and Hopes of Italy, File No. 740.0011 PW/7-645, *FR*, The Conference of Berlin (The Potsdam Conference) 1945, 1: 308–9.

16. Sixth Plenary Meeting, Sunday, 22 July 1945, 5 P.M., Thompson Minutes, Truman Papers, *FR*, The Conference of Berlin (The Potsdam Conference) 1945, 2: 254, 265, quote 265.

17. Sixth Plenary Meeting, *FR*, Conference of Berlin (Potsdam Conference) 1945, 2: 244–66, quote 265.

18. Bills, *Libyan Arena*, 9, 32, quote 9; James F. Byrnes, *Speaking Frankly* (New York: Harper & Brothers, 1947), 76–77. On British disengagement in the Middle East during the period of the Labour government (1945–51) see Wm. Roger Louis, *The British Empire in the Middle East, 1945–1951: Arab Nationalism, the United States, and Postwar Imperialism* (Oxford: Clarendon Press, 1984).

19. Bills, *Libyan Arena*, 24–25, 58.

20. Suggested Directive from the Council of Foreign Ministers to Govern Them in the Drafting of a Treaty of Peace with Italy, September 14, 1945, Memorandum

by the United States Delegation, C.F.M. (45) 16, *FR*, 1945, The Conference of Berlin (The Potsdam Conference), 2: 179; C. Grove Haines, "The Problem of the Italian Colonies," *Middle East Journal* 1, 4 (October 1947): 421–22.

21. James Reston, "U.S. Chiefs Divided on Italy's Colonies," *New York Times*, 2 September 1945. See Bills for an analysis of the significance of the Reston article. *Libyan Arena*, 46–47.

22. Harvey E. Goldberg, *Jewish Life in Muslim Libya: Rivals and Relatives* (Chicago: University of Chicago Press, 1990), 109–22. The impact of the riots on the Jewish community was soon clear; Libyan Jews began to emigrate in increasing numbers, finding a new home in Israel after the creation of a Jewish state in 1948.

23. Byrnes, *Speaking Frankly*, 92–97; Bills, *Libyan Arena*, 50–52.

24. Majid Khadduri, *Modern Libya: A Study in Political Development* (Baltimore: Johns Hopkins University Press, 1963), 117–18.

25. Ibid., 118–20. The Egyptian Abdul Rahman Azzam studied medicine in England and traveled in nationalist circles in Egypt and Tunisia before arriving in Libya toward the end of World War I. Embracing the cause of unity and resistance, "He was as close as Libya would get to a genuine Arab nationalist." Lisa Anderson, "The Development of Nationalist Sentiment in Libya, 1908–1922," in *The Origins of Arab Nationalism*, ed. Rashid Khalidi, Lisa Anderson, Muhammad Muslih, and Reeva S. Simon (New York: Columbia University Press, 1991), 236. On the ideological development of Abdul Rahman Azzam, see Ralph M. Coury, *The Making of An Egyptian Arab Nationalist: The Early Years of Azzam Pasha, 1893–1936* (Reading, Pa.: Ithaca Press, 1999).

26. The Italian Ambassador (Tarchiani) to the Counselor of the Department of State (Cohen), 25 July 1946, CFM Files, *FR*, Paris Peace Conference: Proceedings, 1946, vol. 3, 17–18; Eleventh Plenary Meeting, August 10, 1946, 4 p.m., CFM Files, ibid., 182; United States Delegation Memorandum of Conversation (Byrnes-De Gasperi Conversation, August 22, 1946, 9:30 a.m.), CFM Files, ibid., 267–69; Draft Peace Treaty with Italy, Prepared by the Council of Foreign Ministers, Palais du Luxembourg, Paris, July 18, 1946, CFM Files, ibid., vol. 4, 12.

27. Report by the Committee on Italian Colonies to the Council of Foreign Ministers, C.F.M. (46) 221 (Revised), 11 July 1946, *FR*, Council of Foreign Ministers, vol. 2, 1946, 899–900; "Treaty of Peace with Italy," *Treaties and Other International Agreements of the United States of America, 1776–1949*, vol. 4: *Multilateral, 1946–1949*, comp. Charles I. Bevans (Washington, D.C.: U.S. Government Printing Office, 1970): 311–402.

28. United States Delegation Record, Council of Foreign Ministers, Second Session, Fourth Meeting, Paris, 29 April 1946, 4 p.m., CFM Files: Lot M-88: Box 2063: US Delegation Minutes, *FR*, Council of Foreign Ministers, vol. 2, 1946, 155–64.

29. United States Delegation Record, Council of Foreign Ministers, Second Session, First Informal Meeting, Paris, 2 May 2 1946, 5 p.m., CFM Files, ibid., 221–22; Fifteenth Meeting, Palais du Luxembourg, Paris, 10 May 1946, 11 a.m., CFM. Files, ibid., 334–38; Tenth Informal Meeting, Palais du Luxembourg, Paris, 20 June 20 1946, 5 p.m., CFM Files, ibid., 558–63.

30. Haines, "Problem of the Italian Colonies," 417–19, quotes 419. On French policy in the Levant see Philip S. Khoury, *Syria and the French Mandate: The Politics of Arab Nationalism, 1920–1945* (Princeton, N.J.: Princeton University Press, 1987).

31. Denis Mack Smith, *Modern Italy: A Political History* (Ann Arbor: University of Michigan Press, 1997), 424; Bills, *Libyan Arena*, 133–36.

32. Bills, *Libyan Arena*, 137.

33. Louis, *British Empire in the Middle East*, 105, 300–302.

34. Council of Foreign Ministers, Commission of Investigation, *Report on Libya*, 1948, Khadduri, *Modern Libya*, 120–24. For context on political activity in Cyrenaica see De Candole, *Idris*, 89–92.

35. Richard P. Stebbins, *The United States in World Affairs, 1949* (New York: Harper & Brothers for the Council on Foreign Relations, 1950), 355–59; Bills, *Libyan Arena*, 142.

36. John C. Campbell, *The United States in World Affairs, 1948–1949* (New York: Harper & Brothers for the Council on Foreign Relations, 1949), 437.

37. Statement by the United States Representative to the United Nations General Assembly (Dulles) before the General Assembly Political and Security Committee, 6 April 1949, in *Documents on American Foreign Relations*, vol. 11 (1 January–31 December 1949), ed. Raymond Dennett and Robert K. Turner (Princeton, N.J.: Princeton University Press for the World Peace Foundation, 1950), 683–86, quote 684. A full discussion of the complexity of the negotiations at the United Nations is beyond the scope of this study. The reader is referred to the monumental work by the UN architect of Libyan independence, Adrian Pelt, *Libyan Independence and the United Nations: A Case of Planned Decolonization* (New Haven, Conn.: Yale University Press for the Carnegie Endowment for International Peace, 1970) and Benjamin Rivlin, *The United Nations and the Italian Colonies* (New York: Carnegie Endowment for International Peace, 1950).

38. Henry Serrano Villard, *Libya: The New Arab Kingdom of North Africa* (Ithaca, N.Y.: Cornell University Press, 1956), 33–34.

39. Statement by the United States Representative to the United Nations (Austin) before the Plenary Session of the General Assembly, 17 May 1949, in *Documents on American Foreign Relations*, 11: 686–89, quote 687.

40. Wright, "British and Italians in Libya in 1943," 35.

41. Draft Resolution on the Disposition of the Former Italian Colonies, Submitted by the United States to the United Nations General Assembly Political and Security Committee, 10 October 1949, in *Documents on American Foreign Relations*, 11: 690–91; Resolution on the Disposition of the Former Italian Colonies, Adopted by the United Nations General Assembly, November 21, 1949, in *Documents on American Foreign Relations*, 11: 692–93.

42. The Secretary of State to the Consulate in Tripoli, 5 May 1950, 357.AG/5-350: Telegram, *FR*, 1950, vol. 5, The Near East, South Asia and Africa, 1621–22; Khadduri, *Modern Libya*, 137–40. On the low level of national identity prevailing in Libya in 1948 see Benjamin Rivlin, "Unity and Nationalism in Libya," *Middle East Journal* 3, 1 (January 1949), 31–44.

43. Position Paper Prepared in the Department of State, 6 November 1951, United States Position on Probable Soviet and Arab Challenges Regarding US and UK Military Bases in Libya, SD/A/C.1/374/Add 1/Rev.1, IO Files: Lot 71 D 440, *FR*, 1951, vol. 5, The Near East and Africa, 1359–61; Memorandum of Conversation, Prepared in the Embassy in the United Kingdom, 19 September 1950, Subject: Communism in Africa, 780.00/9–1950, *FR*, 1950, 5: 1551–52.

44. Memorandum by the Under Secretary of State (Webb) to the Executive Secretary of the National Security Council (Lay), 30 April 1951, Subject: Final Progress Report on NSC 19/5, "Disposition of the Former Italian Colonies," *FR*, 1951, 5: 1318–20; Memorandum of Informal United States-United Kingdom Discussions, 19 September 1950, 780.00/9-1850, *FR*, 1950, 5: 296–302.

45. The Ambassador in France (Bruce) to the Secretary of State, 31 March 1950, *FR*, 1950, vol. 5, The Near East, South Asia, and Africa, 1774; Record of the Under Secretary's Meeting, 16 October 1950, Oral Report on Trip to London, Paris, and Tangier, undated, Under Secretary's Meetings: Lot 53 D 250: Minutes of Meetings, *FR*, 1950, 5: 216; Villard, *Libya*, 33. On French concerns about Libyan independence see André Martel, *La Libye, 1835–1990: Essai géopolitique historique* (Paris: Presses Universitaires de France, 1991), 164–65.

46. The Consul General at Tripoli (Lynch) to the Department of State, 9 November 1951, 711.56373/11-951, *FR*, 1951, 5: 1361–63; The Secretary of Defense (Marshall) to the Secretary of State, January 9, 1951, Secretary's Letters: Lot 56 D 459, *FR*, 1951, 5: 1313–15; The Secretary of State to the Consulate in Tripoli, May 5, 1950, 357.AG/5-350: Telegram, *FR*, 1950, 5: 1621–23.

Chapter 5. Independence at a Price

1. Memorandum by the Politico-Military Adviser in the Bureau of Near Eastern, South Asian, and African Affairs (Robertson), 14 November 1949, U.S. Strategic Position in the Eastern Mediterranean and Middle East, 711.9011/11-1449, *FR*, 1949, vol. 6, The Near East, South Asia, and Africa, 56–59, quotes 56. For a penetrating analysis of events in the Northern Tier see Bruce Robellet Kuniholm, *The Origins of the Cold War in the Near East: Great Power Conflict and Diplomacy in Iran, Turkey, and Greece* (Princeton, N.J.: Princeton University Press, 1980).

2. U.S. Strategic Position, *FR*, 1949, 6: 57–58.

3. Ibid., 58–59, quotes 59. U.S. military requirements in Tripolitania were detailed four days after the memo on the U.S. strategic position. Memorandum of Conversation, by the Deputy Director of the Office of African and Near Eastern Affairs (Moose), 18 November 1949, United States Military Requirements in Tripolitania, PPS Files, Lot 64/D/563, Libya, *FR*, 1949, 6: 59–60.

4. Memorandum by the Director of the Office of Near Eastern and African Affairs (Henderson) to the Under Secretary of State (Lovett), 28 August 1947, 841.2383/8-2847, *FR*, 1947, vol. 5, The Near East and Africa, 800–802, quote 802. The United States and United Kingdom maintained a close partnership in the Middle East following the end of World War II. Peter L. Hahn, "Discord or Partnership? British and American Policy Toward Egypt, 1942–56," in *Demise of the British Empire in the Middle East: Britain's Responses to Nationalist Movements, 1943–55*, ed. Michael J. Cohen and Martin Kolinsky (London: Frank Cass, 1988), 162–82.

5. The First Secretary of the Embassy in the United Kingdom (Palmer) to the Assistant Secretary of State for Near Eastern, South Asian, and African Affairs (McGhee), 15 November 1950, 711.56373/11-1550, *FR*, 1950, vol. 5, 1635–38; The Director of the Office of African Affairs (Bourgerie) to the First Secretary of the

Embassy in the United Kingdom (Palmer), 11 December 1950, 711.56373/11-1550, *FR*, 1950, 5: 1638–39.

6. The Secretary of State to the Consulate in Tripoli, 5 May 1950, 357.AG/5-350: Telegram, *FR*, 1950, 5: 1621–22, quotes 1621.

7. Summary of Remarks by the Assistant Secretary of State for Near Eastern, South Asian, and African Affairs (McGhee) to a Bureau of Near Eastern, South Asian, and African Affairs Staff Meeting, 24 October 1950, Summary by Mr. McGhee of Conclusions of Tangier Conference and Recent Visits to Paris and London, 120.4371/11-150, *FR*, 1950, 5: 1569–73, quotes 1570. On Arab nationalist political activity in Cyrenaica in 1948–1951, see E. A. V. De Candole, *The Life and Times of King Idris of Libya* (n.p., 1988), 89–92.

8. Summary by Mr. McGhee, *FR*, 1950, 5: 1571.

9. Memorandum by the Assistant Secretary of State for Near Eastern, South Asian, and African Affairs (McGhee) to the Secretary of State, 6 November 1950, Summary of the Tangier Conference, 120.4371/11-650, *FR*, 1950, 5: 1573–80, quotes 1574.

10. Ibid., 1573.

11. The Consul General at Tripoli (Lynch) to the Acting Secretary of State, 19 May 1950, 711.56373/5-1950: Telegram, *FR*, 1950, 5: 1624–26, quote 1625; The Acting Secretary of State to the Consulate in Tripoli, May 9, 1950, 711.56373/5-950: Telegram, *FR*, 1950, 5: 1623–24.

12. Memorandum of Negotiations for Libyan Bases, General Counsel Hill to Mr. Finletter, July 11, 1951, *Declassified Documents Reference System* (Washington, D.C.: Carrollton Press, microfiche series, various years), 1992-1235: 1 (hereafter *DDRS* 1992-1235: 1). In the *DDRS*, the number immediately following refers to the year in which the document was declassified, the second number is the catalog number of the document, and the third is the page number.

13. Memorandum of Informal United States-United Kingdom Discussion in Connection With the Visit to London of Assistant Secretary of State McGhee, 19 September 1950, 780.00/9-1850, *FR*, 1950, 5: 1631–33, quote 1633; The Consul at Geneva (Ward) to the Department of State, 17 October 1951, 357.AG/10-1751: Telegram, *FR*, 1951, 5: 1344–45; The Secretary of State to the Embassy in the United Kingdom, 17 October 1951, 357.AG/10-1751: Telegram, *FR*, 1951, 5: 1345.

14. Memorandum by the Assistant Secretary of State for Near Eastern, South Asian, and African Affairs (McGhee) to the Secretary of State, 27 December 1950, Proposed US Political and Military Actions Required to Assist the Countries of the Middle East in the Defense of the Area Against Aggression, 27 December 1950, S/P-NSC Files: Lot 61 D 167: "Eastern Mediterranean and Middle East," *FR*, 1951, 5: 4–14, quotes 4, 10. On Great Britain's weak domestic economic position in the postwar period see Rodney Wilson, "Economic Aspects of Arab Nationalism," in *Demise of the British Empire in the Middle East*, 64–78.

15. "Libya: Report of the United Nations Commissioner in Libya; Reports of the Administering Powers in Libya," in Adrian Pelt, *Libyan Independence and the United Nations: A Case of Planned Decolonization* (New Haven, Conn.: Yale University Press, 1970), 893–901; The Consul General at Tripoli (Lynch) to the Secretary of State, 1 November 1950, 357.AG/11-150: Telegram, *FR*, 1950, 5: 1634–35.

16. Memorandum by the Under Secretary of State (Webb) to the Executive

Secretary of the National Security Council (Lay), 30 April1951, Final Progress Report on NSC 19/5, "Disposition of the Former Italian Colonies," S/P-NSC Files: Lot 61 D 167: "Italian Colonies," *FR*, 1951, 5: 1250–53, 1318–20, quote 1319.

17. The Consul General at Tripoli (Lynch) to the Department of State, 2 June 1951, 711.56373/6-251: Telegram, *FR*, 1951, 5: 1325–26, quote 1326.

18. The Consul General at Tripoli (Lynch) to the Department of State, 20 July 1951, 711.56373/7-2051: Telegram, *FR*, 1951, 5: 1332–33, quote 1332.

19. Agreement Between The Government of Libya and the Government of the United States of America, 19 October 1951, 711.56373/12-451, *FR*, 1951, 5: 1347–56. Article 7 was later modified, at the insistence of the Libyan government, to provide for payment of equitable rent for whatever base areas were occupied by U.S. military forces. The Acting Secretary of Defense (Foster) to the Secretary of State, 4 December 1951, 711.56373/12-451, *FR*, 1951, 5: 1364–65.

20. The Acting Secretary of Defense (Foster) to the Secretary of State, 4 December 1951, 711.56373/12-451, *FR*, 1951, 5: 1364–65, quote 1365; The Secretary of State to the Consulate General at Tripoli, December 21, 1951, 711.56373/12-1951: Telegram, *FR*, 1951, 5: 1367; The Consul General at Tripoli (Lynch) to the Department of State, November 9, 1951, 711.56373/11–951: Telegram, *FR*, 1951, 5: 1361–63; Richard P. Stebbins, *The United States in World Affairs, 1951* (New York: Harper & Brothers, 1952), 265–66; *New York Times*, 20 December 1951. For context on French policy in North Africa see Annie Lacroix-Riz, *Les protectorats d'Afrique du Nord entre la France et Washington de débarquement à l'indépendance: Maroc et Tunisie, 1942–1956* (Paris: L'Harmattan, 1988), 109 Ali Muhammad 15.

21. The Consul General at Tripoli (Lynch) to the Department of State, October 30, 1951, 711.56373/10-3051: Telegram, *FR*, 1951, 5: 1358.

22. Memorandum for the National Security Council Senior Staff, September 12, 1952, The Current Situation in North Africa, INR-NIE files, *FR*, 1952–54, vol. 11, Africa and South Asia, Part 1, 131–42, quotes 140.

23. *FR*, 1952–54, 11, 1: 139–42, quote 142.

24. Draft Policy Statement Prepared by the National Security Council Staff for the National Security Council Planning Board, August 18, 1953, Statement of Policy Proposed by the National Security Council on the Position of the United States with Respect to North Africa, S/P-NSC files, lot 61 D 167, "North Africa," *FR*, 1952–54, 11, 1: 150–52, quote 152.

25. National Intelligence Estimate, August 31, 1954, Probable Developments in North Africa, INR-NIE files, NIE-71-54, *FR*, 1952–54, 11, 1: 153–70, quotes 168, 169. For context see William H. Lewis and Robert Gordon, "Libya After Two Years of Independence, "*Middle East Journal* 8, 1 (Winter 1954): 41–53.

26. National Intelligence Estimate, Probable Developments in North Africa, *FR*, 1952–54, 11, 1: 169. The NIE assessment was later challenged by Mustafa Ahmed Ben-Halim, the controversial prime minister of Libya from April 1954 to March 1957. According to Ben-Halim, King Idris "did not appreciate the dynamism of history and never realised that Britain's greatness was at an end by 1945, that she had ceased to be a dominant power and had become a country of the second rank." On the other hand, Ben-Halim did indicate that King Idris clearly recognized the British capacity for manipulation and intrigue. "I have to acknowledge that the King's fear of British plots was well founded and indicated his far-sightedness and shrewdness. He was much more experienced than I in fathoming the capacity of

the British for intrigue" Mustafa Ahmed Ben-Halim, *Libya: The Years of Hope* (London: AAS Media, 1998), 53-55, quotes 53, 54.

27. Lacroix-Riz, *Les protectorats d'Afrique du Nord*, 181–96. In a classic case of policy divergence, the Libyan government was facilitating the supply of arms and equipment to Algerian rebels opposing French rule at the same time that the United States was seeking to avoid actions which might weaken the French position. Ben-Halim, *Libya*, 201–3.

28. National Intelligence Estimate, Probable Developments in North Africa, *FR*, 1952–54, 11, 1: 169–70, quotes 170.

29. The Minister in Libya (Villard) to the Department of State, 21 January 1953, 711.56373/1-2153: Telegram, *FR*, 1952–54, 11, 1: 570–71, quote 570–71; The Consul at Benghazi (More) to the Department of State, 2 September 1952, 711.56373/9-252: Telegram, *FR*, 1952–54, 11, 1: 545–47.

30. Villard, *Libya*, 9; The Ambassador to Jordan (Green) to the Department of State, 5 January 1953, 711.56376/1-553: Telegram, *FR*, 1952–54, 11, 1: 566–67.

31 The Minister in Libya (Villard) to the Department of State, 12 June 1954, 711.56373/6-1254: Telegram, *FR*, 1952–54, 11, 1: 588–90, quote 588.

32 Department of State, *Bulletin* 31 (1954), quotes 396–97; The Secretary of State to the Legation in Libya, 20 1954, 711.56373/7-2054: Telegram, *FR*, 1952–54, 11, 1: 590–91; The Secretary of State to the Legation in Libya, 29 July 1954, 033.7311/7-2954: Circular airgram, *FR*, 1952–54, 11, 1: 591–93. For a copy of the 1954 base rights agreement see Majid Khadduri, *Modern Libya: A Study in Political Development* (Baltimore: Johns Hopkins University Press, 1963), 383–97. For context on American policy concerns in the summer of 1954 see Stephen E. Ambrose, *Eisenhower: The President, 1952–1969* (London: Allen and Unwin, 1984), 186–211.

33. Villard, *Libya*, 142. The Libyan government had concluded a treaty of friendship and alliance, together with a financial agreement, with the United Kingdom on 29 July 1953. Libya later concluded a treaty of peace and friendship with France on 10 August 1955. Martel, *La Libye*, 179–80. French policy in North Africa in 1955 threatened embarrassment for the United States as the French sought to retain troops in the Fezzan after Washington had counseled the Libyan government to pursue a policy of moderation on the issue. Daily Intelligence Abstracts No. 353, Operations Coordinating Board, 21 April 1955, *DDRS* 1992-2148: 1.

34. Letter From the Ambassador in Libya (Tappin) to the Assistant Secretary of State for Near Eastern, South Asian, and African Affairs (Allen), March 11, 1955, S/P-NSC Files: Lot 62 D 1, *FR*, 1955–1957, vol. 18, Africa, 415–19, quotes 415–16.

35. Ben-Halim, *Libya*, 108–17. Ben-Halim's recently published memoirs, as fascinating as they are, must be treated with caution. In addition to being recognized as authoritarian and personally ambitious, he was considered by many to be devious and dishonest. "He has been accused of accumulating illegal earnings at every stage of his political career." Mansour O. El-Kikhia, *Libya's Qaddafi: The Politics of Contradiction* (Gainesville: University Press of Florida, 1997), 36–37, 64–66. On Ben-Halim's financial misdealings see also Laton McCartney, *Friends in High Places: The Bechtel Story* (New York: Simon and Schuster, 1988), 145–50.

36. Despatch from the Embassy in Libya to the Department of State, 30 November 1955, Libyan Exchange of Diplomatic Representatives with USSR and the United States Position in Libya, 601.6173/11, *FR*, 1955–57, 18: 421–25, quote 421–22. The Soviet Union in 1952–55 had repeatedly vetoed Libyan membership

in the United Nations. The establishment of diplomatic relations with the Soviets paved the way for Libya's admission to the United Nations in December 1955 in a package deal that included a total of sixteen new members.

37. Telegram from the Department of State to the Embassy in Libya, 19 January 1956, 773.5-MSP/1-1956, *FR*, 1955–57, 18: 426–27, quote 427. Massimiliano Cricco, "La Libia nella politica delle grandi potenze (1951–1969)," Ph.D. dissertation, Università degli Studi di Fireze, 1999, 38–46.

38. Letter from the Ambassador in Libya (Tappin) to the Deputy Assistant Secretary of State for Near Eastern, South Asian, and African Affairs (Palmer), 1 January 1957, AF/AFS Files: Lot 62 D 406, Miscellaneous, *FR*, 1955–57, 18: 459–62, quote 459. As Ambassador Tappin responded aggressively and positively to Prime Minister Ben-Halim's efforts to raise U.S. aid levels, he became at the same time a severe critic of the Libyan prime minister and the tactics he employed. In a 7 February 1956 telegram to the Department of State, for example, Tappin described Ben-Halim as "bloated with power and possessed of insatiable appetite." He went on to characterize Ben-Halim as having a split personality in which he was "dangerously intelligent, opportunistic, young, shrewd and ambitious both for political power and personal gain" on the one hand and yet very persuasive in his argument that the long range future of Libya was tied to the West on the other. Telegram from the Embassy in Libya to the Department of State, 7 February 1956, Central Files, 773.5-MSP/2-756, *FR*, 1955–57, 18: 436–38, quotes 437.

39. Telegram from the Embassy in Libya to the Department of State, 22 March 1957, 120.1580/3-2257, *FR*, 1955–57, 18: 477–79, quote 477. Prime Minister Ben-Halim recounts with a sense of glee his successful efforts to play off the United States against the Soviet Union in order to increase economic assistance levels. Ben-Halim, *Libya*, 127–32.

40. A very large volume of literature is available on the Suez crisis. For a concise, readable account of Suez see Hugh Thomas, *Suez* (New York: Harper & Row, 1966). In discussing the withdrawal of Western aid to the Aswan High dam, Thomas suggests that this "was the first time that aid to underdeveloped countries had been openly used by the West as an instrument of policy." Thomas, *Suez*, 25. His statement totally ignores the fact that the West had been using economic aid as an instrument of policy in Libya well before its independence in December 1951. In the course of the Suez crisis, the British ambassador in Tripoli emphatically warned Prime Minister Eden that the use of British troops stationed in Libya in operations against Egypt would produce violent reactions in Libya in which British troops would have to be used to restore order. Robert Rhodes James, *Anthony Eden* (London: Weidenfeld and Nicolson, 1986), 491.

41. Memorandum of Discussion at the 321st Meeting of the National Security Council, Washington, 2 May 1957, Eisenhower Library, Whitman File, NSC Discussions, *FR*, 1955–57, 18: 481–85, quote 484. The United States stepped up its economic and military assistance to Libya in 1958. Following strong Libyan representation in April 1958, the British finally agreed to an annual aid level of $9.1 million for five years. On the profound and long-lasting impact the 1956 Suez crisis had on British policy toward Libya, see Alison Pargeter, "Anglo-Libyan Relations and the Suez Crisis," *Journal of North African Studies* 5, 2 (Summer 2000): 41–58.

42. Letter from the Acting Secretary of State to the Secretary of Defense

(Wilson), 12 November 1955, 773.5-MSP/11-1255, *FR*, 1955–57, 18: 419–21, quote 419.

43. The Outlook for US Interests in Libya, 19 June 1956, NIE 36.5-56, *FR*, 1955–57, 18: 454–55, quote 455. For a Libyan perspective on the development of Arab nationalism in Libya see Mohammed Zahi El-Mogherbi "Arab Nationalism and Political Instability in Monarchical Libya: A Study in Political Ideology," M.A. thesis, Kansas State University, 1973.

44. National Security Council Report, 29 June 1957, U.S. Policy Toward Libya, NSC 5716/1, *FR*, 1955–57, 18: 490–95, quote 492.

45. Summary Staff Material, U.S. Considering Moves to Counter Egyptian Influence in Libya, Office of the Director, International Cooperation Administration, 30 November 1956, *DDRS* 1985-2808: 1–2.

46. Robert A. Divine, *Eisenhower and the Cold War* (Oxford: Oxford University Press, 1981), 91–92.

47. Faiz S. Abu-Jaber, *American-Arab Relations from Wilson to Nixon* (Washington, D.C.: University Press of America, 1979), 175–76; George Lenczowski, *The Middle East in World Affairs*, 4th ed. (Ithaca, N.Y.: Cornell University Press, 1980), 796–99.

48. Report by the Vice President, 5 April 1957, Report to the President on the Vice President's Visit to Africa (28 February– 21 March 1957), S/P-NSC Files: Lot 62 D 1, North Africa, *FR*, 1955–57, 18: 57–66, quote 63.

49. Memorandum of Information, Current US-Libyan Relations, Department of the Navy, Office of the Chief of Naval Operations, 15 October 1957, *DDRS* 1984-1578: 1.

50. Memorandum of Discussion at the 406th Meeting of the National Security Council, Washington, 13 May 1959, Eisenhower Library, Whitman File, NSC Records, *FR*, 1958-1960, vol. 13, Arab-Israeli Dispute, United Arab Republic, North Africa: 729–30.

51. Personal Message from the President to the King, Department of State, 22 July 1958, *DDRS* 1982-2578: 1–3; Letter to Libyan Prime Minister, From Edward E. Wright to the Acting Secretary, 18 February 1959, *DDRS* 1984-2530: 1; Message to King Idris of Libya on the Law of the Sea, Memorandum for the President from Secretary of State Christian A. Herter, 23April 1960, *DDRS* 1984-2118: 1; Law of the Sea, Letter from the President to King Idris, Department of State, 25 April 1960, *DDRS* 1982-1780: 1–2. For context on American foreign policy in the so-called "Sputnik era" see Michael S. Sherry, *In the Shadow of War: The United States Since the 1930s* (New Haven, Conn.: Yale University Press, 1995), 214–33.

52. Memorandum of Discussion at the 422d Meeting of the National Security Council, Washington, 29 October 1959, Eisenhower Library, Whitman File, NSC Records, *FR*, 1958–60, 13: 733–34.

53. Implications of Petroleum Developments on U.S. Operations in Libya, National Security Council, Operations Coordinating Board Special Report, 23 September 1959, *DDRS* 1986-2132: 1–4, quote 4.

54. National Security Council Report, 15 March 1960, Statement of U.S. Policy Toward Libya, S/P-NSC Files: Lot 62 D 1, *FR*, 1958–60, 13: 740–49, quotes 740, 743; U.S. Policy Toward Libya, National Security Council, NSC 6004/1, 15 March 1960, *DDRS* 1984-1989: 1–40. The United States and Libya agreed in June 1960 to an amended economic assistance agreement that provided Libya with $10 million a

year in economic assistance in 1960–64, followed by $1 million annually in 1965–71.

55. Sherry, *In the Shadow of War*, 233–36, quotes 233–34; Ambrose, *Eisenhower: The President*, 605–17.

56. John Lewis Gaddis, *Strategies of Containment: A Critical Appraisal of Postwar American National Security Policy* (New York: Oxford University Press, 1982), 212; Sherry, *In the Shadow of War*, 242–44.

57. Wheelus Air Base Background Paper, Visit of the Libyan Crown Prince, 16–24 October 1962, CPV-III-G, 11 October 1962, *DDRS* 1983-1042: 1–4, quote 2.

58. Discussion at the 436th Meeting of the National Security Council, National Security Council Memorandum, 10 March 1960, *DDRS* 1991-1991: 1–16; Memorandum From the Assistant Secretary of State for African Affairs (Williams) to Secretary of State Rusk, 6 September 1963, *FR*, 1961–1963, vol. 21, Africa: 156–57. On the politics of the United Kingdom of Libya see Elizabeth R. Hayford, "The Politics of the Kingdom of Libya in Historical Perspective," Ph.D. dissertation, Tufts University, 1971, and Salaheddin Hasan, "The Genesis of the Political Leadership of Libya, 1952–1969: Historical Origins and Development of Its Component Parts," Ph.D. dissertation, George Washington University, 1973.

59. Memorandum from Robert W. Komer of the National Security Council Staff to President Kennedy, 15 October 1962, *FR*, 1961–63, 21: 142–44, quote 142; Visit of the Libyan Crown Prince, 16–24 October 1962, *DDRS* 1984-2532: 1–2; H. B. Sharabi, "Libya's Pattern of Growth," *Current History* (January 1963): 41–45; Khadduri, *Modern Libya*, 314–17.

60. Memorandum from D. D. Newsom to R. W. Komer, Prime Minister Fikini of Libya, 29 September 1963, *DDRS* 1991-3499: 1–2, quotes 1–2.

61. Memorandum for Mr. McGeorge Bundy, Libyan Prime Minister Fekini's Meeting with President Kennedy, Department of State, 27 September 1963, *DDRS* 1988-2709: 1–3, quote 2.

62. Telegram from the Department of State to the Embassy in Tripoli, Libya, 7 October 1963, *FR*, 1961–63, 21: 159–60, quote 159; Telegram from the Department of State to the Embassy in Benghazi, Libya, 29 June 1963, *FR*, 1961–63, 21: 154; Moncef Djaziri, *État et société en Libye: Islam, politique et modernité* (Paris: L'Harmattan, 1996), 54.

63. Jules Davids, *The United States in World Affairs* (New York: Harper and Row, 1965), 256–57, quote 256; Mustafa Sedd El-Ghariani, "Libya's Foreign Policy: The Role of the Country's Environmental and Leadership Factors, 1960–1973." M.A. thesis, Western Michigan University, 1979, 127–29.

64. Ali Muhammad Shembesh, "The Analysis of Libya's Foreign Policy, 1962–1973: A Study of the Impact of Environmental and Leadership Factors," Ph.D. dissertation, Emory University, 1975, 190–93; Ben-Halim, *Libya*, 87–97; De Candole, *Idris*, 133–35; Djaziri, *État et société*, 54–55.

65. Telegram from the Department of State to the Embassy Office in Baida, Libya, 8 March 1964, *FR*, 1964–68, vol. 24, Africa: 2–3, Internet edition; Memorandum from the President's Special Assistant for National Security Affairs (Bundy) and Robert W. Komer of the National Security Staff to President Johnson, 17 March 1964, *FR*, 1964–68, 24: 4, Internet edition.

66. Memorandum from Robert W. Komer of the National Security Council Staff

to President Johnson, 8 August 1964, *FR*, 1964–68, 24: 5, Internet edition; Telegram from the Embassy in Libya to the Department of State, 30 March 1965, *FR*, 1964–68, 24: 1–2, Internet edition.

67. Letter from President Johnson to King Idris, 1 September 1965, *FR*, 1964–68, 24: 5–6, Internet edition; Memorandum from Robert W. Komer of the National Security Council Staff to President Johnson, 31 August 1965, *FR*, 1964–68, 24: 4–5, Internet edition.

68. Telegram from the Department of State to the Embassy in Libya, 7 June 1967, *FR*, 1964–68, 24: 4–5, Internet edition; Telegram from the Department of State to the Embassy in Libya, 13 June 1967, *FR*, 1964–68, 24: 5–6, Internet edition.

69. Memorandum from W. W. Rostow to the President, The White House, 17 June 1967, *DDRS* 1984-2120: 1. On the impact of the 1967 war see Cricco, "La Libia nella politica delle grandi potenze," 141–48.

70. Memorandum from the President's Special Assistant (Rostow) to President Johnson, 11 April 1968, *FR*, 1964–68, 24: 10–11, Internet edition; William H. Lewis, "Libya: The End of Monarchy," *Current History* (January 1970): 36–37; El-Ghariani, "Libya's Foreign Policy," 98–99, 124–26.

71. Ruth First, *Libya: The Elusive Revolution* (Harmondsworth: Penguin, 1974), 75–86; Wright, *Libya*, 89–118; Ragaei El Mallakh, "The Economics of Rapid Growth," *Middle East Journal* 23, 3 (Summer 1969): 308–20; Lewis, "Libya," 36.

72. "British Denied Libyan SOS on '69 Coup, Records Show," *New York Times*, 2 January 2002.

Chapter 6. One September Revolution

1. Mu'ammar al-Qaddafi dominated the RCC from the outset, and all major policy statements bore the imprint of his personality and thinking. Many observers, like Henri Pierre Habib, tended to underestimate the extent of Qaddafi's power, describing him as simply first among equals in a collegial executive body of military officers. *Politics and Government of Revolutionary Libya* (Montreal: Cercle du Livre de France, 1975), 172–74.

2. Muammar Qaddafi, *Escape to Hell and Other Stories* (Montreal: Stanké, 1998), 48–49.

3. Salah El Saadany, *Egypt and Libya from Inside, 1969–1976: The Qaddafi Revolution and the Eventual Break in Relations, by the Former Egyptian Ambassador to Libya* (Jefferson, N.C.: McFarland, 1994), 5–11. While the Egyptian revolution clearly influenced the Libyan revolution, the available evidence suggests that the Libyan coup d'état caught the Egyptian government completely by surprise. Nothing has come to light in subsequent years to support the suggestion of contemporary America policy makers that the Libyan revolution was inspired, planned, and executed from Cairo.

4. "The Libyan Revolution in the Words of Its Leaders: Proclamations, Statements, Addresses, Declarations, and Interviews from September 1 to Announcement of the Counter-Plot (December 10)," *Middle East Journal* 24, 2 (Spring 1970): 218. Appropriately enough, the passwords employed by the Free Unionist

Officers' Movement during the coup d'état were "Palestine is ours" and "Jerusalem." Habib, *Politics*, 96.

5. Meredith O. Ansell and Ibrahim Massaud al-Arif, eds., *The Libyan Revolution: A Sourcebook of Legal and Historical Documents*, vol. 1, *September 1, 1969–August 30, 1970* (Stoughton, Wis.: Oleander, 1972), 108–13, quote 108; Libyan Arab Republic, Ministry of Information and Culture, *The Revolutionary March* (Tripoli: n.p., 1974), 13–14.

6. Ansell and al-Arif, *Libyan Revolution*, 108–13, quotes 108, 110.

7. Libyan Arab Republic, Ministry of Information and Culture, *Delivered by Col. Mo'ammar el-Gadhafi: 1. The Broadlines of the Third Theory; 2. The Aspects of the Third Theory; 3. The Concept of Jihad; 4. The Divine Concept of Islam* (Tripoli: General Administration for Information, 1973), 41–42.

8. *Foreign Broadcast Information Services, Daily Report: Middle East and North Africa* (hereafter *FBIS-MEA*), Washington, D.C., 4 March 1981: I10; *Jamahiriya Mail* (Tripoli), 18 November 1978.

9. "Interview of Col. Mu'ammar al-Qaddafi on U.A.R. Television on 2 Sha'ban 1389 = 14 October 1969," in Ansell and al-Arif, *Libyan Revolution*, 79–85, quote 79.

10. "Address Delivered by Col. Mu'ammar al-Qaddafi in Tripoli on 4 Sha'ban 1389 = 16 October 1969," in Ansell and al-Arif, *Libyan Revolution*, 88.

11. Libyan Arab Republic, *Broadlines*, 28–29, quote 28; "Law No. 56 of 1970 on the Protection of Morality in Public Places," in Ansell and al-Arif, *Libyan Revolution*, 217–18.

12. "Address Delivered by Col. Mu'ammar al-Qaddafi in Tripoli on 4 Sha'ban 1389 = 16 October 1969," in Ansell and al-Arif, *Libyan Revolution*, 86–95, quote 90.

13. Ahmed M. Ashiurakis, *A Concise History of the Libyan Struggle for Freedom* (Tripoli: General Publishing, Distributing & Advertising Co., 1976), 82–87; Elizabeth R. Hayford, "The Politics of the Kingdom of Libya in Historical Perspective," Ph.D. dissertation., Tufts University, 1971, 425, 483–84; "Evacuation Celebrations," *Progressive Libya* (July 1973): 1, 6. American evacuation of Wheelus Field on 11 June, nine days prior to the designated date, took the revolutionary government by surprise since extensive formalities had been scheduled for 20 June. American forces evacuated the base early due to concerns about the over-charged emotional atmosphere in Libya at the time. El Saadany, *Egypt and Libya*, 48–49.

14. El Saadany, *Egypt and Libya*, 25–28, 38. When Qaddafi first met Nasser on 1 December 1969, he reportedly "offered all of Libya's capabilities for the forth-coming battle with Israel, pointing out that this was the main purpose behind the Mirage deal, which would significantly bolster the air power of Egypt." El Saadany, *Egypt and Libya*, 28.

15. "Resolution by the Revolutionary Command Council Issuing Certain Regulations in Connection with Banks," in Ansell and al-Arif, *Libyan Revolution*, 102–4; Yusif A. Sayigh, *Arab Oil Policies in the 1970s: Opportunity and Responsibility* (London: Croom Helm, 1983), 44–49; Ruth First, *Libya: The Elusive Revolution* (Harmondsworth: Penguin, 1974), 210. For a more detailed discussion of Libyan oil policy during the first eighteen years of the revolution, see Ronald Bruce St John, *Qaddafi's World Design: Libyan Foreign Policy, 1969–1987* (London: Saqi, 1987), 107–24.

16. Mohamed R. Buzakuk, "Libya Took the Lead," *Progressive Libya* (December

1972): 6; Edith Penrose, "The Development of Crisis," in *The Oil Crisis*, ed. Raymond Vernon (New York: W.W. Norton, 1976), 40; Frank C. Waddams, *The Libyan Oil Industry* (London: Croom Helm, 1980), 230–36.

17. J. A. Allan, *Libya: The Experience of Oil* (London: Croom Helm, 1981), 186–87, 309–10; Judith Gurney, *Libya: The Political Economy of Oil* (Oxford: Oxford University Press, 1996), 58–61; Waddams, *Libyan Oil Industry*, 236–40.

18. Libyan Arab Republic, Ministry of Information and Culture, *The Revolution of 1st September: The Fourth Anniversary* (Benghazi: General Administration for Information, 1973), 226; Mohamed R. Buzakuk, "More Price Increases for Short-Haul Crudes," *Progressive Libya* (February 1973): 8; First, *Libya*, 203–4, 209–11; "BP's Lawsuit Against NPC Rejected," *Progressive Libya* (July 1973): 2.

19. St John, *Qaddafi's World Design*, 116–18.

20. Enzo Rossi, *Malta on the Brink: From Western Democracy to Libyan Satellite*, European Security Studies 5 (London: Institute for European Defence & Strategic Studies, 1986); "Gathafi Receives Mintof of Malta," *Progressive Libya* (February 1973): 4; *FBIS-MEA*, 4 September 1980: 11; *Middle East Economic Digest* 26, 12 (19–25 March 1982): 32.

21. Ronald Bruce St John, "Libyan Debacle in Sub-Saharan Africa, 1969–1987," in *The Green and the Black*, ed. René Lemarchand (Bloomington: Indiana University Press, 1988), 126–29. Qaddafi was boasting by late 1973 that he had isolated Israel from Africa. Mu'Ammar el Qathafi, *Discourses* (Valetta: Adam Publishers, 1975), 32, 118–19.

22. Qaddafi, *Escape to Hell*, 167–81, quotes 171–73.

23. Gadhafi, *Broadlines*, 14; "Interview with Colonel Kaddafi," *Progressive Libya* (May–June 1976): 1–2.

24. Muammar Al Qathafi, *The Green Book, Part III: The Social Basis of the Third Universal Theory* (Tripoli: Public Establishment for Publishing, Advertising and Distribution, 1979); Libyan Arab Republic, Ministry of Information and Culture, *The Fundamentals of the Third International Theory* (Tripoli: General Administration for Information, 1974), 3, 13–16. Qaddafi persistently denied an economic basis for this theory. "Gathafi's Press Conference in Paris," *Progressive Libya* (November–December 1973): 4.

25. Fouad Ajami, *The Arab Predicament: Arab Political Thought and Practice Since 1967* (Cambridge: Cambridge University Press, 1981), 199–200.

26. Libyan Arab Republic, Ministry of Information and Culture, *The Third International Theory: The Divine Concept of Islam and the Popular Revolution in Libya* (Tripoli: General Administration for Information, 1973), 11–15; Gadhafi, *Divine Concept of Islam*, 87–117; Gadhafi, *Aspects of the Third Theory*, 38.

27. Gadhafi, *Aspects of the Third Theory*, 42–43; *FBIS-MEA*, 14 July 1980: 11; *Al-Fajr-al-Jadid*, 20 February 1978: 3; U.S. Department of Commerce, Office of Technical Services, *Joint Publications Research Service* (Washington, D.C.) 70813, No. 1772, 21 February 1978: 135–36, 140 (hereafter *JPRS*); Ann Elizabeth Mayer, "Islamic Resurgence or New Prophethood: The Role of Islam in Qadhdafi's Ideology," in *Islamic Resurgence in the Arab World*, ed. Ali E. Hillal Dessouki (New York: Praeger, 1982), 196–220.

28. Knut S. Vikor, *Sufi and Scholar on the Desert Edge: Muhammad b. Ali al-Sanusi and His Brotherhood* (Evanston, Ill.: Northwestern University Press, 1995), 218–40; E. E. Evans-Pritchard, *The Sanusi of Cyrenaica* (Oxford: Oxford University Press,

1949), 1–28; Marius K. Deeb, "Militant Islam and Its Critics: The Case of Libya," in *Islamism and Secularism in North Africa*, ed. John Ruedy (New York: St. Martin's Press, 1996), 187–97.

29. *FBIS-MEA*, 25 January 1982: Q4; *FBIS-MEA*, 12 August 1980: I1; Marius K. Deeb and Mary-Jane Deeb, *Libya Since the Revolution: Aspects of Social and Political Development* (New York: Praeger, 1982), 93–108.

30. Gadhafi, *Concept of Jihad*, 53.

31. *FBIS-MEA*, 4 March 1981: I11; Oriana Fallaci, "Iranians Are Our Brothers: An Interview with Col. Muammar el-Qaddafi of Libya," *New York Times Magazine*, 16 December 1979: 125; "Col. El-Gathafi's Press Conference," *Progressive Libya* (June 1973): 8. Terrorism is defined here as the use by a group for political ends of covert violence which is usually directed against a government but may be against another group, class, or party. Ronald Bruce St John, "Terrorism and Libyan Foreign Policy, 1981–1986," *World Today* 42, 7 (July 1986): 111.

32. *FBIS-MEA*, 11 March 1981: Q3; *FBIS-MEA*, 18 October 1978: I6–I7.

33. "Resolution Establishing the Jihad Fund," in Ansell and al-Arif, *Libyan Revolution*, 115–17; "Law No. 44 of 1970 Imposing the Jihad Tax," in Ansell and al-Arif, *Libyan Revolution*, 131; "The Libyan Revolution in the Words of Its Leaders," 218–19; Qathafi, *Discourses*, 48–49.

34. El Saadany, *Egypt and Libya*, 6–11, quotes 8, 10.

35. Fouad Ajami, "The End of Pan-Arabism," *Foreign Affairs* 57, 2 (Winter 1978/79): 355–73, quote 357; Mohammad Hassanein Heikal, "Egyptian Foreign Policy," *Foreign Affairs* 56, 4 (July 1978): 719–22.

36. Mu'ammar al-Qadhdhafi, "A Visit to Fezzan," in *Man, State, and Society in the Contemporary Maghrib*, ed. I. William Zartman (New York: Praeger, 1973), 131–36, quote 133; Libyan Arab Republic, Ministry of Information and Culture, *Aspects of First of September Revolution* (Tripoli: General Administration for Information, 1973), 9–11.

37. Qadhdhafi, "Visit to Fezzan," quotes 133–34; Qathafi, *Discourses*, 69–90; *FBIS-MEA*, 5 March 1980: I7; *FBIS-MEA*, 9 June 1980: I2.

38. For additional detail on early merger attempts, see Nathan Alexander [Ronald Bruce St John]. "The Foreign Policy of Libya: Inflexibility amid Change," *Orbis* 24, 4 (Winter 1981): 832–38. In contrast to the Libyan approach, Baath ideology generally envisioned a union of the better-endowed Arab states with those whose progress was hampered by a lack of capital and natural resources. Gordon H. Torrey, "The Bath—Ideology and Practice," *Middle East Journal* 23, 4 (Autumn 1969): 451.

39. *FBIS-MEA*, 2 September 1980: I3; *FBIS-MEA*,10 September 1980: I4–I7; *FBIS-MEA*, 2 September 1981: Q4–Q5; *Middle East Economic Digest* 24, 51/52 (19–25 December 1980): 98.

40. St John, "Libyan Debacle in Sub-Saharan Africa," 125–38.

41. Leonard Binder, *The Ideological Revolution in the Middle East* (New York: Wiley, 1964), 241.

42. Qathafi, *Discourses*, 25–29, quote 29; Binder, *Ideological Revolution*, 240–51.

43. "Libyan Revolution in the Words of Its Leaders," 211.

44. Ibid., 212.

45. Libyan Arab Republic, *Fundamentals*, 5–6; *FBIS-MEA*, 4 March 1981: I10; *FBIS-MEA*, 14 May 1979: I5.

46. Qathafi, *Discourses*, 25–29, 47, 87; Gadhafi, *Broadlines*, 9–14, 23–26; Libyan Arab Republic, *Revolution of 1st September*, 250.

47. Seth P. Tillman, *The United States in the Middle East: Interests and Obstacles* (Bloomington: Indiana University Press, 1982), 123–274; Bernard Reich, "United States Middle East Policy," *Current History* 76, 443 (January 1979): 6–8, 41–42; Ethan Nadelmann, "Setting the Stage: American Policy Toward the Middle East, 1961–1966," *International Journal of Middle East Studies* 14, 4 (November 1982): 435–57.

48. John K. Cooley, *Libyan Sandstorm: The Complete Account of Qaddafi's Revolution* (New York: Holt, Rinehart and Winston, 1982), 13–14. There is general agreement that Western diplomats and intelligence services were initially surprised and confused by the coup. Judith Miller, *God Has Ninety-Nine Names: Reporting from a Militant Middle East* (New York: Simon and Schuster, 1996), 215; P. Edward Haley, *Qaddafi and the United States Since 1969* (New York: Praeger, 1984), 21, 24; Guy Arnold, *The Maverick State: Gaddafi and the New World Order* (London: Cassell, 1996), 89.

49. Adriana Bush, *Reagan: An American Story* (New York: TV Books, 1998), 219.

50. Henry Kissinger, *Years of Upheaval* (Boston: Little, Brown, 1982), 859–60.

51. Quoted in Kissinger, *Years of Upheaval*, 860; Mahmoud G. ElWarfally, *Imagery and Ideology in U.S. Policy Toward Libya, 1969–1982* (Pittsburgh: University of Pittsburgh Press, 1988), 85–86.

52. Department of State, *Bulletin*, 29 September 1969.

53. El Saadany, *Egypt and Libya*, 75–77; ElWarfally, *Imagery and Ideology*, 76–77.

54. Waddams, *Libyan Oil Industry*, 251–60; ElWarfally, *Imagery and Ideology*, 80–81. On Libyan crude oil exports by destination, 1962–93, see Gurney, *Libya*, 108, 129.

55. Newsom, statement before the House Foreign Affairs Committee, 19 July 1971; quoted in ElWarfally, *Imagery and Ideology*, 81.

56. Cooley, *Libyan Sandstorm*, 80–100; William Gutteridge, ed., *Libya: Still a Threat to Western Interests?* Conflict Studies160 (London: Institute for the Study of Conflict, 1984), 17; Haley, *Qaddafi*, 24.

57. Colin Legum, ed., *Africa Contemporary Record: Annual Survey and Documents*, vol. 5, 1972–73 (New York: Holmes and Meier, 1973), B54; Legum, *Africa Contemporary Record*, vol. 10, 1977–78, A78; ElWarfally, *Imagery and Ideology*, 88–89.

58. Vernon Loeb, "Fallout for a CIA Affidavit," *Washington Post*, 24 April 2000; Peter Maas, "Selling Out," *New York Times Magazine*, 13 April 1986; Seymour M. Hersh, "The Qaddafi Connection," *New York Times Magazine*, 14 June 1981.

59. United States Policy Toward North Africa: Statement by Assistant Secretary Newsom Before the Subcommittees on Africa and the Near East of the House Committee on Foreign Affairs, July 19, 1972, Richard P. Stebbins and Elaine P. Adam, eds., *American Foreign Relations: A Documentary Record, 1972* (New York: New York University Press, 1976), 371–78, quotes 374–75; Ronald Bruce St John, "Libya's Foreign and Domestic Policies," *Current History* 80, 470 (December 1981): 426–27.

60. Lisa Anderson, "Qadhdhafi and the Kremlin," *Problems of Communism* 34 (September–October 1985): 29–44; Roger F. Pajak, "Arms and Oil: The Soviet-Libyan Arms Supply Relationship," *Middle East Review* 13, 2 (Winter 1980–81): 51–56; *Progressive Libya* (May–June 1975): 2–3.

61. Ronald Bruce St John, "The Soviet Penetration of Libya," *World Today* 38, 4 (April 1982): 131–38; *FBIS-MEA*, 12 June 979: I3 and 30 April 1981: Q1–Q3.

62. *FBIS-MEA*, 12 October 1978: I6; 27 July 1981: Q1; and 2 September 1981: Q12–Q14; *Middle East Economic Digest* 25, 36 (4–10 September 1981): 26.

63. Brian L. Davis, *Qaddafi, Terrorism, and the Origins of the U.S. Attack on Libya* (New York: Praeger, 1990), 35; Dirk Vandewalle, *Libya Since Independence: Oil and State-Building* (Ithaca, N.Y.: Cornell University Press, 1998), 113; John K. Cooley, "The Libyan Menace," *Foreign Policy* 42 (Spring 1981): 84. Ambassador Palmer asked to be recalled in 1972 because the Libyan government refused to deal with him. Haley, *Qaddafi*, 24.

64. Michael S. Sherry, *In the Shadow of War: The United States Since the 1930s* (New Haven, Conn.: Yale University Press, 1995), 337–38, quote 338. Arguing that American credibility was at stake around the globe, Henry Kissinger was an especially strong advocate of the use of force in the *Mayaguez* affair. Although the Ford administration billed the event as a foreign policy triumph, the sad statistics were forty-one American military men killed and nine wounded, together with an untold number of Cambodians, to rescue forty American seamen. William Shawcross, *Sideshow: Kissinger, Nixon, and the Destruction of Cambodia* (New York: Simon and Schuster, 1979), 433–35. For a more detailed discussion of the *Mayaguez* affair, see Ralph Wetterhahn, *The Last Battle: The Mayaguez Incident and the End of the Vietnam War* (New York: Carroll and Graf, 2001).

65. Cooley, *Libyan Sandstorm*, 265, 284; Davis, *Qaddafi*, 37–38.

66. St John, "Libya's Foreign and Domestic Policies," 426–27; Raymond H. Cleveland et al., *A Global Perspective on Transnational Terrorism: A Case Study of Libya*, Research Report 25 (Maxwell Air Force Base Alabama: Air War College, 1977); ElWarfally, *Imagery and Ideology*, 106–8. The author disagrees with the suggestion of Guy Arnold (*Maverick State*, 91–92) that the deterioration in American-Libyan relations reached a point of no return as early as 1976. Even though the Carter administration was soon disenchanted with the Qaddafi regime, there was a noticeable effort on both sides over the next four years to discover areas of accord.

67. Cooley, *Libyan Sandstorm*, 80–82; Simons, *Libya*, 317.

68. "State-Sponsored Terrorism," Statement by the Secretary of Defense (Weinberger), 21 January 1987, *American Foreign Policy: Current Documents* (Washington, D.C.: U.S. Government Printing Office, 1987), 235; Claudia Wright, "Libya and the West: Headlong into Confrontation?" *International Affairs* 8, 1 (Winter 1981–82): 24–25; Gutteridge, *Libya*, 17–18; Frank Lennon, "Libya Seeks Personal Contacts to Counter Official Sanctions," *Middle East Economic Digest* 22, 32 (11 August 1978): 4.

69. Youssef M. Ibrahim, "Qaddafi Calls the $220,000 Loan Part of Billy Carter Business Deals," *New York Times*, 10 August 1980; *Inquiry into the Matter of Billy Carter and Libya*, Report together with additional views of the Committee on the Judiciary, Subcommittee to Investigate Individuals Representing the Interests of Foreign Governments to the United States, Senate (2 October 1980) (Washington, D.C.: U.S. Government Printing Office, 1980): 7; "Billy Carter Investigations—Your Personal Notes," Memorandum for the President, 8 September 1980, *DDRS* 1994–1713: 1–3; "Text of U.S. Documents on Billy's Trip," *New York Times*, 3 August 1980. Frank Terpil, a former U.S. government employee hired by the Libyan government in the mid-1970s and later arraigned on arms-trafficking charges, translated for Billy Carter during his visit to the tenth anniversary celebrations in September 1979. Cooley, *Libyan Sandstorm*, 176.

70. "NSC Role in Aircraft Sales to Libya," 16 September 1986, *DDRS* 1994-1634: 1–3; Johnny Rizq and Robin Allen, "Libya Presses for Decision on Boeings," *Middle East Economic Digest* 23, 50 (14 December 1979): 15.

71. "Al-Qadhdhafi Addresses Celebration on Removal of U.S. Bases," *FBIS-MEA*, 12 June 1979: I1-I2.

72. "Tripoli Demonstration at U.S. Embassy Reported," *FBIS-MEA*, 3 December 1979: I1; Department of State, *Bulletin*, October 1980: 61; Eugene Mannoni, "Le danger Kadhafi," *Le Point* 386 (11 février 1990): 47–53; "A Prophet with an Illusion," *Africa* 94 (June 1979): 50–51. Ambassador William L. Eagleton, Jr., chargé d'affaires at the U.S. embassy in Tripoli at the time, believes television coverage of the mobs in Teheran may have inspired the attack on the U.S. embassy. Personal correspondence, 31 August 2000.

73. Memorandum of Conversation, President Carter, Zbigniew Brzezinski, and Ali El-Houdari, 6 December 1979, *DDRS* 1994-1712: 1–2, quote 1. Chargé d'affaires Eagleton returned to Tripoli from consultations in Washington about this time with a message from President Carter to Qaddafi that included the additional condition that Qaddafi give personal assurances regarding the security of the embassy and its personnel. Qaddafi refused to receive Eagleton, despite his repeated requests for an interview, and later told a reporter that he would deal with the Americans only after a people's committee, similar to those being organized by the Libyans in their embassies around the world, had been formed by the Americans to take over the U.S. embassy. Personal correspondence, 31 August 2000.

74. Personal correspondence, 31 August 2000, 2.

75. President Carter's reply and covering letter, 4 August 1980, to Senator Birch Bayh, Chairman, Subcommittee of the Committee on the Judiciary, in *Inquiry into the Matter of Billy Carter and Libya*, hearings before the subcommittee to investigate the activities of individuals representing the interests of foreign governments, 96th Congress, Second Session, 3, Appendix, 1479; quoted in Cooley, *Libyan Sandstorm*, 176.

76. Christopher S. Wren, "Libya's Identity Blurred by Ties With East, West and Terrorism," *New York Times*, 14 October 1979.

77. Richard D. Lyons, "Suspect Libyan Terrorists Were Watched by F.B.I.," *New York Times*, 9 May 1980; Youssef M. Ibrahim, "Foreign Workers in Libya Subjected to Harassment," *New York Times*, 27 August 1980.

78. Patrick Blum, "Gafsa Attack Raises Shockwaves," *Middle East Economic Digest* (8 February 1980): 42; Peter Blackburn, "Tunisia Blames Libya for Night Attack," *Middle East Economic Digest* 24, 5 (1 February 1980): 39.

79. Mannoni, "Le danger Kadhafi,"; "US Embassy Closes," *Middle East Economic Digest* 24, 7 (15 February 1980) 37; Daniel Pipes, "No One Likes the Colonel," *American Spectator* 14, 3 (March 1981): 18–22. Following the attack on the French embassy, Chargé d'Affaires Eagleton recommended that the U.S. embassy in Tripoli be closed on the grounds its security could not be assured. Personal correspondence, 31 August 2000.

80. "Jallud Comments on 'Liquidating' Libyan Expatriates," *FBIS-MEA*, 6 June 1980: I1-I2; "Four Libya Diplomats Are Expelled by U.S. For Harassing Exiles," *New York Times*, 5 May 1980. On 1 September 1979, Qaddafi called on Libyans living abroad to organize popular marches and to occupy their embassies. Libyan embassies everywhere soon became people's bureaus, with the ambassador

replaced by a people's committee. Mohammed Wahby, "People power diplomacy for Libya," *Middle East Economic Digest* 23, 36 (7 September 1979): 18.

81. *Washington Post,* 22 October 1980; Richard Halloran, "Libyans Are Challenging U.S. Forces in War of Nerves," *New York Times,* 24 October 1980.

Chapter 7. Reagan Agonistes

1. Barry Rubin, "The Reagan Administration and the Middle East," in *Eagle Defiant: United States Foreign Policy in the 1980s,* ed. Kenneth A. Oye, Robert J. Lieber, and Donald Rothchild (Boston: Little, Brown, 1983), 367. For context see Daniel Yankelovich and Larry Kaagan, "Assertive America," in *The Reagan Foreign Policy,* ed. William G. Hyland (New York: Meridian, 1987), 1–18.

2. Robert S. Barrett, "U.S. Policy in North Africa," *American-Arab Affairs* 13 (Summer 1985): 41–42; Tim Zimmerman, "The American Bombing of Libya: A Success for Coercive Diplomacy?" *Survival* 29, 3 (May/June 1987): 208–9; Robert E. Osgood, "The Revitalization of Containment," in *Reagan Foreign Policy,* ed. Hyland, 45. The activist approach of the Reagan administration sparked an intellectual debate among Middle East specialists and policy analysts over Libya and terrorism. While not sympathetic to many of the arguments raised in this debate, Brian Davis (*Qaddafi, Terrorism, and the Origins of the U.S. Attack on Libya* [New York: Praeger, 1990], 38–47) provides a thought-provoking analysis of the discussion.

3. Nathan Alexander [Ronald Bruce St John], "The Foreign Policy of Libya: Inflexibility amid Change," *Orbis* 24, 4 (Winter 1981): 819–46; Ronald Bruce St John, "Libya's 'New' Foreign Policy," *Contemporary Review* 243, 1410 (July 1983): 15–18. The author strongly disagrees with analysts like Mansour O. El-Kikhia, author of a well-written and perceptive study of Qaddafi's Libya, who suggest that Libyan foreign policy was in disarray in the late 1970s or early 1980s (El-Kikhia, *Libya's Qaddafi: The Politics of Contradiction* [Gainesville: University Press of Florida, 1997], 112). On the contrary, inflexibility in the face of constant global change best characterized that policy.

4. J. A. Allan, "Libya Accommodates to Lower Oil Revenues: Economic and Political Adjustments," *International Journal of Middle East Studies* 15, 2 (August 1983): 377–85; Shukri Ghanem, "The Oil Industry and the Libyan Economy: The Past, the Present, and the Likely Future," in *The Economic Development of Libya,* ed. Bichard Khader and Bashir El-Wifati (London: Croom Helm, 1987), 67–68.

5. Pamela Chasek, "Revolution Across the Sea: Libyan Foreign Policy in Central America," in *Central America & the Middle East: The Internationalization of the Crises,* ed. Damián J. Fernández (Miami: Florida International University Press, 1990), 150–76.

6. "Libya Is an African Problem," Testimony by the Assistant Secretary of State Designate for African Affairs (Crocker) Before the Senate Foreign Relations Committee (6 April 1981), *American Foreign Policy: Current Documents* (Washington, D.C.: U.S. Government Printing Office, 1981), 1148. While the literature on Libyan intervention in Chad is vast, the following are especially recommended: J. Millard Burr and Robert O. Collins, *Africa's Thirty Years War: Libya, Chad, and the Sudan,*

1963–1993 (Boulder, Colo.: Westview Press, 1999); Sam C. Nolutshungu, *Limits of Anarchy: Intervention and State Formation in Chad* (Charlottesville: University Press of Virginia, 1996); Guy Jérémie Ngansop, *Tchad: Vingt ans de crise* (Paris: L'Harmattan, 1986); Bernard Lanne, *Tchad-Libye: La querelle des frontières* (Paris: Karthala, 1982).

7. "Possible Libyan Assassination Attempt," Central Intelligence Agency, National Foreign Assessment Center, August 24, 1981, *DDRS* 1988-1937: 1; "Reports of Libyan Assassination Squads," Transcript of an Interview with President Reagan (30 November 1981), *American Foreign Policy: Current Documents*, 1981, 795–96.

8. Ronald Bruce St John, *Qaddafi's World Design: Libyan Foreign Policy, 1969–1987* (London: Saqi Books, 1987), 136.

9. "Libyan Activities," Statement by the Assistant Secretary of State for African Affairs (Crocker) Before Subcommittees of the Senate Foreign Relations Committee (8 July 1981), *American Foreign Policy: Current Documents*, 1981), 1148–51, quotes 1148–49, 1150.

10. "Al-Qadhdhafi Address," *FBIS-MEA*, 2 September 1981: Q3–Q19, quotes Q12–Q13; St John, "The Soviet Penetration of Libya," *World Today* 38, 4 (April 1982): 135–36; "U.S. Planes Attacked by Libyan Aircraft," Department of State *Bulletin* (October 1981): 57–60.

11. "Closing of the Libyan People's Bureau in Washington," Transcript of a Department of State Special Briefing (6 May 1981), *American Foreign Policy: Current Documents*, 1981,787; St John, *Qaddafi's World Design*, 82; "Request for U.S. Citizens to Leave Libya," Statement by the Secretary of State (Haig) (10 December 1981), *American Foreign Policy: Current Documents*, 1981, 796.

12. While the literature on the legal aspects of the Gulf of Sirte controversy is voluminous, the following articles provide a good introduction. Alessandro Silj, "The Gulf of Sidra Incident: March–April 1986," *International Spectator* 28, 1 (January–March 1993): 75–105; Stephen R. Langford, *Libya: The Gulf of Sirte Closing Line*, IBRU Boundary Briefing 3 (Durham: International Boundaries Research Unit, 1990); Roger Cooling Haerr, "The Gulf of Sidra," *San Diego Law Review* 24, 751 (1987): 751–67; Yehuda Z. Blum, "The Gulf of Sidra Incident," *American Journal of International Law* 80 (1986): 668–77; Francesco Francioni, "The Status of the Gulf of Sirte in International Law," *Syracuse Journal of International Law and Commerce* 11 (1984): 311–26. The Gulf of Sirte is also known as the Gulf of Sidra.

13. Claudia Wright, "Libya and the West: Headlong into Confrontation?" *International Affairs* 58, 1 (Winter 1981–82): 16

14. David Ignatius, "U.S. Seeks to Mobilize Opponents of Khadafy in Libya and Outside," *Wall Street Journal*, 14 July 1981; "Kaddafi's Dangerous Game," *Newsweek*, 20 July 1981; "Searching for Hit Teams," *Time*, 21 December 1981; Mahmoud G. El-Warfally, *Imagery and Ideology in U.S. Policy Toward Libya, 1969–1982* (Pittsburgh: University of Pittsburgh Press, 1988), 175–78.

15. Donald Rothchild and John Ravenhill, "From Carter to Reagan: The Global Perspective on Africa Becomes Ascendant," in *Eagle Defiant*, ed. Oye, Lieber, and Rothchild, 352–53; St John, "Libya's Foreign and Domestic Policies," *Current History* 80, 470 (December 1981): 426–29, 434–35; Bernard Gwertzman, "U.S. Pledges to Aid African Countries That Resist Libyans," *New York Times*, 3 June 1981.

16. St John, "Soviet Penetration of Libya," 137–38.

17. For the European reaction to the American call for sanctions see St John,

"Terrorism and Libyan Foreign Policy, 1981–1986," *The World Today* 42, 7 (July 1986): 113–14.

18. George P. Shultz, *Turmoil and Triumph: My Years as Secretary of State* (New York: Scribner's, 1993), 677; Ellen Laipson, "U.S. Policy in Northern Africa," *American-Arab Affairs* 6 (Autumn 1983): 52–53; *New York Times*, 11 March 1982; *International Herald Tribune*, 17–18 December 1983.

19. "Denial of Any U.S. Role in Failure of OAU Summit in Tripoli," Remarks by Vice President Bush, Lagos (13 November 1982), *American Foreign Policy: Current Documents*, 1982, 1263.

20. Wright, "Libya and the West," 14; St John, *Qaddafi's World Design*, 82–83.

21. Dirk Vandewalle, *Libya Since Independence: Oil and State-Building* (Ithaca, N.Y.: Cornell University Press, 1998), 113–14.

22. St John, "Terrorism and Libyan Foreign Policy," 112. In discussing the oil embargo imposed by the Reagan administration in 1982, Judith Gurney (*Libya: The Political Economy of Oil* [Oxford: Oxford University Press, 1996], 70) concludes that the U.S. ban on the import of Libyan crude oil "did not seriously affect Libyan production as the government had little difficulty finding west and east European markets to absorb the exports formerly intended for the USA." The author finds this analysis incomplete because crude oil production in Libya clearly dropped from 1981 to 1984, as indicated in Gurney's chart, "Libyan Crude Oil Production" (*Libya*, 92). Technically true, the suggestion that European markets made up the U.S. shortfall overlooks the fact that total Libyan crude oil exports declined every year from 1981 to 1985. See Gurney's "Libyan Crude Oil Exports by Destination (1980–1993)" (*Libya*, 129).

23. *Middle East Economic Digest* 29, 49 (7–13 December 1985): 30.

24. Michael Ritchie, "Libya: Qaddafi Warns of Further Austerity," *Middle East Economic Digest* 29, 36 (7–13 September 1985): 20–21; *Financial Times*, 10 September 1985; John Damis, "Morocco, Libya and the Treaty of Union," *American-Arab Affairs* 13 (Summer 1985): 44–55.

25. Tony Walker, "Gaddafi's Libya: Why Testing Times Lie Ahead," *Financial Times*, 10 September 1985.

26. H. S. McKenzie and B. O. Elsaleh, "The Libyan Great Man-Made River Project: Project Overview," *Proceedings of the Institute of Civil Engineers: Water, Maritime and Energy* 106 (June 1994): 103–22; J. A. Allan, "The Great Man-Made River: Progress and Prospects of Libya's Great Water Carrier," *Libyan Studies* 19 (1988): 141–46; Teresa English, "Libya's GMR Defies Its Critics," *Middle East Economic Digest* 33, 37 (22 September 1989): 4–5; Toby Odone, "Doubts Surround Libya's Ambitious Irrigation Plans," *Middle East Economic Digest* 27, 49 (9 December 1983): 26–28. On the early involvement of Brown and Root in the American political process see Robert A. Caro, *The Years of Lyndon Johnson: The Path to Power* (New York: Vintage Books, 1990), 1: 450, 458–68, 473–74, 577–78, 607–8; Robert Dallek, *Lone Star Rising: Lyndon Johnson and His Times, 1908–1960* (New York: Oxford University Press, 1991), 402, 450.

27. Lisa Anderson, "Qadhdhafi and His Opposition," *Middle East Journal* 40, 2 (Spring 1986): 225–37; George Joffé, "Islamic Opposition in Libya," *Third World Quarterly* 10, 2 (April 1988): 615–31.

28. Lisa Anderson, "Ignore Qaddafi," *New York Times*, 17 December 1981; Robert Bailey, "Libyan Order Marks Further Airbus Success," *Middle East Economic Digest* 25, 48 (27 November 1981): 20; Helena Cobban, "Europe Learns to Live with Qaddafi—Despite His Deeds in the Past," *Christian Science Monitor*, 11 December 1981.

29. Rothchild and Ravenhill, "From Carter to Reagan," 360–63, quote 362–63. For context see Coral Bell, "From Carter to Reagan," in *Reagan Foreign Policy*, ed. Hyland, 57–77.

30. "Notifying Libya Not to Interfere with the AWACS Airplanes in Sudan," Transcript of a Press Conference by the Secretary of State (Shultz) (20 March 1984), *American Foreign Policy: Current Documents*, 1984, 894.

31. The pressure of the Reagan administration on the Libyan government caused a growing number of apologists for the Qaddafi regime to surface in this time frame. For example, see Bob Abdrabboh, ed., *Libya in the 1980's: Challenges & Changes* (Washington, D.C.: International Economics and Research, Inc., 1985); Mohamed O'Bai Samura, *The Libyan Revolution: Its Lessons for Africa* (Washington, D.C.: International Institute for Policy and Development Studies, 1995); Themba Sono, ed., *Libya: The Vilified Revolution* (Langley, Md.: Progress Press Publications, 1984); *Understanding Libya's Role in World Politics* (Washington, D.C.: People's Committee for Students of the Socialist People's Libyan Arab Jamahiriya, 1984).

32. "Prohibition of Libyan Petroleum Products," Executive Order 12538, Issued by President Reagan (15 November 1985), *American Foreign Policy: Current Documents*, 1985, 602; Bob Woodward, "CIA Reportedly Plans to Undermine Qadhafi," *International Herald Tribune*, 4 November 1985; St John, *Qaddafi's World Design*, 83. Western European governments had been arguing for years that it made no sense for the United States to impose a partial economic embargo on Libya but continue to contribute billions of dollars annually to the Libyan treasury in the form of oil receipts. "Libyan Troops in Chad; American Oil Firms in Libya," Transcript of the Department of State Daily Press Briefing (20 November 1984), *American Foreign Policy: Current Documents*, 1984, 904–5.

33. Untitled Document, Hand-Written Date, 20 February 20 1987, *DDRS* 1991-0046: 1.

34. Noam Chomsky, *Pirates & Emperors: International Terrorism in the Real World* (New York: Claremont Research and Publications, 1986), 128–31; Ehud Ya'ari, "Abu Nidal's New Brand of Terrorism," *Wall Street Journal*, 31 December 1985; David B. Ottaway, "U.S., Egypt Believe Libya Masterminded EgyptAir Hijacking," *International Herald Tribune*, 28 November 1985; Shultz, *Turmoil and Triumph*, 677.

35. *Financial Times*, 16 April 1986; *International Herald Tribune*, 23 April 1986.

36. *Financial Times*, 29 April 1986.

37. "Libya: Imports Face a Sharp Cutback," *Middle East Economic Digest* 30, 15 (12–18 April 1986): 39; *Jeune Afrique*, 19 February 1986: 52; Tony Walker, "The Financial Squeeze on Qaddafi," *Financial Times*, 22 April 1986.

38. *Le Monde*, 27 March 1986.

39. Jonathan Marcus, "French Policy and Middle East Conflicts: Change and Continuity," *The World Today* (February 1986): 28; *Italian Business Trends* (24 January 1986): 2–4.

40. Paul Wilkinson, "State-Sponsored International Terrorism: The Problems of Response," *The World Today* (July 1984): 294; *International Herald Tribune*, 9 January 1986 and 19–20 April 1986; *Wall Street Journal* (Europe), 24 April 1986.

41. "Qadhafi . . . A Pariah in the World Community," Statement by the President (7 January 1986), *American Foreign Policy: Current Documents*, 1986, 446–47.

42. "U.S. Goals Toward Libya," Prepared Statement by the Assistant Secretary of State for Near Eastern and South Asian Affairs (Murphy) (28 January 1986), *American Foreign Policy: Current Documents*, 1986, 448–49.

43. Shultz, *Turmoil and Triumph*, 669–78; *International Herald Tribune*, 9 January 1986, 25–26 January 1986; *Middle East Economic Digest* 29, 19 (10–16 May 1985): 47; *Middle East Economic Digest* 29, 47 (23–29 November 1985): 31.

44. Jane Mayer and Doyle McManus, *Landslide: The Unmaking of the President, 1984–1988* (Boston: Houghton Mifflin, 1988), 221. There is widespread agreement that the Reagan administration targeted the Qaddafi regime largely because it was vulnerable. For examples see Judith Miller, *God Has Ninety-Nine Names: Reporting from a Militant Middle East* (New York: Simon and Schuster, 1996), 225; Chomsky, *Pirates and Emperors*, 131–33; Simons, *Libya*, 324–32.

45. "US to Reject Fresh Bid for Talks from Gadaffi," *Financial Times*, 3 April 1986; St John, *Qaddafi's World Design*, 84; *International Herald Tribune*, 26 March 1986.

46. *New York Times*, 23 March 1986; Shultz, *Turmoil and Triumph*, 678–79.

47. Shultz, *Turmoil and Triumph*, 683; Davis, *Qaddafi*, 115–18. For details of the intercepts see David Locke Hall, *The Reagan Wars: A Constitutional Perspective on War Powers and the Presidency* (Boulder, Colo.: Westview Press, 1991), 213–14. On the weakness of the La Belle justification see Simons, *Libya*, 342–43. Reagan biographers, on the other hand, generally concentrate on the La Belle bombing to the exclusion of other motivations for the 1986 air raid. For example, see Frances Fitzgerald, *Way Out There in the Blue: Reagan, Star Wars, and the End of the Cold War* (New York: Simon and Schuster, 2000), 332.

48. "U.S. Air Strikes Against Libya," Statement by the President (14 April 1986), *American Foreign Policy: Current Documents*, 1986, 450–51. The journalist Seymour M. Hersh later concluded that the primary aim of the Tripoli bombings was to kill Qaddafi ("Target Qaddafi," *New York Times Magazine*, 22 February 1987).

49. "US Calls Libya Raid a Success; 'Choice Is Theirs,' Reagan Says; Moscow Cancels Shultz Talks," *New York Times*, 16 April 1986; Edmund Morris, *Dutch: A Memoir of Ronald Reagan* (New York: Random House, 1999), 586; Chomsky, *Pirates and Emperors*, 142–46. For military details on the U.S. raid on Libya see Joseph T. Stanik, *"Swift and Effective Retribution": The U.S. Sixth Fleet and the Confrontation with Qaddafi*, U.S. Navy in the Modern World Series 3 (Washington, D.C.: U.S. Government Printing Office, 1996) and Col. Robert E. Venkus, *Raid on Qaddafi: The Untold Story of History's Longest Fighter Mission by the Pilot Who Directed It* (New York: St. Martin's Press, 1992). Many legal scholars argued the raid was a clear violation of international law and possibly American law. Ann Elizabeth Mayer, "In Search of Sacred Law: The Meandering Course of Qadhafi's Legal Policy," in *Qadhafi's Libya, 1969 to 1994*, ed. Dirk Vandewalle (New York: St. Martin's Press, 1995), 128.

50. "OPEC Condemns U.S. Attack But Rules Out Oil Embargo," *International Herald Tribune*, 16 April 1986; *Wall Street Journal*, 21 April 1986 and 26–27 April 1986; R. W. Apple, Jr., "Middle East Experts Fear Libya Raid May Harm Interests of Moderate Arab States," *International Herald Tribune*, 22 April 1986.

51. Karen Elliott House, "The Mideast That Wants Qadhafi Toppled," *Wall Street Journal*, 17 April 1986; "U.S. Dismays Allies and Outrages Foes With Libya Bombing," *Wall Street Journal*, 16 April 1986; Frederick Kempe, "U.S. Foreign Policy Comes Under Fire After Libya Raid," *Wall Street Journal*, 21 April 1986.

52. Shultz, *Turmoil and Triumph*, 687.

53. François Soudan, "Le Kaddafi nouveau arrive," *Jeune Afrique* 1355–1356 (24 et 31 Decembre 1986): 34–36; "Al-Qadhdhafi Addresses Revolutionary Anniversary Rally," *FBIS-MEA*, 2 September 1986: Q1–Q24; Gerald F. Seib, "Gadhafi Reemerges Before Libyan Public, Confident, But More Cautious on Terrorism," *Wall Street Journal*, 2 September 1986; "Qadhdhafi Reaffirms Libyan Objectives," *FBIS-MEA*, 5 May 1986: Q4. The available evidence does not support the conclusion of Gottfried and others who suggest the 1986 bombing of Libya caused the Qaddafi regime to modify its international policies and behavior in "a gradual about-face." Ted Gottfried, *Libya: Desert Land in Conflict* (Brookfield, Conn.: Millbrook Press, 1994), 128. See Chomsky (*Pirates and Emperors*, 147–49) on American newspaper editorial support for the notion that the raid had prompted Qaddafi to reorient his foreign policy and terminate support for terrorism.

54. "Al-Qadhadhafi Addresses Revolution Anniversary Rally," *FBIS-MEA*, 2 September 1986: Q1–Q24, quotes Q1.

55. Philip Shehadi, "After a Lull, Committees in Libya Urge Attacks on U.S. Interests, Allies," *International Herald Tribune*, 27 August 1986; Hanspeter Mattes, "The Rise and Fall of the Revolutionary Committees," in *Qadhafi's Libya, 1969–1994*, ed. Dirk Vandewalle (New York: St. Martin's Press, 1995), 89–112; St John, *Historical Dictionary of Libya*, 3rd ed. (Lanham, Md.: Scarecrow Press, 1998), 220–22.

56. Tony Walker, "Defections Highlight Dissatisfaction in Libya's Military," *Financial Times*, 4 March 1987; David Hawley, "Libya Displays a New Militancy," *Middle East Economic Digest* 30, 36 (6–12 September 1986): 11; Nora Boustany, "Poorer But Still, It Seems, Loyal," *Financial Times*, 6 September 1986; "Libyan Opposition," *FBIS-MEA*, 1 July 1986: Q1; R.W. Apple Jr., "U.S. Hopes Libyan Military Will Seek Qadhafi's Removal," *International Herald Tribune*," 6 April 1986.

57. "Opposition," *FBIS-MEA*, 15 May 1986: Q1–Q2; Lisa Anderson, "Libya's Qaddafi: Still in Command?" *Current History* 86, 517 (February 1987): 65; Mary-Jane Deeb, *Libya's Foreign Policy in North Africa* (Boulder, Colo.: Westview Press, 1991), 172–73.

58. "Austerity Measures Implemented," *FBIS-MEA*, 30 May 1986: Q1; "Libya Bans English," *Financial Times*, 23 May 1986; Edward Schumacher, "The United States and Libya," *Foreign Affairs* 65, 2 (Winter 1986/87): 340–41.

59. Ihsan A. Hijazi, "Libya, Soviet at Odds After U. S. Air Raid," *International Herald Tribune*, 7 May 1986; James M. Markham, "Gorbachev Says Libya Raid May Hurt U.S.-Soviet Ties," *New York Times*, 19 April 1986; "Moscow Cancels Meeting, Citing U.S. Raid on Libya," *Wall Street Journal*, 16 April 1986.

60. Robert D. Hershey, Jr., "U.S. Oil Companies End All Operations in Libya," *International Herald Tribune*, 1 July 1986; Robert S. Greenberger, "U.S. to Prohibit Some Exports Tied to Libya," *Wall Street Journal*, 28 May 1986; Frances Ghilès, "US Groups Told to Stop Libya Oil Operations," *Financial Times*, 5 June 1986.

61. David Hawley, "Tripoli in Isolation," *Middle East Economic Digest* 30, 31 (2–8 August 1986): 4–6; Gurney, *Libya*, 70–71.

62. "State-Sponsored Terrorism," Statement by the Secretary of Defense (Weinberger) (January 21, 1987), *American Foreign Policy: Current Documents*, 1986, 230–32, quotes 230–31.

63. "In Collapse of Terror Talks, Jittery Allies," *International Herald Tribune*, 7–8 February 1987; Richard B. Strauss, "U.S. Policy On Libya Is Wavering," *International Herald Tribune*, 9 September 1986; David K. Shipler, "Where Will Reagan's Libyan Battle Plan Lead?" *New York Times*, 20 April 1986; Sheena Phillips, "The European Response," in *Mad Dogs: The US Raids on Libya*, ed. Mary Kaldor and Paul Anderson (London: Pluto Press, 1986), 41–47.

64. Robert Windrem, "Pan Am Bombing Part of Libya Plot," Special Report from MSNBC, Internet Edition, 16 February 2000; Robert Keatley, "Experts on Terrorism Fear It May Rise After U.S. Attacks," *Wall Street Journal*, 16 April 1986; Blaine Harden, "U.S. Aide At Embassy Is Shot in Khartoum," *International Herald Tribune*, 17 April 1986; John Winn Miller, "Italy May Scale Down Ties With Libya After Island Raid," *Wall Street Journal*, 18 April 1986.

65. James M. Markham, "Europeans Say Walters Was Sketchy on Libya," *International Herald Tribune*, 6–7 September 1986; Quentin Peel, "Walters Makes Discreet Calls on European Allies," *Financial Times*, 3 September 1986; David White, "Walters Denies 'Making Demands' over Libya," *Financial Times*, 2 September 1986.

66. Robin Allen, "Gulf States Warm to the Soviet Union," *Middle East Economic Digest* 31, 4 (24–30 January 1987): 2–3; David Hawley, "Libya: EEC Reaction Underlines Divisions," *Middle East Economic Digest* 30, 17 (26 April–2 May 1986): 6–8; Patrick Seale, "Qadhafi Is a Small Part of a Big Problem," *International Herald Tribune*, 25 April 1986.

67. John Walcott and Gerald F. Seib, "Col. Gadhafi and U.S. Again May Be Heading Toward Confrontation," *Wall Street Journal*, 25 August 1986; Bernard Weinraub, "U.S. Asserts Readiness to Thwart Gadhafi," *International Herald Tribune*, 27 August 1986; "Tripoli exige de preuves," *La Suisse*, 31 August 1986; "Think Before You Do Anything, Colonel," *Economist*, 30 August 1986; John Walcott, "U.S. Tries to Capitalize on Current Pressure to Bring About Libyan Leader's Downfall," *Wall Street Journal*, 2 September 1986; "US Steps Up Destabilisation Campaign," *Middle East Economic Digest* 30, 36 (6–12 September 1986): 25.

68. Bob Woodward, "U.S. Strategy of Deceit on Libya Reported," *International Herald Tribune*, 3 October 1986; John Walcott, "Campaign Against Gadhafi Backfires on White House," *Wall Street Journal*, 6 October 1986; Bernard Weinraub, "Reagan Confirms Secret Plan to Unnerve Gadhafi," *International Herald Tribune*, 4–5 October 1986.

69. Lou Cannon, *Ronald Reagan: The Role of a Lifetime* (New York: Public Affairs, 1991), 580; John Walcott and Ellen Hume, "Reverses like Iran Threaten to Unravel Reagan Foreign Policy," *Wall Street Journal*, 14 November 1986.

70. James Schlesinger, "Reykjavik and Revelations: A Turn of the Tide?" in *Reagan Foreign Policy*, ed. Hyland, 239–59; Roberto Suro, "Italian Cites U.S.-Libya Secret Link," *International Herald Tribune*, 20–21 December 1986.

71. Victor Mallet, "Gadaffi Rounds on Summit Delegates in Harare," *Financial Times*, 5 September 1996; "Gaddafi: Non-Aligned Useless," *Jerusalem Post*, 5 September 1996; Anderson, "Libya's Qaddafi," 87; Schumacher, "United States and Libya," 344.

72. James M. Markham, "Europeans Feeling a Drift in U.S. Policy," *International Herald Tribune*, 11 February 1987; St John, *Qaddafi's World Design*, 85.

73. John Orman, *Comparing Presidential Behavior: Carter, Reagan, and the Macho Presidential Style* (New York: Greenwood Press, 1987), 113–14.

74. "An Unusual and Extraordinary Threat," Letter from President Reagan to the Speaker of the House of Representatives (Wright) (12 January 1988), *American Foreign Policy: Current Documents*, 1988, 431–32.

75. "Prospects for an Improved Relationship with Libya," Statement Issued by the Department of State (15 March 1988), *American Foreign Policy: Current Documents*, 1988, 432.

76. *New York Times*, 24 December 1987; Michael R. Gordon, "U.S. Suspects Libyans of Chemical Arms Site," *International Herald Tribune*, 26–27 December 1987. Construction of the production facility at Rabta began in 1984, shortly after chemical weapons were used in the Iran-Iraq war. W. Andrew Terrill, "Libya and the Quest for Chemical Weapons," *Conflict Quarterly* 14, 1 (1994): 48–49.

77. Thomas C. Wiegele, *The Clandestine Building of Libya's Chemical Weapons Factory: A Study in International Collusion* (Carbondale: Southern Illinois University Press, 1992), 24–26.

78. "US Criticises Gaddafi over Chemical Arms," *South China Morning Post*, 16 September 1988; Don Oberdorfer, "U.S. Troubled by Plant Japanese Built in Libya," *International Herald Tribune*, 17-18 September 1988; "Japanese Involved in Chemical Weapons Charge," *Middle East Economic Digest* 32, 39 (30 September 1988): 37; David B. Ottaway, "CIA Director Says Libya Is Building a Large Chemical Weapons Plant," *International Herald Tribune*, 27 October 1988; Lou Cannon and David Ottaway, "U.S. Weighs Strike on Libyan Complex," *International Herald Tribune*, 23 December 1988.

79. "Qaddafi Denies Chemical Arms Assertion," *International Herald Tribune*, 28 October 1988; Jennifer Parmelee, "Courting West, Gadhafi Knock on Europe's Door," *International Herald Tribune*, 26–27 November 1988; Jennifer Parmelee, "A Visit to Libyan Plant Proves Inconclusive," *International Herald Tribune*, 9 January 1989; Wiegele, *Clandestine Building*, 30–33.

80. "International Cooperation Against Libyan Chemical Weapons Production," Press Conference by Secretary of State Shultz, Vienna (17 January 1989), *American Foreign Policy: Current Documents*, 1989, 455; Stephen Engelberg and Michael R. Gordon, "U.S. Presses Bonn on Libya Gas Factory," *International Herald Tribune*, 2 January 1989; Robert J. McCartney, "Bonn Lists 4 Firms in Libya Affair," *International Herald Tribune*, 10 January 1989; Wiegele, *Clandestine Building*, 35–45, 70–112.

81. Edward Cody, "Chad, Libya Agree on Cease-Fire," *International Herald Tribune*, 12–13 September 1987; Hamza Kaidi, "Tchad-Libye: Le cessez-le-feu ne tiendra pas," *Jeune Afrique* 1394 (23 Septembre 1987): 28–32; Youssef M. Ibrahim, "Libya and Chad to End War and Restore Ties," *International Herald Tribune*, 4 October 1988.

82. "Gadaffi Presses Arabs to Develop Atom Bomb," *Times* (London), 3 September 1987; Gaddafi's A-bomb Agenda," *South China Morning Post*, 4 November 1987.

83. "Libya Plans to Scrap Military," *South China Morning Post*, 2 September 1988.

84. David Ottaway, "U.S. Sees Gadhafi Hand in Terrorist Acts," *International Herald Tribune*, 3 June 1988; "Libyan Agents Accused of Terrorism Boost in West," *South China Sunday Morning Post*, 5 June 1988.

85. "Libyan Attack on U.S. Aircraft," Statement by the Secretary of Defense (Carlucci) (4 January 1989), *American Foreign Policy: Current Documents*, 1989, 453–54.

86. Molly Moore and George C. Wilson, "Gadhafi Pledges to Reply," *International Herald Tribune*, 5 January 1989; Joseph Fitchett, "U.S. Downs 2 Libyan Fighters in Clash over Mediterranean," *International Herald Tribune*, 5 January 1989; George C. Wilson, "Pentagon Calls Libyan a 'Liar' For Saying MiGs Were Unarmed," *International Herald Tribune*, 6 January 1989; Joseph Fitchett, "U.S. Says Allies Accept Charges Against Libyans," *International Herald Tribune*, 7–8 January 1989; Serge Schmemann, "Bonn's Libya Crisis: Complex Anxieties," *International Herald Tribune*, 17 January 1989.

87. "Modification of U.S. Sanctions Against Libya," Statement by the President's Press Secretary (Fitzwater) (19 January 1989), *American Foreign Policy: Current Documents*, 1989, 455–56.

Chapter 8. U.S.-Libyan Relations in the Post-Cold War Era

1. Michael S. Sherry, *In the Shadow of War: The United States Since the 1930s* (New Haven, Conn.: Yale University Press, 1995), 431–32.

2. "Gaddafi Invites Bush to Talks in ad hoc Briefing," *South China Morning Post*, 8 January 1989.

3. "Body Returned by Libya Was That of Pilot," *International Herald Tribune*, 16 January 1989; *Keesing's Contemporary Archives* 35, 3 (March 1989): 36572; Mary-Jane Deeb, "New Thinking in Libya," *Current History* 89, 546 (April 1990): 178.

4. "Continued Libyan Support for International Terrorism," Daily Press Briefing by the Department of State Spokesman (Tutwiler), 26 October 1989, *American Foreign Policy: Current Documents*, 1989, 458; "CIA Chief Links Firms to Gas Plants," *International Herald Tribune*, 10 February 1989; David B. Ottaway, "U.S. Continues Attack on Libya Over Terror," *International Herald Tribune*, 20 January 1989.

5. Mansour O. El-Kikhia, *Libya's Qaddafi: The Politics of Contradiction* (Gainesville: University Press of Florida, 1997), 143–44.

6. Robert S. Litwak, *Rogue States and U.S. Foreign Policy: Containment After the Cold War* (Washington, D.C.: Woodrow Wilson Center Press, 2000), 49–56; George P. Shultz, *Turmoil and Triumph: My Years as Secretary of State* (New York: Scribner, 1993), 643–88.

7. Michael T. Klare, *Rogue States and Nuclear Outlaws: America's Search for a New Foreign Policy* (New York: Hill and Wang, 1996), 18–24; Debra von Opstal and Andrew C. Goldberg, *Meeting the Mavericks: Regional Challenges for the Next President*, Significant Issues Series 10, 7 (Washington, D.C.: Center for Strategic and International Studies, 1988), xiii.

8. Michael T. Klare, "An Anachronistic Policy: The Strategic Obsolescence of the 'Rogue Doctrine,'" *Harvard International Review* 22, 2 (Summer 2000): 46–47. For context see Sherry, *In the Shadow of War*, 431–97.

9. Klare, "An Anachronistic Policy," 47–48; Richard Falkenrath, "Weapons of Mass Reaction: Rogue States and Weapons of Mass Destruction," *Harvard International Review* 22, 2 (Summer 2000): 52–55. For an in-depth discussion of the remaking of U.S. military policy see Klare, *Rogue States and Nuclear Outlaws*, 3–34.

10. *Public Papers of the Presidents of the United States: George Bush, 1990* (Washington, D.C.: U.S. Government Printing Office, 1991), 2: 1089–94, quote 1090.

11. *Public Papers: George Bush*, 2: 1091–92.

12. Department of Defense, *Defense Strategy for the 1990s: The Regional Defense Strategy* (Washington, D.C.: Department of Defense, 1993); Litwak, *Rogue States and U.S. Foreign Policy*, 28–29; Klare, "An Anachronistic Policy," 48–49.

13. Carl E. Vuono, "National Security and the Army of the 1990s," *Parameters* (Summer 1991): 12.

14. Klare, "An Anachronistic Policy," 49.

15. Litwak, *Rogue States and U.S. Foreign Policy*, xiv; Secretary of State Madeleine K. Albright, "Remarks and Q&A Session at Howard University," 14 April 1998 <http://secretary.state.gov/www/statements/1998/980414.html>.

16. Litwak, *Rogue States and U.S. Foreign Policy*, 8–9.

17. Meghan L. O'Sullivan, "Sanctioning 'Rogue States,'" *Harvard International Review* 22, 2 (Summer 2000): 56–57; Anthony Lake, "Confronting Backlash States," *Foreign Affairs* 73, 2 (March/April 1994): 45–46.

18. "Al-Talhi Cited on Ties with U.S.," *FBIS-NES*-89-003, 5 January 1989: 15. Quoted in Thomas C. Wiegele, *The Clandestine Building of Libya's Chemical Weapons Factory: A Study in International Collusion* (Carbondale: Southern Illinois University Press, 1992), 53.

19. Wiegele, *Clandestine Building*, 56–69, quote 68–69.

20. Edward Cody, "Banning Toxic Arms: Without Arabs, No Pact," *International Herald Tribune*, 13 January 1989.

21. Juan Tamayo, "Troubled Gadaffi Woos Bush Administration," *South China Morning Post*, 1 July 1989; Craig R. Whitney, "Gorbachev Says Bush Threatens Arms Talk Pace," *International Herald Tribune*, 7 April 1989; "Sudanese Plan New Coalition," *International Herald Tribune*, 6 March 1989.

22. "Evidence That Libya's Rabta Plant Producing Chemical Weapons," Press Briefing by the President's Press Secretary (Fitzwater), 7 March 1990, *American Foreign Policy: Current Documents*, 1989, 615–16; *New York Times*, 7 March 1990; Serge Schemann, "Grim Kohl Endures Broadside on Libya, *International Herald Tribune*, 19 January 1989; Wiegele, *Clandestine Building*, 115–16. On the potential utility of chemical weapons for Libya, see W. Andrew Terrill, "Libya and the Quest for Chemical Weapons," *Conflict Quarterly* 14, 1 (1994): 53–58.

23. Quoted in David Hoffman, "Bush Calls Libya Fire's Origin Hazy," *International Herald Tribune*, 19 March 1990; "Indications That Rabta Fire a Deception Effort," Daily Press Briefing by the Department of State Deputy Spokesman (Boucher), 18 June 1990, *American Foreign Policy: Current Documents*, 1989, 617.

24. "Central Bank Restricts Letters of Credit," *Middle East Economic Digest* 34, 32 (17 August 1990): 28; Jiann-Yuh Wang, "Un accident est si vite arrivé . . . ," *Jeune Afrique* 1525 (26 mars 1990): 12–14; "Libya Detains Suspects, Alleging Rabta Sabotage," *International Herald Tribune* (20 March 1990).

25. "Libya Plans to Re-Open Disputed Rabta Plant," *Washington Times*, 12 March 1991; Terrill, "Libya," 51; Dennis Whiteley, "Libyan Plant Fire a Hoax," *International Herald Tribune*, 10 April 1990; Wiegele, *Clandestine Building*, 116–17.

26. "Talk of a 2d Libya Toxic Gas Plant," *International Herald Tribune*, 19 June 1990; "German Businessman Pleads Guilty in Case of Libyan Chemical Factory,"

International Herald Tribune, 14 June 1990; "Libyan Arms Deal Denied by Official," *South China Morning Post*, 12 June 1990.

27. "Thailand: Libya Gives Pledge," *Far Eastern Economic Review* (6 October 1994): 13; Philip Shenon, "Work by the Thais in Libya Prompts a Warning by U.S.," *New York Times*, 26 October 1993; Douglas Jehl, "U.S. Says That Libya Is Building a 2d Plant to Make Poison Gas," *New York Times*, 18 February 1993; Elaine Sciolino and Eric Schmitt, "Libya Expands Chemical Arms, U.S. Agents Say," *New York Times*, 22 January 1992.

28. Richard Bassett, "Experts Shudder at the Explosive Truth," *South China Morning Post*, 24 March 1990; Craig R. Whitney, "Communists Sent Tons of Explosives to Libya, Havel Reveals," *International Herald Tribune*, 23 March 1990; Sennen Andriamir Ado, "Chronologie d'une déroute," *Jeune Afrique* 1563 (12–18 decembre 1990): 18–20.

29. Michael R. Gordon, "Libya Makes Strides in Extending Jet Range," *International Herald Tribune*, 30 March 1990.

30. Jean-Louis Vassallucci, "Les bons comptes de Kaddafi," *Jeune Afrique* 1600 (28 août–3 septembre 1991): 42–43; Omar Fayeq, "Libya's Gains and Losses from the Gulf Crisis," *Middle East International* 402 (14 June 1991): 17–18; "Nine Western, North African States Forge Ties," *Bangkok Post*, 12 October 1990; Abdelaziz Dahmani, "Ils se verront tous les deux mois," *Jeune Afrique* 1522 (5 Mars 1990): 18–19. For a thoughtful analysis of the internal and external pressures affecting Libyan foreign policy in this time frame see Deeb, "New Thinking in Libya," 149–52, 177–78.

31. "Cheney Has Mixed Record In Business Executive Role," *New York Times*, 24 August 2000; Michael Cooper, "Cheney Strongly Defends His Record as Chief of Halliburton," *New York Times*, 25 August 2000; "Dongah Builds Water Project in Libya," *Korea Herald*, 1 September 2000, Internet edition; Roula Khalaf, "Gadaffi Taps Desert Waters in Bid to Make a Big Splash," *Financial Times*, 11 September 1996.

32. "Libya's Continuing Support for Terrorism," Daily Press Briefing by the Department of State Deputy Spokesman (Boucher), 19 December 1990, *American Foreign Policy: Current Documents*, 1990, 618; Frédéric Dorce, "Les mouches de Kaddafi," *Jeune Afrique* 1530 (30 avril 1990): 7; Jennifer Parmelee, "U.S., Libya and a Fly," *International Herald Tribune*, 20 April 1990.

33. "Au bureau populaire arabe libyen à Paris," *Jeune Afrique* 1597 (7–13 août 1991): 29; "350 Libyans Leave Kenya for New Life in US," *Bangkok Post*, 18 May 1991; Clifford Kraus, "How U.S. Failed to Get Gadhafi Out," *International Herald Tribune*, 13 March 1991.

34. Judith Miller, *God Has Ninety-Nine Names: Reporting from a Militant Middle East* (New York: Simon and Schuster, 1996), 232–33; Jane Hunter, "Bush keeps the heat on Qadhafi," *Middle East International* 421 (20 March 1992): 19; Caryle Murphy, "U.S. Could Push Libyans Too far, Diplomats Warn," *International Herald Tribune*, 14 February 1992.

35. "Chip Links Libya to Lockerbie Bomb," *International Herald Tribune*, 19 December 1990; Michael Wines, "Signs Emerge of Libyan Involvement in Pan Am Bombing," *International Herald Tribune*, 11 October 1990; "Probe into Gaddafi's role in Pan Am crash," *South China Morning Post*, 30 January 1989.

36. "Paris Confirms Joint Talks on Libya Sanctions," *International Herald*

Tribune, 20 December 1991; "Britain, U.S. Ask Lockerbie Payments," *International Herald Tribune*," 28 November 1991; Gilbert Lam Kaboré, "Qui a piégé le DC 10 d'UTA," *Jeune Afrique* 1549 (5–11 septembre 1990): 9; "La Libye serait impliquée dans l'attentat du DC-10 d'UTA," *Le Monde*, 27 août 1990.

37. "OIC Talks Back Libya, Accuse Israel of Racism," *Bangkok Post*, 10 December 1991; "G-77 Snubs Libya," *Bangkok Post*, 25 November 1991; "Arab League Cautions U.S. Against Military Strike," *International Herald Tribune*, 18 November 1991.

38. "Text of U.N. Resolution Asking Libya's Help," *New York Times*, 22 January 1992.

39. Paul Lewis, "U.N. Tightens Sanctions Against Libya," *New York Times*, 12 November 1993; "UN Votes Sanctions on Libya; China and 4 Others Abstain," *International Herald Tribune*, 1 April 1992; "U.S. Blocks Firms Said To Be Libyan," *International Herald Tribune*, 30 March 1992.

40. "Maghreb Union to Back Libya at UN," *International Herald Tribune*, 12–13 December 1992; "Libya Renounces Terrorism but Retains Suspects," *International Herald Tribune*, 15 May 1992; Max Rodenbeck, "Arabs Resigned But Angry over Libya Sanctions," *Middle East International* 424 (1 May 1992): 3; "Libya Vows Not to Hand over Bomb Suspects," *Bangkok Post*, 30 March 1992; Caryle Murphy, "Gadhafi Calls for Compromise," *International Herald Tribune*, 3 February 1992.

41. "Al-Qadhdhafi Comments on Relations with West," *FBIS-NES*-92-174, 8 September 1992: 14.

42. "Al-Qadhdhafi Condemns U.S., West, Lauds Bush Loss," *FBIS-NES*-93-001, 4 January 1993: 18–19.

43. Klare, "An Anachronistic Policy," 30–31, 48–49; Noam Chomsky, "In a League of Its Own: Assessing US Rogue Behavior," *Harvard International Review* 22, 2 (Summer 2000): 69–70. For an in-depth discussion of the security debate at the outset of the Clinton administration, see Klare, *Rogue States and Nuclear Outlaws*, 97–119.

44. O'Sullivan, "Sanctioning Rogue States," 56–60; Klare, "An Anachronistic Policy," 49.

45. Lake, "Confronting Backlash States," 45–46.

46. Lake, "Confronting Backlash States," 46.

47. Litwak, *Rogue States and U.S. Foreign Policy*, 26.

48. Alfred Hermida, "Qadhafi Stands Firm," *Middle East International* 448 (16 April 1993): 8–9; Jacky Rowland, "Impasse over Lockerbie," *Middle East International* 447 (2 April 1993): 13; Elaine Sciolino, "Christopher Signals a Tougher U.S. Line Toward Iran," *New York Times*, 31 March 1993; Jehl, "U.S. Says That Libya Is Building a 2d Plant"; "Report of New Poison Gas Plant Being Built," *FBIS-NES*-93-016, 27 January 1993: 13.

49. Paul Lewis, "U.N. Tightens Sanctions Against Libya," *New York Times*, 12 November 1993; Paul Lewis, "Russia Tying Sanctions Against Libya to a Loan," *New York Times*, 31 October 1993; Frank J. Prial, "Libya Given Deadline to Extradite Suspects in Pan Am Jet Bombing," *New York Times*, 14 August 1993; Michael R. Gordon, "U.S. Warns Moscow on Sale of Key Rocket Fuel to Libya," *New York Times*, 23 June 1993.

50. "Envoy to Arab League Queried on Lockerbie, Ties with West," *FBIS-NES*-93-134, 15 July 1993: 14–16, quote 15.

51. Youssef M. Ibrahim, "Missing Libyan's Wife Reports Bribe Effort," *New York*

Times, 18 May 1994; Mark Nicholson, "Clinton Plea over Libyan Dissident," *Financial Times*, 21 December 1993; Elaine Sciolino, "U.S. Asks Egypt's Help on Missing Libya Dissident," *New York Times*, 19 December 1993; "Qaddafi Calls Libya a Mecca for Guerrillas," *New York Times*, 18 December 1993; Jim Hoagland, "Boxed In, Gadhafi Again Consorts with Terror," *International Herald Tribune*, 16 December 1993.

52. Roula Khalaf, "US Sanctions Are Gadaffi's Greatest Fear," *Financial Times*, 30 October 1996; Chris Hedges, "Libyan Chief Threatens to Defy Flight Ban and Quit U.N.," *New York Times*, 6 April 1995; George Graham and Robert Corzine, "US Seeks New UN Sanctions Against Libya," *Financial Times*, 29 March 1995.

53. Roula Khalaf, "Britain to Expel Libyan Diplomat for Spying," *Financial Times*, 12 December 1995; "Libya Expels Palestinians and Many Are Stranded," *New York Times*, 12 September 1995.

54. "Libya Demands U.S. Surrender Pilots, Planners," *Journal Star*, 16 April 1996; Tim Weiner, "Libya Completing Huge Plant for Chemical Arms, U.S. Says," *New York Times*, 25 February 1996. A Stuttgart state court in June 2001 found Roland Franz Berger guilty both of offenses under German arms control and export laws and violations of UN sanctions against Libya. Berger was allegedly involved in delivering and assembling at Tarhuna in 1994 equipment to be used in the production of mustard gas and Sarin. *Associated Press*, 19 June 2001, Internet edition.

55. "France to Fight U.S. Sanctions on Iran, Libya," *Asian Wall Street Journal*, 8 August 1996; Nancy Dunne, "Clinton Plea to US Allies over Iran and Libya," *Financial Times*, 6 August 1996; Robert S. Greenberger, "Sanctions Voted on Firms Investing in Iran and Libya," *Wall Street Journal*, 20 June 1996. The Clinton administration also moved to block the application of Louis Farrakhan, the leader of the Nation of Islam, to receive the Qaddafi International Prize for Human Rights worth $250,000, together with a gift of $1 billion which Qaddafi pledged to Farrakhan during his visit to Tripoli in January 1996. Farrakhan later accepted the human rights award but declined the monetary prize. "Farrakhan Delays $250,000 Libyan Prize," *New York Times*, 31 August 1996.

56. Douglas Jehl, "Rumors and Secrecy Cloud Issue: Is Qaddafi O.K.?" *New York Times*, 18 October 1998; Ray Takeyh, "Qadhafi and the Challenge of Militant Islam," *Washington Quarterly* 21, 3 (Summer 1998): 159–73; Stephen Hedges and Terry Atlas, "Targeting Masters of Terror," *South China Morning Post*, 23 August 1998; Roula Khalaf, "US Sanctions Are Gadaffi's Greatest Fear," *Financial Times*, 30 October 1996; "Libyan Rebels 'Kill 26'," *Financial Times*, 19 August 1996; Roula Khalaf and Shahira Idriss, "Rioting in Libya Leaves 'up to 50' Dead," *Financial Times*, 15 July 1996. David Shayler, a former British intelligence agent, later charged that British intelligence was involved in a plot to assassinate Qaddafi in 1996. Martin Bright, "How a Bomb in Libya Led to a Legal Earthquake," *Guardian*, 23 July 2000, Internet edition; Sarah Lyall, "Ex-Intelligence Agent Arrested in Britain on Return from Exile," *New York Times*, 22 August 2000.

57. "Mandela Asks Shift in Lockerbie Bomb Trial," *New York Times*, 26 October 1997; Joseph Fitchett, "Mandela Begins Visit to Gadhafi as U.S. Protests," *International Herald Tribune*, 23 October 1997; Douglas Jehl, "Defying UN, Arabs Give Gadhafi Landing Rights," *International Herald Tribune*, 22 September 1997; "Vatican Establishes Full Ties With Libya," *New York Times*, 11 March 1997.

58. "Libya Accepts Pan Am Trial in The Hague," *International Herald Tribune*, 27 August 1998; Steven Erlanger, "U.S. Proposes a Compromise to Libya," *International Herald Tribune*, 25 August 1998; Guy de Jonquieres, "EU Companies 'May Escape Iran-Libya Sanctions Threat,'" *Financial Times*, 11 May 1998; David Buchan, "Libya Claims Victory in Lockerbie Ruling," *Financial Times*, 28 February–1 March 1998; Craig R. Whitney, "World Court Says It Will Rule On 2 Libyans in Pan Am Case," *New York Times*, 28 February 1998.

59. Anne Swardson, "Tripoli Hands Over Pan Am 103 Suspects, *International Herald Tribune*, 6 April 1999; "United Nations Sanctions Attacked," *International Herald Tribune*, 27 October 1998.

60. Mary-Jane Deeb, "Qadhafi's Changed Policy: Causes and Consequences," *Middle East Policy* 7, 2 (February 2000): 146–53; Ray Takeyh, "Libya and Africa," Testimony before the U.S. House of Representatives Subcommittee on Africa, 22 July 1999, Internet edition.

61. Tim Niblock, *"Pariah States" & Sanctions in the Middle East: Iraq, Libya, Sudan* (Boulder, Colo.: Lynne Rienner, 2001), 93–94; Middle East Institute, "US Sanctions on Iran and Libya: What Have We Learned?" *Policy Briefs*, 29 May 2001, Internet edition.

62. Raymond Bonner, "Gadhafi Holds a 5-Nation Summit on Congo," *International Herald Tribune*, 1 October 1999; Emma Thomasson, "Mandela Greets Gadafi, Last Official Guest," *Reuters*, 13 June 1999, Internet edition; Colum Lynch, "Khadafy Commands Loyalty in Africa Despite 18 Years of US Sanctions," *Boston Globe*, 8 May 1999, Internet edition.

63. Barbara Slavin, "Influencing a Progressive Man," *USA Today*, 11 May 2000; Howard Schneider, "Libya Seeking Investors, Moves from Fringe Toward Mainstream," *Washington Post*, 20 July 1999, Internet edition; Sidy Gaye, "OAU Summit Kadhafi Calls for Pan African Congress, *PANA*, 13 July 1999, Internet edition. For a detailed assessment of Libyan policy in Africa after 1969, see Ronald Bruce St John, "Libya in Africa: Looking Back, Moving Forward," *Journal of Libyan Studies* 1, 1 (Summer 2000): 18–32.

64. Gamal Nkrumah, "Confidence in Ourselves," *Al-Ahram Weekly* 476 (6–12 April 2000), Internet edition; "Faster African Union Sought," *Financial Times*, 10 September 1999; "Libya: African Leaders Meet," *New York Times*, 9 September 1999; Nicholas Phythian, "Gaddafi Revives 1960s African Unity Dream," *Reuters*, 5 September 1999, Internet edition.

65. David Buchan, "Rift with Libya to End After 15 Years," *Financial Times*, 8 July 1999; Nicole Winfield, "U.S. Refuses to Lift Libya Sanctions," *Associated Press*, 2 July 1999, Internet edition; Gaylord Shaw, "Lawsuit Against Libya Allowed," *Newsday*, 15 June 1999, Internet edition; Judith Miller, "U.S. Firm on Libya Sanctions," *International Herald Tribune*, 13 June 1999; "Libya to Meet With the U.S. on Sanctions," *New York Times*, 6 June 1999.

66. Ronald E. Neumann, Testimony Before the House International Relations Africa Sub-Committee, 22 July 1999, Internet edition; Department of the Treasury, Office of Foreign Assets Control, "New Rules of the Commercial Sale of Food, Medicine, and Medical Equipment Under Existing Unilateral Sanctions Regimes," 27 July 1999, Internet edition.

67. John Lancaster, "U.S. Moves Toward Better Ties to Libya," *Washington Post*, 24 December 1999, Internet edition; "Terrorisme: Washington adresse un satisfecit

inhabituel à la Libye," *Le Monde*, 2 December 1999; "U.S. Law Seen Hampering Air-bus Supply to Libya," *Reuters*, 30 November 1999, Internet edition; Mark Suzman, "U.S. to Modify Iran and Libya Sanctions," *Financial Times*, 27 July 1999.

68. Alessandra Stanley, "D'Alema Is First Western Leader to Call on Gadhafi in 8 Years," *International Herald Tribune*, 2 December 1999; Dominic Evans, "Britain's New Envoy to Libya Seeks Fresh Start," *Reuters*, 6 December 1999, Internet edition; Mark Huband, "Trade Mission Seeks Deals in Post-Sanctions Libya," *Financial Times*, 7 October 1999.

69. U.S. Department of State, Bureau of Democracy, Human Rights, and Labor, *Human Rights Reports for 1999: Libya*, 25 February 2000, Internet edition; "Libya Rejects U.S. Monitoring," *Associated Press*, 5 December 1999, Internet edition; Vijay Joshi, "Gadhafi Denounces Terrorism," *Associated Press*, 3 December 1999, Internet edition; James Blitz, "Italy Pursues Goal of More Libya Trade," *Financial Times*, 3 December 1999; "Amnesty International, "30 Years On-Time for Action," 31 August 1999, Internet edition; Amnesty International, *Annual Report, 1999: Libya*, Internet edition; "Statement of A. Omar Turbi, Libyan American Human Rights Activist," Subcommittee on Africa, *Hearing U.S.-Libya Relations: New Era*, 22 July 1999, Internet edition.

70. Ronald E. Neumann, "Libya: A U.S. Policy Perspective," *Middle East Policy* 7, 2 (February 2000): 142–45, quotes 143–45; White House, Office of the Press Secretary, "Continuation of Libyan Emergency," 29 December 1999, mimeograph.

71. "Libya Trying to Buy a North Korean Ballistic Missile," *El Pais*, 16 January 2000, Internet edition; David Buchan, "UK Protests at Libya's Smuggling of Scud Missile Parts," *Financial Times*, 10 January 2000; "Libya Smuggling Scud Missile Parts, Britain Says," *New York Times*, 10 January 2000; Nicholas Rufford, "Libyans Smuggled Scuds through UK," *Sunday Times*, 9 January 2000, Internet edition.

72. Barbara Crossette, "Letter to Qaddafi Released," *New York Times*, 26 August 2000; "Text of Annan Letter Released," *Financial Times*, 26–27 August 2000; Barbara Slavin, "Albright Won't Release Bombing Letter," *USA Today*, 18 February 2000, Internet edition.

73. "Review of Libya Restraints," *New York Times*, 22 March 2000; U.S. Department of State, Daily Press Briefing, 22 March 2000, Internet edition; U.S. Department of State, Daily Press Briefing, 28 February 2000, Internet edition; Colum Lynch and John Lancaster, *Washington Post Service*, 28 February 2000, Internet edition; George Gedda, "US-Libya Ties Become a Possibility," *Associated Press*, 26 January 2000, Internet edition.

74. Holger Jensen, "U.S. Wonders if Gadhafi Is Ready to Act Civilized," *Rocky Mountain News*, 18 April 2000, Internet edition; Bill Gertz, "Beijing Delivered Missile Technology to Libya, U.S. says," *Washington Times*, 13 April 2000, Internet edition; Howard Schneider, "Libya Seeks to Restore Broken Ties at Summit," *Washington Post*, 3 April 2000, Internet edition; Ray Takeyh, "Qadhafi's New Political Order," *Policywatch* 445 (9 March 2000), Internet edition; Roula Khalaf, "Gadaffi Returns to 'People Power,'" *Financial Times*, 4–5 March 2000; Rupert Cornwell, "Libya Must Have a Head of State, Gaddafi Decrees," *Independent*, 3 March 2000, Internet edition.

75. Donald G. McNeil, Jr., "Trial of 2 Accused in Pan Am Bombing Finally Under Way," *New York Times*, 4 May 2000; Ian Bickerton, "Lockerbie Murder Trial

Starts Today," *Financial Times*, 3 May 2000. A large volume of material was published on the Lockerbie case even before the trial began; unfortunately, most of it was highly polemical in content. For example, see Charles Flores, *Shadows of Lockerbie: An Insight into the British-Libyan Relations* (Malta: Edam Publishing House, 1997) and Simons, *Libya*, 3–87.

76. On the indictment and charges in the Lockerbie trial see the University of Glasgow School of Law website www.law.gla.ac.uk.

77. Donald G. McNeil, Jr. "Lockerbie Trial Hears Police Minutiae, Defense Hints and, at Day's End, List of Dead," *New York Times*, 6 May 2000; T. R. Reid, "Doubts Persist About Lockerbie Evidence," *Washington Post*, 30 April 2000, Internet edition.

78. Betsy Pisik, "Trial to Start in Lockerbie bombing," *Washington Times*, 1 May 2000, Internet edition.

79. "Lockerbie Bombing 'Nothing To Do with Libya,'" *Sky News World*, 3 May 2000, Internet edition; Ray Takeyh, "The Lockerbie Trial, Round One," *Policywatch* 465 (26 May 2000), Internet edition; Giles Elgood, "Gaddafi Distances Libya from Lockerbie trial," *Reuters*, 3 May 2000, Internet edition.

80. Barbara Slavin, "Libya Has Changed with the World; U.S. Must, Too," *USA Today*, 12 May 2000, Internet edition; "Sanctions Force US firms to Skip Libya Oil Meeting," *Reuters*, 8 May 2000, Internet edition; Tom Hundley, "U.S. Accused of Cruise Missile Diplomacy," *Chicago Tribune*, 28 May 2000, Internet edition.

81. In the High Court of Justiciary at Camp Zeist (Case No: 1475/99), Opinion of the Court, delivered by Lord Sutherland in causa Her Majesty's Advocate v Abdelbaset Ali Mohmed Al Megrahi and Al Amin Khalifa, Mimeograph copy, quotes 81–82; Donald G. McNeil Jr., "Libyan Convicted by Scottish Court in '88 Pan Am Blast, *New York Times*, 1 February 2001; John Mason and Ian Bickerton, "Lockerbie Verdict Welcomed But Sanctions Set to Continue," *Financial Times*, 1 February 2001.

82. U.S. Department of State, "Overview of State-Sponsored Terrorism," 1 May 2000, Internet edition: 3–4.

83. U.S. Department of State, "On-the-Record Briefing on the *1999 Annual "Patterns of Global Terrorism" Report*, 1 May 2000, Internet edition: 4.

84. Department of State, "On-the-Record Briefing," 9.

85. U.S. Department of State, International Information Programs, "Neumann's Senate Testimony on U.S. Policy Toward Libya," 4 May 2000, Internet edition: 1–5, quote 5.

86. Christopher Marquis, "U.S. Declares 'Rogue Nations' Are Now 'States of Concern,'" *New York Times*, 20 June 2000; Barbara Slavin, "U.S. Does Away With 'Rogue State' Tag," *USA Today*, 20 June 2000.

87. Falkenrath, "Weapons of Mass Reaction," 52–53; O'Sullivan, "Sanctioning 'Rogue States,'" 57–60.

88. "Letter from the President: Continuing the Libya Emergency," White House Press Office, 4 January 2001, mimeograph; "Libya Dismisses U.S. Economic Sanctions Renewal Decision," *JANA* News Agency (Tripoli), 5 January 2001, Internet edition; Neil MacFarquhar, "Qaddafi Rants Against the U.S. in a Welcoming After Bomb Trial," *New York Times*, 2 February 2001.

89. "Joint Statement by President George W. Bush and Prime Minister Tony

Blair," White House, 23 February 2001, mimeograph; "Sanctions on the Way Out," *Middle East Economic Digest*, 4 May 2001, Internet edition; Ray Takeyh, "The Rogue Who Came in from the Cold," *Foreign Affairs* 8, 3 (May/June 2001): 62–72; Middle East Institute, "US Sanctions on Iran and Libya: What Have We Learned?" *Policy Briefs*, 29 May 2001, Internet edition; Robert Fife, "Ottawa Ran Libya Plan by U.S.," *National Post*, 3 July 2001, Internet edition.

90. Alison Mitchell, "Senate Extends Sanctions on Libya and Iran," *New York Times*, 26 July 2001; *Oxford Analytica*, "Libya: Investment Outlook," 19 July 2001, Internet edition; Tom Doggett, "White House Urges Shorter Iran, Libya Sanctions," *Reuters*, 28 June 2001, Internet edition.

91. "Libya: Beckoning and Rebuffing, An Erratic Charm Offensive from Tripoli," *Economist Intelligence Unit*, 8 September 2001, Internet edition; "Libya Condemns US Sanctions Extension," *JANA* News Agency (Tripoli), 28 July 2001, Internet edition; Edward Alden, "U.S. to extend sanctions on Libya and Iran," *Financial Times*, 27 July 2001.

92. "Gaddafi Says U.S. Anthrax 'Worst Form of Terrorism,'" *Reuters*, 18 October 2001; Internet edition; "Libyans Express Sympathy for U.S. Victims," *Boston Herald*, 12 September 2001, Internet edition; Caroline Drees, "Mideast Leaders Condemn, Citizens Cheer Attacks," *Associated Press*, 12 September 2001, Internet edition.

Select Bibliography

Abu-Jaber, Faiz S. *American-Arab Relations from Wilson to Nixon.* Washington, D.C.: University Press of America, 1979.

Ahmida, Ali Abdullatif. *The Making of Modern Libya: State Formation, Colonization, and Resistance, 1830–1932.* Albany: State University of New York Press, 1994.

Ajami, Fouad. *The Arab Predicament: Arab Political Thought and Practice Since 1967.* Cambridge: Cambridge University Press, 1981.

———. "The End of Pan-Arabism." *Foreign Affairs* 57, 2 (Winter 1978/79): 355–73.

Albrecht-Carrié, René. *Italy from Napoleon to Mussolini.* New York: Columbia University Press, 1950.

Alexander, Nathan [Ronald Bruce St John]. "The Foreign Policy of Libya: Inflexibility amid Change," *Orbis* 24, 4 (Winter 1981): 819–46.

———. "Libya: The Continuous Revolution." *Middle Eastern Studies* 17, 2 (April 1981): 210–27.

Allan, J. A. *Libya: The Experience of Oil.* London: Croom Helm, 1981.

———. "Libya Accommodates to Lower Oil Revenues: Economic and Political Adjustments." *International Journal of Middle East Studies* 15, 2 (August 1983): 377–85.

———. *Libya Since Independence: Economic and Political Development.* London: Croom Helm, 1982.

Anderson, Frank. "Qadhafi's Libya: The Limits of Optimism." *Middle East Policy* 6, 4 (June 1999): 68–79.

Anderson, Lisa. "The Development of Nationalist Sentiment in Libya, 1908–1922." In *The Origins of Arab Nationalism,* ed. Rashid Khalidi, Lisa Anderson, Muhammad Muslih, and Reeva S. Simon, 225–42. New York: Columbia University Press, 1991.

———. "Legitimacy, Identity, and the Writing of History in Libya." In *Statecraft in the Middle East: Oil, Historical Memory, and Popular Culture,* ed. Eric Davis and Nicolas Gavrielides, 71–91. Miami: Florida International University Press, 1991.

———. "Qadhdhafi and His Opposition." *Middle East Journal* 40, 2 (Spring 1986): 225–37.

———. "Qadhdhafi and the Kremlin." *Problems of Communism* 34 (September–October 1985): 29–44.

———. *The State and Social Transformation in Tunisia and Libya, 1830–1980.* Princeton, N.J.: Princeton University Press, 1986.

———. "The Tripoli Republic, 1918–1922." In *Social & Economic Development of Libya,* ed. E. G. H. Joffé and K. S. McLachlan, 43–65. Cambridgeshire: Middle East & North African Studies Press, 1982.

Ansell, Meredith O. and Ibrahim Massaud al-Arif, eds. *The Libyan Revolution: A Sourcebook of Legal and Historical Documents*, Vol. 1, *1 September 1969–30 August 1970*. Stoughton, Wis.: Oleander Press, 1972.

Arab, Mohamed Khalifa. "The Effect of the Leader's Belief System on Foreign Policy: The Case of Libya." Ph.D. dissertation, Florida State University, 1988.

Arnold, Guy. *The Maverick State: Gaddafi and the New World Order*. London: Cassell, 1996.

Ashiurakis, Ahmed M. *A Concise History of the Libyan Struggle for Freedom*. Tripoli: General Publishing, Distributing & Advertising Co., 1976.

Askew, William C. *Europe and Italy's Acquisition of Libya, 1911–1912*. Durham, N.C.: Duke University Press, 1942.

Ayoub, Mahmoud Mustafa. *Islam and the Third Universal Theory: The Religious Thought of Mu'ammar al-Qadhadhafi*. London: KPI, 1987.

Barclay, Thomas. *The Turco-Italian War and Its Problems*. London: Constable, 1912.

Barger, John. "After Qadhafi: Prospects for Political Party Formation and Democratisation in Libya." *Journal of North African Studies* 4, 1 (Spring 1999): 62–77.

Barker, P. and K. S. McLachlan. "Development of the Libyan Oil Industry." In *Libya Since Independence: Economic and Political Development*, ed. J. A. Allan, 37–54. London: Croom Helm, 1982.

Bearman, Jonathan. *Qadhafi's Libya*. London: Zed Books, 1986.

Ben-Halim, Mustafa Ahmed. *Libya: The Years of Hope: The Memoirs of Mustafa Ahmed Ben-Halim*. London: AAS Media Publishers, 1998.

Bills, Scott L. *The Libyan Arena: The United States, Britain, and the Council of Ministers, 1945–1948*. Kent, Ohio: The Kent State University Press, 1995.

Binder, Leonard. *The Ideological Revolution in the Middle East*. New York: Wiley, 1964.

Birks, J. S. and C. A. Sinclair. "The Libyan Arab Jamahiriya: Labour Migration Sustains Dualistic Development." *Maghreb Review* 4, 3 (June–July 1979): 95–102.

Blackburn, Peter. "Tunisia Blames Libya for Night Attack." *Middle East Economic Digest* 24, 5 (1 February 1980): 39.

Blum, Patrick. "Gafsa Attack Raises Shockwaves." *Middle East Economic Digest* (8 February 1980): 42.

Burgat, François. "La Libye des contraintes: l'idéologie à l'épreuve de l'Infitah." In *Maghreb: les années de transition*, ed. Bassma Kodmani-Darwish, 107–22. Paris: Masson S.A., 1990.

Burr, J. Millard and Robert O. Collins. *Africa's Thirty Years' War: Chad, Libya, and the Sudan, 1963–1993*. Boulder, Colo.: Westview Press, 1999.

Byrnes, James F. *Speaking Frankly*. New York: Harper, 1947.

Cachia, Anthony J. *Libya Under the Second Ottoman Occupation (1835–1911)*. Tripoli: Government Press, 1945.

Callies de Salies, Bruno. *Le Maghreb en mutation: Entre tradition et modernité*. Paris: Masionneuve et Larose, 1999.

Cannon, Lou. *Ronald Reagan: The Role of a Lifetime*. New York: Public Affairs, 1991.

Carvely, Andrew. "Libya: International Relations and Political Purposes." *International Journal* 28, 4 (Autumn 1973): 707–28.

Case, Josephine Young. *Written in Sand*. Boston: Houghton Mifflin, 1945.

Chasek, Pamela. "Revolution Across the Sea: Libyan Foreign Policy in Central

America." In *Central America & the Middle East*, ed. Damián J. Fernández, 150–76. Miami: Florida International University Press, 1990.

Childs, Timothy W. *Italo-Turkish Diplomacy and the War over Libya, 1911–1912*. Leiden: E.J. Brill, 1990.

Chomsky, Noam. "In a League of Its Own: Assessing US Rogue Behavior." *Harvard International Review* 22, 2 (Summer 2000): 68–71.

———. *Pirates & Emperors: International Terrorism in the Real World*. New York: Claremont Research & Publications, 1986.

Cleveland, Raymond H., Charles T. Heifner, George S. Cudd, Martin Dome, and Benjamin F. Fruehauf. *A Global Perspective on Transnational Terrorism: A Case Study of Libya*. Research Report 25. Air War College, United States Air Force, Maxwell Air Force Base, Alabama.

Cleveland, William L. *A History of the Modern Middle East*. Boulder, Colo.: Westview Press, Inc., 1994.

Cooley, John K. *Libyan Sandstorm: The Complete Account of Qaddafi's Revolution*. New York: Holt, Rinehart and Winston, 1982.

Council on Foreign Relations. *The United States in World Affairs: An Account of American Foreign Relations*. New York: Harper, 1932–67.

Cricco, Massimiliano. "La Libia nella politica delle grandi potenze (1951–1969)." Ph.D. dissertation, Università degli Studi di Firenze, 1999.

Cumming, Duncan. "Libya in the First World War." In *Libya in History*, ed. Fawzi F. Gadallah, 383–92. Benghazi: University of Libya, 1968.

Davis, Brian L. *Qaddafi, Terrorism, and the Origins of the U.S. Attack on Libya*. New York: Praeger, 1990.

Davis, John. *Libyan Politics: Tribe and Revolution*. London: I.B. Tauris, 1987.

Dearden, Seton. *A Nest of Corsairs: The Fighting Karamanlis of Tripoli*. London: John Murray, 1976.

De Candole, E. A. V. *The Life and Times of King Idris of Libya*. n.p.: for the author, 1988.

Deeb, Marius. "Militant Islam and Its Critics: The Case of Libya." In *Islamism and Secularism in North Africa*, edited by John Ruedy, 187–97. New York: St. Martin's Press, 1996.

Deeb, Mary-Jane. "The Arab Maghrib Union in the Context of Regional and International Politics." *Middle East Insight* 6, 5 (Spring 1989): 42–46.

———. *Libya's Foreign Policy in North Africa*. Boulder, Colo.: Westview Press, Inc., 1991.

———. "New Thinking in Libya." *Current History* 89, 546 (April 1990): 149–52, 177–78.

———. "Qadhafi's Changed Policy: Causes and Consequences." *Middle East Policy* 7, 2 (February 2000): 146–53.

Deeb, Marius K. and Mary-Jane Deeb. *Libya Since the Revolution: Aspects of Social and Political Development*. New York: Praeger, 1982.

De Felice, Renzo. *Jews in an Arab Land: Libya, 1835–1970*. Austin: University of Texas Press, 1985.

Devine, Robert A. *Eisenhower and the Cold War*. Oxford: Oxford University Press, 1981.

Djaziri, Moncef. *État et société en Libye: Islam, politique et modernité*. Paris: L'Harmattan, 1996.

Evans-Pritchard, E. E. *The Sanusi of Cyrenaica.* Oxford: Oxford University Press, 1949.

Falkenrath, Richard. "Weapons of Mass Reaction: Rogue States and Weapons of Mass Destruction." *Harvard International Review* 22, 2 (Summer 2000): 52–55.

Fallaci, Oriana. "Iranians Are Our Brothers: An Interview with Col. Muammar el-Qaddafi of Libya." *New York Times Magazine,* December 16, 1979, 40–41.

Farley, Rawle. *Planning for Development in Libya: The Exceptional Economy in the Developing World.* New York: Praeger, 1971.

El Fathaly, Omar I. and Monte Palmer. *Political Development and Social Change in Libya.* Lexington, Mass.: D.C. Heath, 1980.

El Fathaly, Omar I., Monte Palmer, and Richard Chackerian. *Political Development and Bureaucracy in Libya.* Lexington, Mass.: D.C. Heath, 1977.

Field, James A. *America and the Mediterranean World, 1776–1882.* Princeton, N.J.: Princeton University Press, 1969.

———. "A Scheme in Regard to Cyrenaica," *Mississippi Valley Historical Review* 44, 3 (December 1957): 445–68.

First, Ruth. *Libya: The Elusive Revolution.* Harmondsworth: Penguin, 1974.

Fisher, Sir Godfrey. *Barbary Legend: War, Trade and Piracy in North Africa, 1415–1830.* Oxford: Clarendon Press, 1957.

Fitzgerald, Frances. *Way Out There in the Blue: Reagan, Star Wars and the End of the Cold War.* New York: Simon and Schuster, 2000.

Flores, Charles. *Shadows of Lockerbie: An Insight into the British-Libyan Relations.* Valletta, Malta: Edam, 1997.

Folayan, Kola. *Tripoli During the Reign of Yusuf Pasha Qaramanli.* Ile-Ife, Nigeria: University of Ife Press, 1979.

———. "Tripoli and the War with the U.S.A., 1801–5." *Journal of African History* 13, 2 (1972): 261–70.

Gaddis, John Lewis. *Strategies of Containment: A Critical Appraisal of Postwar American National Security Policy.* New York: Oxford University Press, 1982.

El-Ghariani, Mustafa Sedd. "Libya's Foreign Policy: The Role of the Country's Environmental and Leadership Factors, 1960–1973." M.A. thesis, Western Michigan University, 1979.

Goldberg, Harvey E. *Jewish Life in Muslim Libya: Rivals & Relatives.* Chicago: University of Chicago Press, 1990.

Goudarzi, Gus H. *Geology and Mineral Resources of Libya—A Reconnaissance.* Geological Survey Professional Paper. Washington, D.C.: U.S. Government Printing Office, 1970.

Gurney, Judith. *Libya: The Political Economy of Oil.* Oxford: Oxford University Press, 1996.

Habib, Henri Pierre. *Politics and Government of Revolutionary Libya.* Montreal: Cercle du Livre de France, 1975.

Hahn, Peter L. "Discord or partnership? British and American policy toward Egypt, 1942–56." In *Demise of the British Empire in the Middle East: Britain's Responses to Nationalist Movements, 1943–55,* ed. Michael J. Cohen and Martin Kolinsky, 162–82. London: Frank Cass Publishers, 1988.

Haim, Sylvia G., ed. *Arab Nationalism: An Anthology.* Berkeley: University of California Press, 1962.

Haines, C. Grove. "The Problem of the Italian Colonies." *Middle East Journal* 1, 4 (October 1947): 417–31.

Haley, P. Edward. *Qaddafi and the United States since 1969.* New York: Praeger, 1984.

Halloran, Richard. "Libyans Are Challenging U.S. Forces in War of Nerves," *New York Times,* 24 October 1980.

Harris, Lillian Craig. *Libya: Qadhafi's Revolution and the Modern State.* Boulder, Colo.: Westview Press, 1986.

———. "North African Union: Fact or Fantasy?" *Arab Affairs* 12 (1990): 52–60.

Hasan Sury, Salaheddin. "The Genesis of the Political Leadership of Libya, 1952–1969: Historical Origins and Development of Its Component Parts." Ph.D. dissertation, The George Washington University, 1973.

———. "The Political Development of Libya, 1952–1969: Institutions, Policies, and Ideology." In *Libya since Independence: Economic and Political Development,* ed. J. A. Allan, 121–36. London: Croom Helm, 1982.

Hayford, Elizabeth R. "The Politics of the Kingdom of Libya in Historical Perspective." Ph.D. dissertation., Tufts University, 1971.

Heikal, Mohammad Hassanein. "Egyptian Foreign Policy." *Foreign Affairs* 56, 4 (July 1978): 719–22.

Hottinger, Arnold. "L'expansionisme Libyen: Machrek, Maghreb et Afrique Noire." *Politique étrangère* 46, 1 (March 1981): 137–49.

Hudson, Michael C. "The Middle East under *Pax Americana*: How new, how orderly?" *Third World Quarterly* 13, 2 (1992): 301–16.

Hume, L. J. "Preparations for Civil War in Tripoli in the 1820s: Ali Karamanli, Hassuna D'Ghies and Jeremy Bentham." *Journal of African History* 21, 3 (1980): 311–22.

Hyland, William G., ed. *The Reagan Foreign Policy.* New York: Meridian, 1987.

Ibrahim, Youssef M. "Foreign Workers in Libya Subjected to Harassment." *New York Times,* 27 August 1980.

Irwin, Ray W. *The Diplomatic Relations of the United States with the Barbary Powers, 1776–1816.* Chapel Hill: University of North Carolina Press, 1931.

Ismael, Tareq Y. and Jacqueline S. Ismael. "The Socialist People's Libyan Arab Great Jamahiriyah (SPLAJ)." In *Politics and Government in the Middle East and North Africa,* ed. Tareq Y. Ismael and Jacqueline S. Ismael, 487–512. Miami: Florida International University Press, 1991.

James, Robert Rhodes. *Anthony Eden.* London: Weidenfeld and Nicolson, 1986.

Joffé, George. "Islamic Opposition in Libya." *Third World Quarterly* 10, 2 (April 1988): 615–31.

———. "Qadhafi's Islam in Local Historical Perspective." In *Qadhafi's Libya, 1969 to 1994,* ed. Dirk Vandewalle, 139–54. New York: St. Martin's 1995.

Khadduri, Majid. *Modern Libya: A Study in Political Development.* Baltimore: Johns Hopkins University Press, 1963.

El-Kikhia, Mansour O. *Libya's Qaddafi: The Politics of Contradiction.* Gainesville: University Press of Florida, 1997.

Klare, Michael T. "An Anachronistic Policy: The Strategic Obsolescence of the 'Rogue Doctrine.'" *Harvard International Review* 22, 2 (Summer 2000): 46–51.

———. *Rogue States and Nuclear Outlaws: America's Search for a New Foreign Policy.* New York: Hill and Wang, 1995.

Kuniholm, Bruce Robellet. *The Origins of the Cold War in the Near East: Great Power Conflict and Diplomacy in Iran, Turkey, and Greece.* Princeton, N.J.: Princeton University Press, 1980.

Lacroix-Riz, Annie. *Les protectorats d'Afrique du Nord entre la France et Washington de débarquement à l'indépendance: Maroc et Tunisie, 1942–1956.* Paris: L'Harmattan, 1988.

Lahwej, Younis Ali. "Ideology and Power in Libyan Foreign Policy with Reference to Libyan-American Relations from the Revolution to the Lockerbie Affair." Ph.D. dissertation, University of Reading, 1998.

Lake, Anthony. "Confronting Backlash States." *Foreign Affairs* 73, 2 (March/April 1994): 45–55.

Lane-Poole, Stanley. *The Barbary Corsairs.* London: T. Fisher Unwin, 1890.

Lawless, R. I. "Population Geography and Settlement Studies." *Libyan Studies* 20 (1989): 251–58.

Le Gall, Michel. "Forging the Nation-State: Some Issues in the Historiography of Modern Libya." In *The Maghrib in Question: Essays in History and Historiography,* ed. Michel Le Gall and Kenneth Perkins, 95–108. Austin: University of Texas Press, 1997.

——. "The Ottoman Government and the Sanusiyya: A Reappraisal." *International Journal of Middle East Studies* 21, 1 (February 1989): 91–106.

Legum, Colin, ed. *Africa Contemporary Record: Annual Survey and Documents.* New York: Holmes and Meier, various years.

Lemarchand, René, ed. *The Green and the Black: Qadhafi's Policies in Africa.* Bloomington: Indiana University Press, 1988.

Lenczowski, George. *The Middle East in World Affairs.* 4th ed. Ithaca, N.Y.: Cornell University Press, 1980.

Leopold, Richard W. *The Growth of American Foreign Policy: A History.* New York: Knopf, 1962.

Lewis, William H. "Libya: The End of Monarchy." *Current History* (January 1970): 34–48.

Lewis, William H. and Robert Gordon. "Libya After Two Years of Independence." *Middle East Journal* 8, 1 (Winter 1954): 41–53.

Libyan Arab Republic. Embassy of the Libyan Arab Republic. Press Section. *Progressive Libya.* Vols. 1–6 (September 1975–April 1977).

——. Ministry of Information and Culture. *Aspects of First of September Revolution.* Tripoli: General Administration for Information, 1973.

——. Ministry of Information and Culture. *Delivered by Col. Mo'ammar el-Gadhafi: 1. The Broadlines of the Third Theory; 2. The Aspects of the Third Theory; 3. The Concept of Jihad; 4. The Divine Concept of Islam.* Tripoli: General Administration for Information, 1973.

——. Ministry of Information and Culture. *The Fundamentals of the Third International Theory.* Tripoli: General Administration for Information, 1974.

——. Ministry of Information and Culture. *The Revolution of 1st September: The Fourth Anniversary.* Benghazi: General Administration for Information, 1973.

——. Ministry of Information and Culture. *The Revolutionary March.* Tripoli: General Administration for Information, 1974.

——. Ministry of Information and Culture. *The Third International Theory: The Di-

vine Concept of Islam and the Popular Revolution in Libya. Tripoli: General Administration for Information, 1973.

"The Libyan Revolution in the Words of Its Leaders: Proclamations, Statements, Addresses, Declarations, and Interviews from September 1 to Announcement of the Counter-Plot (December 10)," *Middle East Journal* 24, 2 (Spring 1970): 203–19.

Litwak, Robert S. *Rogue States and U.S. Foreign Policy: Containment after the Cold War.* Washington, D.C.: Woodrow Wilson Center Press, 2000.

Louis, Wm. Roger. *The British Empire in the Middle East, 1945–1951: Arab Nationalism, the United States, and Postwar Imperialism.* Oxford: Clarendon Press, 1984.

Lyons, Richard D. "Suspect Libyan Terrorists Were Watched by F.B.I.." *New York Times,* 9 May 1980.

El Mallakh, Ragaei. "The Economics of Rapid Growth." *Middle East Journal* 23, 3 (Summer 1969): 308–20.

Mannoni, Eugene. "Le danger Kadhafi." *Le Point* 386 (11 février 1990): 47–53.

Martel, André. *La Libye, 1835–1990: Essai de géopolitique historique.* Paris: Presses Universitaires de France, 1991.

Mayer, Ann Elizabeth. "Islamic Resurgence or New Prophethood: The Role of Islam in Qadhdafi's Ideology." In *Islamic Resurgence in the Arab World,* ed. Ali E. Hillal Dessouki, 196–220. New York: Praeger, 1982.

———. "Libyan Legislation in Defense of Arabo-Islamic Sexual Mores." *American Journal of Comparative Law* 28 (1980): 287–313.

Mayer, Jane, and Doyle McManus. *Landslide: The Unmaking of the President, 1984–1988.* Boston: Houghton Mifflin, 1988.

McCartney, Laton. *Friends in High Places: The Bechtel Story.* New York: Simon and Schuster, 1988.

Meyer, Gail E. *Egypt and the United States: The Formative Years.* London: Associated University Presses, 1980.

El-Mogherbi, Mohammed Zahi. "Arab Nationalism and Political Instability in Monarchical Libya: A Study in Political Ideology." M.A. thesis, Kansas State University, 1973.

Miller, Judith. *God Has Ninety-Nine Names: Reporting from a Militant Middle East.* New York: Simon and Schuster, 1996.

Monastiri, Taoufik. "Teaching the Revolution: Libyan Education since 1969." In *Qadhafi's Libya, 1969 to 1994,* ed. Dirk Vandewalle, 67–88. New York: St. Martin's Press, 1995.

Monti-Belkaoui, Janice and Ahmed Riahi-Belkaoui. *Qaddafi: The Man and His Policies.* Aldershot: Avebury, 1996.

Murphy, Edward. "Libya Opens Up: A Thaw in Political Relations with the West." *Harvard International Review* 22, 3 (Fall 2000): 8–9.

Niblock, Tim. "Libyan Foreign Policy." In *The Foreign Policies of Middle Eastern States,* ed. Anoush Ehteshami and Ray Hinnebush. Boulder, Colo.: Lynne Reinner Publishers, 2001.

———. *"Pariah States" & Sanctions in the Middle East: Iraq, Libya, Sudan.* Boulder, Colo.: Lynne Reinner Publishers, 2001.

Nolutshungu, Sam C. *Limits of Anarchy: Intervention and State Formation in Chad.* Charlottesville: University Press of Virginia, 1996.

Norman, John. *Labor and Politics in Libya and Arab Africa.* New York: Bookman Associates, 1965.

Nyrop, Richard F. et al. *Area Handbook for Libya.* 2nd ed. Washington, D.C.: U.S. Government Printing Office, 1973.

Ogunbadejo, Oye. "Qaddafi's North African Design." *International Security* 8, 1 (Summer 1983): 154–78.

Orman, John. *Comparing Presidential Behavior: Carter, Reagan, and the Macho Presidential Style.* New York: Greenwood Press, 1987.

O'Sullivan, Meghan L. "Sanctioning 'Rogue States': A Strategy in Decline?" *Harvard International Review* 22, 2 (Summer 2000): 56–60.

Otayek, René. *La politique africaine de la Libye (1969–1985).* Paris: Karthala, 1986.

Parker, Richard B. *North Africa: Regional Tensions and Strategic Concerns.* New York: Praeger, 1984.

Pasha, Aftab Kamal. *Libya and the United States: Qadhafi's Response to Reagan's Challenge.* New Delhi: Detente Publications, 1984.

Pelt, Adrian. *Libyan Independence and the United Nations: A Case of Planned Decolonization.* New Haven, Conn.: Yale University Press, 1970.

Pipes, Daniel. "No One Likes the Colonel." *American Spectator* 14, 3 (March 1981): 18–22.

Qaddafi, Muammar. *Discourses.* Valetta, Malta: Adam Publishers, 1975.

——. *Escape to Hell and Other Stories.* Montréal: Stanké, 1998.

——. *The Green Book. Part I. The Solution of the Problem of Democracy. The Authority of the People.* London: Martin Brian and O'Keefe, 1976.

——. *The Green Book, Part II: The Solution of the Economic Problem: "Socialism".* London: Martin Brian & O'Keefe, 1978.

——. *The Green Book, Part III: The Social Basis of the Third Universal Theory.* Tripoli: Public Establishment for Publishing, Advertising and Distribution, 1979.

——. "A Visit to Fezzan." In *Man, State, and Society in the Contemporary Maghrib,* ed. I. William Zartman, 131–36. New York: Praeger, 1973.

Rainero, Romain. "The Capture, Trial, and Death of Omar al-Mukhtar in the Context of the Fascist Policy for the Reconquest of Libya." In *Omar al-Mukhtar: The Italian Reconquest of Libya,* ed. Enzo Santarelli, Giorgio Rochat, Romain Rainero, and Luigi Goglia, 173–87. London: Darf Publishers, 1986.

Rejeb, Lotfi Ben. "To the Shores of Tripoli: The Impact of Barbary on Early American Nationalism." Ph.D. dissertation, Indiana University, 1981.

Rinehart, Robert. "Historical Setting." In *Libya: A Country Study,* ed. Harold D. Nelson, 1–57. Washington, D.C.: U.S. Government Printing Office, 1979.

Rivlin, Benjamin. *The United Nations and the Italian Colonies.* New York: Carnegie Endowment for International Peace, 1950.

Rizq, Johnny and Robin Allen. "Libya Presses for Decision on Boeings." *Middle East Economic Digest* 23, 50 (14 December 1979): 15.

——. "Unity and Nationalism in Libya." *Middle East Journal* 3, 1 (January 1949): 31–44.

Rossi, Enzo. *Malta on the Brink: From Western Democracy to Libyan Satellite.* European Security Studies 5. London: The Institute for European Defence & Strategic Studies, 1986.

St John, Ronald Bruce. "The Determinants of Libyan Foreign Policy." *Maghreb Review* 8, 3–4 (May–August 1983): 96–103.

——. *Historical Dictionary of Libya.* 3rd ed. Lanham, Md.: Scarecrow Press, 1998.

——. "The Ideology of Mu'ammar al-Qadhdhafi: Theory and Practice." *International Journal of Middle East Studies* 15, 4 (November 1983): 471–90.

——. "Libya in Africa: Looking Back, Moving Forward." *Journal of Libyan Studies* 1, 1 (Summer 2000): 18–32.

——. "Libya's Foreign and Domestic Policies." *Current History* 80, 470 (December 1981): 426–29, 434–35.

——. "Libya's 'New' Foreign Policy." *Contemporary Review* 243, 1410 (July 1983): 15–18.

——. "The Libyan Debacle in Sub-Saharan Africa: 1969–1987." In *The Green and the Black: Qadhafi's Policies in Africa,* ed. René Lemarchand, 125–38. Bloomington: Indiana University Press, 1988.

——. *Qaddafi's World Design: Libyan Foreign Policy, 1969–1987.* London: Saqi Books, 1987.

——. "Qaddafi's World Design Revisited." *Global Affairs* 8, 1 (Winter 1993): 161–73.

——. "The Soviet Penetration of Libya." *The World Today* 38, 4 (April 1982): 131–38.

——. "Terrorism and Libyan Foreign Policy, 1981–1986." *The World Today* 42, 7 (July 1986): 111–15.

——. "Whatever's Happened to Qaddafi?" *The World Today* 43, 4 (April 1987): 58–59.

El Saadany, Salah. *Egypt and Libya from Inside, 1969–1976: The Qaddafi Revolution and the Eventual Break in Relations, by the Former Egyptian Ambassador to Libya.* Jefferson, N.C.: McFarland, 1994.

Samura, Mohamed O'Bai. *The Libyan Revolution: Its Lessons for Africa.* Washington, D.C.: International Institute for Policy and Development Studies, 1985.

Segrè, Claudio G. *Fourth Shore: The Italian Colonization of Libya.* Chicago: University of Chicago Press, 1974.

Sharabi, H. B. "Libya's Pattern of Growth." *Current History* 44 (January 1963): 41–45.

Shawcross, William. *Sideshow: Kissinger, Nixon, and the Destruction of Cambodia.* New York: Simon and Schuster, 1979.

Shembesh, Ali Muhammad. "The Analysis of Libya's Foreign Policy, 1962–1973: A Study of the Impact of Environmental and Leadership Factors." Ph.D. dissertation, Emory University, 1975.

Sherry, Michael S. *In the Shadow of War: The United States Since the 1930s.* New Haven, Conn.: Yale University Press, 1995.

Shultz, George P. *Turmoil and Triumph: My Years as Secretary of State.* New York: Scribner, 1993.

Sicker, Martin. *The Making of a Pariah State: The Adventurist Politics of Muammar Qaddafi.* New York: Praeger, 1987.

Simon, Rachel. *Libya Between Ottomanism and Nationalism: The Ottoman Involvement in Libya During the War with Italy (1911–1919).* Berlin: Klaus Schwarz Verlag, 1987.

Simons, Geoff. *Libya: The Struggle for Survival.* 2nd ed. New York: St. Martin's Press, 1996.

——. "Lockerbie: Lessons for International Law." *Journal of Libyan Studies* 1, 1 (Summer 2000): 33–47.

Smith, Denis Mack. *Modern Italy: A Political History.* Ann Arbor: University of Michigan Press, 1997.

———. *Mussolini's Roman Empire.* London: Longman, 1976.

Sono, Themba, ed. *Libya: The Vilified Revolution.* Langley Park, Md.: Progress Press Publications, 1984.

Stanik, Joseph T. "Swift and Effective Retribution": *The U.S. Sixth Fleet and the Confrontation with Qaddafi.* U.S. Navy in the Modern World Series 3. Washington, D.C.: Department of the Navy, 1996.

Stebbins, Richard P. and Elaine P. Adam, eds., *American Foreign Relations: A Documentary Record.* New York: New York University Press, various years.

Stewart, Adrian. "Desert Battleground: The Libyan Campaigns in the Second World War." *Journal of Libyan Studies* 1, 1 (Summer 2000): 48–60.

Takeyh, Ray. "The Evolving Course of Qaddafi's Foreign Policy." *Journal of Libyan Studies* 1, 2 (Winter 2000): 41–53.

———. "Qadhafi's Libya and the Prospect of Islamic Succession." *Middle East Policy* 7, 2 (February 2000): 154–64.

———. "The Rogue Who Came in From the Cold." *Foreign Affairs* 80, 3 (May–June 2001): 62–72.

Terrill, W. Andrew. "Libya and the Quest for Chemical Weapons." *Conflict Quarterly* 14, 1 (1994): 47–61.

Thomas, Hugh. *Suez.* New York: Harper & Row, 1966.

Thompson, E. P. and Mary Kaldor, eds. *Mad Dogs: The US Raids on Libya.* London, Pluto Press, 1986.

United States of America. *Declassified Documents Reference System.* Washington, D.C.: Carrollton Press, 1975–present.

———. *Foreign Broadcast Information Services. Daily Report: Middle East and North Africa (FBIS-MEA).* Washington, D.C.: Department of Commerce, various years.

———. *Foreign Broadcast Information Services. Daily Report:* (FBIS-NEH).

———. *Joint Publications Research Service.* Washington, D.C.: Department of Commerce, various years. Cited as *JPRS.*

———. Department of State. *American Foreign Policy: Current Documents.* Washington, D.C.: U.S. Government Printing Office, 1961–90.

———. *Bulletin.* Washington, D.C.: Department of State, various years.

———. *Papers Relating to the Foreign Relations of the United States.* Washington, D.C.: U.S. Government Printing Office, 1874–1968. Cited as *FR*

Vandewalle, Dirk. *Libya Since Independence: Oil and State-Building.* Ithaca, N.Y.: Cornell University Press, 1998.

———, ed. *Qadhafi's Libya, 1969–1994.* New York: St. Martin's Press, 1995.

———. "Qadhafi's 'Perestroika': Economic and Political Liberalization in Libya." *Middle East Journal* 45, 2 (Spring 1991): 216–31.

Venkus, Col. Robert E. *Raid on Qaddafi.* New York: St. Martin's Press, 1992.

Vikor, Knut S. *Sufi and Scholar on the Desert Edge: Muhammad b. Ali al-Sanusi and His Brotherhood.* Evanston, Ill.: Northwestern University Press, 1995.

Villard, Henry Serrano. *Libya: The New Arab Kingdom of North Africa.* Ithaca, N.Y.: Cornell University Press, 1956.

Viorst, Milton. "The Colonel in His Labyrinth." *Foreign Affairs* 78, 2 (March–April 1999): 60–75.

Waddams, Frank C. *The Libyan Oil Industry.* London: Croom Helm, 1980.

Wahby, Mohammed. "People Power Diplomacy for Libya," *Middle East Economic Digest* 23, 36 (7 September 1979): 18.

ElWarfally, Mahmoud G. *Imagery and Ideology in U.S. Policy Toward Libya, 1969–1982.* Pittsburgh: University of Pittsburgh Press, 1988.

Wiegele, Thomas C. *The Clandestine Building of Libya's Chemical Weapons Factory: A Study in International Collusion.* Carbondale: Southern Illinois University Press, 1992.

Wilson, Rodney. "Economic Aspects of Arab Nationalism." In *Demise of the British Empire in the Middle East: Britain's Responses to Nationalist Movements, 1943–55*, ed. Michael J. Cohen and Martin Kolinsky, 64–78. London: Frank Cass, 1988.

Woodward, Bob. *Veil: The Secret Wars of the CIA, 1981–1987.* London: Headline, 1987.

World Peace Foundation. *Documents on American Foreign Relations.* various editors and publishers, 1939–78.

Wren, Christopher S. "Libya's Identity Blurred by Ties with East, West and Terrorism." *New York Times*, 14 October 1979.

Wright, John. "British and Italians in Libya in 1943." *Maghreb Review* 15, 1–2 (January–April 1990): 31–36.

———. *Libya, Chad and the Central Sahara.* London: C. Hurst, 1989.

———. "Mussolini, Libya and the 'Sword of Islam'." *Maghreb Review* 12, 1–2 (January–April 1987): 29–33.

Wright, Louis B. and Julia H. MacLeod. *The First Americans in North Africa: William Eaton's Struggle for a Vigorous Policy Against the Barbary Pirates, 1799–1805.* Princeton, N.J.: Princeton University Press, 1945.

Yodfat, Arieh. "The USSR and Libya." *New Outlook* 13, 6 (1970): 37–40.

Yost, David S. "French Policy in Chad and the Libyan Challenge." *Orbis* 21, 1 (Winter 1983): 965–97.

Zartman, I. William and A. G. Kluge. "Heroic Politics: The Foreign Policy of Libya." In *The Foreign Policies of Arab States*, ed. Bahgat Korany and Ali E. Hillal Dessouki, 174–95. Boulder, Colo.: Westview Press, 1984.

Ziadeh, Nicola A. *Sanusiyah: A Study of a Revivalist Movement in Islam.* Leiden: E.J. Brill, 1958.

Index

Acknowledgments

I first visited Libya in 1977, and over the next few years I enjoyed opportunities to travel through much of the country. At the time, only a handful of books were available in English on this North African state. To better understand the environment in which I was living and working, I began to conduct my own primary and secondary research, an effort that later led to the publication of three books and two dozen articles. Over the last few decades, the number of publications available on Libya has increased a hundredfold, but most of them focus on the Qaddafi era, paying little or no attention to the years preceding the 1969 revolution. This is unfortunate because a thorough understanding of the policies pursued by Libya, the Western powers, and the Arab states before the revolution is essential to an understanding of the direction Libya moved after 1969.

The purpose of this book is to show, within the framework of a conventional historical narrative, the experience and interaction of the governments and peoples of Libya and the United States over the last two centuries. I have drawn on a wide range of material, much of it new or unfamiliar, in an effort to convey to the fullest extent the depth, breadth, and complexity of this bilateral relationship. In particular, I have consulted all the published diplomatic correspondence between Libya and the United States in the modern era as well as a wide range of recently declassified documents.

I owe special thanks to numerous Libyan and non-Libyan friends and acquaintances who have facilitated access to materials and information in many different ways. The library staffs at Bradley University, Carnegie Mellon University, and Knox College have been especially generous of their time and talent over a prolonged period. I would also like to acknowledge a few individuals whose inspiration, counsel, or scholarship have made important contributions to this work. They include Ali Abdullatif Ahmida, Tony Allan, Lisa Anderson, Mary-Jane Deeb, Mansour O. El-Kikhia, Kola Folayan, René Lemarchand, Dirk Vandewalle, and John Wright.

In addition, I want to acknowledge several individuals who were kind enough to read and comment on earlier drafts of the present work. They include Tony Allan, Massimiliano Cricco, William L. Eagleton, Jr., Oliver

Miles, Tim Niblock, J. Peter Tripp, and Dirk Vandewalle. I also want to thank Clive Schofield at the International Boundaries Research Unit for the map of Libya. Finally, I would like to thank my wife and two sons for the support they have given me. A work of this order requires an enormous amount of time and energy, much of which would otherwise have been devoted to them. For this reason, I gratefully dedicate this volume to my loving wife, Carol.

Needless to say, none of the above institutions or individuals bears any responsibility for errors of omission or inaccuracies found in the present work. I have aspired to the traditional principles of sound scholarship, which include clarity, accuracy, completeness, and adequate documentation. I ask the reader to judge it on the basis of these criteria.

DATE DUE

#47-0108 Peel Off Pressure Sensitive